Rivals for Power

Rivals for Power

Presidential-Congressional Relations

Fifth Edition

Edited by James A. Thurber

ROWMAN & LITTLEFIELD PUBLISHERS, INC.
Lanham • Boulder • New York • Toronto • Plymouth, UK

Published by Rowman & Littlefield Publishers, Inc.
A wholly owned subsidiary of The Rowman & Littlefield Publishing Group, Inc.
4501 Forbes Boulevard, Suite 200, Lanham, Maryland 20706
www.rowman.com

10 Thornbury Road, Plymouth PL6 7PP, United Kingdom

British Library Cataloguing in Publication Information Available

Library of Congress Cataloging-in-Publication Data
Rivals for power : presidential-congressional relations / edited by James A. Thurber.—Fifth edition.
pages cm
Includes bibliographical references and index.
ISBN 978-1-4422-2257-1 (cloth : alk. paper)—ISBN 978-1-4422-2258-8 (pbk. : alk. paper)—ISBN 978-1-4422-2259-5 (ebook)
1. Presidents—United States. 2. United States. Congress. 3. United States—Politics and government—20th century. I. Thurber, James A., 1943–
JK585.R59 2013
320.973—dc23
2013010503

∞™ The paper used in this publication meets the minimum requirements of American National Standard for Information Sciences Permanence of Paper for Printed Library Materials, ANSI/NISO Z39.48-1992.

Printed in the United States of America

For my wife, Claudia

And my family,
Mark, Kathryn, Greg, Tristan, Bryan and Kelsey

Contents

List of Figures

List of Tables

Preface

This book combines the knowledge of a variety of scholars and practitioners from the White House and the Hill and is designed to explain the political dynamic between the president and the US Congress. The examination of the dynamic rivalry between the president and Congress uses a variety of approaches and perspectives. The title *Rivals for Power: Presidential-Congressional Relations* highlights the continued competition between the two branches, whether the White House and Congress are controlled by the same party or by different parties. The book focuses on the divisions in our democracy that create the rivalries between the president and Congress. It explores the structural, political, and behavioral factors that establish incentives for cooperation and conflict between the two branches.

As director of the Center for Congressional and Presidential Studies at American University, editor of the journal *Congress and the Presidency*, and as a former congressional staff member, I have spent several decades studying and teaching about the relationship between the White House and Congress. Much of my understanding of this complex rivalry comes from a combination of my independent research and the knowledge from scholars, White House staff, members of Congress and staff, the press, and students. All of these are essential sources for this book. I have many people from the White House and the Hill to thank for sharing their knowledge and expertise, not the least are US Senator Hubert H. Humphrey, US Representative David Obey, and former US Representative Lee Hamilton for whom I worked. Many interviews with persons in Congress and the White House were helpful to me in preparing this book. The hundreds of former students who are or have worked for Congress and in the White House have all been a source of knowledge and wisdom for my research.

The fifth edition of *Rivals for Power* is intended for students, scholars, public officials, the media, and the general public. Each chapter is new since the last edition and reports on original research on Congress and the relationship between the president and Congress from unique viewpoints often as players from inside the policy making process. Scholars, journalists, and political practitioners have contributed to this volume. Most of the scholars are experienced hands who have worked in Congress and the White House.

This book relies on the support of Niels Aaboe and Lindsey Schauer and others from Rowman & Littlefield who contributed their expertise and dedication to assure its publication. I thank Rowman & Littlefield for its support of this work as well as the copy editor, Leslie Deakin, and the proofreader, Annette Van Deusen.

At American University, I first want to thank Rebecca Prosky at the Center for Congressional and Presidntial Studies (CCPS) for her research, editing and dedication to excellence in the production of this book. I would like to thank Aaron Ray who provided invaluable research assistance at various stages of the project. I would also like to thank the Dr. Patrick Griffin whose many years at the center and experience on the Hill and in the White House have helped me to better understand the two institutions and their relationship. I also thank Candice J. Nelson,

chair of the Department of Government, who has been a helpful friend and strong supporter of the work of the center.. I also thank my close friend and colleague, Neil Kerwin, president of American University, who has been an unfailing and strong proponent of our efforts to build the Center for Congressional and Presidential Studies and to continue our scholarship about the president and Congress.

I thank all the contributors who have contributed original and important scholarship to each chapter. This book is clearly a collective effort. As editor and author, I take full responsibility for any omissions or errors of fact and interpretation.

I dedicate this book to my family. Thank you, Claudia, Mark, Kathryn, Greg, Tristan, Bryan, and Kelsey for your gifts of love and continued inspiration and support..

Chapter One

An Introduction to Presidential-Congressional Rivalry

James A. Thurber

In his 2013 State of the Union address, President Barack H. Obama stated, "Mr. Speaker, Mr. Vice President, Members of Congress, fellow Americans, fifty-one years ago, John F. Kennedy declared to this chamber that 'the Constitution makes us not rivals for power, but partners for progress.'"[1] This was wishful thinking by President Obama. The relationship between the president and Congress, usually conflictual, is now very far from being cooperative "partners for progress."

The journey from the battles of campaigning to governing is always quick for newly elected presidents, but it was especially rapid for President Barack Obama in 2009 and again in 2013 when he started his second term in office. Presidential campaigns are a test of a candidate's style, strategy, message, organization, and leadership. They have an impact on governing. Ultimately, campaigns are a way for voters to judge how the president will lead and what policies he will attempt to implement. Campaigns are as dynamic as a president's relationship with Congress. The 2008 and 2012 Obama campaigns were the most expensive, and maybe the best-run, presidential campaigns in the history of the United States. *Washington Post* veteran reporter, David S. Broder, declared the 2008 campaign to be the "best campaign I've ever covered."[2] The passage of the $787 billion economic stimulus bill three weeks into Obama's first term and his introduction of a transformational $3.6 trillion budget one month into his administration were also swift and historic, as was the federal government fiscal crisis faced by President Obama and the 113th Congress in 2013. Campaigns and governing do not happen in a vacuum, and they are not predetermined by economic or political circumstances. Successful campaigns must develop a clear message and strategy that mobilizes groups of voters that will help the candidate win, that is, the party loyalists ("the base") and the swing voters (often moderate and ideologically in the middle). President Obama sought support in Congress during his first term in the same way: built a solid base of votes from his party and then tried to reach out for votes from moderate Republicans, but failed to persuade congressional Republicans to support his policy agenda.

From the day of his first inauguration, January 20, 2009, President Obama attempted to use his "political capital" from his successful election campaign to work with Congress. The size of his election victory (53 percent), his popularity as shown in early historically high poll ratings (mid-80 percent job-approval ratings the first month in office), and the natural strength of partisan support in unified party government (solid Democratic majorities in the House and Senate) helped to build a strong relationship with Congress in 2009–2010. However, this important presidential resource, "political capital," is often an intangible and transient force, as shown with its rapid decay in Obama's first four years in office. President Obama's second term was a different story. Post 2012 election was challenging for President Obama; there was no honeymoon in his second term, only continued conflict with a highly partisan and divided Congress.

The 111th Congress (2009–2010), which spanned the first two years of the Obama presidency with a Democratic majority in both chambers, was exceedingly productive, but that was effectively stopped after the 2010 election. After the 2008 elections, Democrats controlled both chambers of Congress and the presidency. Between July 7, 2009 and February 4, 2010, the Democrats held a filibuster-proof super majority of sixty votes in the Senate.[3] They used the advantage of unified party government to enact major legislation including the American Recovery and Reinvestment Act (economic stimulus), the Patient Protection and Affordable Care Act (health insurance reform), and the Dodd-Frank Wall Street Reform and Consumer Protection Act (financial reform). This period of legislative productivity in part inspired a conservative "Tea Party" backlash in the 2010-midterm elections. The Republican Party gained control of the House with eighty-seven new freshmen and narrowed the Democratic majority in the Senate. Therefore, the 112th Congress saw deadlock and historically limited legislative productivity in the run up to the 2012 elections. Although President Obama won a second term in office in 2012 and the Democrats expanded their majority in the Senate, the Republicans maintained their hold on the House, which raised significant questions about the ability of a divided Congress to go beyond deadlock and address major issues facing the nation in the 113th Congress and beyond.

During the 112th Congress (2011–2012), divided government led to gridlock in Congress. Tensions came to a head in May of 2011 when Republicans objected to raising the debt ceiling without instituting a plan to reduce the deficit. This impasse resulted in a downgrade of the nation's credit rating and the creation of a bipartisan congressional committee (the "Supercommittee") to recommend a deficit-reduction plan.[4]

How to address these looming deadlines became a primary theme of the 2012 campaign and the major agenda of the president and Congress. In the November 2012 election, Republicans retained control of the House, Democrats retained control of the Senate, and President Obama was reelected to a second term, thus guaranteeing conflict over how to address the fiscal cliff and other pressing policy issues in the 2012 lame-duck session and beyond. President Obama's political momentum and relations with Congress were undermined by the outcome of the 2010 midterm and 2012 elections, the economic woes of the United States and the world, and the unified political opposition of the Republican congressional leadership to his policy agenda.

It behooves candidates and their campaign managers and, after elected, presidents and their political advisers to evaluate environmental conditions early and develop campaign plans and governing strategies that take advantage of the conditions and to revise those plans when events call for it. Campaign (and presidential leadership) strategy, planning, and tactics must take objective economic and political facts into account. Campaign strategy charts the path to win the election and recognizes that campaigns are dynamic and in constant change, reacting to events and opponents. Presidential coalition-building strategies to get votes in Congress for presidential initiatives have similar dynamics. Well-run campaigns and successful governing strategies start with a plan, with a theme and message, making the best use of resources (e.g., a candidate's or a president's time), reducing liabilities (marginalizing opposition), and establishing a set of clear objectives whose achievement will maximize the probability of winning an election or the votes needed to pass a president's legislative agenda in Congress. This sounds simple, but the key elements of a campaign or leadership strategy and plan are complex and dynamic. Campaign strategies and plans and governing style must take into account a vast number of factors, such as the candidate or president's personality/charisma, the constituencies in the nation and on the Hill, the nature of the policies being advocated, the party organization (or lack of it), the strength of party leadership, the economic situation, political resources/capital available, and the nature of the electorate and the key members of Congress.

At the beginning of his first term, President Obama called for a change in the way Washington works. He hoped for bipartisanship and reached out to the Republicans in Congress. In an unprecedented act, he met with Republican congressional leaders on the Hill during his first week of his presidency in an attempt to build a bipartisan coalition to support his historic $787 billion economic stimulus package. He ended up getting only three Republican senators to support the bill and no Republican votes in the House. Both

Presidents Obama and George W. Bush sought more comity and bipartisan support during the early days in office, only to be rebuffed. Both Presidents Obama and Bush inherited a long-seated rivalry, tough partisanship, and difficulty in building coalitions around their policy initiatives. Where does this conflict come from? What are the roots of the rivalry between the president and Congress? Why does the president's success with Congress vary over time? Whether in a unified or divided party government, the president and Congress are separated and prone to rivalry and find it hard to find "partners for progress."

"The relationship between Congress and the presidency has been one of the abiding mysteries of the American system of government," according to Arthur M. Schlesinger, Jr.[5] In this introduction, I will examine several root causes of the rivalry between the president and Congress: the constitutional design with its formal presidential and congressional powers; different electoral constituencies for the president, the House, and the Senate; varying terms of office; increased partisanship and polarization of Congress; the ongoing competition for power between Congress and the president; the permanent election campaign; narrow majorities in both houses; congressional individualism; the impact of the "increasingly microscopic nature of political analysis" of the media (especially cable television and the Internet) in the twenty-four-hour, seven-days-a-week news cycle; and the nature of interest groups and American pluralism.

The framers of the Constitution bequeathed to Americans one of the most enduring rivalries in government, that between the president and Congress.[6] The Constitution separates the three branches of government (legislative, executive, and judicial), but combines their functions, creating conflict and shared powers.[7] As Richard Neustadt observed, the Constitution created a government "of separated institutions sharing powers," which makes it difficult for presidents to bridge the constitutional gap even in the best of political circumstances. The Constitution gives the president and the Congress different powers, and each is jealous of the other's constitutional prerogatives regardless of context. The Constitution invests Congress with "all legislative Powers" (lawmaking), but it also authorizes the president to recommend and to veto legislation. If the president vetoes a bill, "it shall be reposed by two-thirds of the Senate and the House of Representatives" (Article I, Section 7). Because it is so difficult for Congress to gain a two-thirds' vote, presidential vetoes are usually sustained. Through 2012, presidents had used the veto 2,563 times; 1,066 of these were "pocket vetoes" not subject to congressional override.[8] Congress overrode presidential vetoes 6 percent of the time (109 times) when it had the opportunity to vote on them.[9] President Obama did not use a veto in his first four years in office, fewer than any president since President George W. Bush and President Harding before that. The threat of a veto in the legislative process gives the president an important bargaining tool; however, President Obama and George W. Bush did not use this tool in their first terms in office and President Clinton did not use this tool until 1995, when he vetoed a $16 billion rescission bill. Clinton used the veto in his confrontation with the Republican-led Congress over the cuts in Medicaid, Medicare, welfare, education, and federal environmental programs in the fiscal year 1996 federal budget. This showdown ultimately helped to shut down government and stop the drive of the Contract with America supporters in the House and Senate. The greatest power of the president in divided government is often the power to say no as President Clinton did in his last six years of office and George W. Bush did in his last two years of office. It is easier to stop legislation than it is to pass it. President Clinton embraced that notion in his historic budget battle in 1995 when he said: "This is one of those moments in history when I'm grateful for the wisdom of our Founding Fathers. The Congress gets to propose, but the president has to sign or veto, and that Constitution gave me that authority and one of the reasons for the veto is to prevent excess. They knew what they were doing and we're going to use the Constitution they gave us to stand up for what's right."[10]

Congress is given broad powers in article I, section 8 of the Constitution, but the greatest power of Congress is its authority to pass laws directly binding upon all citizens (lawmaking).

Also of great importance is the power of the purse, the power to authorize and appropriate funds for the president and executive branch agencies. Presidents may propose budgets for the federal government, but Congress has the final say on spending. This creates an automatic rivalry, the conflict over spending and taxing, which has dominated President Obama's relationship with Congress. Congress also has the power to levy and collect taxes, to borrow and coin money, and to regulate foreign and interstate commerce. A central element of the rivalry between the president and Congress has been battles over spending, tax, and trade policy over the last three decades.

The powers to declare war, to provide for a militia, and to adopt laws concerning bankruptcy, naturalization, patents, and copyrights are also bestowed on Congress. The interpretation of presidential and congressional war power has changed over time and is another contemporary source of conflict. Congress has the authority to establish or eliminate executive branch agencies (e.g., intelligence reform of 2004) and create new departments (e.g., Department of Homeland Security in 2002) and to oversee their operations. The Senate must approve cabinet nominees, ambassadors, and Supreme Court and federal judicial appointees before they can take office. A president cannot enter into a binding treaty with a foreign government without a two-thirds' vote of the Senate, nor can the president "declare war," a power the Constitution purposely gives to Congress. All of these constitutional congressional and presidential powers force both institutions to confront each other in governance, which more often than not creates rivalry and conflict.

A dramatic but rarely employed check on the president is impeachment. President Clinton's impeachment was historic and rare. The president and executive branch officials can be impeached (formally accused) by a majority vote in the House and tried in the Senate. If two-thirds of the senators vote to convict, the official is removed from office. Only Presidents Andrew Johnson and Bill Clinton have been tried on impeachment charges. The vote fell one short of the number required to convict Johnson and the Senate did not come close to convicting Clinton. The House Judiciary Committee recommended that Richard M. Nixon be impeached for transgressions in connection with the Watergate burglary involving the Democratic National Committee offices and the ensuing cover-up. Nixon, however, resigned the presidency before a full session of the House could vote on the impeachment issue. The threat of impeachment establishes an important check on the president and executive branch officials, limiting the power of the president.

The framers of the Constitution deliberately fragmented power between the national government and the states (federalism) and among the executive, legislative, and judicial branches (separation of powers).[11] They also divided legislative powers by creating two coequal houses, a bicameral Congress with different constituencies, which further magnifies rivalry and conflict. Although divided, Congress was designed to be independent and powerful, able to check the power of the executive and to be directly linked with the people through popular, periodic elections. The framers wanted an effective and powerful federal government, but they also wanted to limit its power in order to protect personal and property rights. Having experienced the abuses of English monarchs and their colonial governors, the framers were wary of excessive executive authority. They also feared "elective despotism," or excessive legislative power, something the Articles of Confederation had given their own state legislatures.

Congress has the function of lawmaking, oversight, deliberation, and education. Therefore, the framers created three branches of government with none having a monopoly. This separation of powers restricted the power of any one branch, and it required cooperation among the three in order for them to govern effectively. Today, as then, political action requires cooperation between the president and Congress. Yet the Constitution, in the way it divided power between the two branches, created an open invitation for conflict.[12] In sum, in creating a separated presidency and two equal legislative chambers, the framers guaranteed checks and an ongoing rivalry between executive and legislative power.

DIFFERENT CONSTITUENCIES

The US system of government, unlike parliamentary systems throughout the world, elects the executive and members of the legislature independently. The president is elected from vastly broader electoral coalitions (271 electoral votes, generally from eight to twelve "battleground" or competitive states) than are representatives, with narrow constituencies and in homogeneous districts, or senators, who often have heterogeneous state constituencies. Members of Congress, even those who belong to the president's party or hail from his home state, represent specific interests that can conflict with the interests of the president, who represents the nation as a whole. James Madison well understood this dichotomy of interest as an important source of conflict between the president and Congress: "The members of the federal legislature will be likely to attach themselves too much to local objects. . . Measures will too often be decided according to their probable effect, not on the national prosperity and happiness, but on the prejudices, interests, and pursuits of the governments and the people of the individual States."[13] Members of Congress often live in discrete communities and cleverly drawn noncompetitive House districts favoring one party or the other, but especially favoring incumbents. Those incumbents who run for reelection are overwhelmingly successful, in the mid-ninetieth percentile for House members and mid-eightieth for senators.

VARYING TERMS OF OFFICE

The interaction of Congress and the president is shaped not only by their different constituencies and electoral competitiveness, but also by their different terms in office. The constitutional structure of US government, which separates the Congress and the president, sets different terms of office for representatives (two-year terms), senators (six-year terms), and the president (four-year terms), and ensures they will be chosen from different constituency bases. Presidents have only four years, possibly eight, in which to establish their programs. They are expected to set the national policy agenda and usually move rapidly in the first year before their decline in popularity.[14] Presidents are not concerned about reelection after the first four years of office and thus focus on their legacy, protecting their successes and pushing new public policy, thus promising an honored place in history. Other interests are certainly operative, but the drive for reelection for members of Congress is a top priority no matter who is president.[15] Legislators, then, are often reluctant to allow their workload and policy preferences to be dictated by a president who has no political clout or perceived electoral mandate to do so. They are often driven by the short-term motivation to be reelected rather than the long-term policy goals of a president.

Congress moves more slowly than the president; it is deliberative and inefficient primarily because it represents a vast array of local interests. Congress passes new laws slowly and reviews old ones carefully. The decision-making pace of Congress and of the president is not the same because of their different terms of office, electoral base, and perceived constituency mandates. Confronted with major economic problems and two wars, President Obama pursued an ambitious policy agenda in his first administration. He did not back off his campaign promises in 2008 of redeployment in Iraq, quick action to turn the economy around, health-care reform, financial reforms, and other policies. However, Congress had its own pace and its own ideas on the Iraq War, health care, financial reregulation, energy, environment, and education. The result of these varying terms of office is rivalry, conflict, extreme partisanship, and often deadlock over major policies. Candidate Obama promised to change the gridlock of Washington, but failed to do so in his first four years in office.

POLITICAL PARTIES

Another factor influencing the relationship between the president and Congress is the federal system of state-based political parties. They contribute to the independence of members of Congress from the president. The president must work with decentralized political party organizations that often exercise little control over recruitment of candidates who run under their party label, mete out weak discipline, and hold even less leverage over members. Senators and representatives usually run their own races with their own financing. The way they respond to local conditions has little to do with national party platforms or presidential politics. Members often freely pursue their own interests without fear of discipline from the president. Independence from political parties and the president allows legislators to seek benefits for their own constituents and to serve specialized interests. Thomas Mann argues further:

> The changes that swept through the political system during the 1960s and 1970s—the growing cost of campaigns and reliance on contributions from special interests, the rise of television, the expansion and growing political sophistication of interest groups in Washington, and the democratization and decentralization of Congress—may well have weakened the classic iron triangles, but they also heightened the sensitivity of politicians to all forms of outside pressure. [16]

There is a continuing trend in both chambers away from bipartisan cooperation and toward ideological and political loyalty. An analysis of party
unity votes, defined by *Congressional Quarterly* as votes where a majority of
one party votes against a majority of the other, shows that Republicans and
Democrats have record levels of polarization. Party unity has steadily increased since 1960, from the low average party unity score of the mid-60s to
the high 80s from 1993 to 2010 (see table 1.1 below). For example, in the
early years of the Obama presidency and eight years of the Bush presidency,
on votes in which party leaders took clear opposing positions, House and
Senate Republicans voted to support the party position from the high 80 to
low 90 percent of the time, and House and Senate Democrats supported the
party position 94 percent of the time. These party voting patterns have revealed the congressional parties to be much more ideological and polarized.

PARTY CONTROL OF GOVERNMENT

Unified and divided party governments have a most important impact on the
relationship between the president and Congress. Unified party government
returned to America for President Obama's first two years and then returned
to divided party government after the 2010 and 2012 elections. A major
impediment to legislative-executive cooperation is divided government.
There are two varieties of divided government (the condition that exists
when the majority party in either or both houses of Congress differs from the
party of the president): divided party control of Congress and split control of
Congress and the White House. From 1901 through 2014 (114 years), we
have had unified party control of government for sixty-seven years (almost
59 percent of the time) and divided party control of government for forty-
seven years, or 41 percent of the time (see table 1.2 below).

From 1887 to 1954, divided party control of government occurred only
eight years (14 percent of the time), but from President Dwight D. Eisenhower's first year (1953) through President Clinton's fourth year in office (1996),
it occurred twenty-eight years (56 percent of the time). Although President
George W. Bush had unified party government most of the time and President Barack Obama had unified party government for the first two years of
his first term and divided control for his last six years in office, divided party
control of the government is the norm in modern US politics. Presidents are
more likely to be successful in their relationship with Congress with unified
party government than with divided government. This has been especially
true since the post-1980 resurgence of party-line voting and party cohesion in
Congress. *Congressional Quarterly* defines its measure of party-line voting
as the percentage of all votes when a majority of voting Democrats opposes a
majority of voting Republicans. As shown in table 1.3 below, President

James A. Thurber

Table 1.1. Party Unity in Congressional Voting, 1954–2010 (percent)

Year	House All Dem.	House Southern Dem.	House Repub.	Senate All Dem.	Senate Southern Dem.	Senate Repub.
1954	80	—	84	77	—	89
1955	84	68	78	82	78	82
1956	80	79	78	80	75	80
1957	79	71	75	79	81	81
1958	77	67	73	82	76	74
1959	85	77	85	76	63	80
1960	75	62	77	73	60	74
1961	—	—	—	—	—	—
1962	81	—	80	80	—	81
1963	85	—	84	79	—	79
1964	82	—	81	73	—	75
1965	80	55	81	75	55	78
1966	78	55	82	73	52	78
1967	77	53	82	75	59	73
1968	73	48	76	71	57	74
1969	71	47	71	74	53	72
1970	71	52	72	71	49	71
1971	72	48	76	74	56	75
1972	70	44	76	72	43	73
1973	75	55	74	79	52	74
1974	72	51	71	72	41	68
1975	75	53	78	76	48	71
1976	75	52	75	74	46	72
1977	74	55	77	72	48	75
1978	71	53	77	75	54	66
1979	75	60	79	76	62	73
1980	78	64	79	76	64	74
1981	75	57	80	77	64	85
1982	77	62	76	76	62	80
1983	82	67	80	76	70	79
1984	81	68	77	75	61	83
1985	86	76	80	79	68	81

1986	86	76	76	74	59	80
1987	88	78	79	85	80	78
1988	88	81	80	85	78	74
1989	86	77	76	79	69	79
1990	86	78	78	82	75	77
1991	86	78	81	83	73	83
1992	86	79	84	82	70	83
1993	89	83	87	87	78	86
1994	88	83	87	86	77	81
1995	84	75	93	84	76	91
1996	84	76	90	86	75	91
1997	85	78	91	86	75	88
1998	86	79	89	90	85	88
1999	86	77	88	91	86	90
2000	86	80	90	90	80	91
2001	86	77	94	90	79	90
2002	90	82	93	85	69	88
2003	91	85	95	90	76	95
2004	91	83	93	88	76	93
2005	91	84	93	90	81	90
2006	90	82	92	89	77	87
2007	95	85	90	92	93	84
2008	97	—	92	92	—	87
2009	94	—	90	94	—	87
2010	93	—	94	94	—	93

Note: Dem. (Democrats); Repub. (Republicans). "—" indicates not available. Data show percentage of members voting with a majority of their party on party unity votes. Party unity votes are those roll calls on which a majority of Democrats vote against a majority of Republicans. Percentages are calculated to eliminate the impact of absences as follows: unity = (unity)/(unity + opposition).

Sources: 1954–1992: Norman J. Ornstein, Thomas E. Mann, and Michael J. Malbin, eds., *Vital Statistics on Congress, 1993–1994* (Washington, DC: Congressional Quarterly, 1994), 201–02; 1993–2010: *Congressional Quarterly Weekly Report* (*CQ Weekly*) (1993), 3479; (1994), 3659; (1996), 245, 3461; (1998), 33; (1999), 92, 2993; (2001), 67; (2002), 142, 3281; (2004), 48, 2952; (2006), 97; (2007), 38; (2008), 147, 3337; (2011), 36.

Table 1.2.   Unified and Divided Party Control of Government, 1901–2014

Unified party control of government (67 years): 59.2%
Divided party control of government (46 years): 40.7%

Year	Party Control	Number of Years	Percentage
1901–1920	Unified	16	80
	Divided	4	20
1921–1940	Unified	18	90
	Divided	2	10
1941–1960	Unified	12	60
	Divided	8	40
1961–1980	Unified	12	60
	Divided	8	40
1981–2000	Unified	2	10
	Divided	18	90
2001–2014	Unified	7	53.8
	Divided	7	46.2

Totals	Years	Percentage
Unified	67	58.8%
Divided	47	41.2%
Total	114	

Obama's presidential success scores of the mid-ninetieth percentile for his first two years in office set a record since measuring them started with President Eisenhower. Overall, Reagan and Bush had low presidential support scores in Congress because of divided party government. Clinton's victories on votes in Congress during his first two years (1993–1994) in office averaged over 86 percent in the House and Senate and dropped to 36 percent in 1995 when the Republicans captured the Congress.

Although President Obama had significant electoral victories in 2008 and 2012, he faced tough opposition from the House and Senate Republicans. Because the necessity for sixty votes to stop a filibuster, President Obama's margin of support has been very thin in the Senate and almost nonexistent in the House after his first two years in office.

Table 1.3. Presidential Success Scores, 1953–2010. Year / House and Senate Victories (percent).

1953	89.2%	1965	93.1%	1975	61.0%	1987	43.5%	1999	37.8%
1954	82.8	1966	78.9	1976	53.8	1988	47.4	2000	55.0
1955	75.3	1967	78.8	1977	75.4	1989	62.6	2001	87.0
1956	69.2	1968	74.5	1978	78.3	1990	46.8	2002	88.0
1957	68.4	1969	74.8	1979	76.8	1991	54.2	2003	78.7
1958	75.7	1970	76.9	1980	75.1	1992	43.0	2004	72.6
1959	52.9	1971	74.8	1981	82.4	1993	86.4	2005	78.0
1960	65.1	1972	66.3	1982	72.4	1994	86.4	2006	80.9
1961	81.5	1973	50.6	1983	67.1	1995	36.2	2007	38.3
1962	85.4	1974	59.6	1984	65.8	1996	55.1	2008	47.8
1963	87.1	(Nixon)		1985	59.9	1997	53.6	2009	96.6
1964	87.9	1974	58.2	1986	56.5	1998	50.6	2010	85.9
		(Ford)							

Figure 1.1. Presidential Success Scores, 1953–2010. Year / House and Senate Victories (percent). (Companion to table 1.3.)

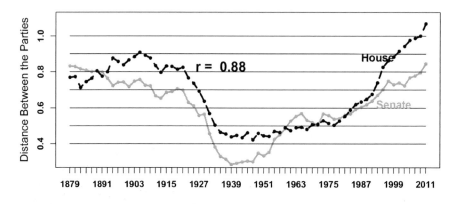

Figure 1.2. Party Polarization, 1879–2012: Distance between the Parties

President George W. Bush had unified Republican government for the first time since 1954, but the closeness of the 2000 election and the tie in the Senate created the foundation for conflict and in effect divided government until he had to face actual divided party government in 2007.

The trend toward ticket splitting between presidential and congressional candidates further exacerbates already strained relations between the president and Congress. Election returns for Congress have increasingly diverged from national presidential returns. During the past forty years, as the power of political parties has declined significantly, there has been a corresponding rise in individualistic candidacies for the presidency, the Senate, and the House, as revealed by the Republican Tea Party Movement. Fewer and fewer members of Congress ride into office on the electoral "coattails" of the president. This has led to the election of presidents who find it difficult to translate electoral support into governing support. This was even the case with Obama's historic 2008 election and was certainly a major factor again in 2012. The short or nonexistent presidential coattails by Obama in 2008 and 2012, Bush I in 1988, Clinton in 1992 and 1998, and Bush II in 2000 and 2004 brings the conclusion that "the emperor has no coat."[17] Bush I was the first candidate since John F. Kennedy to win the White House while his party lost seats in the House. Clinton ran behind all but four members of the House. With the decline of presidential coattails, strong-willed, independent-minded members of Congress are largely beyond the president's control. They are often more responsive to district and specialized interests such as the Republican Tea Party Movement than to the national agenda of the president.

However, unified party control of government does not mean the two branches will work closely together. Divided government does not always mean that the two branches will fight. David Mayhew found that when it comes to passing major legislation or conducting investigations, it "does not seem to make all that much difference whether party control of the American government happens to be unified or divided."[18] However, it is generally easier for presidents to govern during periods of unified party government.

The balance of power between and within the institutions of Congress and the presidency is dynamic and conflict is inevitable, another root cause of the rivalry between the president and Congress, no matter of the same party or not. The congressional institutions of a stable committee system, party leadership organizations, the seniority system, member individualism, and behavioral norms such as reciprocity all have an impact on congressional-presidential relationships. For over two hundred years Congress has continued to represent local interests and to respond (some think too much) to political preferences and public pressures.[19] Nevertheless, the institution has changed dramatically. The reforms of the past forty years have made Congress even more representative and accountable. These reforms have changed the way it makes laws, passes budgets, oversees the executive branch, and confronts or cooperates with presidents. The degree of party centralization or fragmentation of power of congressional leadership among committees and individualism among members has major consequences for Congress's power vis-à-vis the president. It is difficult for the president to build predictable coalitions around a highly fragmented legislature and weak leadership, but it can also play into his favor if divided party government exists. As the congressional leadership is centralized and made more effective by one party, the power of a president of the opposition party is often diminished. This creates more tension between the two branches, with a clash between the president's national policy agenda and the agenda of Congress as shown by the confrontations between President Obama and the House Republicans during his administration.

Pressure to check the power of the president through the War Powers Resolution of 1973 and the Budget and Impoundment Control Act of 1974 brought changes that helped Congress reclaim some of the power it had lost to the president during the previous decades. Many institutional reforms of the 1970s, however, resulted in decentralization, which made Congress more democratic but also less efficient. With the new openness came greater accountability and responsiveness but at the price of efficiency and effectiveness as a lawmaking body.

Although Congress created new ways of checking presidential power in the 1970s, ultimately legislative-executive relationships are not zero-sum games. If one branch gains power, the other does not necessarily lose it. Threats like the terrorist attack on the United States on 9/11 and the economic crisis of 2008–2013 contribute to the policy-making power of both the president and Congress. The war on terrorism, the wars in Iraq and Afghanistan, the continuing economic crisis, and continuing large budget deficits have led to new administrative (and legislative) powers expanding the scope of both branches. Even these crises, however, are not enough to reduce the rivalry between the two institutions and the two parties.

Candidate Obama promised to reduce rivalry between the two branches and to "change the way Washington works" with respect to the way Congress works. He promised to stop the heavy reliance on riders to the appropriations bills as a way to act on significant policy issues. He made promises to reform the abuse of the conference committee by the majority party. He urged Congress to fix the breakdown in the budget process and to stop passing large omnibus spending bills well after the start of the fiscal year (October 1).[20] President Obama also said he would reduce the polarization and would improve the comity and civility between the president and Congress. President Obama and Congress have failed to achieve any of these promises.

THE MISSING MIDDLE: A BARRIER TO COOPERATION BETWEEN THE PRESIDENT AND CONGRESS

A fundamental reason for gridlock and dysfunctionality is the disappearance of the moderates or what some call the vital center in Congress. There has been a steady decline in the number of moderates in Congress since 1960. Figure 1.3 below illustrates this decline in moderate members as measured by DW-NOMINATE scores.[21]

Four decades ago, there was a vigorous middle in Congress. Both parties spanned the ideological divide that exists today. Figure 1.4 below illustrates

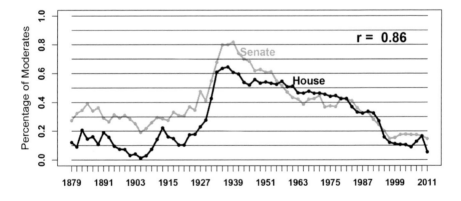

Figure 1.3.   Decline of Congressional Moderates, 1879–2011. Source: Poole and Rosenthal (2012)

the decline in members in each party who overlapped ideologically with the opposition. For much of the twentieth century, each party had a large liberal and conservative wing. On divisive issues such as civil rights, liberal Democrats and Northern moderate Republicans would join forces against the conservatives of the Confederate South. Getting the votes needed to stop a filibuster required a coalition of senators from both parties.

Related to the lack of the middle in each party is the movement of both parties to more extreme partisanship, which has also helped to create congressional dysfunction. In the 1960s, the yearly average was less than 50 percent. Polarization has reduced the frequency of consensus in the House, reduced legislative productivity in the Senate, and increased legislative productivity in the House.[22] In addition, movement of former House members into the Senate has contributed to increased partisan polarization in the upper chamber.[23]

In addition to the challenges of legislating under divided party government in an area of intense polarization, ideological divisions within the Republican Party complicated the efforts of House Speaker John Boehner and Senate Minority Leader Mitch McConnell to organize their members. In the 2011 negotiations between Speaker Boehner and President Obama to reduce the deficit and raise the debt ceiling, a deal was rejected by conservative members of the House Republican caucus. A similar split in the Republican caucus occurred in the 2012 lame-duck session when the Speaker proposed a measure (referred to as Plan B) to avert the fiscal cliff. Although the influence of Tea Party House members seemed to be on the wane after the 2012 election, ideological conservatives, particularly in the House, continued to exert significant influence. Not only does the decline in centrist members increase polarization, but high levels of polarization may in turn drive cen-

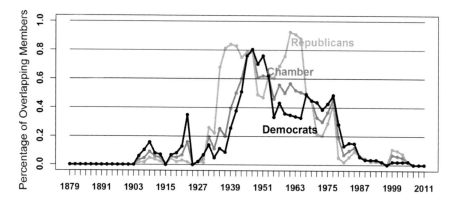

Figure 1.4. Polarization of the House and Senate, 1879–2011. Source: Poole and Rosenthal (2012)

trists out of Congress, having a major impact on the relationship between the president and the Hill. The decision to forgo reelection by two moderate Senators, Democrat Kent Conrad and Republican Olympia Snowe, was attributed in part to the polarized atmosphere in the Senate. Among the potential causes of polarization is the redistricting of House districts. Partisan gerrymandering occurs in most states. Scholars disagree about the role redistricting has played in the increase in polarization. Some argue that redistricting is one driver of polarization in the House. Others dispute the link between gerrymandering and polarization. Despite this disagreement, practitioners perceive that redistricting has negatively impacted Congress and its members. Rep. John Tanner describes the negative consequences of partisan gerrymandering; "When Members come here from these partisan districts that have been gerrymandered . . . they have little incentive to really work across party line in order to reach solutions. If one comes here wanting to work across the aisle, one has to watch one's back, because the highly charged partisans don't like it."[24]

The House has been redistricted to safe seats; only eighty-five seats were competitive in 2010, and eighty-five in 2012.[25] The creation of these safe House districts has led to the election of increasingly "ideologically pure" representatives with a relatively harmonized constituency, little institutional loyalty, and an unprecedented degree of partisan homogeneity within the two parties.

INTEREST GROUPS AND PLURALISM

Candidate Barack Obama ran against interest groups and lobbyists in 2008 claiming that he would change the way Washington works.

Public opinion surveys clearly show an increase over the past seven years of those who believe lobbyists have too much influence and a decline in those who think they have too little.[26] While public perception does not give a true indication of the performance of the lobbying industry itself, it does speak to a misunderstanding held by the American people of what lobbyists do. There is a belief that money can buy congressional votes on tough issues and that the group with the most money wins. President Obama played into these public attitudes when he promised the following in the 2008 campaign: "I intend to tell the corporate lobbyists that their days of setting the agenda in Washington are over, that they had not funded my campaigns, and from my first day as president, I will launch the most sweeping ethics reform in U.S. history. We will make government more open, more accountable and more responsive to the problems of the American people."[27] He later said, "We are going to change how Washington works. They will not run our party. They will not run our White House. They will not drown out the views of the American people."[28]

No matter what President Obama's promises, the passage of his ambitious legislative agenda stimulus was greatly dependent upon the input and support of many interest groups and lobbyists. The antilobbyist theme was not part of the 2012 Obama campaign. President Obama seemed to understand after his first two years in office that it is impossible to govern in the American pluralist representative democracy without federal registered lobbyists, interest groups, and advocates of all kinds. When a president's policy agenda is proposed, especially through his budget, there is a mobilization of interests for and against the thousands of policy decisions and proposals embedded in his fiscal plan, as shown in the lobbying surrounding President Obama's successes in his first term. The competition among a variety of interests has often produced deadlock and stalemate on the nation's most pressing problems. President Obama promised to change that by reducing the role of lobbyists and campaign money for special-interest groups in his administration, but he failed. Interest groups play a central role in the relationship between the president and Congress. Without the help of well-organized groups, the president and Congress cannot easily enact legislation. With them against the president, it is exceedingly difficult to bring about reform. Pluralism (group-based politics) limits the power of the president and Congress to pursue their own agendas and thereby increases the competition between them. Policy-making gridlock (hyperpluralism) often comes from competition among organized interests in society, not simply from divided party control of government. Deadlock over the budget, tax reform, debt and deficit reduction, entitlement reform, immigration, gun control legislation, clean air policy, energy policy, health care policy, education, and the tendency toward "government by continuing resolution" are all examples of the consequences of conflict and a lack of agreement among organized groups outside Congress. The constitutional First Amendment rights, especially freedom of speech, freedom of assembly, freedom of the press, and freedom to petition government for grievances, are the foundation of pluralism in US politics. The decay of political party organizations in the last thirty years in the United States has helped the growth of pluralism.[29] As political parties have lost power to recruit and elect candidates that are loyal to party leaders in government, interest groups have gained political power. The United States is experiencing extreme competition among groups, "hyperpluralism," that makes it almost impossible to define the public good in terms of anything other than the collection of special narrow interests.[30] Hyperpluralism contributes fundamentally to the rivalry between the president and Congress and often leads to deadlock between the two branches of government by making it difficult to make the necessary compromises between the national interests of the president and the parochial interests of members of Congress.[31] However, crisis and presidential leadership can break the deadlock, as with President Bush's post-9/11 policy and President Obama's election in 2008 and his quick action to solve the problem of a failing economy.

CONCLUSIONS AND OVERVIEW OF THE BOOK

How should presidents and Congress be evaluated in their basic governing functions? Where will President Obama and his relationship with Congress stand in history? How much of a president's success and failure and the quality of his leadership are shaped by Congress? What is the impact of Obama's personality, policy preferences, and political style on Congress? What is the influence of political parties, interest groups, public opinion, the media, and elections on presidents and Congress? What are the major constraints on presidents and Congress? What has been the impact of presidential-congressional relations on foreign and domestic policy, the federal budget, on the way decisions are made in Washington? These are some of the important questions addressed in this book. The authors here employ a variety of policy and political perspectives, including approaches from political science, history, law, public administration, economics, psychology, sociology, policy analysis, survey research, and media studies as they assess President Obama and Congress. No single analytic approach or dominant ideology reigns. The authors assess the relationship between President Obama and Congress and how that rivalry compares historically with other presidents and congresses and what it may mean for the American public, the media, interest groups, the Congress, and the world during the next four years. This edition of the book includes a collaboration of academics and practitioners who have written fifteen chapters that focus on the causes and consequences of conflict and cooperation between the president and Congress.

Presidential scholar Stephen J. Wayne assesses President Barack Obama's legislative presidency in his first four years in office in chapter 2, "Obama's First-Term Legislative Presidency: Partisan, Not Personal." Wayne argues that Obama achieved major policy change in his first two years in office by using political capital and at the expense of his party's political standing. President Obama improved that standing in his second two years in office by appealing directly to the American public and by campaigning against congressional Republican policies. In all four years, partisanship overwhelmingly drove the legislative process and policy outcomes. Wayne shows that President Obama's personality, leadership style, and deference to Democratic Party leaders reduced his personal influence and adversely affected his influence in Congress.

Academic-practitioners (both have had extensive experience on the Hill, in the White House, and in the advocacy business) Patrick Griffin and Gary

Andres analyze the implications of polarization on relations between the White House and Congress and how presidents attempt to manage legislative affairs in today's hyperpartisan age in chapter 3, "White House–Congressional Relations in a Polarized Age." They introduce a framework for understanding how presidents work with Congress. They describe the president's institutional constraints and advantages when working with Congress. They evaluate presidential leadership skills and political goals in the context of a fragmented media and an explosion of interest groups that influence White House–congressional relations. From their experience in the White House and on the Hill they describe how the White House manages its relations with Congress in the current hyperpartisan-ideological environment.

James Pfiffner in chapter 4, "Organizing the Twenty-First-Century White House," documents that during the last half of the twentieth century the presidency was transformed from a small office to a collection of specialized bureaucracies that dominates the executive branch. In the process, cabinet secretaries were eclipsed as primary advisers to the president, and conflict between the White House staff and the cabinet increased. The same growth in the size of the White House staff led to the need for a chief of staff to run the White House. This chapter examines these two trends in the George W. Bush and Barack Obama presidencies and their relationship with Congress. Pfiffner also explores the increasingly important role that the vice president has played in recent presidencies.

Roger H. Davidson, congressional scholar, explores the question of presidential and congressional "political time" in chapter 5. The US Constitution sets the clock simply by specifying terms of office: two, four, and six years. But political time may unfold at a faster or slower rate than those measurements. Presidents may face one or more resettings during their four or eight years in the Oval Office. The history of Congress may shift in a single two-year period, or it may extend over a generation or more. In this chapter Davidson describes five modern congressional eras—each with distinctive relationships with the president, political and social environments, leadership goals, member goals, and legislative workloads and outputs. These periods are: Conservative Bipartisan (roughly 1937–1964), Liberal Activist (1965–1978), Postreform (1979–1994), Partisan Conservative (1995–2007), and currently Divided Government (2007–). Davidson concludes that these changing patterns affect not only Capitol Hill behavior but also congressional relationships with the White House and the executive establishment.

In chapter 6, "The President and the Congressional Party Leadership in a Hyperpartisan Era," Barbara Sinclair shows the impact of partisanship on the relationship between the president and the congressional party leaderships. She examines how that relationship looks from 1600 Pennsylvania Avenue and how it looks from Capitol Hill, then investigates the relationship under both unified and divided control. She demonstrates the effects on legislative productivity when partisanship is high and highlights other determinants of cooperation and conflict. Sinclair concludes by commenting on what this portends for the relationship between President Obama and the congressional leadership and for policy outcomes during his second term.

James A. Thurber in chapter 7, "The President, Congress, and Lobbyists: Has President Obama Changed the Way Washington Works?," discusses the role of interest groups in presidential-congressional relations and evaluates the impact of lobbying and ethics reform on Congress and generally policy making in Washington. He concludes that President Obama has failed to change the role of money in elections, the role of lobbyists in policy making, and the lack of bipartisanship.

Ron Elving, senior Washington editor of National Public Radio, evaluates how the power relationship between the president and Congress has changed over the past half century in chapter 8, "The President, Congress, and the Media." Beginning with TV and continuing through the advent of cable and satellite, the personal computer, the Internet, the mobile phone/computer, and the "social media," the media component in the life of federal elected officials has gone from peripheral to central. Elving shows that the latest new media provide speed to the point of being "real time," access to the point of universality, and portability to the point of ubiquity. The changes in media in politics are continuing and may well be accelerating as predominance shifts from "legacy media" such as print and broadcast to more Internet- and cell-based communications. The new technologies expand audiences, enable countless new voices to join the conversation, and alter the advertising economics on which the news industry has been based. This has also altered relationships between traditional reporters and the sources of news in both the executive and legislative branches. It has contributed to a tonal change in many media, concomitant to the rise in partisan and ideological unity within the parties in the House and Senate. More and more members of Congress seeking notice use this confrontational style. This trend also suits media managers who are under pressure to find an audience in order to survive. Elving concludes that the implications of these developments in the media for the president and congressional policy are already beginning to be evident, although the full extent of the changes is still to be seen.

Budget scholar Joseph White explores the battle between the president and Congress over the federal budget in chapter 9. Budgeting is a fundamental function of government, and at the heart of both conflict and cooperation between presidents and Congress. This chapter explains why there is room for cooperation, and how the institutions of budgeting have, at times, behaved in a somewhat cooperative way. The chapter describes the budget process collapse amid unmanageable conflict. Partisan rivalries are one reason for this conflict, but that is not the whole story, according to White. The budget process has broken down under both united Republican and united Democratic government. White concludes that budgeting has involved far too much accusations of blame from the president and from Congress. There has been an excessive focus on the deficit, which made "responsible budgeting" about spending and taxing nearly impossible.

In chapter 10, "The Politics of Federal Regulation: Congress Acts, the President Hones His Policies by Regulations," regulatory lawyer Claudia Hartley Thurber shows how President Obama can accomplish some of his policy objectives without congressional action. In short, the federal departments and agencies are continuing to promulgate rules that implement financial and health-care reforms stemming from Dodd Frank and the Affordable Health Care Act. At the same time, major regulatory agencies such as the Environmental Protection Agency, the Occupational Safety and Health Administration, and the Department of Energy, along with other agencies and independent regulatory commissions are addressing major environmental, health, and safety issues pursuant to the authority granted them in their enabling statutes. Rounding out what President Obama can do are guidelines and Executive Orders. She concludes that divided government and deadlock with Congress need not mean no government.

Lawrence J. Korb and Alexander Rothman of the Center for American Progress analyze the relationship of the president and Congress in foreign policy in chapter 11. They show that although the president may be the most dominant actor shaping US national security and foreign policy, Congress is hardly impotent. They conclude that in his first term, President Obama faced unified opposition from congressional Republicans usually based on partisan politics rather than the substance of the president's policy proposals. Even given the Obama administration's strong record on foreign policy thus far, protecting US national security and interests in the coming decade will require a better working relationship between the president and Congress. Korb and Rothman outline a foreign-policy wish list for the president and Congress in the next four years.

Louis Fisher, constitutional law scholar, describes a number of constitutional conflicts with Congress during President Obama's first term, in chapter 12, "Obama's Constitutional Conflicts with Congress." President Obama's first confrontation started with his failed attempt by executive order to close Guantánamo within a year. Apparently no advisers warned about the risks of congressional opposition and he paid a heavy price in credibility early in his presidency. The decision to prosecute Khalid Sheikh Mohammed in New York City marked another costly setback. Fisher argues that as with previous presidents, President Obama's effort to use signing statements to control public policy was at times awkward and unpersuasive. Fisher also concludes that also of doubtful constitutionality was his use of military force against Libya without first seeking congressional support and authority. He miscalculated both the purpose and the duration of the intervention. Obama's use of recess appointments is currently being litigated and has the potential of a possible ruling that would invalidate decisions taken by the appointees. The scope of the "Fast and Furious" gunrunning scandal could have been limited by a frank and honest statement by the Justice Department, but it chose to release a false letter to Senator Charles Grassley, leading eventually to House contempt of Attorney General Eric Holder and the invocation by President Obama of executive privilege which forces the Justice Department Inspector General to deliver a harsh indictment of conduct by departmental officials.

Congressional scholars Mark J. Oleszek and Walter J. Oleszek analyze the relationship of Congress and the president from the perspective of the Hill in chapter 13. National lawmaking has become increasingly contentious in recent years as deadline-driven negotiations and brinksmanship ("cliffs") between Congress and the president dominate American political life. In this chapter the Oleszeks review President Obama's track record working with Congress during his first term, and offer observations about what we can expect during his second. Using the 2011 debt ceiling showdown between Congress and the president as a case in point, they illustrate how the politics of brinksmanship has come to define the congressional-presidential relationship. They conclude that failure to find compromise encourages brinksmanship politics, which comes at the expense of citizens' trust and confidence in government, the morale of federal workers, and the time and energy that could have been better spent addressing other issues.

In chapter 14, John E. Owens examines how in taking unilateral action, presidents historically have effectively challenged the Congress and the courts to overturn their actions. Presidents from John Adams through Lincoln to Franklin Roosevelt to Barack Obama have stretched executive power to make policy unilaterally by signing administrative orders, executive orders, or executive agreements; by issuing written or verbal proclamations or presidential or national security directives; by writing memoranda; by designating officials; or, more recently, by issuing "findings," some of which may be secret. The Owens' chapter highlights unitary power of the presidencies under Barack Obama and George W. Bush and how the Congress's acquiescence not only prompted important questions about unchecked executive power, but also whether, in respect to counterterrorism policy, the stretching of presidential power and the consequent shift in the balance of presidential-congressional relations would outlive Bush's presidency. This chapter examines detainee policy, drone targeting, state assassination outside the United States, rendition, and torture in terms in that realm. The chapter concludes with a discussion of the congressional-presidential rivalry and the shift in power that has tilted toward the presidency and continues under President Obama, especially with respect to counterterrorism policy.

Chapter 15 concludes the book with an assessment of policies, processes, and politics of congressional-presidential relations and calls for several basic reforms in Congress that James A. Thurber believes will improve the workings of American democracy.

NOTES

1. Barack H. Obama, "State of the Union Address," 2013 State of the Union, Capitol Building, Washington, DC, February 12, 2013.

2. David S. Broder, "The Amazing Race," *Washington Post*, November 2, 2008.

3. On July 7, 2009, Al Franken (D) won the contested Minnesota seat giving the Democrats sixty votes. On February 4, 2010, Scott Brown (R) replaced Paul Kirk (D) in the Massachusetts delegation. However, Ted Kennedy's (D) illness kept him away from the Senate from March to August 2009. Until Kirk replaced Kennedy on September 24, 2009, the Democrats lacked the necessary sixty votes.

4. See James A. Thurber, "Agony, Angst, and the Failure of the Supercommittee," *Extensions* (Summer 2012), Carl Albert Congressional Research and Studies Center, University of Oklahoma.

5. Arthur M. Schlesinger Jr. and Alfred De Grazia, *Congress and the Presidency: Their Role in Modern Times* (Washington, DC: American Enterprise Institute, 1976), 1.

6. See James A. Thurber, "Congress and the Constitution: Two Hundred Years of Stability and Change," in Richard Maidment, ed., *Reflections on the Constitution* (University of Manchester Press, 1989), 51–75.

7. For this constitutional basis of conflict see Richard E. Neustadt, *Presidential Power and the Modern Presidents: The Politics of Leadership from Roosevelt to Reagan* (New York: Free Press, 1990); James L. Sunquist, *The Decline and Resurgence of Congress* (Washington, DC: The Brookings Institution, 1981); Steven A. Shull, *Domestic Policy Formation: Presidential-Congressional Partnership?* (Westport, CT: Greenwood Press, 1983); Michael L. Mezey, *Congress, the President, and Public Policy* (Boulder, CO: Westview Press, 1985); Louis Fisher, *Constitutional Conflicts between Congress and the President*, 4th rev. ed. (Lawrence: University of Kansas, 1996); Louis Fisher, *The Politics of Shared Power: Congress and the Executive* (Washington, DC: CQ Press, 1993); Charles O. Jones, *The Presidency in a Separated System* (Washington, DC: Brookings Institution, 1994); Charles O. Jones, *Separate but Equal Branches: Congress and the Presidency* (New York: Chatham House, 1999); Charles O. Jones, *Clinton and Congress: Risk, Restoration, and Reelection* (Norman: University of Oklahoma Press, 1999).

8. US House of Representatives, History, Art & Archives, "Presidential Vetoes: 1789 to Present," history.house.gov/Institution/Presidential-Vetoes/Presidential-Vetoes/.

9. A pocket veto is the act of the president withholding his approval of a bill after Congress has adjourned. See Harold W. Stanley and Richard G. Niemi, *Vital Statistics on American Politics*, 5th ed. (Washington, DC: CQ Press. 1995), 258. For vetoes and overrides from the 80th to the 103rd Congresses (1947–1994), see Norman J. Ornstein, Thomas E. Mann, and Michael J. Malbin, *Vital Statistics on Congress, 1995–1996* (Washington, DC: Congressional Quarterly Inc., 1996), 167.

10. Todd S. Purdum, "President Warns Congress to Drop Some Budget Cuts," *New York Times*, October 29, 1995.

11. See Jones, *The Presidency in a Separated System.*

12. See George C. Edwards III, *Overreach: Leadership in the Obama Presidency* (Princeton, NJ: Princeton University Press, 2012); George C. Edwards III, *Presidential Influence in Congress* (San Francisco: Freeman, 1980); and Cecil V. Crabb Jr. and Pat M. Holt, *Invitation to Struggle: Congress, the President, and Foreign Policy*, 4th ed. (Washington, DC: CQ Press, 1992).

13. James Madison, "Federalist No. 46," in Clinton Rossiter, ed., *The Federalist Papers* (New York: New American Library, 1961), 296.

14. See Stephen Wayne, *The Legislative Presidency* (New York: Harper and Row, 1978).

15. David R. Mayhew, *Congress: The Electoral Connection* (New Haven, CT: Yale University Press, 1974).

16. Thomas E. Mann, "Breaking the Political Impasse," in Henry J. Aaron, ed., *Setting National Priorities: Policy for the Nineties* (Washington, DC: Brookings Institution, 1990), 302.

17. Nelson Polsby quoted in *Congress and the Nation*, vol. 7, 1985–1988 (Washington, DC: Congressional Quarterly Inc., 1990), 21–22.

18. Mayhew, *Divided We Govern*, 198.

19. See Committee on the Constitutional System, *A Bicentennial Analysis of the American Political Structure* (Washington, DC: Committee on the Constitutional System, 1987).

20. See James A. Thurber, "The Dynamics and Dysfunction of the Congressional Budget Process: From Inception to Deadlock" in Larry Dodd and Bruce Oppenheimer, eds., *Congress Reconsidered* (Washington, DC, Sage and CQ Press, 2013), 319–45 and James A. Thurber, "Twenty-Five Years of Deficit and Conflict: Partisan Roles in Congressional Budget Reform," in Nicole C. Rae and Colton Campbell, eds., *New Majority or Old Minority: The Impact of Republicans in Congress* (Lanham, MD: Rowman & Littlefield, 1999).

21. These scores are a commonly used measure of the ideology of legislators. DW NOMINATE scores are produced by applying a spatial model to roll-call voting in Congress. These scores allow for the comparison of members of different Congresses across time. Poole and Rosenthal (2001) argue that the first ideological dimension, capturing differing views on economic policy, explains most roll-call-voting decisions. A second dimension, capturing views on race, has diminished in importance since the 1960s. For more information on DW-NOMINATE, see Poole, Keith, and Rosenthal, *The Polarization of the Congressional Parties*, 2012. Data and graphs available: http://polarizedamerica.com/political_polarization.asp. See also Keith T. Poole and Howard Rosenthal, "D-NOMINATE after 10 Years: A Comparative Update to Congress: A Political-Economic History of Roll Call Voting," *Legislative Studies Quarterly* 26 (2001): 5–26; Nolan M. McCarty, Keith T. Poole, and Howard Rosenthal, *Income Redistribution and the Realignment of American Politics* (Washington, DC: AEI Press, 1997); Victoria McGrane, "John Tanner Pushes Redistricting Reform," *Policito*, July 24, 2009.

22. Barbara Sinclair, "The President and Congressional Party Leadership in a Polarized Era," in James A. Thurber , ed., *Rivals for Power*, 4th ed. (Rowman & Littlefield, 2009), 83–104.

23. Sean Theriault and David Rohde, "The Gingrich Senators and Party Polarization in the U.S. Senate," *Journal of Politics* 73, no. 4 (October 2011): 1011–24.

24. *Congressional Record*, July 29, 2008, H7285. Also referenced in James A. Thurber, "What's Wrong with Congress and What Should Be Done About It," in Iwan Morgan and Philip Davies, eds., *Broken Government? American Politics in the Obama Era* (London: University of London/Institute for the Study of the Americas Press, 2012).

25. See the *Cook Report*, "Post 2012 Analysis," November 15, 2012.

26. Harris Interactive, www.harrisinteractive.com/.

27. *New Hampshire News*, "The City as Infestation," October 9, 2012, www.nhpr.org/node/14408.

28. NBC News, "DNC Bans Lobbyist Money," June 6, 2008, www.msnbc.msn.com/id/24989468/wid/7468326/.

29. See Joel H. Sibley, "The Rise and Fall of American Political Parties," in L. Sandy Maisel, ed., *The Parties Respond: Changes in American Parties and Campaigns* (Boulder, CO: Westview Press, 1994), 3–18.

30. James A. Thurber, "Political Power and Policy Subsystems in American Politics," in B. Guy Peters and Bert A. Rockman, eds., *Agenda for Excellence: Administering the State* (Chatham, NJ: Chatham House Publishers, 1996), 76–104.

31. See Jonathan Rauch, *Demosclerosis* (New York: Times Books, 1994).

Chapter Two

Obama's First-Term, Legislative Presidency

Partisan, Not Personal

Stephen J. Wayne

Obama's first-term, legislative presidency was a tale of two Congresses: one in which the president achieved most of policy priorities and one in which he did not. It was one in which the president's personal involvement in the legislative process was limited, with health-care reform and negotiations with the House Speaker on the debt limit and government spending being the most notable exceptions.

Obama's operating style, political predilections, and policy preferences generated criticism from both sides of the aisle. Democrats complained about his light hand. They also alleged that he compromised too soon and too much and that he was not sufficiently supportive of their core concerns and positions.[1] Republicans, on the other hand, saw him as a captive of the left, a proponent of big government and big spending, a socialist, distant, unfriendly, and preachy.

These partisan cleavages, highlighted by the news media and heightened by the deepening economic downturn, inflamed political debate, lowered the president's and Congress's approval, and increased public skepticism about government in general and the policies being pursued in particular. In the short run, the hostile political environment facilitated the enactment of most of the president's legislative agenda. When desired economic and social change did not rapidly follow, however, Republican criticism of government overreach, wasteful spending, and growing debt hit a responsive chord, leading to the Democrats' defeat in the 2010 midterm elections and the legislative gridlock during the 112th Congress. That environment, both on Capitol

Hill and within the country, also encouraged the president to use the public
arena to defend his and his party's partisan positions rather than pursue his
own plea for bipartisanship, a position he had advocated in *The Audacity of
Hope*,[2] his 2008 campaign, and his early speeches and remarks in office.
This is the story of Obama's first-term, legislative presidency, transforming
policy and being transformed by politics, of winning the legislative battles,
but losing the public debate, and then using his bully pulpit to restructure that
debate to win reelection.

HITTING THE GROUND RUNNING:
THE PRESIDENT'S LEGISLATIVE TRANSITION

In his 2008 presidential campaign, Barack Obama had promised to transform
policy and politics; he conveyed a confident "yes we can" attitude. That "can
do" attitude contributed to the optimism that followed his historic victory as
the first African American elected president of the United States. It also
added to the administration's initial legislative clout.

So did the magnitude of the economic crisis. In general, crises, when they
first occur, enhance opportunities for presidential leadership. Members of
Congress, much like the general public, look to the president and rally behind
him. President George W. Bush benefited from this "rally round" effect
following the terrorist attacks of September 11, 2001. He gained greater
leverage, quicker action, and more of the policy outcomes he desired than he
would have in a "politics as usual" environment.

The expanded public and congressional influence that results from crisis
decision making motivates presidents to elevate problems to crisis levels,
such as a war on poverty, or declaring the Arab oil embargo as "the moral
equivalent of war," or declaring a health-care crisis, and to keep them at
these levels as long as possible to maximize their public support. They also
have an incentive to prolong crises if they believe it will extend their public
support. Over time, however, if unsatisfactory conditions persist, or if the
cost of overcoming them is too high, presidential popularity and political
influence tend to decline.[3]

Obama used the 2008 financial and economic crisis to help win the 2008
election, demonstrate the need for change, and speed up the legislative process. Even before he took office, he had been advised by Rahm Emanuel, his
first White House chief of staff, "never let a serious crisis go to waste . . . it's
an opportunity to do things you think you could not do before."[4] Obama
followed that advice.

Five weeks after his election victory, he met with his economic and
political advisers. They presented him with their analysis of rapidly deteriorating economic conditions and a plan to halt the slide and prevent a catas-

trophic failure, a large government spending program of about $900 billion; Obama had proposed a $150 billion stimulus package during the 2008 presidential campaign, which his postelection advisers considered to be insufficient.

Accepting their recommendation for a massive government program, the president-elect asked them to fill in the numbers. The next day, he met with congressional Democratic leaders and their principal aides to urge quick passage. Obama had requested the legislation by Inauguration Day, but had to settle for mid-February, President's Day, when he signed the American Recovery and Reinvestment Act into law.

Again, he left most of the legislative details to others, the committee chairs and party leaders. At that point, he had to do so. As president-elect, Obama did not have the resources of the executive branch at his disposal to do the necessary spade work. Moreover, as a former legislator, he believed that giving Congress discretion in writing the bill would contribute to its enactment. And it did.

Delegation to Congress had other advantages. It distanced Obama from the inside game of Washington's legislative politics that he disliked as a senator and wanted to avoid as much as possible as president. He saw his principal presidential roles as setting priorities, making policy decisions, and selling them to the American people, not engaging in the trench warfare that has characterized contemporary presidential-congressional relations. He had an elevated view of the president—apart and above others in the government.

Although Obama's deference to Democratic committee chairs and party leaders enhanced their bargaining position, it did so at the president's expense. It gave them leverage to make the compromises and forge the alliances necessary to enact comprehensive legislation, but it reduced the White House's control over the pace of deliberations. It also limited the ability of the president and his aides to referee the jurisdictional battles among committees and the ego battles among chairs and ranking minority members on such issues as health care, cap-and-trade legislation, and regulations imposed on the financial community.

Delegation also opened up the process to greater press scrutiny. From a theoretical point of view, for a president who preached greater transparency in government, that scrutiny enhanced the democratic character of the system. But from a political perspective, it enabled the Republicans to take pot shots at legislation, to pick it apart, to generate opposition, and embarrass the Democrats and the president. Health care in particular suffered this fate. When Republican criticism in May and June 2009 produced angry public protests that the news media, particular the conservative media, magnified, the president was put on the defensive, a position from which he never recovered on that issue.[5]

Although the president had used the economic crisis as an action-forcing mechanism, he was unable to bridge the legislative partisan divide. Only three Republican senators and no Republican members of the House of Representatives voted for the Recovery and Reinvestment Act, an indication of what was to come during his first term.

During the transition period, the president-elect also persuaded Democrats in the 110th Democratic Congress to release the second stage of bailout funds enacted during the Bush administration; Obama also moved quickly to appoint his White House team. Despite downplaying the importance of Washington experience in his nomination and general election campaigns, he chose people with that experience, particularly on Capitol Hill, to be key staffers for policy formulation and legislative liaison. Their inside knowledge of the people and process gave the administration confidence that it could effectively delegate detailed legislative drafting to Congress and still control the final product, a confidence that in retrospect was misplaced.

PROMISES AND PERFORMANCE: THE TRIUMPH OF PARTISANSHIP

In his 2008 electoral campaign the president had emphasized policy change. He proposed over five hundred new policy initiatives, many of them requiring a legislative format.[6] According to Politifact.com, a website that lists campaign pledges and evaluates progress in accomplishing them, Obama converted about half of them into public policy, compromised on a quarter of them, and failed to gain the rest during his first term.[7]

The president also promised political change. He said that he would unify the country and bridge the partisan divide. He was not successful in doing so, however. Instead of transforming politics, politics transformed Obama, forcing him to be a more partisan president than he had indicated was desirable or that he would do if elected. But he had little choice given the political climate, the diverse policy beliefs in Congress, and the cohesive partisan behavior on both sides of the aisle. Staying partisan was the only way to achieve the legislative policy goals he desired. Besides, the president's political beliefs overlap those of most congressional Democrats. He believes as his party has since the 1930s that government can and should be a positive force in promoting greater economic and social opportunities.

The First Two Years

The scope and substance of the legislative policy initiatives enacted during the 111th Congress was considerable, approaching that of the first two years of the Johnson administration.[8] In addition to the American Recovery and Reinvestment Act, the almost $800 billion stimulus package that provided money for rebuilding the nation's infrastructure, aid to education, computerization of health-care records, grants to promote renewable energy, federal tax incentives, the expansion of unemployment benefits, and grants to states, Congress also passed bills to help families save their homes from foreclosure, require credit card companies to disclose their interest-rate charges, enhance the enforcement and increase the criminal penalties for fraudulent business practices, and provide federal subsidies for new car buyers who traded in their less gasoline-efficient vehicles for more efficient ones.[9]

Other legislation enacted during Obama's first year in office included the Lilly Ledbetter Fair Pay Act that removed the statute of limitations on law suits alleging gender-based salary discrimination; the Children's Health Insurance Act, which President Bush had vetoed twice, that provided states with matching funds for health insurance for children from families with limited incomes that do not qualify for Medicaid; an Omnibus Public Lands bill that designated two million additional acres of wilderness in nine states; the Edward M. Kennedy Serve America Act that expanded opportunities for voluntary national service; and the Family Smoking Prevention and Tobacco Control Act that gave the Food and Drug Administration authority to regulate the sale and advertising of tobacco products.[10]

In 2010, it was more of the same. The Patient Protection and Affordable Care Act (known as ObamaCare) was enacted after protracted and heated public and congressional debate. Health and other benefits for veterans and their families were also passed but without partisan opposition. At the president's urging, Congress enacted a jobs bill that gave tax credits to businesses for hiring the unemployed or underemployed, again extended unemployment insurance, provided new tax cuts and credits for small businesses, and comprehensive legislation to regulate the financial sector, known as the Dodd–Frank Wall Street Reform and Consumer Protection Act.

In the lame-duck session of the 111th Congress, a compromise, negotiated by Vice President Biden and Senate minority leader, Mitch McConnell, extended the Bush income and estate tax cuts for two years as well as unemployment insurance for a year, and allowed votes on the START Treaty with Russia and the military's "Don't Ask, Don't Tell" policy, both of which were approved. From the perspective of the administration and the Democratic majority, it was a very productive Congress.

Obama won because of the partisan cleavage and the Democratic unity that resulted from it. With large majorities in both houses, the Democrats were able to push through much of their legislative agenda. According to the *Congressional Quarterly*, there were more votes in which a majority of Democrats opposed a majority of Republicans than ever before in the US Senate with Senate Democrats backing the president over 90 percent of the time. In the House, key votes were also divided along partisan lines with Democratic support for the president around 80 percent.[11]

When Democrats did not achieve the policy outcomes they desired—the single-payer option for health care, the Dream Act for children of illegal immigrants, and limits to corporate campaign contributions—it was because they lacked a supermajority in the Senate, the sixty votes to break a Republican filibuster after the election of Republican Scott Brown in Massachusetts to replace the late Senator Edward Kennedy.

The Second Two Years

Partisanship continued to drive legislative process in the second part of Obama's first term, but with a very different result. With Congress divided, the parties polarized, and the president magnifying the partisan differences in the public arena, legislative stalemate ensued. There were a few exceptions, most notably the compromise on raising the debt limit and cutting government spending negotiated principally by Senate leaders with the vice president's participation toward the end of the negotiating process, after talks between President Obama and House Speaker John Boehner broke down in the summer of 2011.[12]

The deal in which debt limit increases were to be matched by spending decreases created a joint congressional committee to propose at least $1.2 trillion in additional budget cuts over an eight-year period. The legislation provided that if the committee failed to do so, automatic cuts in government expenditures would occur at the end of 2012, affecting both defense and nondefense spending.[13] It was hoped that the threat of large, across-the-board cuts would pressure the committee to reach an agreement and both legislative houses to support that agreement.

The inability of the committee to find a solution to the fiscal crisis extended that crisis beyond the 2012 election although short-term extensions of the 2 percent reduction in the Social Security payroll tax, unemployment benefits, and increased payments to Medicare providers were achieved as stop-gap measures.[14]

The 112th Congress did reauthorize antiterrorism provisions of the USA Patriot Act, modernize patent law, and enact three free-trade agreements (with Panama, Colombia, and South Korea) that had been negotiated by the Bush administration, but were opposed by Democrats, who feared the agreements would produce job losses at home and continue unfair labor practices abroad. To placate the Democrats and their labor supporters, a jobs bill to provide aid to US workers adversely affected by the trade legislation was also enacted.[15]

As the 2012 election approached, partisan positions hardened and compromise became even more difficult to obtain. Legislative output declined substantially. Only 274 laws were passed by the 112th Congress compared to

385 for the 111th Congress (2009–2010) and 460 for the 110th (2007–2008).[16]

After the election, however, the expiration of the Bush tax cuts, the sequestration of defense and nondefense spending, and the limit on the amount of borrowing that the federal government could do created a fiscal crisis and pressured the administration and party leaders to devise some acceptable policy solution. Neither party wanted to be blamed for inaction that could adversely affect the already fragile economy. A last-minute compromise, negotiated in the Senate, extended most of the cuts for most taxpayers but raised additional revenue by increasing tax rates and limiting tax deductions for higher-income Americans (individuals whose yearly income exceeded $400,000 and families whose total income exceeded $450,000). The budget sequestration was postponed for two months. It and the debt limit remained problems for the next Congress to tackle. The fiscal cliff at the end of 2012 had been averted, but just barely.

GOING PUBLIC AND ITS POLITICAL CONSEQUENCES

The successful enactment of many of Obama's legislative policy goals in his first two years in office did not increase the president's public prestige or extend his personal influence. It had the opposite effect. The failure of the stimulus and other legislation to reverse the economic downturn quickly and significantly reinforced the Republican argument that government was not the solution to the country's economic woes; it was the problem. With high unemployment and low job creation, increasing foreclosures and decreasing property values, and continuing partisan confrontation inhibiting policy accord—all highlighted by the news media and magnified by the 2010 election campaign—fueled public anxieties and reduced confidence and trust in government; job approval ratings for the president and Congress steadily declined from mid-2009 through most of 2012.

Obama had been elected with 53 percent of the vote. Near the end of his first one hundred days he had reach 64 percent in public approval. His numbers then began to drop, reaching a low of 38 percent in August 2010, before the midterm elections. His approval averaged in the mid-forties for the last three years of his first term.[17] (See figure 2.1.)

Congress's ratings fared even more poorly, as they usually do when compared with the president's. After its initial burst of legislative activity in 2009, congressional approval declined from a high of 39 percent in early March of that year to the low twenties and teens for the remainder of Obama's first term.[18] The results of the 2010 elections confirmed the polls; the Democrats lost six seats in the Senate and sixty-three in the House and

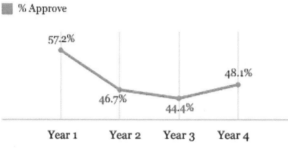

Barack Obama's Yearly Job Approval Averages

■ % Approve

57.2%

46.7%

44.4%

48.1%

Year 1   Year 2   Year 3   Year 4

Gallup Daily tracking

GALLUP

Figure 2.1. Barack Obama's Yearly Job Approval Averages. Source: Jeffrey M. Jones, "Obama Averages 49% Approval in First Term," Gallup Poll, January 21, 2013, www.gallup.com/poll/159965/obama-averages-approval-first-term .aspx.

control of that legislative body. The president and his fellow Democrats were clearly on the political defensive.

The president had won most of the legislative battles but had lost the war in the public arena. Without a legislative majority, and without broad-based support to continue his policy initiatives, he took the path of least resistance, the path that most contemporary presidents (with the possible exception of George H. W. Bush) have taken—he went public.

Presidents resort to their bully pulpit for several reasons. The public expects them to do so. Most of them are good at it and have been successful doing it, winning election to the White House. Their pulpit gives them a louder voice. It helps them prime and shape the news media's agenda. It elevates their status, which they believe enhances their personal influence.

Going public is also relatively easy for most contemporary presidents. They read scripts on a teleprompter; they speak to friendly groups and crowds, carefully selected by the White House, to provide a supportive environment and a sympathetic hearing. The event is choreographed for television; the president speaks behind the seal; the audience responds positively. Even if the president's remarks do not change public opinion,[19] even if Congress does not respond as the administration desires, the president still gets a favorable sound bite, a good picture.

Not only does their pulpit inflate their incumbency advantage, it probably inflates their ego as well. It is their stage. They like being the center of attention. It feeds into perceptions of self-importance and builds self-confidence. For most presidents, the benefits of going public outweigh the costs.

But staying within the public arena also makes the partisan divide more difficult to surmount because it solidifies policy positions, heightens rhetoric, and personalizes issues. It is harder to negotiate in full public view. Electoral calculations become more salient, and interest-group participation may unleash forces that an administration cannot control, as was the case with Clinton and Obama's health-care proposals and Bush's attempt to privatize Social Security.

Going public also consumes considerable White House and presidential time and energy and generates resentment if members of Congress believe that they are being circumvented, neglected, or taken for granted.[20] In the words of Senator Olympia Snowe (R-Maine), "I can understand him [Obama] using the bully pulpit, you know, to enhance his position, but it can't be to the exclusion of ever working with the legislative branch."[21]

During his first term, Obama was accused of not doing enough to cultivate friendships outside his inner circle, a charge to which he reacted defensively when asked about at a news conference following his reelection:

> Personal relationships are important, and obviously I can always do a better job, and the nice thing is, is that now that my girls are getting older, they don't want to spend that much time with me anyway, so I'll be probably calling around, looking for somebody to play cards with me or something, because I'm getting kind of lonely in this big house. [laughter] So maybe a whole bunch of members of the House Republican caucus want to come over and socialize more.[22]

Obama did not regularly host White House meetings with the bipartisan leadership during his first term. With the exception of the president's health-care initiative in which he and Speaker Nancy Pelosi met and spoke with sixty-eight House Democrats during a two-week period in early 2010[23] and his personal negotiations with Speaker Boehner over a grand bargain on spending and debt issues in the summer of 2011, he did not engage in much personal lobbying with members of Congress, although his legislative representatives, Vice President Biden, and his various chiefs of staff obviously did. Both Republicans and Democrats criticized the administration's outreach.[24]

Personal relations are important because they facilitate trust. They can help overcome the institutional and partisan divides. In the words of Senator Tom Harkin, "Personal relations always are better than keeping a distance. It's my observation that President Obama, even when he was here and was on my committee and stuff, he's a very intellectual, focused individual. It never seemed to me that he enjoyed the give and the take of the institution here."[25] Tony Coelho, a former Democratic leader of the House of Representatives echoed a similar refrain. "Clinton loved governing, and my view is that Obama doesn't like governing. . . . In order to be a good president, you've got to love governing. And governing is getting to know the people in the House and the Senate."[26] Economic adviser, Larry Summers, put it this way: "Obama doesn't have the joy of the game. Clinton basically loved negotiating with a bunch of other pols, about anything. Obama, he really [doesn't] like these guys."[27]

President Obama is a better listener before he decides. After reaching a conclusion, he tends to become more lawyer-like, making his points to win the argument. He is also very conscious of his elected position, the status it gives him as chief policy maker and public educator, and the status he believes it should give him as final decision maker.

SUMMARY

The legislative presidency has always been influenced by the partisan political environment, the magnitude of perceived economic and social problems, and the administration itself—its priorities, programmatic proposals, and congressional relations. Richard Neustadt made much of the president's personal skills when he argued the Roosevelt model of strategic mapping, political bargaining, and personal relations was key to a president's policy success on Capitol Hill.[28]

Barack Obama certainly can point to transformative policy change in his first two years in office. Laws to stimulate the economy and help those most adversely affected by it, reform health care, regulate the financial sector, and address a host of other economic and social issues were enacted. Obama shaped that agenda, but it was Democratic partisanship, not the president's heavy or skillful hand, that carried the day. If anything, the president's operating style, his deference to Democratic Party leaders, and his use of the bully pulpit undercut his legislative clout, even within his own party. The scope and content of Obama's legislative presidency increasingly shaped his perception as a partisan president pursuing his party's traditional liberal policies.

With the economy still in the doldrums and little evidence that the expansive legislative activity and the expenditures that accompanied it were producing the desired policy change, public angst turned against the president and congressional Democrats. Their job approval declined and the party suffered major losses in the 2010 midterm elections. Those losses encouraged the president to reduce his legislative activity in favor of a public campaign to reposition himself for reelection and rebuild his political base.

In that campaign he used Republican intransigence in Congress and Republican policy alternatives as a foil to gain a more favorable comparison for himself and his party. Instead of being evaluated on the basis of the expectations he generated, the promises he made, and the imagery he created in 2008, Obama wanted to be judged alongside his GOP opponents, whom both he and the news media held up increasingly to critical scrutiny. He also wanted Democratic policies to be contrasted with those the Republicans were advocating and not to be judged on the basis of their short-term economic results or relatively high cost.

In addition to taking increasing attention from the economic woes, the almost two-year campaign allowed Obama to remain on his presidential pedestal. His pulpit, the electorate's limited choice, and some economic improvement helped restore the country's political balance and enhanced the president and his party's image. The legislative presidency had turned into a public campaign. Obama did not change public opinion but he changed public perceptions and in doing so, demonstrated the powers and prestige of the presidency: taking the initiative, setting the agenda, priming the issues, framing the debate, and shaping (but not controlling) policy outcomes. He did use that campaign to win reelection, hoping that the first term policies would have a more discernible and beneficial second term impact.

NOTES

1. Bob Woodward, *The Price of Politics* (New York: Simon & Schuster, 2012), 332.
2. "I believe any attempt by Democrats to pursue a more sharply partisan and ideological strategy misapprehends the moment we're in. I am convinced that whenever we exaggerate or demonize, oversimplify or overstate our case, we lose. . . . for it's precisely the pursuit of ideological purity, the rigid orthodoxy and the sheer predictability of our current political debate, that keeps us from finding new ways to meet the challenges we face as a country." Barack Obama, *The Audacity of Hope* (New York: Crown, 2006), 39–40.
3. President George W. Bush's approval ratings over the course of the war with Iraq fell from 71 percent at the outbreak of hostilities to a little over 50 percent within a year's time to the low thirties even before the 2008 economic recession and financial crisis. "Trends from A–Z: Presidential Approval Ratings of George W. Bush," Gallup Poll, www.gallup.com/poll/116500/Presidential-Approval-Ratings-George-Bush.aspx.
4. Rahm Emanuel, *Wall Street Journal Digital Network*, November 19, 2008, www.youtube.com/watch?v=_mzcbXi1Tkk.
5. Obama had difficulty responding to allegations about the plan, some of which were outrageous, such as creation of government death panels. With so many other problems requiring his attention, he also found it hard to stay focused on health care, much less frame it to his political advantage. Most problematic, he left himself in a position in which he almost had to accept the bill in whatever form it was enacted if he wanted to claim that he had achieved health-care reform.
6. Angie Drobnic Holan, "A PolitiFact Special Report: Obama's First-Term Campaign Promises," Politifact.com, January 17, 2013, www.politifact.com/truth-o-meter/article/2013/jan/17/politifact-obamas-first-term-campaign-promises/.
7. Bill Adair, Becky Bowers, Angie Drobnic Holan, Louis Jacobson, Molly Moorhead, and J. B. Wogan, "Reflections on the Obameter and Obama's campaign promises," December 28, 2012. www.politifact.com/truth-o-meter/article/2012/dec/28/reflections-obameter-and-obamas-campaign-promises/.

8. In 1964, Congress enacted the Civil Rights Act that prohibited most forms of discrimination based on race, religion, and ethnicity, and the Equal Opportunity Act, which was landmark legislation to begin the fight of the war on poverty. Johnson also signed laws to provide food stamps to the needy, loans for homeowners, and money for mass transit. The legislation also created the administrative structures to implement these programs. In 1965, the Voting Rights Act, designed to end discriminatory practices that prevented citizens from voting; the Elementary and Secondary School Act that provided federal funding for education; and the Medicare and Medicaid programs (the Social Security Act) were made law as was immigration reform (the Immigration Act).

9. The Recovery and Reinvestment Act of 2009; Fraud Enforcement and Recovery Act (May 20, 2009); Helping Families Save Their Homes Act of 2009 (May 20, 2009); The Credit Card Accountability, Responsibility, and Disclosure Act of 2009 (May 22, 2009); and Cash For Clunkers Extension Act (August 6, 2009).

10. Also enacted was legislation to criminalize hate crimes—the Matthew Shepard and James Byrd Jr. Hate Crimes Prevention Act; expand federal funds for the treatment of HIV/AIDS (October 28, 2009)—the Ryan White HIV/AIDS Treatment Extension Act (October 30, 2009); and extend unemployment benefits and provide tax credits for people that purchased a house—the Worker, Homeownership, and Business Assistance Act of 2009 (November 6, 2009).

11. Shawn Zeller, "2010 Vote Studies: Party Unity," *Congressional Quarterly Weekly*, January 3, 2011, library.cqpress.com/cqweekly/document.php?id=weeklyreport112-000003788 817&.

12. For an extensive discussion of these negotiations and why they failed, see Matt Bai, "Obama vs. Boehner: Who Killed the Debt Deal? *New York Times*, March 28, 2012, www.nytimes.com/2012/04/01/magazine/obama-vs-boehner-who-killed-the-debt-deal.html?.

13. Social Security, Medicaid, veterans' benefits, and military pay would be exempted; the reduction in Medicare would be limited to 2 percent.

14. The compromise leading to the Budget Control Act of 2011 is detailed by Woodward in *The Price of Politics*.

15. Leahy-Smith America Invents Act (September 16, 2011); United States-Korea Free Trade Agreement Implementation Act, United States-Colombia Trade Promotion Agreement Implementation Act; United States-Panama Trade Promotion Agreement Implementation Act (October 21, 2011); and The National Defense Authorization Act for Fiscal Year 2012, (December 31, 2011).

16. "Legislation of the United States, 2001-Present," Library of Congress, beta.con gress.gov/legislation?pageSize=25&Legislative_Source=Legislation&.

17. "Trends A–Z: Presidential Approval Ratings—Barack Obama," Gallup Poll, www.gallup.com/poll/116479/Barack-Obama-Presidential-Job-Approval.aspx.

18. Frank Newport, "Congress Begins 2013 With 14% Approval," Gallup Poll, January 11, 2013, www.gallup.com/poll/159812/congress-begins-2013-approval.aspx.

19. George C. Edwards III in his book *On Deaf Ears* (New Haven, CT: Yale University Press, 2003) argues that presidents do not usually succeed in their efforts to change public opinion.

20. When the House minority leader, Nancy Pelosi, excluded from the secret negotiations between President Obama and Speaker John Boehner, learned about the proposed deal and the expectation that a majority of Democrats would support it, she said to a White House aide attending her party's caucus: "Don't insult us. You guys don't know how to count . . . If you're going to ask for House Democrats to put the vote over the top, we want to make sure that our concerns are more fairly reflected." See Woodward, *Price of Politics*, 170.

21. Steven T. Dennis, "Obama's Aloof Behavior with GOP Could Hurt Agenda," *Roll Call*, December 5, 2011, www.rollcall.com/issues/57_68/Obama-Allof-Behavior-gop-hurt-agenda -210744-1.html?zkprintable=t.

22. Barack Obama, "News Conference by the President," The White House, January 14, 2013, www.whitehouse.gov/the-press-office/2013/01/14/news-conference-president.

23. Stephen J. Wayne, *Personality and Politics: Obama For and Against Himself* (Washington, DC: CQ Press, 2012), 135.

24. In an interview with reporter Bob Woodward, House Speaker John Boehner said of the Obama administration: "There was no outreach when we were in the minority. There is no outreach in a majority. You look at both Bush administrations, Clinton's administration, they had a congressional affairs team that was plugged in keeping people up to date. No outreach. Go talk to the Democrats. Because they get treated the same way." Woodward, *Price of Politics*, 376.

25. Woodward, *Price of Politics*, 376.

26. George E. Condon Jr., "Obama Needs Friends in Congress," *The Atlantic*, July 13, 2011, www.theatlantic.com/.../2011/07/obama-needs-friends-in-congress/241902.

27. Woodward, *Price of Politics*, 82.

28. Richard E. Neustadt, *Presidential Power and the Modern Presidents* (New York: Free Press, 1990).

Chapter Three

White House–Congressional Relations in a Polarized Age

Gary Andres and Patrick Griffin

Partisan polarization paints a broad backdrop for the twenty-first-century Congress. Its bold brush strokes now cover nearly every corner of the legislative canvas with bright lines of division, impacting roll-call votes, party-leadership tactics, committee legislative products, and political fundraising to name a few.

Today's conventional wisdom asserts that polarization has reemerged over the past two decades after a hundred year hiatus. Congressional parties in the US House and Senate have once again sorted into two homogeneous, ideological, warring camps. Democrats are now consistently more liberal and Republicans more uniformly conservative than any time since Speaker Thomas Brackett Reed ruled a unified majority with military discipline in the late nineteenth century and the rank-and-file closely followed their leaders like a well-organized militia. In the last twenty years, these volunteer armies of partisans have regrouped and now regularly engage figuratively in hand-to-hand combat, much like they did in the late nineteenth- and early twentieth-century Congress.

Political scientists have offered compelling explanations for the return of polarization and its implications on legislative operations.[1] We do not intend to reiterate or review all the fine scholarly and popular descriptions about the causes and consequences of these hostilities in this chapter, but there's no way to understand the modern Congress—and how the president relates to this institution—without a big hat tip to the power of partisan polarization.

But a broader aperture is needed to fully understand the landscape of today's partisanship in Washington. Based on reading scholarly literature on the topic, one might assume polarization is principally a congressional phenomenon. Our experience suggests otherwise. Partisanship's tentacles ensnare a lot more than just the daily workings around the Capitol. It now grabs most aspects of the Washington establishment—including interest groups and the media. Relations along both ends of Pennsylvania Avenue are also regularly impacted by strong partisan tides. Presidents and entire administrations get covered in its wash. Moreover, presidents who are skillful in using the tools made available to them through interest groups, lobbyists, the media, and technology can successfully leverage their agendas in this hyperpartisan world. In other words, these myriad forces of polarization—and how they are managed—must be factored in when considering a president's success in Washington. Moreover, these same factors must be considered in trying to better understand White House–congressional relations in a partisan age.

But because most scholarly research on partisanship is focused only on Congress, the full extent of our growing polarized politics on relations between presidents and lawmakers—and other aspects of the Washington establishment—is not well understood.

In this chapter we analyze another major spoke in the wheel of twenty-first-century partisan politics: the implications of polarization on White House–congressional relations and how presidents attempt to manage legislative affairs in today's hyperpartisan age.

We propose a framework for understanding how presidents operate in today's hyperpartisan Washington culture. It begins by considering the president's institutional constraints and advantages. We next evaluate his political goals. Finally, we assess how political skills factor into this equation.

But there is another part of the calculation that also deserves consideration. The relationship between the president and Congress doesn't just take place between two governmental actors. Other forces, such as a faster and fragmented media—driven by new technological developments—and an explosion of interest groups also shape White House–congressional relations. These nongovernmental players also impact tactics, strategies, and outcomes of legislative and regulator battles between the branches. We argue that understanding White House–congressional relations in today's more partisan environment requires unpacking all of these factors.

We begin this exploration by outlining the ways today's more partisan political culture has spread well beyond just Congress and now impacts the White House and all its interactions with legislators, outside stakeholders, and the media. The balance of this chapter explores how the White House manages its relations with Congress in this more hyperpartisan environment utilizing the considerations outlined above.

- The president's institutional constraints and advantages
- The president's political goals

• The president's political and legislative skills

These three factors are distinct, but interrelated. For example, one institutional constraint (whether the president faces divided or unified party government) can impact political goals and can also sometimes magnify legislative success or shortcomings. A president facing a determined and hostile congressional majority of the other party might both limit his political goals and also appear less effective in accomplishing his legislative ends—think George W. Bush or Lyndon Johnson in their first terms with unified party control in Congress compared to George H. W. Bush (1989–1993), Bill Clinton after the 1994 election, or Barack Obama after 2010.

The president's institutional constraints and advantages, his political goals and skills are also impacted by modern communications technology and the dramatic growth of interest-group formation, organization, and mobilization over the past twenty years. We integrate the impact of these two important changes later in this chapter.

POLARIZATION AND THE MODERN PRESIDENCY

Viewing polarization only through the prism of Capitol Hill misses a major changed dynamic in the American political system. Presidents are not immune from the spread of partisan polarization that has swept over American politics during the past two decades. As a result, White House–congressional relations are regularly impacted by the partisan waves crashing across both ends of Pennsylvania Avenue.

As Congress has become more sorted into two warring camps, the White House has responded to this spreading partisan brush fire in two ways. First, it supported its own side more aggressively. In other words, presidents tried more deliberately and systematically to make their own congressional team look good. Second, they more aggressively and methodically tried to make their opposition look bad.

This one-two punch of supporting "your own team" while scoring points at the expense of the other puts the president in a unique situation. Instead of trying to find common ground with both parties in Congress, presidents became vocal cheerleaders for their side, taking positions that bolstered their own party while becoming the "critic-in-chief" of the opposition.

Over the past two decades—in both Republican and Democratic White Houses—presidents have routinely singled out their own party for praise and the other for scorn. President Clinton regularly castigated Speaker Newt Gingrich and the Republican Congress for what he called extreme positions on taxes and spending. Presidents George W. Bush and Barack Obama did the same with the opposition party in Congress.

And congressional leaders shot right back.

Of course, skirmishes between presidents and Congress have occurred since the earliest days of the republic. But with the growth of polarization and modern communications and the emergence of partisan-based interest groups (like Heritage Action on the Right and The Center for American Progress on the Left), the frequency of these assaults is growing. The tenor of modern presidential-congressional relations feels qualitatively more partisan. Gestures like George H. W. Bush telling Congress he was reaching out his hand in bipartisan cooperation have been replaced by Barack Obama telling the House Republican Majority Leader, "elections matter and I won." Today there are simply more opportunities for congressional leaders to joust with the president and vice versa in a news cycle that is both expanded and includes many more outlets, from blogs to cable outlets, to Internet news sites, as well as some of the more partisan-based interest groups mentioned above.

The demands of fundraising in both presidential and congressional races also impacts partisan teamwork. Campaign money is now more important than ever and all politicians must allocate more of their time to raising the requisite resources. Presidents routinely hit the road for congressional candidates with increasing frequency, raising money and supporting their party's electoral efforts in ways that would be unheard of in the 1960s and 1970s.

The number of bipartisan congressional leadership meetings at the White House has also decreased in the past twenty years as polarization has grown. Being in the same room together is increasingly awkward in an environment laced with hostile comments in the media with one team attacking the other like a long-running major league rivalry. President George H. W. Bush met with Republicans and Democratic leaders at the White House about twice a month. These meetings decreased in frequency under Presidents Clinton and George W. Bush. Under President Obama they are even more rare, the political equivalent of a lunar eclipse.

Here's a recent illustration of polarization impacting White House–congressional relations. President Obama's conclusion in September 2011 that a major budget deal was not possible led him to a preelection strategy of attacking and blaming the Republicans for their failure to cooperate. At the same time, Republicans anticipated no political consequences in resisting a deal with the president or even cooperating with the equally recalcitrant Congressional Democrats on the Super Committee mandates. As a result, the possibility of a major budget deal to address the deficit—the so-called grand bargain—devolved into finger pointing and mistrust; it was a missed opportunity for bipartisan cooperation. But it was also a recent example of how polarization has impacted White House relations with Congress.

Not only did the "agreement" fall apart, but both sides savaged the other in ways and using communications mediums that literally did not exist twenty years ago.

Outside groups, using sophisticated, targeted communications tools, reached out to respective core supporters on both sides to make their case, citing why either the president or congressional Republicans were wrong to walk away from a deal.

In the end, the entire episode transformed from a bipartisan opportunity for success to a partisan food fight with each side blaming the other for negotiating in bad faith. The Democratic team on the Hill supported President Obama while Republicans said he'd lost his political courage. In the end, both sides used the failure as a political weapon against their opponents in the 2012 election—guaranteeing the partisan vitriol would continue and impact presidential-congressional relations even into the next session of Congress after Obama won his reelection and the Republicans retained their House majority.

MANAGING RELATIONS WITH CONGRESS IN A POLARIZED WORLD

For the president, managing relations with Congress in this hyperpartisan environment is impacted by several factors. Like a promising rookie, every new president's achievements are based on a complicated mix of skill, circumstances, training, and even luck. Polarization only augments the level of difficulty. But we have identified several key variables that impact success. We explore these in the balance of this chapter.

INSTITUTIONAL CONSTRAINTS AND ADVANTAGES

Institutional constraints are the key starting point in understanding presidential-congressional relations. And the impact of these constraints has become even more important in today's hyperpartisan age.

The major variable here is party control—unified versus divided government. When the same party controls both Congress and the White House, the possibility for smooth relations between the branches, although not without challenges, improves considerably. Alternatively, divided government can produce gridlock and increased acrimony between the majority party in Congress and the president.

Party control can also impact the appearance of a president's legislative skills. Unified party control can make the White House look extremely competent and effective in enacting a legislative agenda, particularly if they have large enough majorities not to be constrained by rules of procedure or expected defections. Alternatively, mixed-party government can make a White House look feckless in terms of legislative success. Lyndon Johnson, for example, looked like a master of the legislative process while enjoying large majorities of his party in both the House and Senate from 1964–1968. Gerald Ford—who also came from a congressional leadership background—appeared powerless and even incompetent in terms of getting Congress to pass his agenda while facing massive opposing majorities.

Of course there are exceptions to this rule. Divided government doesn't always guarantee discord. President George H. W. Bush in 1990 and President Bill Clinton in 1997–1998 both negotiated major budget agreements with the opposing party majority. Nor does unified party control always result in smooth sailing. President Clinton could not move comprehensive health insurance reform through a Democratically controlled House and Senate in 1993 and 1994, and George W. Bush failed to enact Social Security reform in the beginning of his second term in 2005 despite controlling majorities in both the House and the Senate. But as a general matter, presidents normally get along better with Congress and find it easier moving their agenda forward when their own party also controls both houses of the legislature.

Partisan polarization has only amplified this reality. President Obama's White House in 2009 and 2010 worked very closely and cooperatively with the Democratic majorities in Congress, as did the Republican majority in Congress with President George W. Bush from 2001–2006. Contrast this to the early 1960s—during a less polarized period—when the House majority, led by Speaker Rayburn, kept many of their own president's agenda bottled up and the "conservative coalition" (Southern Democrats joining with Republicans to form a majority) in the House often passed measures over the White House's objections.[2]

Unified party control also affects more than the lawmaking process. Many observers believe legislative oversight of the executive branch was more benign when Republicans controlled the Congress from 2001–2006 and president George H. W. Bush was in the White House. Legislative oversight became more intense after the Democrats became the congressional majority during the last two years of the Bush administration (2007–2008). But after President Obama was elected in 2008 and the Democrats enjoyed unified party control, legislative oversight waned again. Most recently, after divided government returned following the 2010 election, legislative oversight grew intense again. During this iteration, congressional Republicans focused intensely on the actions of the Obama administration with investigations on matters like the "Fast and Furious" program where guns fell into the hands of drug gangs and Mexico, or the bankruptcy of Solyndra, a solar energy company that received loan guarantees from the Obama administration's Department of Energy based more on ideology and political connections than a sound business plan, at least according to Republicans in charge of the investigation.

POLARIZATION IMPACTS PRESIDENTS DIFFERENTLY THAN CONGRESS

As we argue above, the White House is not immune from the forces of polarization. And developing a full understanding of modern presidential-congressional relations requires incorporating the new realities and challenges of hyperpartisanship as a window to view how these two important institutions get along (or not). But polarization does not impact presidents and legislators in exactly the same way. Below we describe some of the differences and outline the reasons why this is the case.

First, and perhaps most obviously, presidents and Congress are on different campaign cycles. Not only are there practical differences between two-, four-, and six-year terms, but once a president wins reelection, he no longer faces any personal electoral constraints. While this is generally viewed as an opportunity for the president, it can quickly evaporate if not exploited effectively and his lame-duck status becomes paramount. Prior to that, presidents often struggle to pass the most challenging and controversial pieces of their personal agenda within their first year in office. They are not up for reelection for three more years, while their party colleagues face their voters the following year. This was a stinging reality of many Democrats, who supported President Obama's health-care legislation at their own peril, knowing the polls in their districts were hostile to the legislation and failed to return them to office for supporting it.

Second, presidents—unlike congressional leaders—do not face a constituency that elected them on a daily basis. Party leaders run for office twice—once with their constituents and then again to win support of their rank-and-file members. The political calculus for being elected leader of one's caucus is often at odds with the constituencies that send them to Congress in the first place, or possibly more broadly, even the popular sentiment of the country. Senators Byrd and Daschle, both popular leaders of the Democratic caucus, drew serious, and in Daschle's case, deadly, reelection challenges, having to balance the needs of a more liberal caucus with the demands of their more conservative state constituencies. This constraint often was a major consideration in managing the demands of a president of their own party or the opposition.

During preelection 2011–2012 budget negotiations with the White House, congressional leaders had to face their respective caucuses every day, a national expectation to address our fiscal problems that would produce real results, and a president who probably could have benefited from a grand bargain. The reality of that scenario would of course need the cooperation of the Republican Speaker of the House and probably some but not all of the Senate Democrats. While the Speaker had his own very complex Republican Conference politics to sort out, Senate leaders face their own set of challenges.

Senator Reid concluded quickly a "grand bargain" would not be the best path to protecting the largest number of Senate Democratic seats, and thus his majority, that were exposed in the 2012 election. After considerable intraparty haggling behind the scenes, the president decided in the end to align with the Senate Democratic Leader and pull the plug on grand bargain negotiations with the Republicans. While the recent election results seemed to validate the strategy, the president conceivably had more political latitude than Senator Reid to decide whether a deal was in his long-term interest or not. President Clinton chose the opposite option in continuing to work out a ten-year budget deal with the Republican leaders to the chagrin and political detriment of his own congressional party. The grand bargain of that time produced a landslide reelection for Clinton, and expanded majorities in both houses for Republicans at the expense of congressional Democrats.

Third, there are other constituency differences. Presidents report to a national constituency, not a congressional district or state. Obviously a lawmaker from rural Kansas faces a different kind of constituent pressure and interest than the current occupant of the White House. While the tip of that pressure sharpens as a president's reelection comes in focus, his political math gives him many more options to weave together a path to victory than a member of Congress representing a single state or district. While there are some circumstances in the country that the president deservedly gets the blame or credit, a member, even of his own party, may escape without any negative consequence. The 2012 election demonstrates President Obama was able to use his most popular positions on immigration, auto bailout, and concern about the middle class to stitch together a string of like-minded states, leading to his own electoral victory. Yet at the same time, House Republicans were able to appeal enough to their smaller congressional districts to retain a majority.

Fourth, presidents can stay close or far away from the lawmaking process. There are times when a president is knee-deep in the congressional process, going so far as to host negotiating sessions at the White House or sending senior emissaries to Capitol Hill. Or, the president may choose to keep his distance and only engage at the last minute, or not at all. These are tactical choices each White House must make, *but the point is there is a choice.* Legislators engaged in the lawmaking process don't have the same ability to calibrate their engagement with the process.

Fifth, presidents have more tools at their disposal. For example, even if the White House is stymied in terms of its relations with Capitol Hill, individual actions, such as executive orders or other decisions by cabinet level agencies can produce powerful policy outcomes. President Obama chose to pursue the regulation of carbon at the Environmental Protection Agency (EPA) with a series of policy proposals after cap-and-trade legislation failed to pass the Congress.

Sixth, presidents can also attempt to use the power of the bully pulpit to try to convince the public through media appearances, such as televised addresses to the American people. Some political scientists question the direct impact of these tactics; yet there is no doubt the president at least has these opportunities, while congressional leaders only rarely share the chance to "address the nation."[3] And even if these rhetorical forays do nothing but rally core supporters, it's a tactic that none, other than the president, can use.

Moreover, in today's hyperpartisan world, rallying core supporters can be as important as persuading undecided lawmakers.

POLITICAL GOALS

Deciphering the president's political goals is another key factor in gaining a better understanding of White House–congressional relations in a partisan age. Sometimes the president may decide it is in his interest to work with Congress and develop joint accomplishments with lawmakers. Other times, a more overt partisan political approach might better fit the president's objectives.

In a more polarized Washington, political goals can be complex, nuanced, and dynamic. Still, understanding these goals can shed great light on White House–congressional relations, and why certain outcomes occur—or not.

President Clinton began his term in 1993 with majorities in both the House and the Senate. He also assembled a very ambitious domestic legislative agenda. His strategic goal was to be very prescriptive in the content of the legislation, move quickly and very aggressively. Another key element of the strategy was to write the legislation so that it would primarily pass with the support of only Democrats. While he did not initiate this strategy and occasionally resisted this approach, the Democratic leaders in the Congress prevailed on him that this was the most effective way to proceed. This approach did produce a number of positive legislative results; however, it failed most notably in health-care reform initiative. More significantly, it allowed his entire presidency as well as the Democratic congress to be susceptible to the charge of overreaching their mandate.

This allegation along with others resulted in a Republican sweep in the midterm elections, forcing a total revamping of President Clinton's legislative strategy for dealing with the new Republican Congress beginning in January of 1995.

President Clinton's strategy for the new Congress took a while to emerge. The new Republican leaders were proceeding on what they were characterizing as a mandate built upon the Contract with America, a brain child of the new Speaker Gingrich. As the initial strategy emerged from the White House, it was shaping up as a fierce confrontation with the new Republican House.

President Clinton would admit to making some mistakes in his first two years but felt the new leadership of the House was taking the country on a road to disaster. Congressional Democrats were in total support of this strategy and amplified it at every opportunity. This battle was primarily fought in the context of competing comprehensive budget proposals from both sides. After months of haggling and government shut downs, at about a year out from Clinton's reelection, there was a felt consensus that the Democratically aligned strategy prevailed.

Clinton could have remained in sync with the congressional Democrats as they desperately wanted him to do and do nothing to rehabilitate the Republicans before the upcoming election by working with them constructively. As history shows, the president pivoted again with a new set of strategic objectives for working with the same new Congress, which entailed looking for common ground rather than conflict. The Republican leadership also saw it in their self-interest to find legislative areas of cooperation and did. Together, they laid the groundwork for a ten-year deficit-reduction package that passed right after the election, tax cuts for small business, and an incremental but significant piece of health-care legislation for children, among others.

This latest strategic shift left the president's Democratic congressional colleagues in the cold as the 1996 election approached. It had the impression and reality of making them marginal players and replaceable. As a result, the president won reelection and the Republicans kept and expanded their majorities. This strategy appeared to produce the desired result of the electoral moment. However, given the way the relationship between the president and the Republican Congress shifted dramatically shortly after the election to hostile impeachment proceedings, one might conclude a Democratically aligned strategy may have been more productive than triangulation. The bottom line was the president had an option and the Democrats had to vie for themselves.

Conversely, as noted above, by the summer of 2011, President Obama decided his political goal of getting reelected the following year was better served by running against Congress, particularly the Republican-controlled House. Could President Obama have "pulled a Clinton" and triangulated against his party and the Republican House in 2012? Maybe. Our point is that in a more polarized Washington, choosing a strategy of running against the other party seems like the more reflexive and obvious choice—another example of how partisanship shapes political goals, particularly in a hyperpartisan era.

POLARIZATION AND DELEGATING LEGISLATIVE POWER TO PARTY LEADERS

When a president's political goals lead him to keep his distance from Congress, he still needs to make sure lawmakers don't move in a direction adverse to White House interests. We argue that it's easier today—in a more polarized age—for presidents to keep a healthy distance from the lawmaking process (if that is his political goal) because the ideological space between the White House and his party in Congress has shrunk. Gone are the days of Lyndon Johnson when Democrats in the Senate included northern liberals like Hubert Humphrey of Minnesota and southern conservatives like Richard Russell of Georgia.

Closing the ideological gap between lawmakers and their leaders, as well as presidents and their own party leaders, has some important consequences. For example, one of the effects of polarization in Congress is that rank-and-file members delegate power to legislative party leaders during periods of partisan polarization.[4] Our thesis is that presidents often do the same—or at least more than they used to in a less partisan age. As we demonstrate below, when policy preferences between a president and his party in Congress line up closely, it's safe for the White House to let its party leaders do its bidding in legislative negotiations.

An example of this approach occurred in 2011 as the deadline for a debt-ceiling increase approached. Instead of refereeing three-way negotiations between Democrats, Republicans, and his White House, President Obama stepped back and allowed his leaders on Capitol Hill to negotiate a bipartisan package. In a polarized age, President Obama could do that, knowing the final product as negotiated by congressional Democrats would not stray too far from his preferred policy positions on key issues like cuts to Medicaid, and other important priorities.

But there are also times when tensions still exist—even between a president and his own legislative leaders. In these cases something has to give. Either the president convinces his caucus to follow him or the president chooses a direction consistent with his party's strategy on the Hill. We outline some examples of both below.

The Conditional Party Government theory asserts that when ideological cross pressures decline between lawmakers' constituents' preferences and party leadership demands, legislators choose to delegate power to their leadership.[5] The rationale is straightforward: when congressional leadership preferences are closely aligned with a congressman's constituents, following the leaders' wishes produces both legislative success and electoral dividends. Under these conditions, lawmakers essentially trust their leadership to take the ball and run with it. This produces strong party leadership in Congress. As mentioned above, we've seen this phenomenon reemerge in the last two decades.

As the congressional parties have grown increasingly polarized over the last two decades, Republicans and Democrats alike transformed into more homogeneous "teams." And as rank-and-file lawmakers have delegated power to party leaders the clout of leaders has grown.

Our observation of presidential-congressional relations over the past two decades reveals a similar pattern at work between the branches. Just as the rank-and-file members of Congress have increasingly trusted their legislative leadership to do their bidding, so have presidents under some circumstances (President Obama with Senate Democratic Leader Harry Reid and Speaker Nancy Pelosi, President George W. Bush with Speaker Dennis Hastert and Senate Republican Leader Bill Frist).

In other words, as leadership in Congress has been strengthened by the rank-and-file ceding power, in many ways the White House has followed suit. Congressional leaders are stronger BOTH because rank-and-file delegate power to them, *but presidents do as well.*

Strong partisan party leaders in Congress almost instinctively reflect the views of a partisan president—they've got his back and he has theirs—a phenomenon that has fundamentally changed many aspects of White House/legislative relations.

Prior to the period of extreme polarization we now find ourselves in, presidents had to do their own bidding—and it was hard to conclude congressional party leaders "had the president's back." Could President Kennedy, for example, trust Sam Rayburn to carry out the White House legislative agenda or would the Texas Speaker of the House attempt to find middle ground between his southern and northern membership?

Kennedy could not let go of his agenda in a congressional environment filled with powerful Committee chairs and legislative leaders facing a diverse caucus. He had to win the votes on his own.

Today's environment is very different. When Nancy Pelosi was Speaker there was little daylight between her caucus's agenda and President Obama. She could cut the deals and produce the votes knowing nearly everything she did and supported would be in line with the president's preferences. In an environment like that, presidents can delegate authority to leaders, just like the rank-and-file does. As a result, lots of negotiating goes on among party leaders to produce legislation without direct White House involvement.

In unified government, this can produce a lot of partisan legislation with polarized public support (for President Obama, for example, the Affordable Care Act, the Economic Stimulus legislation, and the Wall Street reform known as Dodd/Frank). In divided government it can produce a lot of partisan rancor and polarization, as was the case with President Obama and the Republican House in 2011 and 2012 or earlier between President George W. Bush in 2007 and 2008 with the then Democratic majority in Congress.

Contrast these more recent examples to the 1986 tax bill, Clean Air Act Amendment of 1990, or Welfare Reform near the end of the Clinton administration in 1998. These are all examples of bipartisan accomplishments in less partisan times, negotiated between the White House and individual lawmakers, not among just congressional leaders.

And there are exceptions still happening today. For example, in 2012, during a period of divided party control, Congress did produce legislation that got signed into law despite the politics and polarization of an election year. Food and Drug Administration (FDA) Reform, a Highway bill, and a package that included extension of a payroll tax cut and unemployment insurance all passed with broad bipartisan support. All three measures received little direct input from the White House, yet Democratic Party leaders knew the parameters of the president's policy preferences and could negotiate with Republicans, knowing the end product was acceptable to the president.

WHEN DOES THE WHITE HOUSE CHOOSE *NOT* TO CEDE POWER TO PARTY LEADERS?

Sometimes furthering political goals means presidents do not cede power to party leaders. Even though polarization has reduced the amount of ideological difference between presidents and their party leaders in Congress, there are several reasons why a president's political goals might lead him not to pursue this strategy.

For example, during periods of divided government, it's nearly impossible for presidents to cede power to their party leaders in Congress because the minority party (at least in the House) can accomplish little on its own. President Clinton clearly decided to forgo intraparty alignment in the months leading up to his reelection in 1996. While he started out marching in step with congressional Democrats in opposition to the Republican's budget that they proposed after their congressional victories in 1994, he abandoned that approach once he saw the Republicans were willing to compromise after their government-shutdown strategy failed in 1995. Congressional Democrats would have preferred to have allowed the embarrassment of the shutdowns hang around the Republicans' necks through the 1996 election. But Clinton chose to compromise from a position of strength and got legislative deals on the budget, small-business tax relief, and children's health insurance, to his electoral advantage and theirs. This was very upsetting to congressional Democrats who lost further seats in both the House and Senate.

Yet often the old institutional tensions still exist. In these cases, the White House needs to sort through its strategy and interests with its own party leaders and determine a path forward. But even under these conditions of institutional give and take, today they are done in a more partisan atmosphere—rather than some kind of bipartisan summit.

POLITICAL AND LEGISLATIVE SKILLS

Assessing the president's political and legislative skills is another key to understanding White House–congressional relations in a more partisan age.

Some of these skills are well known and have been key indicators of success for many years—during both hyperpartisan and less polarized eras. Others, however, are more critical in today's fragmented media environment and technologically advanced era. Let's start with some traditional political and legislative skills that help the president at almost any time.

The first is fundraising. The president's role as party-builder is often exemplified by his ability to raise money for congressional challenger candidates and incumbents. Barack Obama, by some accounts, raised about $1 billion for his campaign, the Democratic National Committee, and candidates in 2012.[6] He was a fundraising juggernaut. By actively campaigning for candidates like this, presidents both build good will and potentially their numbers in the House and Senate.

Personal relationships with lawmakers are another key political and legislative skill. This is an intangible, yet valuable asset that can help win support on close key votes to promote the White House agenda. President George H. W. Bush, as a former House member, had many strong relationships with lawmakers on both sides of the aisle that he drew upon frequently to help his relations with Congress. These friendships were formed over a long career in Washington. Presidents Clinton and George W. Bush, as former governors, were less well known in the corridors of the House and the Senate prior to arriving on the scene. Barack Obama only served a short tenure in the Senate before he won election in 2008. Clinton and Bush worked to compensate for their lack of Washington experience to develop these relationships. Critics say Obama has remained aloof.

Process knowledge is yet another tool to help presidents succeed and manage relations with Congress. It's true we normally think of the president of the United States being above the mundane nuances of legislative procedure. But when it comes to moving the White House's agenda, some procedural knowledge can go a long way. Lyndon Johnson certainly used his background as Senate majority leader to influence the levers of power to get Congress to consider his agenda. Listening to his process discussions with legislative leaders as revealed on the Johnson tapes underscores how he used process knowledge to help advance his White House's interests.[7]

More recently, President Obama has been able to enlist Vice President Joe Biden—a former senator with deep knowledge of legislative process—to help advance the White House agenda on a host of negotiations with lawmakers. Working with Republican Senator Mitch McConnell (R-KY) in January of 2013, Biden used his process knowledge to help shepherd an agreement to allow taxes to increase on wealthier Americans, a victory that allowed President Obama to say he fulfilled a major campaign promise.

One more traditional source of legislative and political skill is policy expertise. With the full force of the executive branch and its experts behind him, a president—either personally or through his staff—is in a strong position with respect to programmatic and budget information compared to the Congress. When the White House learns how to harness this advantage, it can usually gain a tactical edge over the legislative branch.

Indeed, one of the reasons why Congress passed the 1974 Budget Impoundment and Control Act was because the legislative branch felt at a disadvantage in terms of information and analysis. The Nixon administration consistently outmaneuvered Congress when it came to government-spending strategy. This new law, among other things, created the Congressional Budget Office to help lawmakers compete with the president's Office of Management and Budget in terms of data, projections, and fiscal forecasting.

Persuasion is the final traditional political and legislative skill we address in this section. Presidents can persuade by using either "inside" or "outside" influence. Inside influence is shaped by factors like personal relationships, as well as policy and procedural knowledge. Outside influence might include using the speeches—the so-called bully pulpit—to shape public opinion in favor of the White House. Normally, a combination of the two is most effective or at least attempted.

The president's ability to move public opinion to an extent that it persuades Congress—all other things equal—has come under some question in recent years.[8] Quiet diplomacy and compromise seem like more of a recipe for success than major White House–backed public relations campaigns.

In addition to considering how these traditional presidential political and legislative skills impact relations with the Congress, there are two other variables we explore in the last part of this section—changes in technology and the increased number of stakeholders in the process. Transformations in both these areas have become more important as polarization has increased and created challenges and opportunities for presidents' interactions and success in managing relations with Congress.

THE IPHONE IS THE NEW BULLY PULPIT

The speed of modern communications and the fragmentation of the media also provide new challenges and opportunities to how presidents manage relations with Congress. The news cycle used to be a daily occurrence, capped by the evening news program on one of the major networks or the morning headlines generated by a wire service or nationally read daily newspaper. In the Clinton administration, there was a daily ritual of several senior staff gathering in the White House Chief of Staff's office every day at around 6:00 p.m. to watch each of the three networks nightly news feeds. In doing so the team assessed the progress they made that day by monitoring the movement of good stories up and bad ones down among the top three leads of each network. Today the back and forth can and does occur many times during the day, some say in two-hour news cycles or even more, before the network anchor shows up for work in New York.

Using technology to educate, organize, and mobilize supporters is another new tactic available for presidents to lobby Congress. This new strategy will be put to the test in the 113th Congress for the first time as President Obama attempts to use the database that proved so successful in identifying and motivating supporters in 2012 and translate this electoral support to legislative advocacy. It remains unclear whether the tactic will work. Does political support in elections endure and translate to people taking the time to advocate for the president with Congress? The Obama White House will try to use the millions of voters that they communicated with during the campaign and ask them to urge Congress to support the president's agenda. The answer to this question will have significant implications for presidential-congressional relations as well as adding new meaning to the term "permanent campaign."

FROM SANDLOT TO YANKEE STADIUM:
EXPANDING THE NUMBER OF PLAYERS

Modern-day interest-group politics also test the president's legislative and political skills. White House–congressional relations used to occur in closed settings—lubricated by bourbon and branch in the White House private residence, a frank negotiation in the Oval Office, or a handshake in a Senate hideaway. No more. Today there are both more players and spectators. The number of individuals and stakeholders used to be small and manageable. But over the past thirty years, the roster of players has grown exponentially. These outside agents dramatically shape the tone, content, strategies, and tactics of White House–congressional relations. The game has expanded from small to big—from sandlot to Yankee Stadium.

The larger number of entrants on the playing field provides both challenges and opportunities for how presidents advance their legislative agendas. Successful presidents can exploit these opportunities, mobilizing outside groups such as individual lobbyists, business trade associations, consumer groups, unions, environmental activists, or corporations to advance the White House agenda.

One of the best recent examples of a White House activating outside groups was President Obama's efforts with parts of the health-care community when it came to passage of the Affordable Care Act (aka ObamaCare).

Groups like the pharmaceutical manufacturers (PhRma), the American Medical Association, and the American Hospital Association could have represented major obstacles to passage of the new health-care law. Instead, the White House recognized the importance of bringing these groups into the fold early to ensure they did not mobilize active opposition to the bill.

Working with politically aligned stakeholders (for Democrats, unions, environmental groups, consumer groups; for Republicans, business associations, conservative social and economic groups) is another area that tests a president's legislative and political skill. Unlike the example above, where the White House had to actively lobby health interests to help with passage of the legislation, there are many stakeholder groups or even more ideological think tanks that lean Democratic or others that lean Republican that are ready, willing, and able to help their team in the White House.

As the number of interest groups has expanded, it's become increasingly important for the White House to identify those that are politically aligned with Republicans or Democrats and move quickly to win their support for the president's legislative agenda, or to enlist these groups' support in fighting off hostile proposals from Capitol Hill—particularly in mixed party government situations.

Here's the bottom line. Management, persuasion, and leveraging outside groups was not a prerequisite to presidential success in managing relations with Capitol Hill in the past because the number of groups was much smaller and their communications channels less robust. Today that has all changed. How presidents manage the expansive array of outside groups is a major test of his political and legislative skill.

CONCLUSION

As we complete the writing of this chapter, Barack Obama is just beginning his second term as president. We can best understand how he will operate in his last four years in office using the model we have outlined.

Constraints and Opportunities

The constraints and opportunities of a reelected president need to be examined in the context of the constitutional definitions of a second term and through the prism of the overall election results.

Constitutionally, the president is now unencumbered by reelection concerns. He does not need to remain mindful of a winning electoral map, fundraising for himself, or holding hands of big donors. However, he does have to balance being liberated and unbeholden to any particular interest with being marginalized as a lame-duck politician who brings nothing to the table as his party turns away to find their next leader. Conventional timeframes for tipping from one status to the next have the clock ticking faster as the mid-term election approaches.

His personal election results could also present constraints or opportunities. Did he win big or small, where and with which constituencies? Were his campaign messages validated or muddled? Does he have a mandate or just another term? Careful analysis of these variables usually translates these results into specific objectives. However, the aggregate interpretation will suggest whether the president will be launching his second term from a position of institutional strength or weakness.

The congressional election results will also shape the institutional constraints and opportunities of a president facing his second term. Has power been redistributed from one party and/or chamber to another? Have we moved from unified party control to divided government, as was the case after the 2010 election? Maybe the election produced a more ambiguous outcome. Did it maintain an institutional status quo, but shift the perception of who had the political advantage?

While this question remains in dispute, many have characterized this last election as a victory for the president, providing him with clear policy mandates. The congressional results were validating but not as decisive. While Democrats made substantial gains in the Senate and marginal ones in the House, their limited success continues to present a major institutional constraint for the president to implementing any mandate that may be associated with his personal victory.

In any event, President Obama concluded that his legislative opportunity in relation to the Congress would be based on an explicit campaign pledge he ran on, to increase the tax burden on the wealthy. His opponents ceded this reality quite quickly after the election but haggled over the configuration of the actual policy until the last minutes of the 112th Congress. This specific provision was hoped to be part of a larger "grand bargain" with the Republicans in the Congress that combined entitlement cuts with tax increases as a major down payment on the deficit trajectory.

Unfortunately, negotiations collapsed. The cornerstone campaign pledge was barely kept and the opportunity to make a major impact on the deficit was missed. The reelection results clearly produced a legislative opportunity that was partially realized. However, the ability to maximize it failed.

History will make the final determination as to what produced the collapse. Some have speculated that the grand bargain was unnecessary or an overreach from the start. Others have charged that the critical players did not have the skill or the will to maneuver through the treacherous waters of making such a deal and alienating their respective bases. In any event, failing to seize this opportunity will likely produce political costs for both leaders and potentially limit other legislative opportunities, particularly for the president.

Another potential presidential legislative opportunity based on the election results is immigration reform. The Hispanic vote throughout the entire United States overwhelmingly supported President Obama's candidacy. These results, combined with the dramatic demographic shifts within this population, will make Hispanics an increasingly influential voting bloc to many individual politicians running for office and especially presidential candidates.

It is widely speculated that this combination of variables may create the impetus for comprehensive bipartisan congressional action on legislation. The reality of this opportunity is yet to be tested. Finding the policy consensus on this complicated topic is just getting underway. But the substantive parameters of common ground seem well within reach. However, the political leaders on either side of this debate will need, once again, to demonstrate the skills necessary not only to fashion the policy options but to find and sell a reasonable compromise to their respective sides.

Presidential Goals

Not unlike a newly elected first-term president, the goals of his second term typically remain a function of his personal aspirations and/or his party and, as suggested above, the specifics of the election results. However, there are two added dimensions that could critically affect the prioritization of these goals, when he pursues them, as well as what he might do to succeed. The first dimension is typically defined by the president's concern about his personal legacy and the historical footprint he is likely to leave. The second is the conventional wisdom that the window to solidify or expand this legacy is a small one that usually ends at or before the midterm elections of his second term.

In many cases, a reelected president has already put a down payment on his legacy in his first term. Sometimes the impression is muddled and needs to be refined and/or expanded. It is likely that President Obama believes that the Affordable Health Care Act will comprise a major portion of his legacy but it is unlikely one that will completely satisfy him. There has been much speculation as to what issue he might choose to enhance his legacy in the second term. It was initially assumed that a comprehensive deficit-reduction package would be priority number one. While the possibility for that has waned considerably for a variety of reasons, his strategy appeared to have been to act quickly and be prepared to push hard against the far left of his party, if he were to include substantial entitlement reform.

It is an open question whether a deliberate strategy of his or the Republicans will force a revisiting of the deficit as a defining issue or whether he will move on to one of the other issues he mentioned in his Inaugural address. Among others, he mentioned gun control, immigration reform, and climate change.

A decidedly failed attempt in his opening efforts at this second-term agenda could have lasting impact on his ability to successfully make progress on any or all of the other legislative objectives. While that has yet to be determined, another possible strategic direction might be to focus less on accomplishing legislative victories and more on broadening the base of the Democratic Party. The president might approach this by attempting to assert his and his party's leadership on a variety of issues with broad appeal to expanding constituencies. This strategy would focus less on making policy accommodations to reach legislative compromise with the Republicans and more on defining them as out of touch with the new America and without a political future in electoral politics. Or as Speaker Boehner stated, "The Democrats want to annihilate the GOP." This approach—if the president chooses to take it—might represent the apex of polarization in terms of White House–congressional relations—a trend, as we have noted in this chapter, that has been steadily on the rise over the past two decades.

Political and Legislative Skills

While Lyndon Johnson set the bar pretty high for being an effective legislator-president, no modern president has been without the skills and talents to demonstrate some measure of effectiveness on issues that mattered to them. They may not have the precise combinations of skills needed to handle every matter or even their own reelections.

It is also hard to imagine a presidential skill set that would be unique to a second term that couldn't be of some value throughout his tenure. However, the specific skill set President Obama will actually need as he starts his second term will be a function of the institutional opportunities and challenges as he perceives them and specific objectives as he ultimately defines them.

In any event, he will need to remain agile in his approach and what it might take to be successful. The operating environment of divided government has certain obvious challenges. Regardless of how he begins, the strategic conditions in which he will have to function will be dynamic. They will be shaped by his opposition's reactions as well as those from his own congressional party. Knowing when to confront and to cooperate with both entities will be paramount to any hope of success. Having long-standing and trusting relationships with members of the opposition becomes a real asset when attempting to make these delicate calibrations. This tension will be inevitably complicated further by unanticipated and uncontrollable events. Domestically, natural disasters, abrupt changes in the economy (sometimes positive), scandal, and deaths all can dramatically alter the playing field. International developments that can threaten our national security and economic stability are also factors. Nevertheless, there are probably no circumstances in which the president's ability to communicate to Congress and directly to the country won't be important. The real question will be, to what end? If is to convince his opposition that they need to cooperate with him legislatively, he will have to find the balance between using his strength to bring them to a table he has set and having the leadership and grace to inspire cooperation from the opposition without them feeling decimated. A negotiating dynamic in divided government that produces nothing positive for the opposition is not likely sustainable. Doing nothing becomes as politically viable or better than even minimal cooperation. Similarly, convincing his own party that his legislative objectives will work equally well for them as they face their midterm elections could be equally as challenging.

On the other hand, if producing a political message framework rather than legislative outcomes is the intent, a communication skill set with the bully pulpit is probably all that is required.

The three major institutional players in this dance are the president, his Senate Democrats, particularly those up for reelection in 2014, and the House Republicans and their leadership. All of their strategic calculations will be assessed through the prism of the midterm elections. The president, knowing the clock is ticking on his relevance, will be assessing his ability to truly add to his legislative legacy and risk failing at that approach. The Senate Democrats will be trying to determine if legislative cooperation strengthens their ability to maintain control of the Senate in 2014 or weakens it. House Republicans, haunted by the footsteps of intraparty primary challenges that may expand if a cooperation strategy is embraced, will weigh a similar calculation.

Any way you cut it, a simple math assessment suggests the stakes are quite high for all of the key institutional players to embrace a conventional cooperation approach to governing over the next two years. Absent unanticipated action enforcing events, partisan attempts to highlight differences are more likely the accepted course, leaving 2014 as a way to measure the political price of continued partisan gridlock.

Partisan polarization has deeply influenced the way presidents and Congress waltz together in today's "dance of legislation." President Obama and the 113th Congress are no exception. And while future chapters remain to be written, the odds of an outbreak of bipartisan cooperation are unlikely. Elections—and the hope for one-party control—may arbitrate policy outcomes more heavily in the future than the legislative bargaining table. But unless and until one party dominates Washington with overwhelming majorities, partisanship will shape the relationship on both ends of Pennsylvania Avenue for the foreseeable future.

NOTES

1. Sean M. Theriault, *Party Polarization in the Congress* (New York: Cambridge University Press, 2008).

2. John F. Manley, "The Conservative Coalition in Congress," *American Behavioral Scientist* 17 (1973): 223–47.

3. George C. Edwards, *On Deaf Ears: The Limits of the Bully Pulpit* (New Haven, CT: Yale University Press, 2003).

4. See, for example, John Aldrich, *Why Parties? The Origins and Transformation of Party Politics in America* (Chicago: University of Chicago Press, 1995); Gary Cox and Mathew McCubbins, *Legislative Leviathan: Party Leadership in the House*, 2nd ed. (New York: Cambridge University Press, 2007); David Rhode, *Parties and Leaders in the Post-Reform House* (Chicago: University of Chicago Press, 1991).

5. Cox and McCubbins, *Legislative Leviathan*.

6. Nicholas Confessore and Jo Craven McGinty, "Obama, Romney and Their Parties on Track to Raise $2 Billion," *New York Times*, October 25, 2012.

7. LBJ Presidential Library, www.lbjlib.utexas.edu/johnson/archives.hom/dictabelt.hom/content.asp.

8. Edwards, *On Deaf Ears*.

Chapter Four

Organizing the Twenty-First-Century White House

James P. Pfiffner

Since the writing of the Constitution, the presidency has been transformed from a small institution primarily concerned with executing public policy and conducting foreign relations to a huge organization of thousands of professionals that dominates the politics and government of the United States. The presidency of today is the result of major shifts in US politics and government of the late twentieth century. The White House Office has grown from several personal advisers in the Roosevelt administration to the huge bureaucracy of specialists that it is today. This chapter will analyze the effects of these shifts on the internal management of the presidency by examining three major trends: (1) centralization, (2) the Office of Chief of Staff, and (3) the role of the vice president.

For most of American history, cabinet secretaries were the main advisers of presidents, but since the mid-twentieth century they have been eclipsed by the growing White House staff. Rather than delegating responsibilities to cabinet secretaries and depending on them for advice, presidents now rely on their White House aides who are much closer, physically and symbolically. With larger White House staffs, presidents have had to pay more attention to managing their own offices. The management and control job is now too large for the president to handle, and the Office of Chief of Staff has developed to fill that role, among others. Perhaps the most important development in recent presidents has been in the role of the vice president. Even though the vice presidency of Richard Cheney will probably not be duplicated in the future, he set important precedents that will have a significant impact on future presidencies.

CENTRALIZING CONTROL IN THE WHITE HOUSE

Before the mid-twentieth century, presidents had staff help, but they tended to be personal advisers, generalists, and performers of clerical chores who were often relatives. Their primary advisers on policy were members of their cabinets, the secretaries of the major departments of the government. But since the emergence of a professional White House staff after World War II, presidential aides now dominate administration policy making.

After the Great Depression and World War II the role of the federal government had grown tremendously, and President Eisenhower institution-alized the White House staff in important ways, by creating the Office of Chief of Staff and designing offices with specialized functions, for example the Office of Legislative Liaison. Eisenhower, however, continued to rely primarily on his cabinet secretaries for advice. He used the cabinet as a policy-consulting body that would advise him on the large questions of ad-ministration policy, and he held regular cabinet meetings to solicit their advice. He created a cabinet secretariat to prepare agendas for cabinet meet-ings and for follow up with implementation. He also delegated a range of discretion to cabinet heads to influence and implement policies in their areas of jurisdiction.

Presidents Kennedy and Johnson rejected the role the cabinet played in the Eisenhower administration and began to use White House staffers as their chief advisers on major policy priorities. By the end of the Johnson adminis-tration, the role of the federal government had again expanded, with the War on Poverty and Great Society programs. In reaction to this growth in execu-tive branch programs, President Nixon sought to rein in the bureaucracies and impose presidential control on policy implementation. He suspected that career civil servants were committed to the policies of Democratic social programs; he even suspected that his own cabinet appointees were too sym-pathetic to the programs they were charged with implementing. In response, Nixon began to centralize policy making in the White House staff. The national security staff was increased significantly under Henry Kissinger, who centralized all major foreign-policy initiatives under his control. On the domestic-policy side, John Ehrlichman recruited a large White House staff for the Domestic Policy Council. The effect of these institutional innovations was to give the White House staff the capacity to conduct policy develop-ment independent of the policy experts in the departments and agencies of the executive branch. The number of White House staffers consequently increased from 250 to more than five hundred.

Presidents Ford and Carter initially sought to rein in the White House staff and rely primarily on their cabinet secretaries for policy advice. But they were soon disillusioned by what their own staffers saw as policy advo-cacy from cabinet members that was not closely enough attuned to White

House priorities. Each of them reacted by centralizing control in their White House staffs and increasing the size and capacity of the White House Office. President Reagan, with a clear set of priorities, continued to centralize control in the White House, and expanded that control to political appointees throughout the executive branch. The George H. W. Bush and Clinton administrations, with fourteen cabinet departments, followed suit.

In remarks about her eight years as secretary of health and human services during the Clinton administration, Donna Shalala illustrated the common attitude of cabinet secretaries toward the White House staff. She was asked about the effect of the impeachment of the president on her cabinet department. She replied that it made her job much easier because the White House staff was so absorbed in impeachment proceedings that it left her alone to manage her department: "He got distracted and we got focused."[1]

By the end of the twentieth century the number of personnel within the Executive Office of the President totaled more than two thousand. The capacity of the White House to develop policy was firmly established; and the primary advisers to the president were in the White House staff, not the cabinet.

President Bush and Centralization

Despite President George W. Bush's care in recruiting an experienced and well-credentialed cabinet, he was not about to reverse the trend of the past four decades of power gravitating to the White House. Early in his administration, all of the major policy priorities were dominated by White House staffers rather than led from the cabinet. As one high-level White House official characterized his approach: "The Bush brand is few priorities, run out of the White House, with no *interference* from the Cabinet. . . . The function of the Bush Cabinet is to provide a chorus of support for White House policies and technical expertise for implementing them" (emphasis added).[2]

When President Bush was inaugurated in 2001, he had designated his whole cabinet and had a fully functioning White House staff ready to run administration policy making. For instance, the administration's education initiative was handled by the domestic-policy adviser, Margaret LaMontagne Spellings, rather than Education Secretary Roderick Paige. On medical issues, such as government financing of prescription drugs, the patients' bill of rights, and stem-cell research, the action was in the White House rather than with Health and Human Services Secretary Tommy Thompson. The administration's tax-cut proposals were not led by Treasury Secretary Paul O'Neill but by White House staffers, particularly the National Economic Council director, Lawrence Lindsey. Vice President Cheney dominated the administration's energy-policy proposals rather than Secretary of Energy Spencer Abraham.[3]

The centralization of control in the Bush White House was reinforced by its reaction to the atrocities of 9/11 that led to the primacy of national security policy for administration. National security policy was tightly controlled by Vice President Cheney, who acted as Bush's prime minister or, in effect, the chief operating officer. This was as President Bush wanted it; his approach to governing was to keep his eye on the big picture and delegate implementation and details to others.

President Bush's style of leadership was to articulate a vision, set priorities, and then delegate implementation to his vice president and his loyal staff team. In his autobiography, *A Charge to Keep*, he put it this way: "My job is to set the agenda and tone and framework, to lay out the principles by which we operate and make decisions, and then delegate much of the process to them."[4] President Bush preferred short memos, oral briefings, and crisp meetings. His circle of advisers was relatively small. According to President of the American Enterprise Institute Christopher DeMuth, "It's a too tightly managed decision-making process. When they make decisions, a very small number of people are in the room, and it has a certain effect of constricting the range of alternatives being offered."[5]

His White House staff was legendary for its tight message discipline and absence of unauthorized leaks. President Bush saw himself as the one who listens to advice and then makes the tough calls. "I listen to all voices, but mine is the final decision. . . . I'm the decider, and I decide what's best."[6] In contrast to his father or Bill Clinton, who would agonize over important decisions, Bush would decide and move on. The detached Bush style resembled the style of President Reagan, but it contrasted sharply with those of Presidents Clinton and Obama, who delved into the details of policies and played active roles in policy making.

Bush described his personal approach to decision making as intuitive: "I can only go by my instincts." He did not believe in elaborate deliberation or in explaining his thinking to his White House staff. As he told Bob Woodward: "I'm the commander—see, I don't need to explain—I do not need to explain why I say things. That's the interesting thing about being the president. Maybe somebody needs to explain to me why they say something, but I don't feel like I owe anybody an explanation"[7] In contrast to President Bush, Barack Obama had a much more regularized policy process, approached decisions analytically, and was collaborative in his deliberations; but he agreed with Bush on centralized White House control.

President Obama and Centralization

President Obama began his administration with the intention of running all major policy initiatives out of the White House, with the exception of legal policy on detainees, which he delegated to his attorney general and friend,

Eric Holder. Obama's experiment with delegation foundered at the hands of the White House staff, illustrating the imperative of centralized White House control of policy. President Obama was criticized for his use of policy "czars" in his White House staff to coordinate policies that cut across the jurisdictions of different departments. Predictably, these political realities were resented by his cabinet and denounced by external critics.

Cabinet secretaries in the Obama administration often resented their treatment by Chief of Staff Rahm Emanuel, who they felt treated them as his "minions" rather than as major administration officials.[8] They were required to send weekly reports to Emanuel, who returned them with specific comments and instructions.[9] As in other administrations, cabinet secretaries often felt that the president paid too much attention to his inner circle of campaigners (in this case his campaign loyalists Valerie Jarrett, David Axelrod, and Robert Gibbs) and did not grant enough access to old Washington hands and cabinet officials.

The administration intended from the very beginning to handle its signature policy priority, health-care financing reform, in the White House. During the transition, when Obama asked former Senate leader Tom Daschle to be secretary of health and human services, Daschle insisted that he also be designated as the White House czar of health-care reform. The request for this unique designation reflected Daschle's understanding that the real action in policy making would take place in the White House rather than in cabinet departments. When Daschle withdrew his nomination because of tax problems, Obama appointed Nancy-Ann DeParle to be White House health czar and former governor of Kansas, Kathleen Sebelius, to head health and human services. In testimony before Congress in early February 2010, Sebelius admitted her secondary role in health-care reform. "I am not a principal in the negotiations, nor is my staff." She said that they would provide "technical support" to Congress but they did not play a role in negotiating over the shape of the health-care legislation.[10]

There were exceptions to White House centralization and resentment of members of the cabinet. Treasury Secretary Timothy Geithner took the lead on administration financial policy, though Lawrence Summers, the Council of Economic Advisers, and Rahm Emanuel were equally important. Robert Gates and Hillary Clinton were often at the White House and influenced foreign and national security policy. In all administrations the "inner cabinet" of the original four departments of Defense, State, Treasury, and Justice are closer to the president, particularly if they are headed by personal friends of the president.

The exception that proved the rule of centralized White House control was Obama's initial intention to delegate the legal aspects of detainee policy to his attorney general, Eric Holder. Holder accepted the position with the understanding that he would make legal decisions independently of the

White House, though of course the president would have the final say. President Obama also wanted to be seen as not letting politics interfere with legal principles. Thus he delegated some of the key legal decisions regarding detainee policy to Attorney General Holder. Obama told Holder to make decisions on the merits of the law rather than on political grounds. Exercising his delegated authority, Holder decided to try the 9/11 terrorist suspects in criminal court rather than military tribunals, and he chose New York City as the venue. The decision caused a political uproar, with congressional leaders threatening legislation to mandate military commission trials and New York Mayor Bloomberg backing off of his initial support of Holder's venue decision. Thus Obama faced the dilemma of backing the initial decision of Holder about the best legal strategy for handling detainees or bowing to political pressure.

Holder's decisions reinforced White House staffers' suspicion that he was not sufficiently sensitive to the president's political interests. Holder was aware of the conflict and tried to maintain a balance. "I hope that whatever decision I make would not have a negative impact on the president's agenda. But that can't be a part of my decision."[11] White House staffers, however, felt that Holder was more concerned with his own legal reputation than the political success of the president. According to a lawyer close to the Obama White House, White House staffers "think he wants to protect his own image, and to make himself untouchable politically, the way Reno did, by doing the righteous thing."[12] Political aides in the White House were so concerned about what they considered Holder's tin ear for politics that they suggested appointing a "minder" in the Justice Department who had more sensitive "political antennae" than Holder.[13]

Ultimately, the White House staff, particularly Chief of Staff Emanuel, convinced Obama that the political repercussions of Holder's decisions were more important than Holder's legal judgments and his independence from the White House. Obama in the spring of 2009 decided that some detainees would be tried in civil courts, but most would be tried by military commissions or detained indefinitely without trial. Thus ended Obama's experiment with delegation of policy making to cabinet secretaries. The centralization of control of high-visibility legal policy in the White House illustrates pressures faced by all contemporary presidents to ensure that departmental perspectives do not undercut broader presidential interests.

During his first year, Obama also wanted tight, personal control over national-security policy making. According to one senior aide, "President Obama is his own Henry Kissinger—no one else plays that role. . . . This president wants all the trains routed through the Oval Office."[14] By the end of his first year in office the Obama White House had established a "regular order" for the national-security policy process. There was a systematic set of procedures for paper flow, consultation, and sign-off; the process was managed and enforced by deputy national security adviser Tom Donilon and Rahm Emanuel. The daily 9:30 a.m. national security briefings were conducted by Donilon, who also ran the "deputies meetings" of the National Security Council, the heart of the interagency process. Reflecting his centrality to the national-security policy process, Donilon became national security adviser when General Jones retired. Obama's personal engagement went so far as to assert his control of the details of Afghanistan policy by personally dictating the November 2009 policy memorandum that specified the thirty-thousand troop buildup in Afghanistan

One of the essential roles of White House staffers is to coordinate administration policy that spans more than one department of the executive branch. The need is based on the reality that "where you stand depends on where you sit." That is, one's stance on a policy issue is heavily influenced by one's official position. For instance, secretaries of state will predictably be concerned primarily with diplomacy, and secretaries of defense will primarily be concerned with military policy. Their advice to the president on foreign-policy issues will necessarily reflect their formal roles and duties. The president, however, must take into account both diplomatic and military factors in making policy. With the complexity of foreign-policy issues, it is imperative for the president to get advice from staffers whose perspective is presidential rather than tied to one department. The growth of the National Security Council staff in the White House reflects this reality. The role of national security adviser is now firmly established in the White House, and it is broadly seen as legitimate and necessary. Yet President Obama was severely criticized by members of Congress for establishing "czars" in other policy areas. Though all modern presidents have had White House staffers who acted as policy "czars," President Obama designated more of them than previous presidents.[15]

The term "czar" has no generally accepted definition within the context of American government. It is a term loosely used by journalists to refer to members of a president's administration who seem to be in charge of a particular policy area. More accurately, the term "czar" in the American context refers to members of the White House staff who have been designated by the president to coordinate specific policy areas that involve more than one department or agency. In contrast to officers of the United States, such as cabinet secretaries, members of the White House staff are appointed by the president without Senate confirmation. They are legally authorized only to advise the president; they cannot make authoritative decisions for the government of the United States.

The most controversial of Obama's czars were White House staff appointees who were charged with or perceived as exercising authority in executing the law that only officers of the government should have, such as cabinet secretaries and other Senate-confirmed positions. For instance, he designated a director of recovery for auto communities and workers to direct funds from the economic-stimulus legislation to help communities affected by the near collapse of the auto industry. He also appointed a "car czar" to distribute money provided for saving General Motors and Chrysler from bankruptcy. There were also several coordinators of policy toward major bodies of water that affected several states, such as the Great Lakes and the Chesapeake Bay. In a questionable tactic, Obama appointed Elizabeth Warren (later Senator) to help establish the newly created Bureau of Consumer Financial Protection. The problem was that because Warren could not overcome Republican opposition to her appointment, Obama tried to skirt the constitutional requirement of Senate confirmation by appointing her to the White House staff.[16]

In another example, Carol Browner (head of the Environmental Protection Agency [EPA] in the Clinton administration) was tasked with overseeing administration agencies concerned with energy and climate change. These agencies included the White House Council on Environmental Quality, the EPA, as well as the Departments of Energy, Defense, and Interior. In announcing his choice of Browner, Obama described the role that he expected White House czars to play; she would provide "coordination across the government" and ensure "my personal engagement as president" in environmental policy. He said that she would have authority to "demand integration among different agencies; cooperation between federal, state and local governments; and partnership with the private sector."[17]

Aside from constitutional issues, the managerial problem with White House czars is that they confuse the chain of command and leave open the question of who is in charge of administration policy. Czars are often frustrated because they lack the authority to carry out their responsibilities. That is, they do not control budgets or appointments, and they cannot order cabinet secretaries to do their bidding. For example, past drug czars (heads of the Office of National Drug Control Policy) expressed frustration because they could not authoritatively coordinate the Federal Bureau of Investigations (FBI), Drug Enforcement Administration (DEA), Coast Guard, Department of Housing and Urban Development (HUD), and other agencies that implement drug-control policies.

Thus President Obama continued the twentieth-century trend of centralizing control in the White House staff, ensuring the frustration of cabinet secretaries. But in the modern presidency, coordination of administration policy from the president's perspective is essential. The challenge is to maintain a healthy balance between too much centralization and the opposite problem of lack of coordination of policy making and implementation in departments and agencies.

WHITE HOUSE ORGANIZATION AND THE CHIEF OF STAFF

Along with the great expansion of the role of the national government in the United States came the increase of the numbers of people who serve the president rather than work in a department or agency. With hundreds of professionals in the White House Office divided into their own areas of expertise (e.g., national security, personnel recruitment, legislative liaison, communications, etc.), internal control and coordination became essential.

President Eisenhower established the Office of Chief of Staff early in his first term, based on his military experience. The main task of Chief of Staff Sherman Adams was to keep issues off the president's desk unless they clearly needed presidential attention. The White House had a clear hierarchy, and Adams was at the top of it, guarding access to the president. In contrast, John Kennedy and Lyndon Johnson ran their White Houses with an advisory model that was more "collegial," meaning that there was no strict hierarchical control of White House staffers and a number of staffers reporting to the president directly. The hierarchical model creates a more orderly White House, though it narrows the perspectives that the president receives. The collegial model allows more access to the president from staffers with different perspectives, but at the cost of increased presidential time and attention.

With the sharp increase in the numbers of staffers and their expanded role in the presidency during the Nixon administration, the collegial model of organization became untenable. H. R. Haldeman was Nixon's chief of staff and ruled the White House with an iron hand. He controlled access to the president, with the exception of Henry Kissinger, and he controlled all presidential papers. Presidents Ford and Carter each tried to run the White House using the collegial model, but both gave up in frustration. The size of the White House staff and its expanded functions created the need for someone short of the president to be in charge. After trying to run the White House by himself, President Ford concluded that working without a chief of staff "is putting too big a burden on the president himself. You need a filter, a person that you have total confidence in who works so closely with you that in effect his is almost an alter ego. I just can't imagine a president not having an effective chief of staff."[18]

The role of chief of staff that developed in the twentieth century was to impose order on the policy process, manage the White House staff, deal with conflicts among members of the cabinet, advise the president, and make the trains run on time. But in recent administrations, presidents have also expected their chiefs of staff to take more public roles as spokespersons for the administration, negotiating with Congress, setting the policy agenda, and providing outreach to key constituencies.[19] This was particularly evident in President Obama's chiefs of staff, though not in the Bush administration, as will be explained below.

President Bush's White House

At the beginning of his administration, President Bush appointed Andrew Card as his chief of staff. Card was an experienced Washington insider and Bush loyalist since 1980. He had worked in the White House for Ronald Reagan and had been deputy chief of staff to John Sununu in the George H. W. Bush administration before being appointed Secretary of Transportation; he also ran the 2000 Republican National Convention for George W. Bush. Card served admirably in directing routine processes and work flow in the White House and acting as a trusted adviser to the president. But the Bush White House was so dominated by Vice President Cheney that Card could not play the traditional role of chief of staff. This section will analyze the dominant role Vice President Cheney played in the Bush White House. The factors that allowed him to do so will be covered in the section on the vice presidency.

Before he became vice president, Richard Cheney had emphasized the importance of a regular and disciplined policy process in the White House. "The process of moving paper in and out of the Oval Office, who gets involved in the meetings, who does the president listen to, who gets a chance to talk to him before he makes a decision, is absolutely critical. It has to be managed in such a way that it has integrity."[20] Dick Cheney well understood the importance of a regularized policy development process to the president's understanding of a broad range of policy options. "It's very, very important when you set up shop to make certain that you have a guaranteed flow . . . that everybody's got their shot at the decision memo. You know if there's going to be a meeting, the right people are going to be in the meeting, that the president has a chance to listen to all of that and then make a decision."[21]

When Cheney became vice president, however, he was able to exploit the lack of a regularized policy process to his own advantage. In some of the most important policy decisions of the Bush presidency Cheney circumvented any regularized process. On domestic issues Treasury Secretary Paul O'Neill thought that the Bush White House had no serious domestic policy process. "It was a broken process . . . or rather no process at all; there seemed to be no apparatus to assess policy and deliberate effectively, to create coherent governance."[22]

In the policy areas that mattered to Cheney—business, environment, national security, budget, and executive power under the Constitution—he dominated administration policy. For instance, in environmental policy he engineered the reversal of one of President Bush's campaign positions. EPA Director Christine Todd Whitman, who had cleared the issue with Andrew Card, gave a speech at an international conference, committing the United States to a policy to reduce carbon emissions. When Cheney heard about the speech, he convinced President Bush to sign a letter to members of Congress that in effect reversed his position. The policy change was not cleared with the EPA or the State Department before Bush signed the letter, which undercut Whitman. After further frustration with the vice president's office, Whitman resigned from the administration.[23]

On the national security side of policy making, Cheney and his staffers were able to get the president's approval without subjecting their policy preferences to the scrutiny of those in the administration who ordinarily would be expected to provide advice to the president.

For instance, the Military Commissions Order of November 13, 2001 was secretly prepared by Cheney advisers and kept secret from others in the administration who normally would have important expertise to bear on the legal and military issues, such as Secretary of State Colin Powell and National Security Adviser Condoleezza Rice. When Attorney General John Ashcroft saw a draft of the order, he was upset that the Justice Department would not have a role in deciding which terrorist suspects would be tried by military commission and which in the criminal justice system. When he went to the White House to object, he found that the vice president was in charge of the order and that John Yoo of the Office of Legal Counsel, nominally Ashcroft's subordinate, had recommended that the US court system be avoided. Ashcroft wanted to see the president personally about the issue, but Cheney denied him access to the president.[24]

Normally, such an important policy document would be staffed out and routed through other White House and administration officials. But Cheney personally took the document to President Bush in his private dining room to clear it with him and subsequently to sign it. White House aides present said they did not know that the vice president had been involved in drafting the memo. Thus Cheney had engineered President Bush's approval and signature without any regular policy process or sign-off by relevant White House and Cabinet officials.

Similarly, President Bush's decision to declare that the Geneva Conventions did not apply to the US war with al Qaeda was engineered by Cheney's aide, David Addington, over the objections of State Department lawyers. When Secretary of State Powell, who was out of the country, heard that Bush was ready to sign the document suspending the Geneva Conventions, he returned and demanded a formal National Security Council meeting to discuss the issue.[25] Powell objected to the decision because he considered it abandoning an important US obligation and might lead to the mistreatment of US soldiers in the future. Powell's arguments, however, were undercut when the vice president's office leaked counter arguments refuting Powell's points to the conservative *Washington Times* newspaper before the meeting. The newspaper article implied that Powell was caving in to pressure from the political left. President Bush rejected Powell's plea for reconsidering the issue and signed the memorandum on February 7, 2002.

This decision was important because suspending US compliance with the Geneva Conventions constituted the renunciation of a treaty and led to the torture and abuse of detainees in the war on terror.[26] Vice President Cheney had been successful in excluding from the early decision process those who might have disagreed with his draft of the order; he got his way, but the decision led to a flawed legal framework for dealing with detainees in the war on terror. The consequences of excluding outside input on the decision came when the Supreme Court, in *Hamdan v. Rumsfeld*, struck down the military commission's plan because they were not authorized in accord with US law or the Uniform Code of Military Justice.

The vice president also steered administration intelligence policy. One important administration initiative was kept secret from most of the top White House staffers and almost led to the resignation of Bush appointees at the Justice Department. The secret Terrorist Surveillance Program conducted by the National Security Agency was designed to intercept suspected terrorist communications within the United States without going through the warrants required by the Foreign Intelligence Surveillance Act. The legal justification for the program was written by Cheney lawyer David Addington but kept secret from those running the program as well as most other national security officials in the administration.[27]

After reviewing the dubious legal reasoning justifying the program, Attorney General John Ashcroft refused to sign off on an extension of the program unless it was changed to comply with the law. When it became clear that a number of top Bush appointees in the Justice Department were ready to resign if the program went forward unchanged, Cheney did not tell the president. It was only when Bush met personally with the acting attorney general, James Comey (Ashcroft was in the hospital), that the president understood the extent of the Department of Justice objections and decided to make changes in the program. That Cheney did not make the president aware of the impending resignations illustrates how pervasive Cheney's control of White House policy and process was.

Chief of Staff Andrew Card was replaced by Joshua Bolton for the last two years of the Bush administration. Even though the power of Vice President Cheney had waned a bit, Bolton was not able to play the role of the traditional, strong chief of staff. The broader point of these examples is to illustrate the reality that Vice President Cheney so dominated the Bush administration in most important areas of policy making that the chief of staff was relegated to the routine processes of administration rather than the usual role of presidential chiefs of staff. With the coming of the Obama administration in 2009, the chief of staff role returned to its earlier prominence.

President Obama's Chiefs of Staff

Shortly after his election, President-elect Obama designated Rahm Emanuel to be his chief of staff. It was clear from the beginning that Emanuel would be a traditionally strong chief of staff as he oversaw the recruitment of other White House staffers and President Obama's selection of cabinet secretaries. Emanuel and his successors as chief of staff fit with Obama's desire to have an orderly policy process in the White House. Lawrence Summers, Obama's chief economic adviser, noted Obama's White House "stands out for having both intense presidential involvement and reasonable organizational order."[28] As Summers mentioned, Obama engaged himself in the details of policy, though the hierarchical model of White House organization was modified by the direct access of several close advisers (David Axelrod, Valerie Jarrett, and Tom Donilon) who did not have to go through Emanuel to reach the president.

Emanuel had experience as deputy chief of staff in the Clinton administration, and was a member of the House of Representatives rising in the Democratic leadership when Obama convinced him to join his administration. The chief of staff role in any presidency is a formidable task; and it would be particularly difficult in Obama's high-maintenance White House staff structure. Emanuel would have to ride herd on the many policy czars, smooth ruffled feathers, corral large egos, guard access to the president, make the trains run on time, negotiate between White House staffers and cabinet secretaries, and get all of the separate political and policy threads to go through the eye of the needle at the same time.

By all accounts, Emanuel was up to the job. In addition to his impressive political experience, Emanuel was known for his abrasive personality, vulgar language, volatile temperament, and tactical brilliance. He represented the "Tammany Hall" part of the White House staff, which favored practical political victories. His approach occasionally conflicted with the "keepers of the flame" who had been with Obama for years and worked in his campaign. These were the idealists who wanted Obama to hold true to his campaign values and work for large-scale social change. Each side represented one aspect of the president's mind. Emanuel specialized in what he called "the art of the possible," and he was a master of "transactional politics," that is, making deals and compromises, rather than approaching policy from an ideological perspective.

Emanuel was central to the Obama administration in its first year in office, acting as a primary lobbyist of Congress, major liaison with the Washington press corps, and traffic cop in the White House. Emanuel's office was the nerve center of the White House, with all paperwork and policy advice required to run the gauntlet of Emanuel's scrutiny before going to the president. Emanuel was central to all of Obama's major policy decisions and negotiations with Congress. He was not a "neutral" broker in his advice to Obama, and his preferred policy positions tended to favor tactical judgments rather than ideological convictions, in contrast to Vice President Cheney in the Bush administration.

Emanuel was seen by Obama critics as the root of flawed Obama policies. Critics on the right saw him as an advocate of big government and partisanship; critics on the left saw him as being too willing to betray Obama's campaign promises and compromise with Republicans. He was attacked for being one of the Chicago insiders who supposedly insulated Obama from broader sources of advice. He was also defended for being a realist who tried to save Obama from idealistic policies (such as the closing of Guantánamo, the civil trials of 9/11 suspects, and comprehensive health-care reform) favored by his supporters on the left.

Emanuel's style as chief of staff can perhaps be best illustrated by contrasting him with his temporary successor, Pete Rouse. A month before the midterm elections in 2010, Emanuel announced that he was leaving the White House to return to Chicago to run for mayor, a long-time goal of his. When Emanuel left, President Obama appointed his former Senate chief of staff, Pete Rouse, to fill Emanuel's shoes. Rouse had previously served as chief of staff to Senator Thomas Daschle; he was so skilled in his job that he was known as the "101st Senator." Rouse had been with the White House from the beginning of the administration as a "senior adviser" to the president. His duties were not fixed, but ranged across White House trouble spots, particularly friction among staffers. Rouse intended to be "acting" chief of staff until Obama named a formal replacement for Emanuel.

In temperament Rouse was much more similar to Obama than to Emanuel. He was low-key rather than histrionic, in contrast to Emanuel, and he seldom or never used foul language. Perhaps the president summed it up best when he praised Rouse as "completely ego-free."[29] Rouse was thus much more of an honest broker, internal manager, and behind-the-scenes actor than was Emanuel, who had strong views on policy issues and how they related to political realities.

After the 2010 elections in which Republicans swept the elections, picking up six seats in the Senate and sixty-three seats in the House, President Obama appointed William Daley of Chicago to take over the chief of staff job. Daley had been secretary of commerce in the Clinton administration, had pushed the North American Free Trade Agreement (NAFTA) through Congress against Democratic opposition, and had subsequently been a business executive. His background seemed well suited to mend Obama relations with the business community, and he was seen as a moderate Democrat who would better fit the public mood after the 2010 Republican electoral victories.

Daley was also expected to mend fences with the cabinet. Cabinet secretaries continued to complain that Emanuel relegated them to minor roles and kept them from advising the president about their portfolios. Emanuel was seen as unrelentingly negative, hectoring, and attempting to micromanage them. They also complained about the White House staff "czars" who kept them away from the president. In addition to Daley's appointment, the White House also created a "Cabinet Communications Director" in order to "better coordinate with and utilize members of the Cabinet."[30] Daley was also expected to play a more public role, acting as a "public surrogate" for President Obama, according to David Axelrod.[31]

Over the next year, Daley was able to placate the cabinet, but was not as successful at coordinating the White House staff, which continued to be dominated by the inner circle of those closest to the president from early campaign days.[32] Daley also alienated Democrats on the Hill by publicly saying that "both Democrats and Republicans have really made it very difficult for the president to be anything like a chief executive."[33] In addition, on Daley's watch, White House negotiations with House Republicans for a "grand bargain" on deficit reduction had failed to yield a solution in the summer of 2011 (though this could hardly be blamed on Daley).

As a result, in October 2011 Obama shifted Daley's role to liaison with the cabinet and outside visitors. Pete Rouse was again tasked with the more traditional chief of staff role of handling the White House staff and making the trains run on time. The shift may also have foreshadowed the president's strategy for the coming election year during which he would back away from courting Republicans in the House and the business community and make a more populist appeal to the electorate.

In January 2012 Obama appointed his Office of Management and Budget (OMB) director, Jack Lew, to be his new chief of staff. Lew had been OMB director in the Clinton administration, and he was Hillary Clinton's deputy secretary of state for management and resources in the Obama administration. Given his expertise and experience, Lew was expected to play an important role in negotiating with Congress over deficit reduction. Lew was also seen as a progressive and in tune with President Obama's policy priorities for the election year. Lew's role as negotiator was emphasized by President Obama, who said, "Jack's economic advice has been invaluable and he has my complete trust, both because of his mastery of the numbers but because of the values behind those numbers."[34]

Obama's chiefs of staff returned the position to its more traditional role as presidential enforcer and master of the White House policy process. The aberration in the development of the office represented by the Bush administration is not likely to be repeated in future presidencies. The reasons for this are due to the unique talents and background brought to the Bush White House by Vice President Cheney, as will be explained below.

THE RISE OF THE VICE PRESIDENCY

Through the middle of the twentieth century, the vice presidency had been seen as a secondary office, without much power associated with it and a source of frustration to its occupants. John Adams called it the "most insignificant office that ever the invention of man contrived or his imagination conceived."[35] Harry Truman was not even informed of the Manhattan Project until after Franklin Roosevelt was dead. President Eisenhower relegated Richard Nixon to international travel and ceremonial duties, and when asked in 1960 to name Nixon's contributions to his presidency said, "If you give me a week, I might think of one. I don't remember."[36] Lyndon Johnson was looked down upon by John Kennedy's staffers, and in the last year of his presidency he did not let Hubert Humphrey participate in deliberations about Vietnam. Spiro Agnew was driven to resign from the Nixon administration by revelations of his corruption, and Nelson Rockefeller was sidelined by Gerald Ford's chiefs of staff, Donald Rumsfeld and Richard Cheney.[37]

Part of the reason for this unforeseen reality of American politics was that vice presidents were often chosen for electoral reasons to "balance the ticket," with the vice presidential candidate expected to please a particular constituency or represent an important faction of the political party that the presidential candidate wanted to court. At times, the vice president was the presidential candidate's main rival for the nomination. Once in office, presidential staffs often viewed the vice president as a potential rival to the president and carefully ensured that publicity or credit for public policies accrued to the president. Friction was exacerbated when vice presidential staffs felt that their principal was being sidelined and shut out of important policy deliberations.

It was President Jimmy Carter, however, who transformed the Office of Vice President when he chose Walter Mondale as his vice president in 1976. Carter did not choose Mondale for electoral reasons but for personal compatibility, Washington experience, and substantive expertise. Carter valued Mondale's advice, met with him regularly, and gave Mondale important, trouble-shooting assignments. Carter reinforced his personal judgments with important resources, not available to vice presidents in the past: an office in the West Wing with easy access to the Oval Office, the right to attend any White House meeting, integration of some staff between the president and vice president, and access to document distribution within the White House.[38]

These precedents were extended to subsequent vice presidents, though Vice Presidents George H. W. Bush and Dan Quayle were not accorded the same access or assignments from Presidents Reagan or Bush. The enhanced vice presidency was continued when Bill Clinton chose Al Gore for personal compatibility and substantive expertise. Gore played important roles in the

Clinton administration on environmental issues, national defense, telecommunications policy, and the National Performance Review management initiative.

The Cheney Vice Presidency

By the time that Richard Cheney became vice president, the office had become institutionalized with an enlarged staff and the precedents mentioned above. But Cheney brought with him unique characteristics and experience that enabled him to dominate much of the important policy making in the administration of George W. Bush, as illustrated in previous sections above.[39]

Dick Cheney had much broader governmental and foreign policy experience than had President Bush or most other presidential candidates, for that matter (excluding vice presidential experience). He had been a congressional staffer, worked at the Office of Economic Opportunity, was deputy chief of staff to President Ford (at the age of thirty), and became chief of staff when Donald Rumsfeld was appointed secretary of defense. Later he represented Wyoming in the House of Representatives and was secretary of defense in the George H. W. Bush administration. In addition, he had business experience as chief executive of the large engineering firm, Halliburton. All of these professional experiences, none of which President Bush had, gave him invaluable advantages when he became vice president.

Cheney conducted George Bush's search for a vice presidential running mate, and after a lengthy vetting of a number of possible nominees, accepted Bush's offer to become his vice presidential running mate. Immediately after the election, despite the lack of a declared winner, Cheney got a head start in organizing the Bush administration when he was put in charge of the transition and set up his headquarters in Arlington, Virginia. He used his extensive contacts to place throughout the government at subcabinet levels people with whom he had worked before and who would be loyal to him.

From the beginning, Cheney worked on integrating his own staff as fully as possible with the president's own staff. In an important stroke, he had the budget categories of the office of the president and vice president merged into a single executive office, symbolically and fiscally combining the power of the two offices. As the White House organization was established, Cheney assured that none of the previous privileges accorded to vice presidents were lost, and he went further than any other vice presidents by merging some of his staffers with those of the president. Two of his staffers were accorded the highest staff title in the White House, assistant to the president, and two became deputy assistants to the president. This ensured that his people would have access to all policy meetings and guarantee that Cheney would never be out of the loop in policy making. Cheney also established a parallel staff structure with counterparts to presidential staffers on his own staff. After two months, Cheney had a staff of eighty-five for national security alone as well as a separate congressional relations staff. [40]

Cheney was not interested in social policies, such as faith-based initiatives, abortion, cell research, gay marriage, and so on, and he left those issues to President Bush's staff. The policy areas that Cheney focused on, and often dominated, included national security, intelligence, environment, business regulation, judicial appointments, tax policy, and budget issues. According to Cheney, President Bush told him, "I'd have the opportunity to be a major participant in the process, to get involved in whatever issues I wanted to get involved in." [41]

One factor contributing to Cheney's power was his declaration that he was not interested in any further political office, that is, running for the presidency after President Bush's terms. This made him seem less of a threat to steal the limelight from President Bush. The president enjoyed the public dimensions of politics, which Cheney eschewed, leaving Cheney to work on the details of policy making and implementation.

Cheney's role in the Bush administration fit well with President Bush's management style. Like President Reagan, but unlike Presidents Clinton and Obama, George Bush saw himself as a big-picture leader willing to delegate details and implementation to others. This played to Cheney's strength, which was policy substance. His mastery of policy substance and detail allowed Cheney to heavily influence the Bush policy agenda and frame issues for the president. His influence was enhanced by his ability to reach several layers down into the bureaucracy to tilt policy recommendations so that when they reached the president, his influence was not obvious and he could present his own recommendations to the president with a light hand. For instance, Cheney would preview the president's daily intelligence briefing and influence how issues were presented to the president, with Cheney present.

As a consequence of Cheney's experience, his personal network in the administration, his staff and personal expertise, access to the president, and the lack of a regularized policy process, the vice president was able to dominate the Bush administration as few other people short of the president had been able to do in the modern presidency. Colin Powell concluded that "things didn't get really get decided until the president had met with Cheney alone." [42]

Joseph Biden as Vice President

When Obama chose Joe Biden as a running mate in August 2008, he knew he was adding depth and experience to the Democratic ticket. Biden came to the vice presidency after an impressive career in national politics. He had been a senator since his election in 1972; he served on the Senate foreign relations committee for decades, and was its chair in 2008. He ran for the Democratic nomination for president in 1988 and was an early candidate for the nomination in 2008. After becoming vice president, Biden rejected the Cheney model of the vice presidency; but saw himself as a valuable adviser to the president, an emissary to foreign nations, and liaison to his long-time friends in Congress.

Before taking office Biden visited Iraq and Afghanistan to talk with their leaders, and he continued to visit Iraq regularly during Obama's first term and came to represent the United States during the drawdown of US forces. He played a key role in negotiating the administration's stimulus bill in Congress, and Obama put him in charge of overseeing its implementation. In the debt-ceiling crisis in the summer of 2011, Biden was the most active and important representative of the president in dealing with both Democrats and Republicans on the Hill.

Biden fit well into President Obama's approach to decision making. Unlike President Bush, Obama worked on mastering the details of the policy under consideration and took an analytical approach. He ensured that there was an orderly process and careful deliberation with a wide range of options considered. This is where Biden's contributions were important. When the vice president was willing to disagree with a seeming staff consensus, it legitimized the option for others to voice their own skepticism without worrying about being excluded from further deliberations.

In addition to his specific policy assignments and regular negotiations with members of Congress, Biden's most important role was to act as a high-level counselor to the president on major foreign-policy decisions. In the fall of 2009 President Obama spent several months reevaluating the US commitment of troops in Afghanistan. After taking office in 2009, at the request of the military, he sent twenty-one thousand more troops, bringing the total to sixty-eight thousand. With US forces not making major progress in the summer of 2009, General Stanley McChrystal sought more troops to implement a counterinsurgency strategy in the conflict. McChrystal sent a confidential memo to Obama with options of increasing troop strength to forty, twenty, or twelve thousand, and the military made it clear that forty thousand was the minimum necessary. President Obama was determined to take the time to master the military details in order to make an informed decision. In a series of ten formal meetings over two months in the fall of 2009, President Obama deliberated with his civilian and military advisers. Though political opponents accused him of "dithering," Obama carefully worked through all of the available options.

The key issue was how solid the government of President Hamid Karzai was and how effective the counterinsurgency strategy would be. Over the weeks of deliberation, the president's advisers engaged in a wide-ranging and thorough process of deliberation. Military leaders, along with Secretary Gates and Secretary Clinton, firmly advocated increasing the US troop presence significantly, by forty thousand. President Obama, however, expressed skepticism about the wisdom of sending that many additional troops.

During these deliberations, Vice President Biden played a key role in providing an alternative option to the military proposals to increase the number of troops and widen the war. Obama told Biden, "I want you to say exactly what you think. And I want you to ask the toughest questions you can think of."[43] Obama was, in effect, assigning Biden the role of "devil's advocate" to question the wisdom of the consensus among military leaders. Biden argued forcefully for a "counterterrorism" strategy that would focus on defeating al Qaeda rather than on building a government in Afghanistan that Afghans would support. He argued for not expanding the commitment of US troops but pulling back to defended bases. Rather than attempting to defeat the Taliban throughout the country, Biden argued that US forces should be used to strike any al Qaeda forces in Afghanistan or near the border in Pakistan. Although several other civilian advisers favored Biden's scaled-back option, in the end President Obama decided to go forward with a "surge" of thirty thousand troops but with a drawdown beginning in the fall of 2011.

Another major national-security decision in which Biden played a key role was the decision of whether to send special forces to capture or kill Osama bin Laden. In the spring of 2011, circumstantial evidence was accumulated by the CIA that indicated that bin Laden was hiding in a large house in Abbottabad, Pakistan. Briefings on the possibility of bin Laden's location were tightly held, and deliberations were secret. Even though the circumstantial evidence was strong, there were no photographs or other hard evidence that bin Laden was actually there. The consequences of the decision were far reaching. Capturing or killing bin Laden would be an important victory for the United States in the war on al Qaeda. But a failed attempt would be a disaster and probably cost the lives of many US troops. His advisers were all aware that in 1980 President Carter ordered a raid to try to free US hostages in Tehran, but in the staging for the attack two US helicopters collided, killing several personnel and aborting the attempt to free the hostages. Even a successful raid on a house with innocent inhabitants would be a terrible mess and an embarrassment. The United States would also be risking the ire of the government of Pakistan, a key ally in US counterterrorism and a country with deep ambivalence toward the United States.

In the National Security Council meeting on April 29, 2011 to advise the president on the final decision of whether to authorize the raid, Obama asked each of his advisers their judgment. Most of his advisers were ambivalent, reflecting the reality that the evidence was genuinely ambiguous. The exceptions were CIA Director Leon Panetta, who unequivocally favored the attack and Vice President Biden, who advised against an attack until the evidence of bin Laden's presence was more firmly established. "Mr. President, my suggestion is, don't go."[44] The raid was successful, bin Laden was killed, and it was a great victory for the US war with al Qaeda. A week after the attack, President Obama recalled "At the end of the day, this was still a 55-45 situation. Had he [bin Laden] not been there, then there would have been some significant consequences."[45]

The point in these examples of Biden's role in the Obama presidency is not that his advice was rejected, but that Biden was willing to explicitly disagree with a consensus and give his frank advice to the president. The soliciting of opposing points of view was central to President Obama's style of decision making and in contrast to that of George W. Bush.[46] Eventually, Obama's policy on the war in Afghanistan came close to that of Biden's. Biden's views on financial reform and the bailout of the auto companies also were influential to Obama's final policies.

In summary, Biden had a good working relationship with President Obama and was an across-the-board adviser. His policy assignments were selective but important. President Obama benefitted from Biden's decades of experience in US foreign policy by making him a special emissary to many countries. His negotiating trips to Iraq were essential to the US disengagement with the war. He played an important role in US relations with Russia and China. He negotiated with the Senate in the ratification of the START Treaty with Russia. He was a key negotiator in the economic recovery act and oversaw its implementation early in the administration. He was important in winning the lame-duck congressional tax compromise after the 2010 elections and in negotiations over the debt ceiling crisis in 2011. In the last hours of 2012, he was the key negotiator in arriving at a compromise to avoid the sharp increases in taxes and drastic spending cuts, known as the "fiscal cliff." Scholar of the vice presidency, Joel Goldstein, concluded that "Biden has been one of the most consequential vice presidents in U.S. history."[47]

CONCLUSION

Presidents George W. Bush and Barack Obama reinforce the major trends of the twentieth century in organizing their White Houses. The centralization of control that began in the 1970s was inevitable, given the growth in functions of the US government and the fragmentation in the executive branch and Congress. The only future restraint on centralization will come from within; if centralization continues, the White House will suffer from overload, and delegation will become necessary. Managing the White House itself has become a major challenge, let alone trying to manage the whole executive branch. The chief of staff's job has become necessary and more complex.

White House czars may seem necessary for coordination, but czars themselves have to be managed. It has taken two centuries, but the Office of Vice President has now come into its own as an important asset for presidents to use to their advantage. Future presidents will likely keep this in mind when they choose their running mates.

NOTES

1. Remarks at the Annual Meeting of the National Academy of Public Administration, November 15, 2012. The author was present.

2. Jim VandeHei and Glenn Kessler, "President to Consider Changes for New Term," *Washington Post*, November 5, 2004.

3. Ellen Nakashima and Dana Milbank, "Bush Cabinet Takes Back Seat in Driving Policy," *Washington Post*, September 5, 2001.

4. Mike Allen, "Management Style Shows Weaknesses," *Washington Post*, June 2, 2004.

5. Ron Suskind, "Faith, Certainty and the Presidency of George W. Bush," *New York Times Magazine*, October 17, 2004.

6. White House, "President Nominated Rob Portman as OMB Director and Susan Schwab for USTR," April 18, 2006, georgewbush-whitehouse.archives.gov/news/releases/2006/04/20060418-1.html.

7. Both quotes from Bob Woodward, *Bush at War* (New York: Simon & Schuster, 2002), 145–46.

8. Edward Luce, "America: A Fearsome Foursome," *Financial Times*, February 3, 2010.

9. Peter Baker and Jeff Zeleny, "Staff Chief Wields Power Freely, but Influence Comes with Risk," *New York Times*, August 16, 2010.

10. Robert Pear, "Health Official Can't Guarantee Openness in Talks," *New York Times*, February 4, 2010.

11. Daniel Klaidman, "Independent's Day," *Newsweek*, July 20, 2009.

12. Jane Mayer, "The Trial," *New Yorker*, February 15, 2010.

13. Jodi Kantor and Charlie Savage, "Getting the Message," *New York Times*, February 15, 2010.

14. Edward Luce and Daniel Dombey, "US Foreign Policy: Waiting on the Sun King," *Financial Times*, March 30, 2010.

15. For a history of White House policy "czars" and a critique of their constitutional legitimacy, see Mitchel A. Sollenberger and Mark J. Rozell, *The President's Czars: Undermining Congress and the Constitution* (Lawrence: University Press of Kansas, 2012).

16. Sollenberger and Rozell, *The President's Czars*, 146–60.

17. Michael Shear and Ceci Connolly, "Obama Assembles Powerful West Wing," *Washington Post*, January 8, 2009.

18. Martha Kumar and Terry Sullivan, eds., *The White House World* (College Station: Texas A&M University Press), 111.

19. See Bruce Schulman, "The Power and Politics Behind the Chief of Staff," *Politico*, January 18, 2012, 23.

20. Barton Gellman and Jo Becker, "'A Different Understanding with the President,'" *Washington Post*, June 24, 2007.

21. Quoted in Barton Gellman, *Angler: The Cheney Vice Presidency* (New York: Penguin, 2008), 86–87.

22. Ron Suskind, "Why Are These Men Laughing?" *Esquire*, January 2003, www.ronsuskind.com/articles/000032.htm, accessed September 27, 2006.

23. Gellman, *Angler*, 81–86.

24. Gellman and Becker, "'A Different Understanding with the President,'" 1.

25. This account is based on the analysis of Gellman in *Angler*, 162–71.

26. See James P. Pfiffner, *Torture as Public Policy* (Boulder, CO: Paradigm Publishers, 2010).

27. For details see James P. Pfiffner, *Power Play: The Bush Presidency and the Constitution* (Washington, DC: Brookings, 2008), chap. 7.

28. Quoted in James Fallows, "Obama, Explained," *The Atlantic*, March 2012.

29. Anne E. Kornblut, "Emanuel's Replacement Is Known as a Fixer," *Washington Post*, October 1, 2010.

30. Anne E. Kornblut, "Daley Aims to Mend Rifts within Obama Team," *Washington Post*, March 9, 2011.

31. Sheryl Gay Stolberg, "Obama's Top Aide a Tough, Decisive Negotiator," *New York Times*, January 8, 2011.

32. Paul Starobin, "The Rise and Fall of Bill Daley: An Inside Account, *The New Republic*, January 18, 2012.

33. Anne E. Kornblut, "Daley Shifting Roles, Officials Say," *Washington Post*, November 9, 2011.

34. Quoted by Mara Liasson, "Low-Profile Power Player Jack Lew May Be in Line for Treasury Post," National Public Radio, December 18, 2012.

35. White House, "About the White House," www.whitehouse.gov/about/presidents/john adams.

36. Eisenhower news conference, August 24, 1960, posted on *The American Presidency Project*, University of California–Santa Barbara, www.presidency.ucsb.edu/ws/in dex.php?pid=11915.

37. For an authoritative book on the vice presidency, see Joel Goldstein, *The Modern American Vice Presidency: The Transformation of a Political Institution* (Princeton, NJ: Princeton University Press, 1982).

38. Joel Goldstein, "How the Vice President Can Serve as the President's Most Unbiased Adviser," *History News Service*, December 5, 2009.

39. This section is based on Gellman, *Angler*; and Joel Goldstein, "Cheney: Vice Presidential Power and the War on Terror," paper presented at the American Political Science Association annual meeting, September 5, 2009, Toronto, Ontario, Canada.

40. See Shirley Anne Warshaw, *The Co-Presidency of Bush and Cheney* (Stanford University Press, 2009), chap. 4.

41. Quoted in Warshaw, *Co-Presidency*, 59.

42. Bob Woodward, *Plan of Attack* (New York: Simon & Schuster, 2004), 392.

43. Bob Woodward, *Obama's Wars* (New York: Simon & Schuster, 2010), 160.

44. Peter L. Bergen, "Warrior in Chief," *New York Times*, April 28, 2012; Mark Lander, "Biden Recounts Back-and-Forth on Bin Laden Raid," *New York Times*, January 31, 2012.

45. Joby Warrick and Karin Brulliard, "Obama Says He OKd bin Laden Raid Despite Warnings," *Washington Post*, May 9, 2011.

46. See James P. Pfiffner, "Decision Making in the Bush White House," *Presidential Studies Quarterly* (June 2009): 363–84.

47. Joel Goldstein, "Sorry, Folks—Biden Is Here to Stay," *Washington Post*, August 28, 2010. See also Joel Goldstein, "Firing Reaffirms Joe Biden's Significance to Administration," *Politico*, June 30, 2010.

Chapter Five

The Presidency and Congressional Time

Roger H. Davidson

The legislative workload, along with institutional arrangements for coping with it, is a major component of the structure and substance of legislative-executive relations. Given the Constitution and the political history of the United States, it could not be otherwise. Articles I and II, after all, lay out the interleaved lawmaking responsibilities of the two branches—from initiation ("He [the president] shall from time to time recommend to their [Congress'] consideration such measures as he shall judge necessary and expedient. . . .") to implementation ("He shall take care that the laws be faithfully executed. . . ."). Beginning with George Washington, activist presidents have always inserted themselves into the legislative process. Franklin D. Roosevelt and his modern successors institutionalized "the legislative presidency"; today's chief executives are expected to submit their legislative agendas to Congress and to provide their allies on Capitol Hill with leadership and guidance.

Yet congressional-presidential ties are often frayed, even hostile. In the seven decades since World War II, nearly all presidents have suffered from erosion of legislative support during their tenure in office. At some point, almost all faced a Congress controlled wholly or in part by the opposition party. Only John F. Kennedy, Lyndon Johnson, and Jimmy Carter had the luxury of working solely with their own Capitol Hill majorities. Yet Johnson pulled out of his 1968 reelection race because of public rancor over the Vietnam War; Carter lost his 1980 reelection bid.

Bill Clinton—although reelected handily to a second term—was impeached by the House (though not convicted by the Senate) for sexual improprieties with a White House intern. Also reelected to a second term, George

W. Bush saw his support plummet amid vocal opposition from Democrats, Independents, and even factions among his fellow Republicans. Disapproval of his administration—especially the Iraq War and the failure to cope with the devastation after Hurricane Katrina in 2005—led to election losses in 2006 and 2008, giving Democrats control of both legislative chambers. Bush retired to private life, declining to attend the GOP's 2008 and 2012 national conventions.[1] His successor, Democrat Barack Obama, had a stormy but fruitful first two years; but he and his party endured a "pasting" (his own term) in the 2010 congressional elections, giving Republicans control of the House and strengthening their minority position in the Senate.

As for Congress, one attribute sets it apart from virtually all of the world's other national assemblies: it is a working body that writes, processes, and refines laws that are typically its own handiworks; and it relies to a large degree on "in-house" resources. Scholars have paid scant attention to legislative business as a research topic. Yet Congress's agenda and workload shape not only the behavior and operations of the Senate and House of Representatives, but also the two chambers' relationships with the executive branch. What is more, the legislative workload reminds us of "what Congress actually does and how it does it, with all its duties and all its occupations, with all its devices of management and resources of power."[2]

Legislative activity is, of course, only one aspect of the interactions between presidents and congresses. Executive communications to Congress, for example, have grown so rapidly over the past two generations that almost as many of them are referred to committees as are bills and resolutions. Implementing and overseeing the laws and agencies created by Congress, not to mention scrutinizing administrative and judicial rule making, are other functions that repeatedly propel the president and Congress into joint action. Given the breadth and reach of modern government, these oversight duties remain burdensome even when few new statutes are produced. Yet oversight is closely linked to lawmaking: it flows from previously enacted statutes, and it influences how the statutes are carried out or revised.

Making federal appointments is another joint enterprise that has become more burdensome at both ends of Pennsylvania Avenue. In days gone by, presidential nominations were usually handled perfunctorily, following the belief that presidents deserved to have executive-branch leaders of their own choosing. Today, however, nominees' qualifications, records, and financial activities are vetted within the White House by the Presidential Personnel Office and examined on Capitol Hill by the committees with jurisdiction over the relevant agencies.

Even federal court appointments—whose selection is clearly a joint duty of the president and the Senate (which is charged with giving "advice and consent")—historically provoked little congressional participation. Not until 1925 did the Senate Judiciary Committee hear a court nominee: Harlan Fiske

Stone, who was easily confirmed, serving later as Chief Justice (1941–1946). Confirmation hearings became common only in the 1950s. But they were still not required: Chief Justice Earl Warren (1953–1969), a towering figure in the court's history, was not asked to testify—when confirmed, he was already sitting on the court as an interim appointee. Nowadays, writes Robert A. Katzmann (a political scientist now serving as a US Circuit Court judge), "Hearings have become a staple of the confirmation process. The expectation that nominees will testify is firmly rooted."[3] Not only the committee, but also numerous lobby groups, scrutinize nominees' writings and judicial opinions; the media often cover the hearings. In short, congressional outputs are diverse in content and variable over time.

THINKING ABOUT POLITICAL TIME

Thinking in terms of political time ought to come naturally to students of US politics. After all, the Constitution separates the two policy-making branches, the presidency and Congress, chronologically as well as functionally. The interlocking system of terms of office—four years for the president, two years for representatives, and staggered six-year terms for senators—creates a perpetual timetable for electoral renewal or replacement of officials. The constitutional system was designed as an intricate machine of interlocked moving parts—and that machine could very well be a timepiece.[4]

The two policy-making branches run on different but related time frames; rarely do they experience change at precisely the same moment or at exactly the same rate. Because presidents are limited to four or eight years, they are forced to focus on pressing policy issues and to seek quick results. By contrast the houses of Congress display a measure of continuity, sustained by overlapping tenure and by the presence of experienced careerists. As a result policies are typically incubated and nurtured by Capitol Hill policy entrepreneurs, oftentimes years or even decades before someone in the White House decides to elevate the item to a short-list for urgent action.

These divergent time perspectives suggest why it is misleading to tell political time strictly according to elections. Every new Congress is to some degree unique; but not every election makes substantial changes in the two chambers. As a continuing body the Senate is more resistant to change: despite respectable turnover rates, the average senator nowadays has served nearly three six-year terms. The House of Representatives formally reconstitutes itself every two years, but only rarely is it as radically transformed as in the recent past: the Republicans, led by Newt Gingrich, seized control in 1995 after fifty years in the minority. Twelve years later the Democrats regained control, only to fall to the GOP's landslide election of 2010—their largest majority in sixty-four years. Both change and continuity are evidenced in recent elections. Even in the 2010 upheaval, more than 80 percent of all incumbents won reelection (although a number of incumbents chose retirement rather than probable defeat). For the 113th Congress (2013–2015), eleven senators and eighty-seven representatives were newcomers; half the members of both bodies had served for less than ten years.

Categorizing by presidencies might seem a simpler matter, and indeed most historians and political scientists use particular presidencies as their unit of analysis. But even here things are not always what they seem. First, an administration may undergo substantial midcourse corrections—caused by midterm elections, crises, or other events. Such occurrences can alter a president's governing strategy and effectiveness.[5] Bill Clinton's first term was derailed after only two years, when the opposition Republicans won control of Capitol Hill. George W. Bush's first term was transformed by the events of 9/11; his second term was enfeebled by plunging public support. Obama's presidency was transformed by the Republicans' landslide House victory in 2010. Second, essential presidential governing strategies or styles may conceivably extend beyond a single administration—as, for example, in the Nixon–Ford or Reagan–Bush successions.

Political scientists tend to measure political time in terms of underlying and enduring political party coalitions. These "party systems" are initiated by realigning elections or periods: most notably, Andrew Jackson's election in 1828; the Republican Party's ascendancy from 1860; the "system of 1896" that strengthened the GOP's dominance; and Franklin D. Roosevelt's election in 1932—a period of Democratic rule that extended into the 1980s. To this list we may add several recent shifts: a "postreform" period of economic torpor and political uncertainty; Republican rule beginning in 1994 and lasting for a dozen years; and finally a period of divided government that began in 2006.

Such a categorization assumes the underpinning of mass-based parties that can effectively mobilize loyal supporters in elections—unless and until these stable loyalties are disturbed either by short-term forces or by more permanent reordering of party divisions.[6] The theory conforms to political development during the heyday of US political parties, roughly from the 1830s through the 1960s; and it fits reasonably with events since that time: an era increasingly marked by intense top-down partisan organization and elite mobilization, though with lower overall rates of participation. Despite its flaws, party-alignment theory yields provocative insights into changes in presidential and congressional policy making.[7]

CONGRESSIONAL WORKLOAD AND OUTPUTS

Both the president and Congress today confront a number and variety of demands unmatched in all but the most turbulent years of the past. The history of Congress readily demonstrates that "the volume of output demands as well as . . . their complexity, uniformity, and volatility, vary greatly over time."[8] Aggregate legislative statistics from the last six decades show how variable these workload measures can be.

One workload indicator is the number of bills and resolutions introduced by senators and representatives. In both chambers, bill introduction followed a long-term growth from the mid-1940s through the 1970s, followed by gradual decline. In the House, a portion of the decline can be traced to changes in cosponsorship rules and the rise of mega-bills. Both chambers, however, have experienced parallel buildup and then a period of extraordinary legislative activity, followed by contraction. Since the late 1990s, there has been a modest rise in the volume of bills: in today's two-year congresses, from eight thousand to ten thousand public bills and joint resolutions are introduced. From four hundred to eight hundred public laws are enacted.

Bill introduction and sponsorship vary widely among individual senators and representatives. Some lawmakers are inveterate sponsors of bills and resolutions; others shy away from sponsoring measures. In the late 1940s, House members on average authored about eighteen bills or resolutions, compared to thirty-three for senators. Bill sponsorship peaked in the later 1960s, when the average member in both bodies authored almost fifty measures per Congress. Then in the late 1970s the figures plummeted, reaching a plateau that remains to this day. Today's lawmakers introduce fewer measures than those who served in Congress in the post–World War II period— some thirty per senator and fewer than half that number per representative.

Legislators today are doubly disadvantaged: not only do they introduce fewer bills and resolutions; but their proposals are less likely to be approved by the full chamber. A Senate measure introduced in the 1940s had better than an even chance of passage in some form; the odds are now less than one in four. A House measure used to have nearly one chance in four of passage; today the odds are less than half that.[9] This trend stems from two trends: (1) an increased emphasis on broad-scale legislative vehicles—omnibus bills, usually shaped by party or committee leaders, that serve as catch-alls for scores of specific provisions, and (2) the gradual elimination or contraction of large numbers of administrative or noncontroversial matters that were once the subject of separate bills.

Recorded votes on the House and Senate floors underscore these shifts in legislative activity. The numbers of recorded votes, traditionally quite low, accelerated in the 1960s and then exploded in the 1970s. The rise in floor activity was linked directly to changes in rules and procedures that made it easier for members to offer floor amendments and gain recorded votes. This shifted power perceptibly from the committee rooms to the chambers themselves. Party and committee leaders, especially in the House, soon fought back with procedural tactics aimed at limiting contentious floor votes. Accordingly, the number of recorded votes fell off markedly after 1978. In the Senate votes have stabilized to about six hundred to eight hundred per Congress, compared to one thousand or more in the 1970s. President Obama's only experience with unified government, the Democratic 111th Congress (2009–2011), produced 383 public laws, starting with the Lilly Ledbetter Act and ending with the landmark Affordable Care Act.[10]

The end products of lawmaking are bills and resolutions that survive the complex legislative process to become law. Working in tandem, Congress and the executive strictly regulate the flow of legislative outputs. Of the thousands of bills and resolutions introduced in the House and Senate in a given Congress, only about 5.5 percent find their way into the statute books. The size and shape of the legislative product are a function not only of political support or opposition but also of changing rules specifying which matters must be resolved by statute and which can be handled by other means.

Overall legislative output figures—measures passed by the two chambers, measures signed into law—look quite different from the input and activity figures described thus far. The number of enacted public bills (those dealing with general legislative issues) began at a high level after World War II, peaking at midcentury. The GOP-controlled postwar 80th Congress (1947–1949)—derided as "awful" by President Truman in his 1948 campaign—actually passed no less than 906 public laws. Levels have fallen since then. Only a modest upsurge in the volume of public laws occurred during the activist era of the 1960s and 1970s, More recently, there has been a steep decline: the 112th Congress (2011–2013) passed a mere 173 public laws.[11] Of this most recent Congress, there was no end of expert and public scorn at its failure to pass even essential and noncontroversial legislation. "It's been like watching paint dry," remarked Senator Bob Corker (R-TN).[12]

The shrinkage in the volume of substantive legislation is commonly attributed to the policy "gridlock" that has resulted from close party competition and heightened cohesion within the two parties. Many blame also an underlying polarization among the electorate—especially the core partisans who are more likely to vote in party primaries and midterm elections.

The shrinkage is also, however, a byproduct of the increasingly common stratagem of packaging legislative proposals into massive measures—for example, continuing resolutions, reconciliation bills, tax-reform packages, and broad-scale reauthorizations. This is attested by the steady growth in the length of public statutes. Between 1947 and the present day, the average public law has ballooned from 2.5 pages to more than thirteen pages. As recently as the 1960s, more than two-thirds of all public laws took up no more than a single page; nowadays very few are that brief. And the proportion of truly lengthy enactments—twenty-one pages or more—grew three-fold in that same period. Legalistic verbosity is only partly to blame; legislative packaging is also at work.

These statistical trends, especially the activity and workload figures, lend strong support to the thesis that contemporary lawmaking has passed through a series of five distinct stages or eras (see table 5.1). Legislative-executive relations follow different paths during each of these periods. The first was a relatively static era dominated by a bipartisan conservative coalition (roughly 1937–1964); the second was an era of liberal activism and reform (1965–1978); the third was an era of contraction, fiscal restraint, and political stalemate (1979–1992); the fourth congressional era (1995–2007), while marked by elements of stalemate, was increasingly driven by a conservative partisan majority. Most recently, the tectonic plates of US party loyalty have shifted toward bipartisan stalemate—at first favoring the Democrats who, recapturing the House and Senate in 2007, opposed the late Bush administration and then responded to the Obama administration's agenda (2009–2011). Afterward, a Democratic president faced a Democratic Senate but an unyielding House Republican majority.

Like any artifacts of historical categorization, these eras are bound to arouse debate over their precise definitions and boundaries, and perhaps even over their utility in illuminating legislative-executive relations. Historical developments, after all, are continuous and multifaceted, rarely yielding unambiguous boundaries. Although our primary data sets begin in 1947, we can extend the first era back to the second Roosevelt administration (1937–1941) by turning to fragmentary statistical indicators and a wealth of qualitative data. The boundaries of the second, liberal, era are also problematic: reformist skirmishes broke out over a period of years starting in the late 1950s; by the time the climax occurred in 1974–1975, the era's energy was already waning. The third, postreform, era was one of instability in which elements of the prior period coexisted uneasily with subsequent economic and political trends. The years of the fourth, conservative, era also resist rigid boundaries.

The current fifth era reflects both rigid partisanship and political instability: It begins with a gradual rise in progressivism during George W. Bush's later years, leading in 2008 to consolidation of Democratic control with President Obama's election. But Democratic hegemony was torn down only two years later, with almost unprecedented GOP gains, giving them control of the House. In 2012 the Democrats struck back with Obama's reelection and gains in both houses—although still short of the hoped-for House majority or a Senate filibuster-proof of sixty.

Table 5.1. Political/Operational Eras of the Modern Congress

Congressional Era	Approximate Dates*	Environmental Forces	Leadership Mode	Member Goals	Activity Workload
Bipartisan Conservative	1937–1964	Intra-party divisions	Chairmen of "corporate committees"	Public policy; internal influence sought by careerists; reelection stressed by marginal members	Stable routine
Liberal Activist	1965–1978	Liberal majorities	Democratic caucus	Public policy now competes with reelection for most members; internal influence	Rising legislative innovation; jurisdictional expansion
Postreform	1979–1994	Divided government	Party leaders versus committee majorities	Public policy sought by many, internal influence by a few; reelection important for most members	Declining (jurisdictional protectionism, oversight
Partisan Conservative	1995–2007	Inter-party conflict	Republican leadership	Public policy predominant; careerism rebounds after initial decline; reelection stressed by marginal members	Short-term party committee productivity
Divided Government	2007–	Inter-party conflict; ideological parties	Deadline-driven, about fiscal or "sunset" issues	Public policy predominant, often ideologically driven	Low some

These dates are approximations, based on certain turning points that seem most clearly to herald a passage from one regime to another—for example, the 1964 electoral surge that gave the Democrats two-to-one majorities in both houses, the the Republicans that led to their wider victories in 1980, and the GOP takeover of both chambers in 1992. Of course, there arbitrariness in erecting these landmarks. These "regimes" are actually products of gradual and incremental changes in environment and operations. Democratic gains in 1958, for example, set the stage for an outpouring of liberal legislation President Kennedy's assassination in 1963. More recently, the Republican regime was not fully operative until the aftermath terrorist attacks of September 11, 2001. The most recent era has yet to reveal itself: its dimensions, not to mention its longevity term policy implications, are yet to be determined.

Despite these caveats, it is intriguing how closely these five eras coincide with changing journalistic and scholarly understandings of the legislative process. The "textbook Congress" that emerged from the first era was well researched and descriptively persuasive.[13] The same can be said for the liberal activist, or reform, era—which produced numerous journalistic and textbook analyses. Scholarly consensus even emerged on the nature and characteristics of the postreform era—with its emphasis on candidate-centered politics and cutback policy making.[14] The fourth era—marked by close competition between cohesive party cadres—is described by scholars as a state of "conditional party government."[15] The current era as yet lacks convincing definition or boundaries—although current observers would likely use the terms "gridlock" or "dysfunctional" to describe its outputs.

THE BIPARTISAN CONSERVATIVE ERA (1937–1964)

The bipartisan conservative era outlasted several presidents of widely varying goals and skills. Roosevelt failed after 1936 to keep Capitol Hill safe for New Deal initiatives; after 1940 he was preoccupied with the war effort. Truman repeatedly broke his lance in efforts to push legislation through conservative congresses—most memorably in housing, labor–management relations, civil rights, and medical care. Eisenhower's moderate right-of-center legislative instincts were a better fit with the objectives of the conservative coalition that ruled Capitol Hill. More aggressive than Eisenhower, Kennedy enjoyed considerable success in a transitional period when the old order in Congress was crumbling.

According to popular legend, Franklin D. Roosevelt overwhelmed Congress with his New Deal programs, dictating legislation that gained virtually automatic approval. The facts by no means support this legend. Aside from the emergency measures approved quickly in the spring of 1933, during the first months of his administration, Roosevelt's legislative record drew heavily on proposals already introduced and incubated on Capitol Hill. This interbranch cooperation increased in the late 1930s. For the years 1931–1940, Lawrence H. Chamberlain found joint presidential-congressional influence at work in 52 percent of the major pieces of legislation; the president prevailed in 37 percent of the cases and Congress in 11 percent.[16] His findings affirmed "the joint character of the American legislative process," even in years of powerful presidential leadership.

The New Deal soon gave way to a long period of bipartisan conservative dominance, which lasted roughly from the second Roosevelt administration through the mid-1960s. Both parties were split internally between progressive, internationalist wings and reactionary wings. Although the progressives tended to dominate presidential selections, the conservatives held sway on

Capitol Hill. An oligarchy of senior leaders, oftentimes called "the barons" or "the old bulls," wielded the gavels and commanded the votes in committees and on the floor. Whichever party was in power, congressional leaders overrepresented safe one-party regions (Democrats in the rural South and urban North, Republicans in the rural Northeast and Midwest). The narrow legislative agenda reflected the will of the conservative bipartisan majority that controlled so much domestic policy making.

This Capitol Hill regime proved a hostile environment for activist presidents and their ambitious legislative agendas. "For God's sake," a congressional spokesman telephoned the White House in April 1938, "don't send us any more controversial legislation!" Recounting this anecdote from Franklin Roosevelt's second term, James MacGregor Burns summed up legislative-executive relations as "deadlock on the Potomac."[17]

Harry Truman's clashes with Congress began early and continued throughout his administration. "Except for the modified Employment Act of 1946," related Robert J. Donovan, "the [Democratic] Seventy-ninth Congress had squelched practically every piece of social and economic legislation Truman had requested."[18] Truman's other congresses were equally frustrating, although in different ways. The Republican 80th Congress (1947–1949) "gave [Truman] his most enduring image. Facing an opposition-controlled legislative body almost certain to reject any domestic program he proposed, he adopted the role of an opportunist."[19]

Truman campaigned successfully in 1948 by attacking the "awful, do-nothing 80th Congress"—by no means a do-nothing body. Yet the Democratic 81st Congress (1949–1951) rejected virtually all of Truman's major Fair Deal initiatives; and the 82nd, marked by depleted Democratic majorities and the Korean War stalemate, was even more hostile to new domestic legislation.

The 1950s were years of outward quiescence accompanied by underlying, accelerating demands for action and innovation. Dwight Eisenhower (1953–1961), whose legislative goals were far more modest than Truman's, was increasingly placed in the position of offering scaled-down alternatives to measures launched on Capitol Hill by coalitions of activist Democrats and moderate Republicans.

The legislative workload throughout this era was, accordingly, relatively stable and manageable from year to year. A large proportion of the bills and resolutions were routine and dealt with matters not yet delegated to the executive branch for resolution—for example, immigration cases, land claims, and private legislation. Demands were building, however, for bolder legislation to address civil rights, housing, unemployment, and other concerns of urban and suburban voters.

On Capitol Hill, the powerhouse committees (the taxing and spending panels plus House Rules) were cohesive groups—"corporate," Richard F.

Fenno, Jr. termed them—with firm leadership and rigorous internal norms of behavior.[20] They put a tight lid on new legislation, especially in fiscal affairs. The appropriations committees, in particular, stood as guardians of the US Treasury, holding in check the more ambitious and costly goals of the program-oriented authorizing panels.

Power thus gravitated to a cadre of strong committee leaders in both houses. The best of these were able, vivid personalities whose safe constituencies enabled them to lavish their time and skills upon their committees' agendas. If they often behaved autocratically, they usually enjoyed the tolerance if not support of a majority within their committees. Southern Democrats, who chaired many of the key panels during those days, reached across the aisle to build their working majorities, often cultivating close bonds with GOP ranking members and other conservatives.

Journalists and political scientists closely studied mid-twentieth-century congresses, constructing a detailed and persuasive picture of their operations. Borrowing research concepts and techniques from sociology and anthropology, behaviorally trained political scientists illuminated Congress's workings through close personal observation, interviews, and statistical analyses. The Senate of that era was lovingly described by journalist William S. White and systematically analyzed by political scientist Donald R. Matthews.[21] Richard F. Fenno, Jr. wrote powerful, detailed accounts of committee operations and the budgetary process.[22]

The picture of the midcentury Congress that emerged from the scholars' work on Capitol Hill was so persuasive that it was regarded as "the textbook Congress."[23] According to the leading theoretical framework of that period, the institution was viewed as an interlocking pattern of personal relationships in which all the structural and functional parts worked in rough equilibrium. Ironically, by the time observers got around to completing this coherent picture of a tight, closed, internally coherent congressional system, that world was already being turned upside down. Pressures for change and "reform" mounted, heralding a period of liberal activist and reformist politics.

LIBERAL ACTIVIST GOVERNMENT (1965–1978)

The cozy domains of Capitol Hill's barons were eventually demolished by what journalist Hedrick Smith called a "power earthquake."[24] That metaphor was inexact. Although many observers linked the changes to the post-Watergate "class of 1974" and their overthrow of three House committee chairmen, these events signaled the high-water mark rather than the outset of the era of liberal legislative activism and procedural reform.

The process of change began in earnest in the last two Eisenhower years—after the 1958 elections, when the Democrats enlarged their ranks by

sixteen senators and fifty-one representatives, many of them urban and suburban liberals. The elections had immediate effect upon both chambers. Senate Majority Leader Lyndon Johnson's (D-TX) heavy-handed leadership
style visibly softened; in the House a band of liberal activists organized the
Democratic Study Group (DSG), which set about launching a drive for procedural reforms. After Sen. John F. Kennedy (D-MA) won the presidency
two years later, the Senate majority leader's post passed from Johnson to
Mike Mansfield (D-MT), a mild-mannered liberal. In order to clear the way
for Kennedy's agenda, House Speaker Sam Rayburn (D-TX) struggled to
break the conservatives' control of the powerful Rules Committee. The reform era reached its high-water mark in the mid-1970s with successive
waves of changes in committee and floor procedures and, in 1975, the ouster
of three of the barons from their committee chairmanships.

One underlying cause of the upheaval was the policy demands of urban
and suburban voting blocs as well as minority groups—demands already
heeded by activist presidents.[25] The spirit of the era was reflected in the
popular movements that came to prominence: civil rights, feminism, environ-
mentalism, consumerism, and growing opposition to the Vietnam War.
These movements provided not only an extensive legislative agenda, but also
grassroots activists who promoted that agenda—some of whom wound up
serving in the House and Senate. Longer-range causes of the era's liberal
activism included demographic shifts, widened citizen participation, social
upheaval, technological changes in transportation and communications, and
Supreme Court–ordered reapportionment and redistricting that made the
House more responsive to urban and minority interests.

The resulting changes left Congress more open and participant-friendly,
and encouraged legislative innovation and productivity. Individual lawmakers had greater leverage; influence was dispersed among and within the committees. More leaders existed than ever before, and even nonleaders could
exert more influence. More staff aides were on hand to extend the legislative
reach of even the most junior members.

Individual senators and representatives, while enjoying their enhanced
legislative involvement, were forced at the same time to devote increased
attention to constituents back home. No longer was frantic citizen outreach
confined to a few senators from large states and a few representatives from
swing districts; it was practiced by all members (or their staffs) in order to
purchase electoral security at a time of dwindling grassroots party support. In
their office-holding activities, members tended to exchange the role of work-
horse, or legislative specialist, for that of the show horse, becoming legislative generalists, advertisers, and credit seekers.

The reforms were propelled by, and in turn helped to facilitate, an ambitious and expansionist policy agenda, as signified by such themes as John F.
Kennedy's "New Frontier" and Lyndon B. Johnson's "Great Society." This

era witnessed a flood of landmark enactments in civil rights, education, medical insurance, employment and training, science and space, consumer protection, and the environment, not to mention five new cabinet departments and four constitutional amendments. Legislative activity soared by whatever measure one chooses to apply—bills introduced, hearings, reports, hours in session, floor amendments, recorded floor votes, and measures passed. The processing of freestanding bills and resolutions became the centerpiece of committee and subcommittee work.

This legislative outpouring formed a gigantic "bulge in the middle," which David R. Mayhew noted in his study of lawmaking between 1946 and 1990.[26] Fifty-two percent of the 267 major enactments Mayhew identified over the fifty-four-year period were enacted between John F. Kennedy's inauguration in 1961 and the end of Gerald Ford's administration in 1976. Over this period seventy-four measures were produced under eight years of divided party control (Nixon, Ford) and sixty-six under eight years of unified control (Kennedy, Johnson). Johnson's presidency was arguably the most productive in history, legislatively speaking. Yet the most telling point is that the flow of legislation continued unabated during the Republican presidencies of Nixon and Ford. At least in the Kennedy-Johnson-Nixon-Ford years, party control made little difference in the congressional output of major enactments or investigations.

Nixon may have been a conservative president, but the legislative record compiled during his administration was expansive and progressive. This historical irony deserves more careful and dispassionate reassessment by historians and political scientists than it has yet received.[27] Stephen W. Stathis of the Congressional Research Service found fifty-five pieces of "landmark legislation" produced during Nixon's presidency.[28] Only one of these, the War Powers Resolution, was passed over Nixon's veto. The Tax Reform Act of 1969 removed an estimated 5.5 million low-income taxpayers from the tax rolls and reduced taxes for middle-income taxpayers while increasing Social Security benefits and raising taxes for higher-income citizens. Our fundamental environmental legislation dates from this period, including the National Environmental Policy Act (1969); the Water Quality Improvement Act (1970); the Clean Air Amendments (1970); and the Energy Policy and Conservation Act (1975). Such domestic policy protections as the Occupational Safety and Health Act (1970); the Food Stamp Act (1970); the Comprehensive Employment and Training Act (1973); and the Equal Opportunity Act (1972) were also enacted into law. Other achievements involved the space shuttle program, urban mass transit, AMTRAK, coastal-zone management, consumer protection, the eighteen-year-old vote, nuclear nonproliferation, and the very first federal campaign spending laws (later hindered by an unsympathetic Supreme Court).

The liberal juggernaut continued during conservative presidencies for at least two reasons. First, Democrats held solid majorities in both chambers of Congress: an average of fifty-six out of one hundred senators and 245 representatives (a majority is 218). Between 1973 and 1976, Ornstein and his colleagues explained, these forces "attempted a much higher number of veto overrides than any of the other congresses in the previous thirty years, and a large number of their attempts were successful."[29] Second, Nixon and Henry J. Kissinger—his foreign policy adviser and second-term secretary of state—viewed foreign affairs and diplomacy as their prime mission. Nixon's domestic Cabinet members and aides were thus left to negotiate as best they could with Capitol Hill majorities. And Nixon's Cabinet included a number of notable figures.

Vice President Gerald R. Ford, who assumed the presidency when Nixon resigned under threat of impeachment, owed his position to an earlier resignation: that of Vice President Spiro T. Agnew (1969–1973), who left his post under a storm of charges, including bribery and extortion. As the genial and moderate GOP House minority leader, Ford was respected on both sides of the aisle, and was more or less forced upon Nixon—and not only by Republicans. This contributed to the continued legislative productivity during Ford's two and a half years in office.

The decentralization of the 1960s and 1970s was accompanied by a weakening of the appropriations committees' grip over spending and by a strengthening of the power of the authorizing committees (for example, Agriculture, Banking, Commerce). By ingenious use of "backdoor spending" provisions—such as contract authority, budget authority, direct Treasury borrowing, and especially entitlements—the ascendant authorizing committees stripped the appropriations panels of much of their former fiscal guardianship role.[30] Three-quarters of the domestic spending growth between 1970 and 1983 occurred in budget accounts lying outside annual appropriations—that is, beyond the appropriations committees' reach.[31]

Like the earlier period, this reform era was well documented by journalists and scholars.[32] The most popular scholarly paradigm of the era, drawn from economics, focused on Congress's decentralization and fragmentation.[33] Lawmakers were viewed not as role players enmeshed in a complex system of interactions in equilibrium, but as individual entrepreneurs competing in a vast, open marketplace that rewarded self-interested competitiveness with little or no regard for the welfare of the whole institution.

THE POSTREFORM ERA (1979–1994)

The next legislative regime, the postreform era, spanned part or all of the presidencies of Jimmy Carter, Ronald Reagan, and George H. W. Bush. The advent of zero-sum, stalemate politics was popularly associated with President Ronald Reagan, who took office in 1981 pledging to cut taxes, domestic aid, and welfare programs. His election was interpreted at the time as a sea change in American politics; some of Reagan's initiatives—especially the 1981 revenue cuts and repeated threats to veto new domestic spending or taxes—helped to curtail the legislative agenda. However, deteriorating economic conditions and shifting attitudes had already caused President Carter to curtail his legislative agenda.[34] By the 96th Congress (1979–1981) the altered environment led to a decline in the legislative workload.

The advent of what economist Lester Thurow called the "zero-sum society" no doubt lay at the root of the changed political atmosphere.[35] Between World War II and the early 1970s, the nation's productivity levels soared, along with real incomes for average citizens. These engines enabled the nation to raise its standard of living while underwriting an expanding array of public services. But after 1973 both the nation's productivity and individual workers' real income stagnated, in comparison with both our economic rivals and our previous record. Indeed, the 1970s and 1980s were the century's poorest productivity decades.[36] The economy no longer seemed to support the federal government's vast array of services, many of them enacted or enlarged during the liberal activist period.

Lagging productivity affected not only government tax receipts but also citizens' attitudes toward their economic wellbeing. In the late 1970s the economy was buffeted by "stagflation," a combination of high inflation and high unemployment. Serious recessions occurred in the early 1980s and again in the early 1990s. Meanwhile, the government's costly and relatively impervious system of entitlements, coupled with President Reagan's 1981 tax cuts and program reallocations, turned the midcentury's "fiscal dividends" into "structural deficits."

Intellectual fashions and political realities repudiated the notion that government could solve all manner of economic and social ills. Disenchantment with the results of government programs, many of which had been shamelessly oversold to glean support for their enactment, led to widespread demands for a statutory cease-fire: disinvestment, deregulation, and privatization. At the same time, "bracket creep" raised the marginal and real tax rates of millions of citizens and spurred a series of tax revolts that swept through the states to the nation's capital.

In the 1980s the president and Congress were fixated on resolving fiscal and revenue issues, rather than designing new programs or establishing new agencies in response to constituent preferences or national needs. In the domestic realm, the emphasis was on reviewing, adjusting, refining, or cutting back existing programs. "There's not a whole lot of money for any kind of new programs," remarked Sen. Thad Cochran, R-MS, "so we're holding oversight hearings on old programs . . . which may not be all that bad an idea."[37] Accordingly, fewer individual members were tempted to put forward their ideas as freestanding bills or resolutions. Such new schemes as were salable were more likely to be contained in amendments to large-scale legislative vehicles: reauthorizations, continuing appropriations, and debt limit or reconciliation bills.

The constraints of the 1980s reversed the previous era's liberal activism. Government revenues were curtailed by lagging economic productivity, exaggerated after 1981 by tax cuts, program reallocations, and soaring deficits. Few new programs were launched, and few domestic programs were awarded additional funding. Although the public continued to expect Congress to take problem-solving actions, there was equal sentiment for cutting back "big government" and reducing public-sector deficits. Public faith in government's capacity to solve problems plummeted in the wake of criticisms of waste and ineffectiveness of government programs.

Elected officials at both ends of Pennsylvania Avenue sought profit from cutback politics. They engaged in creative bookkeeping to give the appearance of balancing revenues and outlays and trimming the deficit as required by a series of seemingly stringent budgetary process fixes, beginning in 1985. Conservatives seized upon revenue shortfalls as a way of snuffing demands for new programs and new spending. Liberals blamed the situation on the Reagan and Bush administration failures and pledged to protect federal programs favored by middle-class voters. As for the voters, they naturally wanted to have it both ways. As Gary C. Jacobson put it, "They can vote for Republican presidential candidates committed to the diffuse collective goods of low taxes, economic efficiency, and a strong national defense, and for congressional Democrats who promise to minimize the price they have to pay for these goods in forgone benefits."[38]

Cutback politics influenced the postreform Congress in at least six ways. First, fewer bills were sponsored by individual senators and representatives. Second, key policy decisions were packaged into huge "mega-bills," enabling lawmakers to gain support for provisions that would be unlikely to pass as freestanding measures. Third, lawmakers employed techniques of "blame avoidance"—for example, in closing military bases—to protect themselves from the adverse effects of cutbacks. Fourth, many more noncontroversial "commemorative" resolutions were passed—nearly half of all laws produced by congresses in the 1980s. Fifth, party-line voting on Capitol Hill, driven mainly by changes in the parties' demography, climbed toward modern-day highs. Finally, leadership in the House and Senate was markedly stronger than at any time since 1910. Congressional leaders benefited not only from powers conferred by reform-era innovations of the 1960s and 1970s; they also responded to widespread expectations that they were the only people who should, or could, untangle jurisdictional overlaps and orchestrate the legislative schedule.[39]

Confronted by a lagging economy, a divided government, and the public's doubts about the efficacy of government programs, the president and Congress in the postreform era changed the way they approached the legislative workload. Presidents trimmed their agendas and hampered congressional initiatives through a combination of curtailed revenue and veto threats. Interbranch negotiations frequently took the form of high-level summitry. Divided control of the White House and Congress, along with rising party voting on the Hill, placed a premium on tough bargaining between the president, Senate leaders, and House leaders. Congress, for its part, moved away from the decentralized system established during the 1960s and 1970s to facilitate that era's frantic legislative activity. A knowledgeable British scholar put it this way: "There can be little doubt that the Congress of the mid-1980s differed from that of the late 1970s in terms of its emphasis on parliamentary reform, legislative activity, constituency attentiveness and distribution of power." In sum, "the reform orientation of the New [or reform-era] Congress [was] left far behind."[40]

CONSERVATIVE PARTY GOVERNMENT (1995–2006)

The early 1990s brought a new mix of challenges to governmental institutions; some of them continuing long-term trends but others startlingly new. Prolonged economic uncertainty—manifested in sluggish growth, heightened foreign competition, and widely reported job layoffs—weakened citizens' self-confidence and optimism. Widening racial, ethnic, religious, and even sexual fissures, along with a seemingly permanent disadvantaged underclass, fueled growing suspicions that the nation had become uncontrollable and perhaps ungovernable. The public services that most people came in contact with—public schools, police, courts, welfare offices—seemed especially flawed. The end of the Cold War brought only fleeting satisfaction: losing the menace of the Soviet "evil empire" in fact also meant losing a certain sense of national purpose.

Public unrest deepened into what can only be called a crisis of governance. One member of Congress called it a massive "civic temper tantrum."[41] Few institutions escaped public censure. Scarcely more than a year after celebrating the Persian Gulf War in a burst of civic pride, citizens turned President George H. W. Bush out of office in 1992. With an election plurality of only 43 percent, successor Bill Clinton's public-opinion "honeymoon" hardly survived the wedding night; his job ratings remained precarious. Although surveys uncovered public disgust with partisanship and "gridlock," the Democrats' victories that year ended divided government only in a formal sense; two years later, the Republicans captured the House and Senate, dissolving even that deceptive unity.

President Clinton's first two years, with a Democratic Congress, brought mixed results. Having campaigned as a "new" centrist Democrat, Clinton tried to separate himself from the growing liberal ranks of his Capitol Hill party—a strategy known as "triangulation."[42] His greatest achievement, however, attracted not a single Republican vote, and was enacted only when Vice President Al Gore cast the tie-breaking vote in the Senate. This was the Omnibus Budget Reconciliation Act of 1993, which raised taxes on upper-income citizens and—affixed to the booming economy of the later 1990s—wiped out the federal government's deficits by the 1998 fiscal year. On other matters, the centrist strategy dictated cross-party alliances with Republicans. Their support ensured passage of 1993 legislation implementing the North American Free Trade Agreement (NAFTA); only 40 percent of House Democrats voted for it. Other cross-partisan efforts brought forth the Brady Handgun Violence Act, the Family and Medical Leave Act, the Motor Voter Act, a national service law (called Americorps), a crime law, and the odious Defense of Marriage Act (DOMA). But the Clinton administration is remembered as a time of failed initiatives: for example, the collapsed health-care reform plan and the clumsy "Don't Ask, Don't Tell" policy for gays serving in the military.

In the early Clinton years, however, Congress bore the largest measure of public scorn. A series of Capitol Hill scandals targeted five senators who had championed a failed savings-and-loan magnate, forced closure of the House "bank" (payroll office), and cast doubt on the personal ethics of numerous members. By the spring of 1992, only 17 percent of those questioned in a national survey approved of the way Congress was doing its job, whereas 54 percent approved of their own representative's performance. Both figures were all-time lows.[43] Such anger exceeded the usual level of Congress bashing and recalled the public unrest that preceded the reforms adopted in the early 1970s.

Civic unrest dramatically changed the guard on Capitol Hill. The 1992 elections brought 110 new House members (eighty-seven of whom returned two years later) and fourteen new senators. The 1994 contests added eighty-six new representatives and eleven new senators. When the House convened in January 1995, nearly a majority of its members had arrived in the 1990s. Although the Senate changed more slowly, twenty-nine of its members were 1990s arrivals.

Most importantly, the 1994 elections brought Republican control to both chambers—for the first time in forty years in the House, and following an eight-year hiatus in the Senate. The party balance of nearly two generations was overturned. The public policy agenda was transformed. Long-simmering issues suddenly boiled over: downsizing the federal establishment, devolution of power to states and localities, welfare reform, budget stringency, and a regulatory ceasefire. Facing Clinton's struggling presidency, the resurgent

Republicans seized command of policy initiatives, media attention, and public expectations.

As GOP leaders flexed their muscles, activity levels initially soared; innovative procedures were explored, tested, and adopted. House Speaker Newt Gingrich, R-GA, backed by a cohesive party dominated by newcomers (many of them Gingrich recruits), pushed wide-ranging changes in structures and procedures. Cuts were made in the number of committees, committee assignments, and committee staffs; committee and floor procedures were altered; administrative arrangements were streamlined; and most of all, the Speaker and other party leaders gained greater leverage over committee assignments, committee scheduling, floor scheduling, and administrative management. House leaders used all these tools to win committee approval and floor votes for all ten items of their campaign platform, the "Contract with America," within the first hundred days of the 104th Congress (1995). But political stalemate, manifested by the White House and a more contentious Senate, kept most of these proposals out of the statute books—with the exception of congressional accountability (1995) and welfare reform (1996).

Clinton's second term was clouded by persistent partisan competition and the absence of secure Republican majorities. Indeed, the House GOP lost ground in all three elections following their 1994 triumph. Leadership miscalculations can be blamed for much of the erosion. The GOP was blamed for shutting down the federal government in winter 1995–1996, in the midst of fierce battles between budget-cutters on the Hill and a veto-wielding president. Even more dramatic was the 1998–1999 impeachment of President Clinton—a project launched by House Judiciary Committee Republicans and supported by party leaders. The whole affair played poorly with the public: while they deplored the president's sexual misbehavior—the ostensible cause of the proceedings—they nonetheless approved his second-term job performance.[44] Midterm election media ads highlighting the impeachment served only to remind voters that it was GOP leaders who were targeting the president. After the midterm elections, the Senate failed to muster the two-thirds majority needed to convict the president or remove him from office.

The Clinton-era partisan warfare went far beyond clashes over the president's personal life or even federal spending levels. They reflected a bitter struggle between the White House and Capitol Hill Republicans over control of the policy agenda. Most key votes were along party lines: the various impeachment floor votes in both chambers found more than nine out of ten representatives and senators voting with their respective parties—Republicans opposing the president, Democrats supporting him.[45]

Speaker Newt Gingrich, who had engineered the GOP takeover of the House in 1994, faced mounting opposition—including an abortive internal effort to oust him, the 1998 midterm election fiasco, and, finally, reports of his own sexual dalliance. He and his heir apparent, Robert Livingston, both stepped aside in late 1998. The agreed-upon successor, J. Dennis Hastert of Illinois, inherited a fractured and disheartened GOP conference. Eventually he gained mastery of the House, by ceding more powers to the committee chairmen and by consulting widely before reaching final decisions. Yet the GOP leaders' partisanship could be firm: minority Democrats were often excluded from committee markups of bills and leadership decisions on the bills' final contents.

If the Republicans reigned but did not yet rule in the 1995–2001 years, the terrorists' attacks of September 11, 2001, transformed the political environment. First, they shifted George W. Bush's presidency to a wartime enterprise—a metaphor certain to enhance presidential leadership.[46] For another, they immediately transformed Congress into a more reactive, compliant institution. Initially, it hastily approved the use of force against 9/11 perpetrators, and passed the problematic USA Patriot Act (both in 2001), a resolution authorizing use of force against Iraq (2002), and the Military Commissions Act for prosecuting wartime prisoners (2006).

The congressional workload rebounded somewhat during the Republican years—in terms of bills and resolutions introduced, bills per member, and even enactments of public laws. The average page length of public laws continued to rise, reflecting the continuing popularity of large-scale omnibus measures. Although committee meetings tended to subside, hours of floor sessions continued to rise.[47]

DIVIDED GOVERNMENT (2007–)

A final and still-evolving divided-control regime embraces George W. Bush's second administration and at least Barack Obama's first one. Its characteristics are a product of the most coherent, militant, and combatant parties seen since a century ago—very liberal Democrats pitted against very conservative Republicans. Only a very few of the past eras' moderates have survived this hyperpartisanship.[48] Other observers hold that congressional partisanship is rooted in the partisanship of voters—especially in primary and midterm elections, which tend to attract the most active citizens.[49]

The most visible characteristic of recent Congresses is "gridlock," and the end product is often minimal productivity. This avoidance affects not only high-profile policies, but extends even to such traditionally popular legislation as infrastructure (roads and bridges) and agriculture bills, full of "something-for-everyone" benefits. Another characteristic might be described as "kicking the can down the street": that is, passing temporary measures on such essential matters as taxes, appropriations, debt ceilings, and the like. US citizens are fully aware of Congress's failures. Just 9 percent of those surveyed by Indiana University's Center on Congress in November 2012 approved of Congress's current job performance.[50] Respondents gave an overall "D" rating to Congress for its handling of key issues facing the country and keeping excessive partisanship in check.

Post 9/11 developments, including the 2004 elections, appeared to strengthen the Republicans as the dominant party. President George W. Bush's reelection, although no landslide, was achieved through his image as a wartime leader who would protect the nation from terrorists. But his job rating stood at only 51 percent; by the end of 2004, a clear majority of citizens (56 percent) believed that the Iraq war's costs outweighed its benefits. During his second term, his job ratings slid steady downward, as the wars in Iraq and then Afghanistan dragged on and the administration's response to the devastation of Hurricane Katrina—then the costliest national disaster in the nation's history—was judged as inept and unfeeling. On the eve of the 2008 election, surveys pegged Bush's approval level at 25 percent—"the worst of his presidency to date, and just three percentage points higher than Harry Truman's all-time low 22 percent approval rating in 1951."[51]

Public worries about the state of the nation, coupled with disdain for the Bush administration, led to a measurable shift in partisan loyalties favoring the Democrats. When Bush was reelected in 2005, Democratic partisans claimed only a 2 percent margin over the GOP (35 to 33 percent). By October 2008, however, that margin had climbed to 12 percent. Nearly four in ten voters identified with the Democrats, according to the Pew Research Center's surveys. (Independents accounted for 34 percent of the electorate, leaving Republicans in third place with 28 percent.[52]) The Pew Center's surveys of Americans' political values and core attitudes also revealed a landscape more favorable to the Democrats. The reason was "increased public support for the social safety net, signs of rising public concern about income inequality, and a diminished appetite for assertive national security policies."[53]

The 2008 elections extended the Democrats' gains of two years earlier. The top story was the triumph of Barack Obama, their presidential nominee. But the party also gained ground in both chambers of Congress. House Democrats gained twenty-four seats, for a total of 257 (to the Republicans' 178)—approaching the 259 seats the party held in 1994, before the GOP took over control. In the Senate, at least seven additional Democrats were elected, for a total of fifty-eight.[54] Four GOP senators were turned out of office; more than a dozen GOP House members were defeated.

Obama ran on a platform of change—including postpartisan cooperation—but he was elected because of an economic crisis blamed on the Bush administration (and, by association, his party in Congress). His election as an African American was a triumph; but the irony was that he inherited an economic quagmire. (*The Onion*, a humor blog, headlined his election as follows: "Black Man Elected to Nation's Worst Job!") Although he initially reached out to the minority Republicans, his early goal—a gigantic stimulus spending package—was supported by only three GOP senators and none of their representatives. The challenge for liberals in the White House and Capitol Hill was twofold: to prevail against the minority Republicans—whose cohesiveness had surged with the virtual disappearance of their moderate lawmakers—while at the same time mobilizing the Democrats' more diverse members (including centrists who had defeated GOP moderates on their own turf).

No one could predict whether or not the unprecedented spending would jumpstart the economy and produce the needed jobs and capital. The Democratic regime's future, for better or worse, rested upon the perceived success or failure of these unprecedented economic measures. House GOP Whip Eric Cantor of Virginia remarked that the Democrats "assume[d] ownership of the era of the bailout." He contended that the 2010 elections would be "a test for the mandate of change that this administration was elected with. I do think there will be a price to pay."[55]

That price was exacted in the 2010 elections, which Obama himself described as "a pasting." It was an unusually dramatic case of midterm election dynamics, serving as a kind of true-false test about the weak economy and Obama's first two years. Republicans won control of the House and near-control of the Senate. The GOP's 242 House members were the party's largest caucus since the 80th Congress (1947–1949). The hapless Democrats lost sixty-six House seats and six senators (The average midterm loss for presidential parties is 27.8 representatives and 3.6 senators.) "It is an exaggeration, but perhaps a revealing one," analyst Michael Barone observed, "to say that the Republicans swept everything from the George Washington Bridge to the Donner Pass."[56]

President Obama was reelected comfortably in 2012 and Democrats posted gains in both chambers, although falling short of a House majority. It was little comfort that Democratic House candidates nationally outpolled Republicans by some 1.4 million votes—the GOP advantage having been gained mainly through the dark art of gerrymandered districts in states they controlled.[57] Barring unforeseen electoral shifts, his presidential destiny will be chained to divided, hyperpartisan, and even dysfunctional lawmaking bodies. As former Rep. Lee H. Hamilton put it, "So we're left with two parties passing one another in the night, unable to come to terms and unwilling to risk alienating their core constituencies to do so."[58]

PARTY CONTROL AND LEGISLATIVE REGIMES

Party control influences legislative outputs. Many observers further contend that "things go better" when the same party controls both the executive and legislative branches and that divided government is a prescription for confusion, delay, and deadlock. Legislative productivity is, without a doubt, affected by party control. And certainly presidents are more apt to achieve their legislative goals if their partisans comfortably control both chambers.

Equally to the point, shifts in Capitol Hill partisan ratios can yield meaningful changes in policy outputs, quite apart from any questions of party control or alignment. The recession-driven Democrats in 1959–1961, the Johnson landslide class of 1964, the Watergate class of 1974, and the pro-GOP electoral shifts in 1980, 1994, and 2010 were dramatic changes in partisan strength on Capitol Hill that led in turn to policy redirections and procedural innovations. These changes probably far exceeded any underlying shifts in attitudes or voting habits within the electorate as a whole, not to mention long-term partisan realignments.

Yet party control is an incomplete guide to legislative activity and productivity. The administrations of Roosevelt, Truman, Carter, and even George W. Bush testify to the fact that party control of both branches is no guarantee of legislative productivity. By the same token, the Nixon-Ford and Reagan periods saw productivity far beyond what would be expected from divided government. The correlation between party control and legislative productivity seems even more tenuous when we consider Mayhew's intriguing piece of evidence: during what we term the liberal activist era, annual productivity under split party control actually exceeded that under unified control.[59] Legislative productivity and workload, in short, fit imperfectly with traditional political thinking that stresses presidential leadership or the locus of party control of the two branches.

CONCLUSION

Shifting the viewpoint from the Oval Office to Capitol Hill radically changes one's perspective on congressional-executive relations. Rather than measuring political time in terms of successive presidencies, we have sought to identify congressional equivalents. By tracking one cluster of variables— legislative workload and productivity figures—we have identified five distinctive congressional eras or regimes. Examining legislative attributes within each era, and between succeeding eras, casts new light on inter-branch policy making since the New Deal and even helps resolve some puzzling historical anomalies—for example, Franklin Roosevelt's mixed legislative record and the unexpected productivity of the Nixon-Ford period.

Our foray into the thicket of legislative activity and productivity reveals two general truths about modern-day politics and policy making. First, legislative productivity does not necessarily coincide with the tenure of individual presidents. Second, legislative productivity is less determined by party control than one would predict.

Recent events show that Congress's evolution has by no means run its full course, and that such change is influenced but not determined by the White House. Continuing changes in Congress's political environment will produce further alterations in the membership, organization, procedures, and policy-making capacities of the House and Senate. As in the past, these alterations will require leadership, ingenuity, bargaining, and legislative professionalism if Congress is to make its way successfully through the twenty-first century. Will Congress be able to fulfill its constitutional duties and reassert its constitutional prerogatives in a time of militant parties and divided government? Viewing the current state of Congress, the outlook is grim. Yet only future events can shape history's judgment.

NOTES

1. First Lady Laura Bush attended the 2008 convention to recall her husband's achievements and introduce a video, in which the president described the record of Senator John McCain, the GOP's presidential nominee.

2. Woodrow Wilson, *Congressional Government* (1885; reprint, Baltimore, MD: Johns Hopkins University Press, 1981), 56. See also Charles O. Jones, "A Way of Life and Law," *American Political Science Review* 89 (March 1995): 1–9.

3. Robert A. Katzmann, *Courts and Congress* (Washington, DC: Brookings Institution Press/Governance Institute, 1997), 33–34.

4. See Michael G. Kammen, *A Machine that Would Go of Itself: The Constitution in American Culture* (New York: Alfred A. Knopf, 1986).

5. For an account of the post-9/11 changes, see James P. Pfiffner, "The Transformation of the Bush Presidency," in Pfiffner and Roger H. Davidson, eds., *Understanding the Presidency*, 4th ed. (New York: Pearson Longman, 2006), 474–94.

6. The *locus classicus* of party alignment theory is V. O. Key, Jr., "A Theory of Critical Elections," *Journal of Politics* 17 (February 1955): 3–18. More detailed analyses are found in William N. Chambers and Walter Dean Burnham, eds., *The American Party Systems: Stages of Political Development* (New York: Oxford University Press, 1967); Walter Dean Burnham, *Critical Elections and the Mainsprings of American Politics* (New York: Norton, 1970); James L. Sundquist, *Dynamics of the Party System*, rev. ed. (Washington, DC: Brookings Institution Press, 1983), esp. chaps. 1–3; and David R. Mayhew, *Electoral Realignments* (New Haven, CT: Yale University Press, 2002).

7. See, for example, David W. Brady, "Electoral Realignment in the U.S. House of Representatives," in Gerald C. Wright, Jr., Leroy N. Rieselbach, and Lawrence C. Dodd, eds., *Congress and Policy Change* (New York: Agathon Press, 1986), 46–69.

8. Joseph Cooper, "Organization and Innovation in the House of Representatives," in Joseph Cooper and G. Calvin Mackenzie, eds., *The House at Work* (Austin: University of Texas Press, 1980), 332. This essay draws upon statistical data originally compiled by the author, his former colleagues at the Congressional Research Service, and other investigators. The most relevant data are summarized in Norman J. Ornstein, Thomas E. Mann, and Michael J. Malbin, *Vital Statistics on Congress 2001–2002* (Washington, DC: AEI Press, 2002), 145–54.

9. Ornstein, Mann, and Malbin, *Vital Statistics on Congress 2001–2002*, 146–47.

10. Donald Wolfensberger, *Getting Back to Legislating: Reflections of a Congressional Working Group*, Wilson Center, November 27, 2012, appendix B, table 1, p. 19.

11. Jennifer Steinhauer, "Congress Nearing End of Session Where Partisan Input Impeded Output," *New York Times*, September 18, 2012.

12. Rosalind Helderman, "Outgoing Congress Proves to Be Unproductive to the End," *Washington Post*, December 29, 2012.

13. Kenneth A. Shepsle, "The Changing Textbook Congress," in John E. Chubb and Paul E. Peterson, eds., *Can the Government Govern?* (Washington, DC: Brookings Institution Press, 1989), 238–66.

14. See Roger H. Davidson, ed., *The Postreform Congress* (New York: St. Martin's Press, 1992).

15. The seminal work concerning this conceptualization is John H. Aldrich, *Why Parties? The Origin and Transformation of Party Politics in America* (Chicago: University of Chicago Press, 1995).

16. Lawrence H. Chamberlain, *The President, Congress and Legislation* (New York: Columbia University Press, 1946), 450–53.

17. James MacGregor Burns, *Roosevelt: The Lion and the Fox* (New York: Harcourt Brace, 1956), 337, 339.

18. Robert J. Donovan, *Conflict and Crisis: The Presidency of Harry S Truman* (New York: Norton, 1977), 260.

19. Alonzo L. Hamby, "The Mind and Character of Harry S Truman" in Michael J. Lacey, ed., *The Truman Presidency* (Cambridge: Woodrow Wilson International Center for Scholars and Cambridge University Press, 1989), 46.

20. Fenno, *Congressmen in Committees*, 279.

21. William S. White, *Citadel: The Story of the U.S. Senate* (New York: Harper and Brothers, 1956); and Donald R. Matthews, *U.S. Senators and Their World* (Chapel Hill: University of North Carolina Press, 1960).

22. Fenno, *Congressmen in Committees*; Richard F. Fenno, Jr., *The Power of the Purse: The Appropriations Process in Congress* (Boston: Little, Brown, 1966).

23. Shepsle, "Changing Textbook Congress."

24. Hedrick Smith, *The Power Game: How Washington Works* (New York: Random House, 1988), chap. 2.

25. James L. Sundquist, *Politics and Policy: The Eisenhower, Kennedy, and Johnson Years* (Washington, DC: Brookings Institution Press, 1968), chap. 10.

26. David R. Mayhew, *Divided We Govern: Party Control, Lawmaking, and Investigations, 1946–1990* (New Haven, CT: Yale University Press, 1991), 76.

27. See, however, John C. Whitaker, "Nixon's Domestic Policy: Both Liberal and Bold in Retrospect," *Presidential Studies Quarterly* 26 (Winter 1996): 131ff.

28. Stephen W. Stathis, *Landmark Legislation 1774–2002* (Washington, DC: CQ Press, 2003), 275–300.

29. Norman J. Ornstein, Thomas E. Mann, and Michael J. Malbin, *Vital Statistics on Congress 1993–1994* (Washington, DC: CQ Press, 1994), 151.

30. Allen Schick, *Congress and Money: Budgeting, Spending and Taxing* (Washington, DC: The Urban Institute Press, 1980), 424–36.

31. John W. Ellwood, "The Great Exception: The Congressional Budget Process in an Age of Decentralization," in Lawrence C. Dodd and Bruce J. Oppenheimer, eds., *Congress Reconsidered*, 3rd ed. (Washington, DC: CQ Press, 1985), 315–42.

32. See, for example, Roger H. Davidson and Walter J. Oleszek, *Congress against Itself* (Bloomington: Indiana University Press, 1977); James L. Sundquist, *The Decline and Resurgence of Congress* (Washington, DC: Brookings Institution Press, 1981); and Leroy N. Rieselbach, *Congressional Reform: The Changing Modern Congress* (Washington, DC: CQ Press, 1994), esp. chap. 3.

33. David R. Mayhew, *Congress: The Electoral Connection* (New Haven, CT: Yale University Press, 1974).

34. Charles O. Jones, *The Trusteeship Presidency: Jimmy Carter and the U.S. Congress* (Baton Rouge: Louisiana State University Press, 1988), chap. 7.

35. Lester Thurow, *The Zero-Sum Society* (New York: Basic Books, 1980).

36. Paul Krugman, "We're No. 3—So What?" *Washington Post*, March 24, 1990.

37. Quoted in Helen Dewar, "Congress Off to Slowest Start in Years," *Washington Post*, November 21, 1989.

38. Gary C. Jacobson, *The Electoral Origins of Divided Government: Competition in U.S. House Elections*, 1946–1988 (Boulder, CO: Westview Press, 1990), 112.

39. Barbara Sinclair, *Legislators, Leaders, and Lawmaking: The U.S. House of Representatives in the Postreform Era* (Baltimore: Johns Hopkins University Press, 1995), 48–57.

40. Christopher J. Bailey, "Beyond the New Congress: Aspects of Congressional Development in the 1980s," *Parliamentary Affairs* 41 (April 1988): 246.

41. Quoted in Lawrence N. Hansen, "Our Turn: Politicians Talk about Themselves, Politics, the Public, the Press, and Reform," Centel Public Accountability Project (March 1992): 5.

42. The term was invented by Dick Morris, at the time one of Clinton's chief advisers. See Paul J. Quirk and William Cunion, "Clinton's Domestic Policy: The Lessons of a 'New Democrat,'" in Colin Campbell and Bert A. Rockman, eds., *The Clinton Legacy* (New York: Chatham House, 2000), 200–225.

43. Richard Morin and Helen Dewar, "Approval of Congress Hits All-Time Low, Poll Finds," *Washington Post*, March 20, 1992.

44. An analysis from the Capitol Hill perspective is: Nicol C. Rae and Colton C. Campbell, *Impeaching Clinton: Partisan Strife on Capitol Hill* (Lawrence: University Press of Kansas, 2004).

45. Roger H. Davidson, "Congressional Parties, Leaders, and Committees: 1900, 2000, and Beyond," in Jeffrey E. Cohen, Richard Fleisher, and Paul Kantor, eds., *American Political Parties: Decline or Resurgence?* (Washington, DC: CQ Press, 2001), 284–85.

46. See Kathleen Hall Jamieson and Paul Waldman, *The Press Effect: Politicians, Journalists, and the Stories that Shape the Political World* (New York: Oxford University Press, 2003), 150–52.

47. Norman J. Ornstein, Thomas E. Mann, and Michael J. Malbin, *Vital Statistics on Congress, 1999–2000* (Washington, DC: AEI Press, 2000), 146–50.

48. John Aloysius Farrell, "The Eroding Center," *National Journal* 44 (September 29, 2012), 31–33.

49. David Wasserman, "Parallel Universes," *National Journal* 44 (December 15, 2012), 17–20.

50. Emma Dumain, "Survey Sees the Nadir of Congress' Approval Rating," *Roll Call*, December 20, 2012, 6.

51. The Gallup Poll, "Bush Approval Rating Doldrums Continue," Gallup.com, October 30, 2008.

52. Pew Research Center, "Democrats Hold Party ID Edge across Political Battleground," October 30, 2008, pewresearch.org/pubs/1015.

53. Pew Research Center for the People and the Press, *Trends in Political Values and Core Attitudes, 1987–2007*, people-press.org/report/?reportid=312.

54. One race remained undecided: in Minnesota, the Senate candidates—Democrat Al Franken and Republican incumbent Norm Coleman—fought to a virtual tie. After a hand recount, Franken appeared to have won by 225 votes, but the final outcome was determined by the Minnesota Supreme Court, which upheld Franken's victory.

55. Quoted by Michael D. Shear and Paul Kane, "Politically, Stimulus Battle Has Just Begun," *Washington Post*, February 16, 2009.

56. Michael Barone and Chuck McCutcheon, *The Almanac of American Politics 2012* (Chicago: University of Chicago Press/National Journal, 2011), 2.

57. Dana Milbank, "In the House, a Deck Stacked for Republicans," *Washington Post*, January 4, 2013.

58. Lee H. Hamilton, "What the Fiscal Cliff Deal Tells Us about Congress," *Comments on Congress* (Bloomington: Center on Congress at Indiana University, January 9, 2013), 2.

59. Mayhew, *Divided We Govern*, 7.

Chapter Six

The President and the Congressional Party Leadership in a Hyperpartisan Era[1]

Barbara Sinclair

Of the promises Barack Obama made during his 2008 presidential campaign, changing the harsh, high-decibel partisan climate is the one on which he unquestionably had the least the success. Not only was Obama unable to reverse the intense partisanship and high polarization that had developed over the previous several decades, they continued to get worse. What impact did these trends have on his relationship with the congressional leadership and on his legislative success during his first term and how are they likely to affect his second?

A president is judged successful in considerable part by whether his agenda is enacted into law and that makes him dependent on Congress. In the highly polarized political world of the early twenty-first century, that means the president is dependent on the majority party leaderships in the House and Senate. The president plays no role in choosing congressional party leaders, even those of his own party, and yet whether they promote or oppose his agenda is a key determinant of his likely legislative success. The dependence, however, is mutual; the party leaders also want things from the president. The character of the relationship depends on a number of factors, preeminently on whether the president and the congressional majority leaderships are of the same or opposing parties. Yet, even if they are of the same party, differences in their perspectives and goals can make for an uneasy partnership.

This chapter examines how the relationship looks from 1600 Pennsylvania Avenue and how it looks from Capitol Hill; it then investigates the relationship under both unified and divided control during Obama's first term in order to demonstrate the effects of control when partisanship is high and to highlight the varied other determinants of cooperation and conflict. In the final section, I consider what this portends for the relationship between President Obama and the congressional leadership during his second term.

THE VIEW FROM 1600 PENNSYLVANIA AVENUE

Whether the president's immediate goal is enhancing his chances of reelection, burnishing his legacy, or bringing about policy change he believes in, passing his program is a critical means toward accomplishing any of those ends. Consequently congressional action is essential to presidential success. So what does a contemporary president see when he looks down Pennsylvania Avenue to Capitol Hill? Like his predecessors, he sees two legislative bodies with different memberships and rules, both of which need to pass a bill for it to become law. Unlike many of his predecessors, he sees congressional parties that are highly polarized along ideological, that is, policy preference, lines, with most congressional Republicans being strongly conservative and most Democrats, liberal or moderate. [2] Furthermore, this polarization is not simply a Washington phenomenon; rather, constituency sentiment at both the activist and voter level underlies congressional partisan polarization, especially in the House with its smaller and more homogeneous districts.

In the House of Representatives, greater ideological homogeneity made possible the development of a stronger and more activist party leadership. [3] The House is a majority-rule institution; decisions are made by simple majorities and opportunities for minorities to delay, much less block, action are exceedingly limited. The Speaker is both the presiding officer of the chamber and the leader of the majority party. When the majority party is homogeneous, its members have the incentive to grant the Speaker significant powers and resources and to allow him or her to use them aggressively, because the legislation the Speaker will use them to pass is broadly supported in the party. By the mid-1980s, majority-party members had granted their party leadership such new authority and the leadership did, in fact, employ it assertively to pass legislation the members wanted. With the Republican takeover of the House in the 1994 elections, the trend only accelerated.

The majority-party leadership oversees the referral of bills to committee, determines the floor schedule, and controls the drafting of special rules that govern how bills are considered on the floor. The leaders can bypass committees when they consider it necessary or orchestrate postcommittee adjustments to legislation. The leadership can serve as an extremely valuable ally for the president. The leaders can work with (and, if necessary, lean on) the committees to report out the president's program in a form acceptable to him and in a timely fashion; deploy the extensive whip system to rally the votes needed to pass the legislation; and bring the bills to the floor at the most favorable time and under floor procedures that give them the best possible chance for success.[4]

Senate rules are a great deal more permissive that House rules and give individual members much greater prerogatives; consequently the Senate majority leader lacks many of the institutional tools the Speaker possesses. Still, the majority leader does command the initiative in floor scheduling and is the elected leader of the majority party in the chamber. Over the course of the 1980s and 1990s as their memberships became more internally like-minded, the Senate parties, like their House counterparts, organized themselves for joint action.[5] Thus the Senate majority leadership too is potentially a useful ally for the president. The Senate minority leader is, however, potentially a much tougher opponent than his House counterpart.

The president, then, sees majority-party leaderships that can be valuable allies but, by the same token, may alternatively be formidable opponents. Given the high partisan polarization that underlies leadership strength, he can expect a majority-party leadership of his own party to be a great deal more inclined to cooperate with him than one of the other party. If the opposition party controls one or both houses, he knows he and his program have a much rockier road ahead; he may be able to use his own substantial resources to induce Congress to act in the manner he prefers, but he very likely will need to do so through the majority-party leadership, especially in the House.

THE VIEW FROM CAPITOL HILL

Congressional party leaders are elected by their fellow party members in the chamber and need to meet their members' expectations to keep their positions. Members have both electoral and policy goals and expect their leaders to promote those goals by enacting legislation and by engaging in other activities that serve to maintain the party's majority in the chamber and further individual members' reelection. From the leadership's perspective, the question is: does passing the president's program promote those goals?

In a time of high partisan polarization, when the president is of the same party, the answer is usually "yes." Members of Congress are likely to have similar policy goals to those of a president of their party—not infrequently his program includes policy proposals that originated with them; furthermore, members are aware that the president's success or failure will shape the party's reputation and so affect their own electoral fates. To be sure, there will always be differences about particulars and sometimes also about priorities. Different constituencies assure that.

Nevertheless, when control is unified, the House leadership will usually see it in its own interest to act on the president's behalf and employ the formidable resources discussed above to enact much of the president's program. The incentives are similar for the Senate majority leader but the resources at his command are less. Precedent and tradition give the majority leader the task of scheduling legislation for the floor but because sixty votes are required to cut off debate—even on a motion to consider a bill—a unified minority party of forty-one or greater can act as a major barrier to passing legislation in a form the majority party—and often the president—prefers. Since the 1990s, with the increase in partisan polarization, Senate minorities have routinely used filibuster strategies to extract concessions and to kill legislation.

When the congressional majority in a chamber faces a president of the other party, the members' policy and electoral goals are much less likely to impel the leadership toward cooperation with the president. With the parties so polarized along ideological lines, members of a congressional majority party are likely to strongly oppose on policy grounds many of the legislative initiatives of a president of the opposition party. Furthermore they are likely to see his success as a threat to their electoral goals. The party leadership, thus, may consider blocking the president's agenda as the best way of furthering their members' goals.

Still, even under divided control, political circumstance may give party leaders incentives to work with the president. If a newly elected president is perceived to have received a mandate for his agenda, blocking its enactment may be seen as politically perilous, especially for electorally marginal members of the majority. Similarly, a congressional leader has to think hard and long before strongly opposing a broadly popular presidential proposal; among other considerations is whether, even in this period of high partisan polarization, the leader can keep his or her members in line. A crisis can confront both the president and members of Congress with the necessity of responding or appearing incompetent and indifferent; and swift legislative action demands cooperation. Just doing the minimum necessary to keep the government functioning by enacting appropriations (i.e., money) legislation requires that the leadership and the president deal with each other. Yet, even if a congressional leader sees advantages to cooperating with a president, he can do so only to the extent his members are willing to allow.

Political circumstance may sometimes make it difficult or even impossible for party leaders to cooperate with a president of their own party. If supporting the president fundamentally conflicts with furthering member goals, congressional leaders are likely to put their members first, to "dance with the one that brung them."

Congressional party leaders expect a president of their own party to avoid putting them in such a predicament. They expect access and information, to be consulted and to be informed about presidential decisions that affect them and their members. They expect his administration to be flexible about the details of policy proposals when those are important to their members. They expect the president to use his resources to help them pass his program and they want him to employ the bully pulpit effectively so as to make passing his initiatives easier. A president who treats the congressional leaders with respect and never blindsides them maximizes the cooperation that political circumstances allow. Indeed showing respect and scrupulously keeping his promises can lubricate the president's relations with the leaders of the opposition party as well.

In sum, we expect unified versus divided control to be the single most important determinant of cooperation versus conflict between the congressional majority-party leadership and the president, but not the sole determinant.

COOPERATION OR CONFLICT?

In the following sections, I examine the relationship between the president and the congressional leadership under conditions of unified and divided control in recent years to highlight the effect of control and to identify other factors that affect that relationship.[6] President Obama enjoyed unified control with sizeable margins in both chambers during his first two years; in the 2010 elections, Democrats lost control of the House of Representatives and their margin of control in the Senate shrank severely. So contrasting the two congresses—the 111th (2009–2010) and the 112th (2011–2012)—is illustrative.

Unified Control: Obama and the Democratic 111th Congress

The political context at the beginning of Obama's presidency was distinctly favorable to a cooperative relationship between the president and the congressional majority party leadership and to legislative success. Running on an ambitious policy agenda, Obama won the 2008 election with 53 percent of the vote, the first nonincumbent president elected with a majority of the popular vote since 1988. House Democrats began the 111th Congress with a 257 to 178 margin. Senate Democrats, who had struggled through the 110th with a 51 to 49 majority, boosted their numbers to fifty-eight with one seat undecided. Obama and congressional Democrats ran on quite similar issues, as one would expect when the political parties are relatively ideologically homogeneous; thus they began with considerable agreement on a policy agenda broadly defined. The economic crisis fueled a sense of urgency in the public and among policy makers alike, further focusing the attention of the new president and his congressional partisans on the same agenda.

For the leaders of the 111th Congress the incentives to make passing Obama's agenda a central objective were especially great. Public expectations were high and the congressional party as well as Obama would be judged by the extent to which they were met. Furthermore, Democrats had been in the minority in both chambers for most of the 1995–2006 period and, during that time, their policy preferences had been largely rebuffed; pent-up demand for policy change among Democrats was immense.

The House Democratic leadership in the 111th consisted of Speaker Nancy Pelosi (CA), Majority Leader Steny Hoyer (MD), Majority Whip James Clyburn (SC), and a number of other members holding lesser offices. The three top members of the Senate Democratic leadership were Majority Leader Harry Reid (NV), Whip Dick Durbin (IL), and Charles Schumer (NY), vice chair of the Democratic Conference. All were experienced and astute legislators and Pelosi especially was a strongly policy-oriented leader for whom passing major policy change was a priority.

For key White House positions Obama chose savvy operators with extensive congressional experience. Chief of Staff Rahm Emanuel was a former House member who had served as chair of the Democratic Congressional Campaign Committee and chair of the Democratic Caucus; Office of Management and Budget Director Peter Orszag had served as director of the Congressional Budget Office. Head of congressional liaison Phil Schiliro was formerly chief of staff for senior House Democrat Henry Waxman, chairman of the Energy and Commerce Committee; and Senior Adviser Pete Rouse was a thirty-year veteran of the Hill who had served as chief of staff to Senate Majority Leader Tom Daschle as well as to Senator Barack Obama.

Obama and his team started consulting with the Democratic congressional leadership even before Election Day and continued throughout the transition period. Once in office, contact, usually by phone, between top leadership staffers and the White House was constant; Pelosi and Obama spoke frequently as did Reid and Obama.

Obama reached out to congressional Republicans as well, attempting to deliver on his promise of tamping down the partisan hostility in Washington. He sent Emanuel to meet with the Republican leadership soon after the election; he himself called a number of the Republican ranking committee members; Vice President Elect Joe Biden talked to some of his former Senate colleagues; Obama himself consulted Olympia Snowe, a key Senate moderate, on the stimulus package; and on January 5, two days after the new Congress convened, Obama met first with Pelosi and Reid, and then with the Republican and Democratic leadership teams. He continued his outreach, even going to the Hill after he became president to meet with Republicans on the stimulus package.

A context conducive to policy change and political actors astute enough to take advantage of it yielded very considerable legislative success. The massive stimulus bill, health-care reform (Affordable Care Act or ACA), and financial services regulation reform (Dodd-Frank) are best known but much other significant legislation was enacted including the Lilly Ledbetter Fair Pay Act, a major change in the student loan program to free up more money for loans; food safety and child nutrition bills; a credit card regulation bill; legislation to allow the FDA to regulate tobacco; an expansion of the hate crimes covered by federal law; and repeal of "Don't Ask, Don't Tell." The Senate also ratified the New START treaty.

Brief accounts of passing the stimulus bill and the ACA illustrate how important the working relationship between the president and the Democratic congressional leadership was to legislative success and how the context shaped their strategies.

PASSING THE STIMULUS BILL: EARLY SUCCESS AND TROUBLING PORTENDS

By early 2009, a consensus had emerged among experts that, to meet the worst economic crisis since the Great Depression, a very substantial stimulus package was essential.[7] Partly out of necessity because he was not yet president, Obama relied heavily on congressional Democrats to craft the stimulus package. To be sure, Obama team members begin meeting and discussing a potential stimulus bill with the congressional leadership before the November elections and, by mid-December, Obama transition team members and relevant Democratic congressional staffers were meeting almost daily. Nevertheless, as would become a standard Obama strategy, he gave congressional Democrats great leeway, calculating that members who had a major role in shaping legislation would have a much greater stake in its enactment.

Pelosi tapped Appropriations Chairman David Obey as the head negotiator for House Democrats; a considerable proportion of a stimulus bill would be within his committee's jurisdiction and Obey was a politically savvy and tough legislator. On this and the other major agenda items, Pelosi would delegate to her trusted committee leaders but would continuously oversee the process and involve herself deeply when she saw the necessity.

Despite the Obama administration's outreach to Republicans and the inclusion of a large tax-cut component in the stimulus bill, Republicans opposed the majority's bill. In fact, on inauguration evening, a group of Republicans had met and agreed to "show united and unyielding opposition to the president's economic policies."[8] The group included House Minority Whip Eric Cantor; House GOP Deputy Whip Kevin McCarthy; Paul Ryan, top Republican on the House Budget Committee; and Senate Minority Whip John Kyl. Conservatives in Congress and on the airwaves launched an all-out attack on the Democratic plan. At one point in the stimulus battle, opponents seized the initiative in defining the bill, claiming it was not a stimulus at all but just a lot of useless and expensive pork. Urged on by the Democratic congressional leadership, Obama personally took over the job of selling the stimulus bill and did so aggressively, but some ground had been lost.

Demonstrating the control the House majority leadership commands as well as the extent to which Democrats saw passage of the stimulus as essential, the House committees marked up the stimulus bill during the first week of the Obama presidency and the House passed it in the second. The bill was considered on the floor under a rule that "self-executed" (meaning no vote was necessary) an amendment making several last-minute changes to the bill; these postcommittee adjustments included provisions striking money for re-sodding the Mall and family-planning funds. Democratic leaders had decided that these provisions had become lightning rods that were not worth the pain they were causing their members. Better to remove them than try to explain in the face of the conservative onslaught. Of the amendments made in order by the rule, three were sponsored by freshmen Democrats, including one benefiting the textile industry by North Carolinian Larry Kissel. In constructing the rule, the leadership's first concern was facilitating passage of this key agenda item but the leaders were also looking out for their more vulnerable members.

HR1, the stimulus bill, passed the House by 244 to 188; eleven Democrats, mostly more conservative Blue Dogs, voted against the bill; not a single Republican supported it. The Republican whip system was aggressively employed to keep any Republican members from straying; even Joseph Cao, newly elected from a poor, majority-black district, was pressured into opposing the stimulus bill.[9] The Republican House leadership had decided that the party's electoral interest lay in unequivocally and vigorously opposing Obama's and the congressional Democrats' policy agenda. They had no real problem in keeping their members united behind that strategy because those members' core constituencies strongly favored all-out opposition to Obama's agenda; Republican activists, largely severely conservative, were, in fact, far more likely to punish their member of Congress for supporting rather than opposing Obama's legislative priorities.

Because a simple majority can prevail in the House, even unanimous Republican opposition was irrelevant to passage. In the Senate, a minority of forty-one or more can block passage if it uses its prerogative of extended debate. Thus Majority Leader Harry Reid's problem was how to get to sixty votes; with fifty-eight Democrats, he would need several Republican votes and the Republican Senate leadership had made its opposition to the Democratic approach clear. Thus when Senate moderates Ben Nelson, Democrat of Nebraska, and Susan Collins, Republican of Maine, began talks about possible revisions to the committee-reported bill, Reid encouraged their effort. Intense negotiations among these and a larger group of moderates and with Reid and White House officials finally yielded an agreement that could garner sixty votes. It cut the size of the stimulus; at Senator Collins's insistence, aid to the states was significantly reduced and school construction funds were deleted. Yet the many Senate Democrats who supported a bigger package had no real choice but to go along.

After cloture was invoked on the compromise bill with the essential help of three Republicans—Susan Collins and Olympia Snowe, both of Maine, and Arlen Specter of Pennsylvania—and the bill passed the Senate, a compromise between the House and Senate bills was necessary. That would require some serious bargaining, which, as is often the case, took place behind closed doors before a formal meeting of the conference committee. Although the Obama administration had left much of the detailed drafting to Congress, at this point the administration was deeply involved with Chief of Staff Rahm Emanuel and Office of Management and Budget (OMB) Director Peter Orszag acting as point men. Pelosi too was a key negotiator. And the Senate moderates had to be consulted and kept on board. When talks seemed to hit a wall over funding for school construction, the president phoned Pelosi and House Majority Whip Jim Clyburn to make sure that negotiations moved ahead.

The agreement reached by House and Senate negotiators was for a stimulus plan costing about $789 billion. As the leaders had promised, both chambers passed the conference report before the President's Day recess. Obama signed the bill on February 17, less than a month after his inauguration.

PASSING HEALTH-CARE REFORM:
ESSENTIAL BUT EXPENSIVE VICTORY

In contrast, passing health-care reform proved to be a marathon. However, the strategies employed by Obama and the Democratic congressional leaders were largely the same as those used to pass the stimulus bill and the problems and barriers were similar too, though in exaggerated form. The policy issues were more complex; they divided Democrats to a greater extent and thus made putting together winning coalitions a trickier and more delicate enterprise; and they confronted even more adamant GOP opposition.

Obama again did not submit a detailed plan to Congress; he laid out general principles and depended on congressional Democrats to fill in the details. This strategy by no means represented a hands-off approach. The Office for Health Care Reform (OHCR) that Obama created shortly after he became president "acted as liaison between the executive and the legislative branches. Its purpose was to relay White House positions and priorities to Congress and try to influence the direction the bill was taking but not to write the bill itself." [10] Initially the OHCR met with the relevant committees weekly but by summer 2009 meetings with committees and the party leadership were taking place daily. Nancy DeParle, who headed the office, became an almost continuous presence on the Hill.

To get a bill to the floor that could command the necessary majority took intense leadership negotiations at a number of stages of the process and some painful compromises in both chambers. To avoid turf fights, Speaker Pelosi asked the chairmen of the three committees with jurisdiction to negotiate a single bill that then could be introduced in all their committees. Pelosi and her leadership team undertook a months-long campaign of consulting, educating, and negotiating with their members. The leaders knew they could expect no Republican votes at all so they could lose at most thirty-nine Democrats. That meant they would have to get a considerable number of moderate to conservative Democrats on board without losing their liberal members. In the end, Pelosi was forced to delete the "robust" public option, a government-run health-insurance plan that would pay providers at the Medicare care rate plus 5 percent, and to allow a stringent antiabortion amendment to be offered on the floor. Both were decisions House liberals opposed and that Pelosi herself disliked but they were essential to the 220 to 215 victory on November 7, 2009; thirty-nine Democrats voted against the bill. [11]

With fewer procedural powers and the need to attain a supermajority, Senate Majority Leader Reid had a still more difficult task. Both he and Obama hoped to get some Republican support in the Senate. The Finance Committee whose chairman had tried for months to forge a bipartisan deal finally reported out a bill in September with one Republican vote; Health, Education, Labor, and Pensions (HELP), the other committee with jurisdiction, had reported a very different bill months earlier. As on the House side, putting together a bill that could pass required consulting broadly, a task that was directed by the leadership as was the case in the House. Reid, however, knew that he would need sixty votes just to get the bill to the floor and then sixty again to get a vote on final passage; at this point, he also knew that getting any Republican votes would be exceedingly difficult.

In the end, Reid would be required to make a number of compromises unpalatable to his more liberal members. Hardest to take was Joe Lieberman's demand that any form of the public option be dropped and then that the compromise of letting some fifty-five- to sixty-four-year-olds buy into Medicare also be scrapped. Reid, knowing he had to have the vote, acceded. The last holdout, Ben Nelson, was brought on board with compromise abortion language and some special provisions for his state.

At 7 a.m. on Christmas Eve morning, the bill passed the Senate on a straight party line vote of 60 to 39. The Senate had debated the bill for twenty-five days without breaks for weekends since early December, and Democrats had had to win five cloture votes; provisions that a large majority of the Democratic membership strongly supported had been dropped to get the requisite sixty votes. But Reid had gotten a major health-reform bill through the Senate before the end of Obama's first year. He had done so, in Senator Tom Harkin's words, by "exhibit[ing] the patience of Job, the wisdom of Solomon and the endurance of Samson."[12]

The process of forging one bill from the two chambers' different versions was well under way when Republican Scott Brown won a special election to replace Ted Kennedy in the Senate. Brown's victory on an anti-health-care platform in strongly Democratic Massachusetts shocked and scared congressional Democrats. It also deprived Senate Democrats of that crucial sixtieth vote.

In the first days after the January 20 special election, Speaker Pelosi was the strongest voice for finishing the job of enacting major reform. Despite advice to settle for smaller changes in health-care policy, Obama too decided fairly quickly to plow ahead.

Over the course of the months-long battle, the White House had played a significant behind-the-scenes role and Obama himself had sometimes used the bully pulpit as well. Senior White House aides had assisted the congressional leaders in their negotiations; they and Obama had met with innumerable members attempting to keep the process moving and then to persuade them to vote for the bills. Although never doing as much to frame the debate favorably as congressional Democrats wanted him to do, Obama had made an extremely important health-care speech to a joint session of Congress in September. Coming after a brutal August during which many Democrats had been attacked vociferously by Tea Party activists at home, Obama's well-received speech stemmed the panic. Obama had always intended to take a more prominent role in shaping the final language after both chambers had passed a bill. Even before the Brown victory, Obama had chaired lengthy negotiating sessions at the White House. Now a still more prominent role became necessary. Obama convened a health-care summit to which he invited Republican and Democratic congressional leaders; over seven hours of civil and substantive discussion, Obama made the case for thoroughgoing reform and showed that the Republicans lacked a plan.

Obama's PR offensive gave the congressional leadership the time and the cover to implement a plan for finishing health-care reform legislation. The loss of the sixtieth vote in the Senate made the normal ways of resolving differences between the chambers politically impossible because any compromise product would be filibusterable in the Senate. The House could have simply accepted the Senate bill but, since it included some provision that were extremely unpopular with House Democrats—the "Cornhusker Kickback" to get Nelson's vote and a stiff tax on "Cadillac health-care plans," for example—Pelosi insisted she could not get the votes to do so. Fortunately, at the insistence of House Democrats and the White House, the budget resolution passed in spring of 2009 had allowed for a reconciliation bill with health-care provisions. The Budget Act provides that such reconciliation bills are not subject to filibusters.[13] Because Budget Act rules restrict what can be included in reconciliation bills, enacting health-care reform entirely through a reconciliation bill was not feasible; however the main changes House Democrats needed to support the bill could be included in a reconciliation bill.

A full court press involving the White House, other members of the administration, and Obama himself as well as the House Democratic leadership and its entire apparatus of persuasion was required to pass the bills in the House. On March 21 the chamber first passed the Senate bill by 219 to 212 and then the reconciliation bill that fixed the Senate bill on a 220 to 211 vote. Obama signed the Senate bill on March 23. On March 25, the Senate passed the reconciliation bill fifty-six to forty-three and the president signed it on March 30. No Republican supported health-care reform on any of these votes.

THE BENEFITS AND COSTS OF IDEOLOGICALLY HOMOGENEOUS PARTIES: PART I

These legislative victories would have been impossible without a close working relationship between Obama and the congressional party leadership. The party leaders willingly made passing Obama's agenda their first priority because they saw his success as essential to their own and their members' success. They were able to do so much to facilitate the passage of these and other key priority bills because they led a membership that had become increasingly ideologically homogeneous and, in good part as a result, they had amassed formidable powers and resources and the latitude to use them.

The political forces that over time produced a more homogeneous Democratic Party also forged an even more homogeneous Republican Party. When the minority party faces unified government, its members and particularly its leaders may perceive bipartisanship to conflict with their electoral interests. Their rationale: the president and his congressional party will get credit for any successes but, if they support the bills, they will share the blame for any failures. However, if the president won big and seemed to earn a mandate, minority-party members may fear the wrath of their constituents if they oppose him. Yet, with the polarization that has occurred not just in Congress but among voters and especially activists, fewer minority-party members are likely to fear such a reaction. And, of course, when the parties are highly polarized, the minority party will have genuine and severe policy disagreements with the majority. As a result the prospects for much genuine bipartisanship in the 111th Congress were always bleak and there was little Obama could have done about that.

The early battles made it clear that the Senate, where the minority party has so much more power than in the House, would pose the greatest barrier to enacting the Democrats' agenda. Even when Democrats for a time had sixty votes, minority-party obstructionism made passing legislation and confirming nominations a time-consuming slog. Minority Leader Mitch McConnell proved to be adept at holding his members together, forcing Democrats to amass the necessary sixty votes from their own membership most of the time. Over 70 percent of major legislation encountered a filibuster-related problem in the Senate, up from the already high 51 percent average during the Clinton and George W. Bush presidencies. [14]

Unified Republican opposition to the Democrats' agenda extracted a price in legislation that failed; no comprehensive immigration reform bill was ever proposed; the DREAM Act succumbed to a filibuster in the Senate and climate change legislation also died in the Senate. In addition, by making the process very messy and by branding Obama's marquee legislation as wholly partisan, congressional Republicans took a big toll on the popularity of Obama's legislative accomplishments. To a public with limited understanding of how legislatures normally work, the drawn out, contentious, and deal-infused process of getting to sixty in the Senate appeared shady at best and cast a pall of illegitimacy on the resulting legislation. The 2010 elections, which ended so disastrously for Democrats, were mostly the result of the poor economy but congressional Republicans' strategy of all-out opposition appears to have contributed at the margin.

DIVIDED CONTROL: OBAMA, BOEHNER, AND REID IN THE 112TH CONGRESS

In the 2010 midterm elections, Democrats lost over sixty House seats and so control of the chamber; the 112th Congress would begin with a House of 242 Republicans—eighty-seven of them freshmen—and 193 Democrats. Senate Democrats lost six seats but maintained a majority, though one reduced to fifty-three.

In his second two years, thus, Obama would be operating in a very different political context. With far from sixty Democrats in the Senate, Republican Leader Mitch McConnell would be even more influential. And, instead of the like-minded Nancy Pelosi, the House would be led by John Boehner, a conservative Republican. The very ambitious and more hardline Eric Cantor became majority leader, Kevin McCarthy, majority whip, and Paul Ryan, chair of the House Budget Committee. The three under the self-applied label "Young Guns" had contributed significantly to the 2010 victory, recruiting and helping to finance like-minded hardline conservatives. [15] In making leadership decisions, Boehner would always have to be aware that many of the freshmen were closer, both ideologically and personally, to the Young Guns than to their nominal leader. Republican congressional leaders had complained that, during the 111th Congress, Obama seldom consulted them and, when he did, paid little attention to their views. (Of course, Obama argued he had tried repeatedly to compromise with them and they had refused.) Now Obama had no choice but to deal with the Republican leadership.

The surprisingly productive lame-duck (postelection) session of the 111th Congress raised hopes that the 112th might not be doomed to gridlock. The START2 treaty was ratified; the "don't ask, don't tell" policy of the military on homosexuals was repealed, and a deal on extending the Bush tax cuts was reached. But this show of productivity was deceptive. A galaxy of GOP foreign policy and defense superstars from past Republican administrations vocally supported the START treaty and yet Republican senators split thirteen to twenty-six against. DADT repeal, which polls revealed to be broadly supported by the public, picked up eight GOP votes but thirty-one voting against. The tax-cut package was negotiated between President Obama and Senate Minority Leader Mitch McConnell and was passed by bipartisan majorities in both chambers. Republicans got what they valued most—an extension of the Bush tax cuts for everyone, including the most affluent, and the estate tax set at a much lower rate than Democrats preferred. Obama got a continuation of the tax cuts for the middle class, an extension of unemployment insurance for thirteen months, and, instead of some tax reductions for the working poor that were expiring, a 2 percentage-point cut for a year in employees' payroll taxes—all measures the administration considered crucial to keep the economic recovery on track. And both avoided the possibly devastating blame attendant on a big increase in most Americans' taxes come January. Liberal Democrats who objected to tax breaks for the affluent and very conservative Republicans who wanted the tax cuts made permanent disliked the package but were marginalized.

These accomplishments were achieved by the members of the outgoing 111th Congress. The new 112th was very different in composition and outlook. When a party wins a huge victory as Republicans did in 2010 its members are likely to interpret the election results as a mandate. The rise of the Tea Party during 2009 and 2010 strongly influenced the Republican Party and shaped the 2010 campaign. Many of the new Republican members of Congress had been supported and all were influenced by the Tea Party movement. These freshmen fervently believed they had been elected to cut federal spending and the deficit severely, to resist any increases in taxes whatsoever, and to repeal the major accomplishments of Obama's first two years, especially "ObamaCare." As much as the Tea Party movement injected new energy into the Republican Party, it did not represent a discontinuity. Many of the more senior congressional Republicans were enthusiastic supporters of the same agenda; they after all were the members who had fought so intensely and nearly unanimously against the Obama agenda in the 111th Congress. Of the eighty-seven House GOP freshmen, seventy-eight joined the Republican Study Committee, the organization of the most hardline conservative members; in the 112th Congress, the RSC included over 170 of the 242 House Republicans.

Minority Leader Mitch McConnell and new Speaker John Boehner were seasoned leaders and skilled deal makers. Yet their members'—and their own—policy and electoral interests conflicted with Obama's. McConnell, in fall 2010, baldly stated that his top priority was to see that Obama was not reelected. Boehner led a membership with intense and often extreme policy preferences and little tolerance for compromise. Although some pundits saw in the lame duck a promise of a cooperative relationship and even of a grand bargain on deficit reduction, the omens were not favorable.

House Republicans began the 112th by passing the "Repealing the Job-Killing Health Care Law" Act; every Republican voted to repeal and all but three Democrats opposed it. Although all but the most inexperienced know the Democratic Senate would kill any such legislation, House Republicans would vote for ACA repeal over thirty times during the 112th Congress, symbolic of a Congress long on grand gestures but largely incapable of significant real accomplishments. Yet even a gridlocked Congress must pass some legislation simply to keep the government functioning. That in itself would prove to be difficult.

KEEPING THE GOVERNMENT FUNDED: DOING ORDINARY BUSINESS IN EXTRAORDINARY CIRCUMSTANCES

The first order of must-do business was passing appropriations to fund the government's operations. The Democratically controlled 111th Congress had failed to pass the regular appropriations bills by October 1, the beginning of the fiscal year, and had passed short-term stop-gap legislation instead. During the lame-duck session, Senate Republicans blocked legislation appropriating funds through the remainder of FY2011; GOP candidates had promised to cut hundreds of billions of dollars from federal spending and intended to start delivering early in 2011. In December, the outgoing 111th managed only to pass a continuing resolution (CR) maintaining funding at current levels until March 4, 2011.

On April 15, 2011, Obama signed an omnibus appropriations bill that funded the government for the remainder of the fiscal year and cut $39.9 billion in discretionary spending. The process that led to the enactment was prolonged, conflictual, and characterized by brinksmanship, intended and inadvertent.

When Speaker Boehner and Republican appropriators unveiled their proposal in early February, the Obama administration and congressional Democrats condemned the severity of the cuts while hardline conservatives organized in the Republican Study Committee (RSC) objected that they were not nearly enough. The party had promised to cut at least $100 billion in nonsecurity discretionary spending in FY11 and anything less was a betrayal, they argued. Their leaders' contention that, since only seven months of the fiscal year remained, the amount should be prorated did not persuade them. In the face of this resistance, Boehner sent his appropriators back to find more cuts. The House passed the still more draconian HR1 on February 19 with only Republican votes.

Clearly neither Senate Democrats nor the While House would accept the House bill; but the hardline conservative House Republicans were unwilling to compromise. Boehner very much wanted to avoid a government shutdown, which going beyond the March 4 deadline without a bill would entail. The government shutdown in late 1995/early 1996 had grievously wounded Speaker Gingrich and congressional Republicans.[16] Senate Majority Leader Reid attempted to draw Boehner into negotiations and the White House made clear it was open to some cuts. Two short-term CRs were negotiated and passed, each on the eve of the drop-dead date. The true ideological chasm between the parties and the bargaining advantage of playing chicken made reaching even these interim agreements difficult. It was clear to all participants that Boehner could not get the votes to pass any CR without spending cuts, and both short term CRs included cuts—the first $4 billion and the second another $6 billion. But these were relatively easy cuts, ones that had been included in the president's budget, for example. In early March, after the first short-term CR passed, negotiations on the long-term CR began in earnest. Vice President Joseph R. Biden Jr. headed the administration's team in talks with Speaker Boehner, Senate Majority Leader Harry Reid, Senate Minority Leader Mitch McConnell, and House Minority Leader Nancy Pelosi.

An agreement finally came two hours before the shutdown deadline at midnight April 8. Talks behind closed doors and dueling PR efforts came to fruition. During the final days, Obama had called senior leaders to the White House for meetings several times a day. The deal entailed $39 billion in cuts; most of the policy riders House Republicans had added that Obama and Democrats abhorred were dropped.

The prolonged battle over funding the government, one of the most basic tasks of Congress and the president, demonstrated just how difficult policy making in the 112th would be. The ideological divide between Republicans and Democrats was about as deep as it has ever been. Republicans, especially the large hardline group, believed they had been given a popular mandate by the 2010 elections; many abhorred the notion of compromise, seeing it as selling out. Although the omnibus appropriations bill passed handily in both chambers, fifty-nine House Republicans refused to vote for it, convinced their leaders had compromised too much. Speaker Boehner's bargaining position was strengthened by this hard core; when in the future he pushed for more concessions on the basis that they were necessary to sell a deal to his right flank, his opponents had to take him seriously. Yet the battle also exposed Boehner's tenuous control of his membership and consequently his questionable reliability as a bargaining partner.

Obama and congressional Democrats would mostly be relegated to playing policy defense, the appropriations battle suggested. During the early months of 2011 Obama gave his state of the union address and released his budget. Both bowed to the message of the 2010 elections but argued for smart cuts and strategic investments in areas such as education and infrastructure. The House Republicans' budget plan—the Ryan budget as it came to be known after the chair of the House Budget Committee Paul Ryan—commanded more attention and offered a stark contrast with Obama's proposals. The Ryan plan as approved in the budget resolution passed by the House in 2011 and again in 2012 proposed to cut $4 trillion from federal spending over the next ten years, revamp Medicare into voucher plan, and block-grant and cut or freeze spending on other safety-net and social welfare programs, while reducing tax rates, including decreasing the corporate tax from 35 to 25 percent.[17]

In his contest with House Republicans, Obama could expect little help from House Democrats, reduced as House minorities are to near impotence. Senate Democrats and Majority Leader Harry Reid, however, were crucial allies. Although the 2010 elections had seriously reduced his numbers and unnerved some of his more moderate members, Reid as majority leader still controlled floor scheduling. His ability to pass legislation was less than it had been in the 111th Congress since amassing the sixty votes necessary was often impossible; but his power to block was just as great. As House Republicans would send the Senate a stream of legislation totally unacceptable to Obama, Reid could assure that those bills were "dead on arrival." In addition, Republican proposals were often so extreme that Reid had less problem maintaining Democratic unity than he might otherwise have had. Thus Reid could hold votes to show House Republicans that their bills had no chance of becoming law, as he did on HR1, the House GOP's first omnibus appropriations bill. The bill not only failed, it received no Democratic votes.

DEBT CEILING 2011: TO THE BRINK

Congress by law establishes a debt ceiling, a limit on the amount of money the US government can borrow, and periodically has to raise the limit so that the government can pay its bills. Well before the 2010 elections, it became clear that the debt ceiling would be reached sometime in 2011. Although raising the debt ceiling does not increase the deficit and failing to raise it when it is reached would lead to a US government default on its debts, members of Congress hate to vote for an increase. It is an easy vote to demagogue because it is a hard vote to explain to one's constituents. In fact, Eric Cantor and his Young Guns had encouraged GOP candidates to demagogue the issue in their 2010 campaigns, promising not to vote for an increase. [18]

The very serious consequences for the economy of a default was a two-edged sword for the congressional leadership; Boehner and McConnell knew that they could not let a default happen; they also knew that the requirement of congressional action gave them a major weapon for extracting concessions from a president intending to run for reelection. The congressional Republicans saw the upcoming fight as an opportunity to force Obama and congressional Democrats to agree to severe cuts in entitlement programs, which would thus have the Democratic Party's imprint.

Yet Boehner was in a particularly dicey situation; many of his new members had promised to vote against an increase and seemingly did not understand the consequences of default. Furthermore, during the fight over the omnibus appropriations bill, the House GOP leadership had urged their members to vote for a bill they disliked by promising them a big win on the debt ceiling.

On May 2, Treasury Secretary Tim Geithner announced that the debt ceiling had to be increased before August 2, after which the US government would not be able to pay its bills. President Obama designated Vice President Joe Biden to negotiate with congressional leaders. Obama and congressional Democrats knew that they would have to make concessions to get a debt-limit increase. Obama very much wanted a grand bargain that would include spending cuts, entitlement reform, and tax increases; such a comprehensive agreement would help the economy and lower the bitterly partisan tone, thus giving him a policy win and helping his reelection prospects. Congressional Democrats were wary; they feared the Obama might give away too much. Yet, they had no real choice but to go along.

The first meeting of the Biden group took place at the Capitol on May 5. Obama had asked all four congressional leaders to designate up to two members to represent them in the talks. Boehner's choice of Cantor was widely interpreted as a protective move; Cantor would "own" any deal reached and so could not use it to undermine Boehner. McConnell's choice of Jon Kyl, the Senate GOP whip and a hardliner, indicated that McConnell intended to hold out for maximal concessions and, soon after the talks began, McConnell insisted that major cuts in domestic spending and a Medicare overhaul would be the price of Republicans agreeing to raise the debt limit.

The Biden group met numerous times over the course of several weeks and, so long as spending cuts were being discussed, appeared to be making significant progress. However, when Democrats finally insisted on discussing tax increases, Cantor walked out. For House Republicans, any increase in taxes was anathema. With Kyl soon following, the Biden talks fell apart. If a grand bargain was to be reached, Boehner and Obama would have to negotiate directly. As Majority Leader Harry Reid said, "I think it's now, with what Kyl and Cantor [have] done, I think it's in the hands of the Speaker and the president and, sadly, probably me."[19]

The next several weeks saw a flurry of meetings including the full set of leaders, vigorous dueling PR efforts attempting to frame the debate, and, behind the scenes, off-and-on negotiations between Boehner and Obama. Republicans called on Obama to publicly lay out a plan, hoping to force him to take responsibility for unpopular cuts. Democrats accused Republicans of endangering the full faith and credit of the United States and the health of the economy and of an unwillingness to agree to a fair plan including higher taxes on the affluent as well as cuts affecting the less well-off. At several points, the Obama-Boehner talks seemed close to a big—if not a grand—bargain, but in the end they too failed. On July 22, Boehner pulled out. Amid intense acrimony, each side cast blame on the other. The basic problem was again taxes. No deal that Boehner could sell to his members and that Obama and his fellow Democrats in Congress would accept existed.[20]

The Republican congressional leaders knew they could not allow default to occur, even if some of their members did not. McConnell, saying that Republicans must not let themselves be seen as responsible for the bad economy, had on July 12 proposed a complicated plan intended to result in periodic debt limit increases requested by the president that Congress could veto with a two-thirds vote coupled with spending cuts.

The aim was to ensure the United States would not default but also to stick the president with the responsibility of asking for three debt limit increases before the 2012 elections and proposing offsetting budget cuts and congressional Democrats with voting—up to six times—to allow those increases to occur. Both hardline Republicans and most Democrats disliked the plan, but Reid saw it as a possible way out of the dilemma and he and McConnell began to negotiate.

On July 19, House Republicans passed "Cut, Cap and Balance," a bill that would severely cut spending, balance the budget, and put a cap on overall federal spending. Promoted by the hardline Republican Study Committee, the plan was strongly opposed by Democrats, garnering only five Democratic votes in the House. Obama threatened a veto and, on July 22, the Senate tabled it. Although its fate was totally predictable, by allowing a vote on the bill Boehner mollified the Study Committee members and showed them that their preferred path was not realistic. Friday, July 22 was also the day that Boehner pulled out of the talks with Obama.

After the weekend, both Boehner and Reid unveiled widely divergent plans for raising the debt ceiling. The same day, July 25, Obama attempted to increase the pressure for a deal by making a nationally televised address. He urged Americans to call their members of Congress to advocate compromise. "The only reasons [a] . . . balanced approach isn't on its way to becoming law right now is because a significant number of Republicans in Congress are insisting on a different approach—a cuts-only approach," he said. "That is no way to run the greatest country on Earth."[21]

Boehner's plan immediately ran into trouble from both ends of the spectrum. The Obama administration issued a veto threat and Boehner's own hardline members denounced it. Over several agonizing days, Boehner repeatedly revised his plan to get enough votes to pass it. On Friday, he finally succeeded but the version that passed was even more draconian than his initial plan and the Senate quickly killed it. Reid confronted problems as well; he could kill anything that the House sent over but could not amass sixty votes to bring his own plan to an up-or-down vote. With stalemate seemingly threatening again, Obama ratcheted up the pressure by holding a press conference. Again, as with his earlier speech, the result was a flood of phone calls to Capitol Hill.

With the August 2 deadline looming, negotiations again moved to the White House. All weekend, top White House staff, Vice President Biden, and sometimes Obama himself talked with various top leaders. On a Sunday morning talk show, McConnell said a deal was close. At 8:30 p.m., Reid and McConnell announced on the Senate floor that a deal had been reached. Obama made an announcement soon thereafter. Boehner, who would have the most difficult task passing a deal, held a conference call with this membership, working at selling the agreement.

Many hardline Republicans were unhappy with the agreement, as were many progressive Democrats. Nevertheless, on August 1, the House passed the bill 269 to 161; Republicans split 174 to 66; Democrats 95 to 95. The next day, the Senate passed it 74 to 26, with six Democrats and nineteen Republicans voting against it. Shortly thereafter Obama signed the legislation.

The Budget Control Act (BCA) allowed the president to raise the debt limit by up to $2.5 trillion in two steps and subject to disapproval by Congress by a two-thirds vote. The immediate increase in the debt ceiling was to be accompanied by $1 trillion in cuts in defense and domestic discretionary spending over ten years. A Joint Select Committee on Deficit Reduction was to be appointed by the four party leaderships and charged with agreeing on another $1.5 trillion in cuts, with Congress required to vote for the committee's recommendations as a package. If the committee did not agree or Congress did not approve its package, automatic cuts (called sequestration) would take effect. The cuts would come half from defense and half from domestic spending but Medicaid, Social Security, veterans' programs, and many programs targeted to low-income Americans would be largely exempt. Medicare was also mostly protected.[22]

The deal was a mixed bag for all the major actors. Obama got an easy path toward increasing the debt ceiling enough to get beyond the 2012 elections and protected some of the domestic programs Democrats care about most. Yet, having to bargain at all and to agree to big cuts in order to get a debt-ceiling increase was unprecedented and made him look weak. And many Democrats were disgruntled with the results. The House Democratic leadership regained some influence because Democratic votes were needed to pass the deal and the leaders thus had standing to insist that many safety-net programs be protected. Yet the deep cuts in other domestic spending were hard for many Democrats to swallow. For the GOP leadership and Boehner especially, getting a deal that included no revenue increases was a significant victory. And, of course, the cuts, though not as large as many House hardliners wanted, were nevertheless a substantial down payment on the GOP promise to cut government. By managing to pass the deal in the House, Boehner looked stronger than he had most of the year, but the fact that sixty-six members of his Caucus refused to go along was a danger sign.

The messiness and perils-of-Pauline character of the process of reaching agreement took a toll on all the major actors' public standing. The Congress was already unpopular but its public approval decreased further. Although more people blamed Congress than Obama for the impasse, Obama's job approval nevertheless declined significantly and a president's reelection chances are more closely linked to his job approval numbers than are those of individual members of Congress. For the Obama team, the debt-limit fight taught a stark lesson: conciliation and compromise were losing strategies both in policy and electoral terms. Whatever Boehner might himself prefer, he could not deliver his members for any big deal that Democrats could accept. Continuing to try to compromise with congressional Republicans would only make Obama look weak and might well lead to a reelection defeat.

NO MORE MR. NICE GUY

Obama turned to a more confrontational, outward-direct strategy. In a nationally televised speech to Congress, he offered a big jobs bill that he knew congressional Republicans would never accept. He then took to the hustings with the slogan "We Can't Wait." When House Republicans attempted to extract large spending cuts in return for extending the payroll tax cut for another year, Obama and congressional Democrats hung tough and Republicans were forced to concede. Obama had pounded them publicly for months on this popular provision. Similarly, the fear of electoral repercussions persuaded congressional Republicans to pass legislation preventing the student loan interest rate from doubling. Obama again had raised the visibility of the issue through innumerable speeches and public statements. In both of these fights, Reid's adept use of Senate procedure was an essential contributor to success. He forced Republicans to take tough votes on popular provisions and fashioned means of getting to deals.

Still 2012 was predominantly characterized by policy stalemate. The Joint Select Committee on Deficit Reduction—dubbed the Supercommittee—failed to reach any agreement. Its composition of equal numbers of Republicans and Democrats selected by the party leaders and its short timeframe to report probably doomed it to failure from the start. As a consequence of its failure, severe automatic spending cuts would go into effect at the beginning of 2013 unless the BCA was changed. Even bills that are "must pass" and that usually pass easily—the transportation bill, the Federal Aviation Administration reauthorization—were excruciatingly difficult to enact. When the 112th Congress recessed for the 2012 elections, it was being characterized the least productive congress in history.

A NEW BEGINNING?

The 2012 elections awarded Obama a second term as president; in a contest pundits predicted to be razor thin, Obama won handily 51 to 47 percent. Against the odds, Senate Democrats who were defending twenty-three seats in the thirty-three Senate races actually picked up two seats and entered the 113th Congress with fifty-five of the hundred Senate seats. Democratic candidates for the House of Representatives won more votes overall then did Republicans and Democrats increased their numbers in the chamber from 193 to 201, but Republicans maintained control.

Obama and the congressional leaders faced one final major challenge during the lame-duck session of the outgoing 112th Congress. With the Bush tax cuts set to expire at the end of 2012 and the across-the-board sequestration cuts scheduled to go into effect at the beginning of 2013, Congress and the president would need to reach a deal to avoid this "fiscal cliff" that many economists predicted would sink the economy into recession. During the campaign Obama had aggressively advocated higher taxes on the wealthy and he insisted that higher tax rates on upper incomes had to be part of any deal. Although the election results had strengthened Obama's hand, Republicans argued that the voters had simply maintained the status quo and that

House Republicans particularly had just as much a claim to a mandate as Obama did.

Obama and Boehner again attempted to negotiate a deal and, when an agreement was not reached, Boehner tried but failed to pass what he labeled his Plan B, which maintained the Bush tax cuts for all but millionaires. The root problem in both cases was Boehner's inability to sell any deal that Obama and Democrats would accept to his members. To be sure, an appreciable number of Republicans, House members as well as senators, recognized that given Obama's strengthened hand, they would eventually have to accept some tax increases; but a significant number of die-hards in the House did not—enough to sink Plan B—and most Republicans expected huge concessions from Obama in return. Characteristic of policy making in the 112th Congress, a fiscal cliff deal was reached and approved by Congress only hours before the deadline and the expiration of the 112th—and the deal just postponed the sequestration for two months.

The end of the 112th Congress suggested that the 113th would be plagued with much the same problems as its gridlock-prone predecessor. The US system of government meshes very badly with highly polarized parties unless control of the branches—and the chambers—is unified; and even then, Senate rules represent a significant barrier unless the majority party has an unusually large majority. In making deals, leaders can only go as far as their followers will allow; leaders may be able to persuade but they cannot command.

NOTES

1. In addition to the sources cited and media reports, this chapter is based on the author's interviews with members of Congress, congressional staff, and informed observers.

2. See Barbara Sinclair, *Party Wars: Polarization and the Politics of the Policy Process* (Julian Rothbaum Lecture Series, University of Oklahoma Press, 2006); Pietro Nivola and David Brady, eds., *Red and Blue Nation?: Characteristics and Causes of America's Polarized Politics* (Washington, DC: Brookings Institute, 2006); Pietro Nivola and David Brady, eds., *Red and Blue Nation?: Consequences and Correction of America's Polarized Politics* (Washington, DC: Brookings Institute, 2008).

3. David Rohde, *Parties and Leaders in the Postreform House* (Chicago: University of Chicago Press, 1991); Barbara Sinclair, *Legislators, Leaders and Lawmaking* (Baltimore: Johns Hopkins University Press, 1995).

4. For examples, see Barbara Sinclair, "Trying to Govern Positively in a Negative Era: Clinton and the 103rd Congress" in Colin Campbell and Bert A. Rockman, eds., *The Clinton Presidency: First Appraisals* (Chatham, NJ: Chatham House Publishers, 1996); Barbara Sinclair, "Context, Strategy and Chance: George W. Bush and the 107th Congress," in Colin Campbell and Bert Rockman, eds., *The George W. Bush Presidency: An Early Appraisal* (Chatham, NJ: Chatham House Publishers, 2003).

5. Steven S. Smith, "Forces of Change in Senate Party Leadership and Organization," in Lawrence C. Dodd and Bruce I. Oppenheimer, eds., *Congress Reconsidered*, 5th ed. (Washington, DC: CQ Press, 1993).

6. For a more detailed discussion of Clinton's relations with Congress see Sinclair, "Trying to Govern Positively in a Negative Era Clinton and the 103rd Congress," and Barbara Sinclair,

"The President as Legislative Leader," in Colin Campbell and Bert A. Rockman, eds., *The Clinton Legacy* (Chatham, NJ: Chatham House Publishers, 1999). For the same on George W. Bush, see Sinclair, "Context, Strategy and Chance: George W. Bush and the 107th Congress," and Barbara Sinclair, "Living (and Dying?) by the Sword: George W. Bush as Legislative Leader" in Colin Campbell and Bert Rockman, eds., *The Bush Legacy* (Washington, DC: CQ Press, 2007).

7. See Henry Farrell, "Consensus, Dissensus and Economic Ideas: The Rise and Fall of Keynesianism during the Economic Crisis," manuscript, March 9, 2012. Also Michael Grunwald, *The New New Deal: The Hidden Story of Change in the Obama Era* (New York: Simon & Schuster, 2012).

8. Robert Draper, *Do Not Ask What Good We Do: Inside the U.S. House of Representatives* (New York: Free Press, 2012), 26.

9. Alex Isenstadt and Patrick O'Conner, "Unanimous 'no' from House GOP," *Politico*, February 13, 2009.

10. Anne-Laure Beaussier, "The Patient Protection and Affordable Care Act: The Victory of Unorthodox Lawmaking," *Journal of Health Politics, Policy and Law*, June 14, 2012, 775.

11. Carl Hulse, "Sweeping Health Care Plan Passes House," *New York Times*, November 8, 2009.

12. John Stanton and Steven T. Dennis, "Moderates MIA during Demoratic Victory Lap," *Roll Call*, December 23, 2009.

13. On the Budget Act, see James Thurber and Samantha Durst, "The 1990 Budget Enforcement Act: The Decline of Congressional Accountability," in Dodd and Oppenheimer, *Congress Reconsidered*, 5th ed., and Walter J. Oleszek, *Congressional Procedures and the Policy Process*, 7th ed. (Washington, DC: CQ Press, 2007).

14. Barbara Sinclair, "The New World of U.S. Senators," in Lawrence C. Dodd and Bruce I. Oppenheimer, eds., *Congress Reconsidered*, 10th ed. (Washington, DC: CQ Press, 2013).

15. Thomas E. Mann and Norman J. Ornstein, *It's Even Worse Than It Looks: How the American Constitutional System Collided With the New Politics of Extremism* (New York: Basic Books, 2012).

16. Sinclair, "The President as Legislative Leader."

17. *Congressional Quarterly Weekly*, March 26, 2012, 596–99.

18. Mann and Ornstein, *It's Even Worse Than It Looks*, 19.

19. Joseph J. Schatz, "Boehner, Obama Take Over Talks," *Congressional Quarterly Weekly*, June 27, 2011, 1376.

20. See, for example, Peter Wallsten, Lori Montgomery, and Scott Wilson, "Obama's Evolution: Behind the Failed 'Grand Bargain' on the Debt," *Washington Post*, March 17, 2012, and Matt Bai, "Obama vs. Boehner: Who Killed the Debt Deal?," *New York Times*, March 28, 2012.

21. CQ Staff, "Dueling Plans Set Stage for High Drama," *Congressional Quarterly Weekly*, August 1, 2011, 1692.

22. "Highlights of Budget Control Act," *Congressional Quarterly Weekly*, August 8, 2011, 1761–62.

Chapter Seven

The President, Congress, and Lobbyists

Has President Obama Changed the
Way Washington Works? [1]

James A. Thurber

Widespread scandal and public opinion helped to fuel Senator Obama's non-stop attack on the role of lobbyists in American politics starting as the ethics and lobbying reform leader in the US Senate in 2006–2007 and continuing in his 2008 election campaign and repeated with his sustained attempts to change the culture of lobbying and influence in Congress and Washington in his first four years as president. Lobbying is a profession that has been deeply sullied in the early 2000s by the illegal actions and conviction of Jack Abramoff, the criminal convictions of Representatives "Duke" Cunningham (bribes for earmarks) and Bob Ney (accepting illegal gifts from lobbyists), the resignation and conviction of Representative Tom DeLay (illegal use of corporate campaign funds from lobbyists), the conviction (later overturned) of Senator Ted Stevens (illegal gifts from lobbyists), as well as the criminal indictments of twenty-six and conviction of former congressional aides and executive branch employees. In 2009 and 2010, Congressman Charles Rangel (D-NY) was asked to step down as chair of the powerful House Ways and Means Committee and after a lengthy investigation and trial before the House Ethics Committee, he was convicted on eleven counts related to breaking House ethics gift ban and travel rules associated with lobbyists. The House Ethics Committee also investigated Representatives Todd Tiahrt (R-KS), Peter Visclosky (D-ID), John Murtha (D-PA), Norm Dick (D-WA), and Jim Moran (D-VA), all on the House Appropriations Committee, for campaign contributions for earmarks from corporations through PMA, a now-defunct lobbying firm. [2] The rapid increase in campaign spending and lobbying expenditures, negative public attitudes about lobbying, and general anger with Congress also set the political environment for reform.

Are lobbyists distorting what is in the public interest, undermining public trust in Congress and ultimately the integrity of American democracy, as argued by Senator/candidate/President Obama? Has President Obama changed the murky world of the revolving door of lobbyists/advocates in campaigns and government? Has he changed the way Congress and Washington works? These are not new questions[3] for Washington; they echo James Madison's lament in Federalist Paper Number 10.

Complaints are everywhere heard from our most considerate and virtuous citizens, equally the friends of public and private faith, and of public and personal liberty, that our governments are too unstable, that the public good is disregarded in the conflicts of rival parties, and that measures are too often decided, not according to the rules of justice and the rights of the minor party, but by the superior force of an interested and overbearing majority. However anxiously we may wish that these complaints had no foundation, the evidence of known facts will not permit us to deny that they are in some degree true.

This chapter explores the causes, characteristics, and consequences of President Barack Obama's attacks on lobbyists and his attempt to change the way Congress and Washington works. It concludes with a discussion of the barriers President Obama has faced in reforming Congress and pluralist democracy in Washington.

Lobbying and ethics reform started for President Obama when he was a senator and continues into his second term as president. With Obama's leadership and the bipartisan help of Senator McCain, reform of ethics and lobbying in Congress in 2006 resulted in the passage of the most significant reform since 1995, the Honest Leadership and Open Government Act (HLOGA) of 2007.[4] HLOGA attempts to slow or stop the "revolving door" between public service and lobbying, to curb excesses in privately funded travel and gifts, and to enhance disclosure and transparency of lobbying activities. The 1995 Lobbying Disclosure Act (LDA) and HLOGA define lobbying and lobbyists and require those who register under the acts to disclose the identities of people attempting to influence government, the subject matters of their attempts, and the amounts of money they spend to accomplish their goals on a quarterly basis.[5] Senator Obama's goal in HLOGA was supposed to make it easier for the public to know about campaign contributions from lobbyists to lawmakers and to make it easier for the public to be aware of lobbyist advocacy topics, targets, and expenditures. HLOGA prohibits senior Senate staff and Senate officers from lobbying contacts with the entire Senate for two years, instead of just their former employing office. The act also continues to prohibit senior House staff from lobbying their former office or committee for one year after they leave House employment.

Obama continued his pointed criticism of lobbyists, Congress, and the role of money in Washington with his reform agenda in his 2008 election campaign and ethics reforms in his first few months in office. The overwhelming public perception of lobbyists, whether convicted or investigated for malfeasance, is that they are bad, a corrupting influence on government and the way Washington works. This negative public perception was a major cause of President Obama's attacks on lobbyists as part of his campaigning and governing style. The public had high expectations for President Obama changing the way Congress and Washington works by changing the lobbying and influence culture in Washington, a popular issue during and after the 2008 campaign. President Obama has used that public anger with Washington in his attempts to garner support for his policies on the Hill. Fifty-eight percent of the respondents in the 2008 Cooperative Congressional Election Study (CCES) national poll felt Obama would be very likely or somewhat likely to change the way Washington works.[6] After the economic crisis, government corruption was the second-most important issue mentioned by voters in national surveys in 2008 and the most important issue among the electorate in the midterm election of 2006. Anger against Washington politics continued to be a major issue in the 2010 midterm elections. Americans think lobbyists have too much power, as shown in the Harris Interactive survey results to the following question: "Do you think political lobbyists have too much or too little power and influence in Washington?"[7]

The growing number of respondents over the past seven years who believe lobbyists have too much influence and a decline in those who think they have too little reveals a need for reform.[8]

Candidate Barack Obama in 2008 captured the anger with Congress, lobbying, and the way Washington works when he made this promise to the public:

> I intend to tell the corporate lobbyists that their days of setting the agenda in Washington are over, that they had not funded my campaigns, and from my first day as president, I will launch the most sweeping ethics reform in U.S. history. We will make government more open, more accountable and more responsive to the problems of the American people.[9]

Although candidate Obama promised to change the way lobbyists influence Washington politics, as president he has found changing the lobbying industry difficult because of its size, adaptability, and the integral part it plays in America's pluralist democracy. By official estimates, lobbying is the third-largest enterprise in our nation's capital, after government and tourism.[10] As of January 1, 2009, there were over twenty-seven thousand federal-registered lobbyists representing virtually every type of interest in America. The number of registered lobbyists dropped precipitously in the first twelve

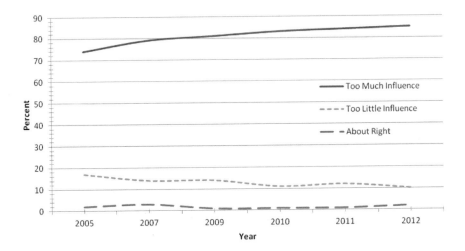

**Figure 7.1. Public Opinion on How Much Influence Lobbyists Have, 2005–2012.
Source: Harris Interactive 2012.**

months of the Obama administration to fourteen thousand and then to 8,500
in 2012. However, the number of persons employed in Washington who are
either lobbyists or are associated with all dimensions of the advocacy industry (registered and unregistered advocates and supporting institutions) has
been estimated to be well over one hundred thousand.[11] Spending by registered lobbyists has increased 62 percent in the last five years from $2 billion
to $3.5 billion in 2010, but that is just the visible, registered activities. The
$3.5 billion is just the tip of the lobbying-expenditures iceberg, because it
includes only what is recorded by registered lobbyists in public records. This
astonishingly averages out to over $18 million in lobbying expenditures each
day Congress was in session in 2012. This does not include money spent for
other forms of lobbying such as grassroots organizing; coalition building;
issue advertising on television, radio, and in the print media; support of think
tanks; issue-related survey research; and advocacy on the Internet. There are
estimates that the total spent on lobbying is closer to $9 billion per year in
Washington—or about three times the officially reported amount. Candidate
Obama promised to change Congress and Washington, something American
people wanted. He started by banning federal registered lobbyists from his
campaign organization.[12]

President Obama used these attacks on lobbyists as a way to build support
for his policy agenda in 2009, especially in the battle over health-care reform
and major changes in financial regulation.[13] President Obama used his executive power to restrict lobbyists from service in government and limit their
access to policy making in the executive branch. Immediately after he was

sworn into office he also directed his departments and agencies to avoid even the appearance of conflicts of interest (EO 13490). President Obama also continued his unrelenting criticism of congressional earmarks.

President Obama is fighting an integral part of pluralist representative democracy in the United States. Lobbyists, interest groups, and advocates of all kinds are increasingly influential and controversial both in American elections and governing, impacting the quality of campaigns and elections and later governing and policy making. Lobbyists influence the way issues and problems are framed and ultimately the way policy is made in Washington. They promote candidates and policies, raise money, sway voters, and continue their influence through major lobbying campaigns after an election. They provide services such as general strategic advice; issue advocacy advertising, polling, and advice about media strategy; and organize get-out-the-vote (GOTV) strategies, general tactical guidance for candidates, and many volunteers.[14] Ultimately President Obama is trying to limit the continuation of these identical services and tactics after elections during major issue battles in the policy process, as seen with his tax and spending agenda, climate change legislation, health-care reform, financial-regulatory reform, immigration policy, gun control, and education policies. A major dilemma for President Obama is sometimes that he likes lobbyists and other times he attacks them; sometimes he tries to stop them and other times he needs them; they have become essential to his legislative strategy.

During his first five years in office, President Obama has attacked lobbyists dozens of times for hindering or stopping his policy agenda, and for undermining democracy and the public interest, while at other times he uses them to help push through reforms. He used criticisms about the role of lobbyists and money in politics to his advantage in building support for health-care reform and financial-regulation reforms, but was later criticized for "selling out" to the special interests when compromises were necessary to pass those historic reforms. For example, in a speech on the need for health-care reform on March 19, 2010, he attacked health-insurance lobbyists for stopping what he felt was in the public interest:

> At the heart of this debate is the question of whether we're going to accept a system that works better for the insurance companies than it does for the American people because if this vote fails, the insurance industry will continue to run amok. They will continue to deny people coverage. They will continue to deny people care. They will continue to jack up premiums 40 or 50 or 60 percent as they have in the last few weeks without any accountability whatsoever. They know this. And that's why their lobbyists are stalking the halls of Congress as we speak, and pouring millions of dollars into negative ads. And that's why they are doing everything they can to kill this bill.[15]

President Obama reiterated his criticisms of lobbyists in his State of the Union message on January 27, 2010 and pledged again to lead the effort to change the way they work in Washington.

> It's time to require lobbyists to disclose each contact they make on behalf of a client with my administration or with Congress. It's time to put strict limits on the contributions that lobbyists give to candidates for federal office. Each time lobbyists game the system or politicians tear each other down instead of lifting this country up, we lose faith. The more those TV pundits reduce serious debates to silly arguments and big issues into sound bites, our citizens turn away. No wonder there's so much cynicism.[16]

However, he publicly praised his "stakeholders" (often federal registered lobbyists) from organizations like the American Association of Retired Persons (AARP), the pharmaceutical industry, the American Hospital Association, the American Medical Association, and yes, the health-insurance industry, in passing his historic health-care reform legislation. What is the difference between lobbyists and nonregistered stakeholder advocates (e.g., former Senator Tom Daschle)—both public advocates for his policies? President Obama's rhetoric makes a difference. Voters think lobbyists are corrupting Congress and Washington, as argued relentlessly by President Obama. However, advocates and lobbyists cite the same source of legitimacy; that is, a fundamental right of free speech, of assembly, and to petition government for grievances, all guaranteed under the First Amendment. A federal registered lobbyist is defined in law and must report quarterly the details of their lobbying activities, clients, and money spent; fines and jail are possible for those who do not comply.[17] Stakeholders and those giving strategic advice and hire federal registered lobbyists in issue campaigns are not held to that standard; their activities and spending are not reported publicly. Generally their advocacy role is nontransparent.

Early in his administration President Obama continued his passion to reform lobbying and the way Congress and Washington works by instituting more regulations to reduce conflicts of interest and to increase transparency about the lobbying industry. He started by restricting participation by federal registered lobbyists on his transition team. He instituted a strong code of ethics for all executive branch appointees, implemented a tough gift ban, passed more transparency rules for decision making, and on his first day in office he issued an executive order restricting the "revolving door" of lobbyists both in and out of government.[18] He also banned direct lobbying for funds and tax breaks from the Troubled Assets Relief Program (TARP) (Public Law 110-343) and the 2009 economic stimulus package bill. Early in President Obama's first term in office he centralized White House control over government ethics and lobbying by hiring lobbying reformer Norm Eisen to head this policy in the transition and later as Special Counsel to the

President for Ethics and Government (the Ethics Czar). Eisen led the drafting of President Obama's two historic executive orders and several presidential memos on lobbying and ethics, as listed in the following text box. President Obama tried to change the way Washington works by attempting to bring more transparency, to encourage more public participation in decision making, to reduce conflicts of interest in his administration, and by pressuring Congress to reform itself.

President Obama's Ethics and Lobbying Reforms, 2009–2010

- Ethics Commitments by Executive Branch Personnel, Executive Order 13490, January 21, 2009.
- Memorandum for the Heads of Executive Departments and Agencies on Transparency and Open Government, January 21, 2009.
- Memorandum for the Heads of Executive Departments and Agencies on Ensuring Responsible Spending of Recovery Act Funds, March 20, 2009.
- Reducing Improper Payments and Eliminating Waste in Federal Programs, Executive Order 13520, November 23, 2009.
- Memorandum for the Heads of Executive Departments and Agencies on Freedom of Information Act, December 18, 2009.
- President Obama's Weekly Address: President Obama Vows to Continue Standing Up to the Special Interests on Behalf of the American People, January 23, 2010.

Source: WhiteHouse.gov, Briefing Room, May 2010.

THE CONSEQUENCES OF OBAMA'S REFORMS FOR CONGRESS AND WASHINGTON

Rhetoric, executive orders, regulations, and law aside, what has been the reality of the congressional and White House "revolving door" in the Obama administration? The lobbyist-White House revolving door in and out of government is prohibited by President Obama's executive order, but it has proven difficult to break old habits in the way Washington works, and exceptions have been granted. Also "advocates," who are not federal registered lobbyists, have heavily populated the Obama White House and departments. Other advocates and other nonfederal registered lobbyists, like former Senator Tom Daschle and former President of the Center for American Progress (CAP) John Podesta, have often had easy access to the White House, as shown on the White House log of visitors.[19] The campaigning and later advocacy activities of former Senator Daschle and CAP President Podesta, who both played key roles in the Obama campaign and his transition, are examples of people with outside interests who have inside access to power in the White House. Although negative publicity about his nonpayment of taxes prevented Daschle from being appointed Secretary of the US Department of Health and Human Services and the White House health policy czar, he played a prominent advocacy role in the White House and on the Hill in the battle for health-care reform and other issues. Because of the new transparency rules in the White House, there is a public record of dozens of meetings between Daschle, Podesta, and White House staff (including the President) during health-care battles in 2009 and 2010.[20]

Campaign consultants-turned-lobbyists/advocates who build strong reciprocal relationships with candidates-turned-elected office holders (presidents) or appointed officials (secretaries of departments) are part of the Washington political culture that President Obama is finding difficult to reform. One of the reasons is that he is also using these relationships to help move his policy agenda as revealed by the log of visitors from a variety of special interests. He has not stopped the prominent role of lobbyists in campaigning in 2008, 2010, and 2012 nor in governing during his first five years in office. The Sunlight Foundation analyzed the White House visitor logs and found, for example, that within a few months of being sworn in, President Obama and his top White House aides met dozens of times with leaders from the pharmaceutical industry, unions, AARP, the American Medical Association, the American Hospital Association, American automobile companies, bankers, Wall Street executives, and other "special interests" to develop health-care and Wall Street reforms that eventually passed in Congress.[21] Sunlight Foundation analysis of Federal Election Commission records and lobbying disclosure records by these organizations also showed sharp increases in campaign contributions and lobbying expenditures for health-care issues from these organizations during 2009 and 2010.[22] The pharmaceutical industry spent over $28 million on lobbyists, $8 million on campaign contributions to both Democrats and Republicans on the Hill, and over $100 million on issue advertising that went to White House Senior Adviser David Axelrod's former firm AKPD (which owed Axelrod $2 million).[23]

These questions about lobbyists and interest groups present several ethical problems for American democracy that President Obama uses in his attacks on lobbyists and the need to reform the way Washington works. The first problem and probably the most prominent one used by President Obama is the enormous amount of campaign money raised and spent by interest groups for candidates and political parties, which raises serious ethical questions about corruption in financing elections.[24] The cost of all presidential and congressional campaigns, including soft money and issue advertising by interest groups, reached approximately $5 billion in the 2008 electoral cycle and $4 billion in the 2010 midterm elections, and $6 billion in 2012, more than doubling the campaign expenditures of four and six years earlier.[25]

President Obama had little impact on reducing the amount of money raised and spent in 2010 and 2012. He helped the congressional Democrats raise large amounts of money from interest groups for the 2010 midterm election. However, President Obama has argued that the amount of issue advertising, independent expenditures, and campaign services raised from interest groups and "super PACs" often dwarfs the input from voters, political parties, and other groups with fewer resources, thereby almost insuring narrow and possibly exclusive interest-group influence on public policy making. The money spent in campaigns (an estimated $6 billion in 2012), added to the increasing amounts used in lobbying issues, is substantial. There was a steep increase in lobbying expenditures by federal registered lobbyists from 1998 to 2012 ($1.43 billion in 1998 to an estimated $3.3 billion in 2012). The increase in the amount of money spent by federal registered lobbyists and others in the advocacy business involved in battles over the stimulus legislation, health-care reform, financial regulation, and climate change (cap and trade) alone was massive in 2009–2010 ($7 billion by registered lobbyists alone). It continued in 2011–2013 over debt and deficit reduction, tax reform, immigration, and gun control. Moreover, not included is the money spent on other lobbyist-related activities such as paid media (issue ads), grassroots, grass tops, coalition building and maintenance, use of the Internet, survey research, supporting think tanks, and a variety of other nonregulated advocacy tactics that many think would triple the actual amount of advocacy spending in Washington. President Obama has not been able to stop this flow of money and influence on Congress. There was an unintended consequence of President Obama's expansive policy agenda; a new spending frenzy by lobbyists and interest groups for and against his reforms on the Hill.

The amount of money spent on campaigns increased substantially in the 2010 midterm election (estimated over $4 billion) and 2012 ($6 billion), partially as a result of the *Citizens United vs. FEC* Supreme Court case.[26] All of these new dollars may well undermine the "common good" through the maximization of narrow interests and the enhancement of oligarchy in the US political system.[27] Candidate Obama has tried to reduce special-interest campaign spending by soliciting small contributions through the Internet and by encouraging people to give to his campaign rather than 527 groups in 2008 and 2012.[28] He has criticized the *Citizens United* decision and has argued that it will make it more difficult for him to change the way money and politics work in Washington.[29] The massive increase in the 2010 and 2012 election-campaign finance from special-interest groups, often nontransparent, confirms President Obama's fears. Congress and Washington have not changed.

A second issue identified by Obama (and scholars) is that interest groups feed the negative effects of the "permanent campaign," defined by Hugh Heclo as "the combination of image making and strategic calculation that turns governing into a perpetual campaign and remakes government into an instrument designed to sustain an elected official's popularity."[30] This results in an unrelenting demand from incumbents for campaign funds that are more easily collected from particular interest groups than broad-based networks. In an era of seeming endless partisan parity, the permanent campaign creates the need for advice from campaign consultants-lobbyists that is broadened beyond the strategy of conducting a winning campaign to include which issues and policies to embrace in order to win the next election. National politics has thus gone past the stage of campaigning to govern and has reached the "more truly corrupted condition of governing to campaign," with campaign consultants and lobbyists playing a central role in the phenomenon.[31] Although President Obama has tried to be the postpartisan president, it has not worked. Although he tried to break the lock of extreme partisanship, wedge issues, and the constant campaigning, President Obama failed to change this characteristic of Congress and the way Washington works. There is little evidence that either he or the Republicans have stopped the permanent campaign. Divided party government in the 112th and 113th Congresses has exacerbated the permanent campaign.

A third problem is when interest groups participate in election campaigns, through money or services, and also hire or use their own lobbyists, serious ethical questions of conflict of interest arise, particularly the question of who is paying for what. Serious consequences for public policy making are likely to occur. Candidate Obama did not stop this practice. President Obama encouraged it during the 2010 midterm election campaign to help elect Democrats to the House and Senate and did not eliminate it in his 2012 campaign. Are the lobbyist-consultants loyal to the issues as lobbyists for their private clients, or to the public interest? President Obama has not stopped the growth in the number and influence of lobbyist/advocate-campaign consultants in the last five years, another measure of changing Congress and Washington.

A fourth problem President Obama has raised stems from a major norm of political life generally: reciprocity. Has President Obama outlawed the norm of reciprocity in the way Congress and Washington works? It is unlikely. Reciprocity is one of the strongest imbedded norms in public life. It is directly related to ethical dilemmas that occur in the linkage among consultants, lobbyists, and members of Congress. The "iron law of reciprocity" is like gravity. That it exists is beyond dispute. Reciprocity is defined as: "To return in kind or degree; the mutual or equivalent exchange or paying back of what one has received; a mutual exchange; mutual dependence, action or influence; a mutual exchange of privileges."[32] Reciprocity is expected in personal relationships and it is a strong influence on political relationships in campaigns, lobbying, governing, and public policy making.

Reciprocity can be the basis of the movement of people through the political and government "revolving door." Reciprocity, campaign contributions, and the drive for political self-preservation (reelection) are central to these ethical dilemmas, something President Obama has not stopped or even slowed. Candidates with the most campaign resources are able to hire campaign professionals with the best reputations, thus improving their probability of winning elections. Most of the campaign contributions (money, volunteers, and services) come from powerful businesses, unions, associations, and interest groups.[33] Well-known campaign consultants also help generate campaign funds, thus helping to build incumbency advantage for the next election. These consultants are successful during an election year and also in off-election years because their business volume relies on both campaigns and lobbying. Electoral success for top campaign consultants often leads to lobbying success or service in government (e.g., President Bush's Karl Rove and President Obama's David Axelrod). Where is their loyalty? How does it change when employment changes? President Obama has not broken the strong linkage of mutual exchange and personal relationships in Congress through his attacks on the way Washington works, nor through his executive orders. Reciprocity is at the heart of contemporary politics in the United States, for President Obama and Congress, but may well be a strong factor that reduces public trust in the Congress and policy-making process. The public's strong negative reaction to spending earmarks, especially in the 2008, 2010, and 2012 elections, is partially about this problem of reciprocity and what is in the public interest.

President Obama has not smashed the reciprocal nexus of campaign consultants and lobbyists in policy-making networks as shown with Congress and in his own White House. His governing style in his first five years in office uses advocates from outside government to build coalitions of support. Some are federal registered lobbyists and many are not; they all represent special interests in America.[34] Campaign consultants and lobbyists/advocates build relationships that help bring money to campaigns to help candidates win and to later influence elected public officials, including the president. President Obama has tried to break those ties, rhetorically and legally, but with limited success. He has proven that he needs those relationships to govern, thus not changing the way Washington works.

Public complaints about the quality of election discourse and lack of trust in government is a fifth problem that President Obama has said stems directly from interest-group activity in elections.[35] The reciprocal close ties of campaign consultants-lobbyists/advocates-public officials were certainly a factor fostering voter cynicism toward government in 2008 and 2010. However, President Obama's attacks on lobbyists may have increased expectations of reform and reinforce and encourage distrust in their role in American democracy. The level of trust in President Obama, Congress, and other governmental institutions has declined significantly during his administration.[36] In fact, it has been declining over the last three decades for a variety of reasons, but one major factor is certainly the public perception about the way money and lobbyists work with Congress and in Washington.[37]

Consequences and Barriers

Has President Obama's lobbying and ethics reforms protected our democratic system from abuses by lobbyists/advocates and campaign consultants? Has he succeeded in changing Congress and the way Washington works with lobbyist and advocates of special interests? Has he helped protect the "public good" over private gain?[38] President Obama has prominently paraphrased and used James Madison's argument in *Federalist* No. 10 that factions or narrow interests undermine the rights of other citizens and that it is the duties of government to regulate the factions so that they do not do harm to others.[39] President Obama also agrees with Madison when he stated that factions (interest groups and lobbyists) are "adverse to the rights of other citizens or the permanent and aggregate interests of the community."[40] President Obama has also used the arguments found in Madison's *Federalist* No. 45 that emphasizes that the public good is a collective or communal interest that is different from the individual rights of special interests. Madison (and Obama) argues that:

> It is too early for politicians to presume or forget that the public good, the real welfare of the great body of the people, is the supreme object to be pursued; and that no form of government whatever has any other value than as it may be fitted for the attainment of this object.[41]

The major lobbying and ethics reforms in 2007 (HLOGA), a major success of Senator Obama, and President Obama's new regulations over lobbyists and public statements criticizing lobbyists, as well meaning as they were intended to be, do not seem to have significantly reduced public and media suspicion of lobbyists and campaign consultants. In the first five years of his administration, President Obama's lobbying reforms and his effort to change the way Washington works, boil down to three basic principles of sound government: transparency, accountability, and enforcement.

First, President Obama has brought some new transparency. Has he brought public policy making into the open? President Obama's transparency initiatives have had limited effect. President Obama has tried to bring an unprecedented amount of transparency to the deliberations in the White House and in the executive-branch agencies. However, with his attacks on lobbyists have come a flood of deregistrations of federal registered lobbyists (declining from twenty-seven thousand to fourteen thousand in 2009 to an estimated eight thousand in 2012), at the same time the "advocates" have increased to approximately ninety thousand, which leads to less transparency of who is lobbying, for whom and what, and how much money is being spent on those advocacy activities. [42]

President Obama has called for more accountability and enforcement of the law and rules related to lobbying and ethics. He has made it clear who is responsible for monitoring and maintaining ethical behavior for the White House and the agencies, the Office of Government Ethics in the White House, and other executive branch departmental ethics offices. The Ethics Committees in the House and Senate have responsibility for enforcing rules of ethics for members of Congress and staff. President Obama's new rules have brought more accountability for lobbyists and executive-branch officials, but ultimately it is the responsibility of Congress to assure accountability through its oversight and investigative function, and through its ability to make its own members account for their behavior. It is the responsibility of the Department of Justice to investigate and prosecute illegal lobbying behavior. There have been over five thousand referrals from Congress to the Department of Justice under LDA and HLOGA since 2007, but there have been no investigations. [43] The House and Senate Ethics Committees have had several high-profile investigations (Representatives Rangel and Waters in 2009 and 2010), but seem to be lapsing into their old habits of overlooking or "enforcement lite" when it comes to members and staff malfeasance.

President Obama's rhetorical goals and ethics rules and lobbying regulations fall far short of fulfilling these three basic principles. Lobbying disclosure, especially with the dramatic decline of federal registered lobbyists in 2009 and 2010, is limited in its reach across the many forms of public issue advocacy. Increased deregistration of lobbyists has resulted in a lack of transparency about who is advocating for whom, on what issue, and most importantly, about how much they are spending on those lobbying campaigns. An unintended consequence of President Obama's attempt to reduce conflicts of interest has seriously limited those with expertise from serving as appointees and on government advisory panels. Little seems to have fundamentally changed in lobbying whether it is done transparently or nontransparently. President Obama has changed the rhetoric, but not the way Washington works.

Accountability and compliance with the law, let alone strong ethical norms, is spotty and often is greatly dependent on media investigation and reporting of questionable behavior. President Obama has not weakened the reciprocal networks among members of Congress, lobbyists-advocates, and campaign consultants, especially when he turns to them to help build coalitions and support for his programs. These networks still dominate major public policy making. It is the norm in the way Congress, the president, and Washington works. President Obama's executive orders have set a new high standard of transparency, accountability, enforcement, and public participation to address these questions, but the implementation, enforcement, and impact of his reforms are not yet transforming Washington. It limits those who can be appointed to executive positions, but it has had little impact on those who participate in decision-making processes, especially nonregistered advocates from specialized interests. Moreover, President Obama has worked closely, often in a nontransparent way, with networks of lobbyists/advocates in crafting the economic-stimulus funding, tax reform, health-care reform, financial-regulatory reforms, the federal budget deficit and debit, climate change legislation, education reform, immigration policy, gun control reform, and a wide array of other issues on his public policy agenda. He has also met with many campaign contributors who have a vested interest in the policy battles, but are not federal registered lobbyists. Is it any different for President Obama to meet with corporate CEOs or union leaders confidentially (which he does regularly) or the lobbyists hired by them (whom he attacks publicly)? Does the transparency inherent in the visitor's log of the White House and executive branch agencies foster better government or merely allow the public to see who gets in to see decision makers?

President Obama's populist rhetoric of greater transparency, more accountability, increased enforcement, and wider participation by the American public has been a popular theme. His failure to reach these goals helped to create the angry backlash against Democrats by the electorate in the historic 2010 midterm election and continues in the 113th Congress.[44] The constitutional and political reality of Washington has so far hobbled President Obama's ability to bring major change to Congress and the way public policies are made. Public attitudes about how Congress works, the role of money, and the place of lobbyists in politics are still very bad. Citizens have gotten even more negative about Congress, and President Obama has lost popular support since he has taken office as shown so clearly by outcome of the historic 2010 midterm elections and in the rhetoric of the 2012 presidential election. Obama has promised change, to be the reform postpartisan president, but he has quickly adapted to the realities of working with Congress and governing. He has tried to reform lobbying and Congress as a senator, candidate, and president, but he has failed to meet the high expectations of the American public to change the role of lobbyists and specialized interests in congressional policy making.

NOTES

    1. See James A. Thurber, "The Contemporary Presidency: Changing the Way Washington Works? Assessing President Obama's Battle with Lobbyists," *Presidential Studies Quarterly* 41, no. 2 (June 2011): 358–74 for an early assessment of President Obama's impact on the way Washington works.

    2. For a criticism of Representative Norm Dick's relationship with Boeing and PMA see Dana Milbank, "Mr. Boeing Is about to Be Mr. Spending," *Washington Post*, May 9, 2010.

3. From James Madison's Federalist Paper Number 10: "Complaints are everywhere heard from our most considerate and virtuous citizens, equally the friends of public and private faith, and of public and personal liberty, that our governments are too unstable, that the public good is disregarded in the conflicts of rival parties, and that measures are too often decided, not according to the rules of justice and the rights of the minor party, but by the superior force of an interested and overbearing majority. However anxiously we may wish that these complaints had no foundation, the evidence, of known facts will not permit us to deny that they are in some degree true."

4. Honest Leadership and Open Government Act of 2007 (Pub. L. 110-81, 121 Stat. 735 [September 14, 2007]).

5. A person who must register as a federal lobbyist : (1) is employed or retained by a client for compensation; (2) has made more than one lobbying contact on behalf of such client; and (3) spends at least 20 percent of his/her time working for that client during a three-month quarter on "lobbying activities" (defined in the LDA).

6. See Center for Congressional and Presidential Studies 2008 Cooperative Congressional Election Study (CCES) voter opinion survey results on President Obama and lobbying reform.

7. Harris Interactive, 2012.

8. While public perception does not give a true indication of the performance of the lobbying industry itself, it may speak to a misunderstanding held by the American people of what lobbyists do.

9. James A. Thurber, "Obama's Battle with Lobbyists," in James A. Thurber, ed. *Obama in Office* (Boulder, CO: Paradigm Publishers, 2011).

10. See James A. Thurber, "Corruption and Scandal in Washington: Have Lobbying and Ethics Reform Made a Difference? Exploring the Relationship among Candidates, Campaign Consultants, Lobbyists, and Elected and Appointed Public Officials," paper for Conference on Political Corruption in America at Loyola Marymount University, Institute for Leadership Studies, February 23, 2009.

11. Sharyl Attkisson, "Behind the Closed Doors of Washington Lobbyists," *CBS News*, October 7, 2012, www.cbsnews.com/8301-3445_162-57527490/behind-the-closed-doors-of-washington-lobbyists/.

12. Both candidates publicly banned federal registered lobbyists from serving on their campaign staffs, but forty-two top campaign staffers for McCain were recently lobbyists and twenty-three top campaign staffers for Obama were recently lobbyists.

13. See Center for Congressional and Presidential Studies 2008 Cooperative Congressional Election Study (CCES) voter opinion survey results on President Obama and lobbying reform.

14. James A. Thurber and Candice J. Nelson, eds., *Campaign Warriors: Campaign Consultants in Elections* (Washington, DC: Brookings Press, 2000) and Stephen K. Medvic, *Political Consultants in U.S. Congressional Elections* (Columbus: Ohio State University Press, 2001).

15. Speech at George Mason University Patriot Center, March 19, 2010.

16. State of the Union Message, January 19, 2010.

17. A lobbyist is an individual (1) who is employed or retained by a client for compensation; (2) who has made more than one lobbying contact on behalf of such client; and (3) who spends at least 20 percent of his/her time working for that client during a three-month quarter on "lobbying activities" (defined in the LDA).

18. See President Obama's January 21, 2009, Executive Order 13490 on the revolving door in "Ethics Commitments by Executive Branch Personnel." The highlights of the Executive Order follow:

> Section 1. *Ethics Pledge.* Every appointee in every executive agency appointed on or after January 20, 2009, shall sign, and upon signing shall be contractually committed to, the following pledge upon becoming an appointee:
>
> As a condition, and in consideration, of my employment in the United States Government in a position invested with the public trust, I commit myself to the following obligations, which I understand are binding on me and are enforceable under law:

1. *Lobbyist Gift Ban.* I will not accept gifts from registered lobbyists or lobbying organizations for the duration of my service as an appointee.
2. *Revolving Door Ban—All Appointees Entering Government.* I will not for a period of 2 years from the date of my appointment participate in any particular matter involving specific parties that is directly and substantially related to my former employer or former clients, including regulations and contracts.
3. *Revolving Door Ban—Lobbyists Entering Government.* If I was a registered lobbyist within the 2 years before the date of my appointment, in addition to abiding by the limitations of paragraph 2, I will not for a period of 2 years after the date of my appointment:

   a. participate in any particular matter on which I lobbied within the 2 years before the date of my appointment;
   b. participate in the specific issue area in which that particular matter falls; or
   c. seek or accept employment with any executive agency that I lobbied within the 2 years before the date of my appointment.

19. See WhiteHouse.gov visitor's log for 2009–2012.

20. As part of President Obama's commitment to government transparency, the White House provides records of White House visitors on an ongoing basis online. In December 2009, the White House began posting all White House visitor records for the period from September 15 onward. In addition, as part of its new policy, they will post records dating from January 20 that are specifically requested on an ongoing basis.

21. See www.sunlightfoundation.com for analysis.

22. www.sunlightfoundation.com.

23. See "Politico Playbook" by Mike Allen, October 27, 2012. www.politico.com/playbook. Axelrod returned to his firm after the 2012 election to make millions of dollars from clients who are interested in influencing public policy.

24. Michael J. Malbin and Thomas J. Gais, *The Day After Reform: Sobering Campaign Finance Lessons from the American States* (Albany, NY: Rockefeller Institute Press, 1998); Robert K. Goidel, Donald A. Gross, and Todd G. Shields, *Money Matters* (Lanham, MD: Rowman & Littlefield, 1999); and David Magleby and Candice J. Nelson, *The Money Chase: Congressional Campaign Finance Reform* (Washington, DC: Brookings Press, 1990).

25. Burdett Loomis, "The Industry of Politics," unpublished manuscript, Department of Political Science, University of Kansas (November 2001), 1.

26. *Citizens United v. Federal Election Commission* was a landmark decision by the US Supreme Court holding that corporate funding of independent political broadcasts in candidate elections cannot be limited under the First Amendment. The 5 to 4 decision resulted from a dispute over whether the non-profit corporation Citizens United could air via video-on-demand a critical film about Hillary Clinton, and whether the group could advertise the film in broadcast ads featuring Clinton's image, in apparent violation of the 2002 Bipartisan Campaign Reform Act commonly known as the McCain-Feingold Act.

27. See Jeffrey A. Winters and Benjamin I. Page, "Oligarchy in the United States?" *Perspectives on Politics* 7, no. 4 (December 2009): 731–51.

28. A 527 organization or 527 group is a type of American tax-exempt organization named after a section of the US Tax Code. A 527 group is created primarily to influence the nomination, election, appointment, or defeat of candidates for public office. Although candidate committees and political action committees are also created under Section 527, the term is generally used to refer to political organizations that are not regulated by the Federal Election Commission or by a state elections commission, and are not subject to the same contribution limits as PACs.

29. On January 21, 2010, President Obama stated: "With its ruling today, the Supreme Court has given a green light to a new stampede of special interest money in our politics. It is a major victory for big oil, Wall Street banks, health insurance companies and the other powerful interests that marshal their power every day in Washington to drown out the voices of everyday

Americans. This ruling gives the special interests and their lobbyists even more power in Washington—while undermining the influence of average Americans who make small contributions to support their preferred candidates. That's why I am instructing my Administration to get to work immediately with Congress on this issue. We are going to talk with bipartisan Congressional leaders to develop a forceful response to this decision. The public interest requires nothing less."

30. Hugh Heclo, "Campaigning and Governing: A Conspectus," in Norman Ornstein and Thomas Mann, eds., *The Permanent Campaign and Its Future* (Washington, DC: American Enterprise Institute and the Brookings Institution, 2000), 3; and see Sidney Blumenthal, *The Permanent Campaign* (New York: Simon & Schuster, 1982), 7, for definition of the permanent campaign.

31. Heclo, "Campaigning and Governing: A Conspectus," 34.

32. *Webster's New Ninth Collegiate Dictionary* (Springfield, MA: Merriam-Webster, 1983), 983.

33. Makinson, "What's Ethics Got to Do with It?" in Candice J. Nelson, David Dulio, and Stephen K. Medvic, eds., *Shades of Gray: Campaign Ethics* (Washington, DC: Brookings Press, 2002).

34. James A. Thurber, "Political Power and Policy Subsystems in American Politics," in Guy Peters and Bert A. Rockman, eds., *Agenda for Excellence: Administering the State* (Chatham NJ: Chatham House, 1996), 76–104.

35. Jeffrey H. Birnbaum, *The Money Men: The Real Story of Fund-raising's Influence on Political Power in America* (New York: Crown Publishers, 2000), and Kenneth R. Mayer and David T. Canon, *The Dysfunctional Congress? The Individual Roots of an Institutional Dilemma* (Boulder, CO: Westview Press, 1999).

36. Gary K. Jacobson, "Obama and the Polarized Public," in James A. Thurber, ed., *Obama: The First Two Years* (Boulder, CO: Paradigm Press, 2011), 19–40.

37. Haynes Johnson and David S. Broder, *The System: The American Way of Politics at the Breaking Point* (Boston: Little, Brown, 1996), and Gary C. Jacobson, *The Politics of Congressional Elections* (New York: Longman, 2001), 86–88.

38. See James L. Connor, "Principles for the Ethical Conduct of Lobbying," Woodstock Theological Center, Georgetown University, 2–3, for a discussion of lobbying and the public good.

39. James Madison, "No. 10," in *The Federalist Papers*, 2nd ed. (New York: A Mentor Book, New American Library, 1962), 79.

40. Madison, *The Federalist Papers*, No. 10, 83

41. Madison, *The Federalist Papers*, No. 45, 289.

42. Thurber, "Corruption and Scandal in Washington: Have Lobbying and Ethics Reform Made a Difference?"

43. This is reported by a legislative assistant on the Senate Rules Committee to the author in May 2012.

44. Gary C. Jacobson, "Obama and the Polarized Public," in James A. Thurber, ed., *Obama in Office* (Boulder, CO: Paradigm Publishers, 2011).

Chapter Eight

The President, Congress, and the Media

Ron Elving

On the last Sunday of 2012, the White House and Congress faced a deadline. By the terms of a deal the two rival institutions had reached to resolve a previous crisis, New Year's Day 2013 would bring a 10 percent cut in discretionary federal spending on both defense and nondefense programs. At the same time, federal income and payroll taxes were to rise dramatically, as reductions enacted a decade earlier and extended in 2010 finally expired. A rare consensus of economists foresaw such sudden spending cuts and tax hikes knocking the national economy back into recession. [1]

Weeks earlier, Federal Reserve Board Chairman Ben Bernanke had referred to the pending policy changes as "a fiscal cliff," a vivid phrase that swiftly became media shorthand for a raft of tax-and-spend issues, budget deficits, and accumulating national debt. Cable news networks featured on-screen clocks counting down to the instant the nation would take the plunge.

The cliff, of course, was no more than a metaphor, intended to attract attention. In reality, to avert this purported precipice, President Obama and congressional leaders needed only to cobble together a successor agreement to their last budget deal. Both chambers of Congress were in session, despite the weekend and the holiday season. Yet negotiations remained frozen between the White House and the Speaker of the House John Boehner, as well as between the Senate's majority and minority leaders. For several days, the leaders seemed unable to find anyone to talk to. [2]

But if the official halls of power were silent, a high-decibel conversation was happening elsewhere. The Sunday morning papers were full of stories and analyses and editorials. President Obama was making his case on NBC's "Meet the Press," and a bevy of senators from both parties were making their own partisan remarks on the other Sunday morning "chat shows"—"Fox News Sunday," CBS's "Face the Nation," CNN's "State of the Nation," and ABC's "This Week." Their remarks were also being distributed by their staffs and redistributed by thousands of "followers" on Twitter and "friends" on Facebook, who told their Facebook friends what they were watching. Others could catch up later by hearing the shows replayed on C-SPAN or by calling up the best moments on YouTube.

Late on that Sunday, the Republican Senate leader, Mitch McConnell of Kentucky, came to the Senate floor and told a handful of colleagues and a far larger audience on C-SPAN that he was ready to move ahead "but I need a dance partner." Shortly thereafter, he and Vice President Joe Biden began discussing the terms that would become the next negotiated settlement and pass the Senate by overwhelming vote the following day.

The next night, with the cliff just hours away, House Democratic Leader Nancy Pelosi held an impromptu news conference in a hallway in the Capitol. When a reporter asked whether the House Republicans would allow a floor vote on the McConnell-Biden compromise, Pelosi looked out on the gaggle of reporters with a smile and said: "All I know about what the majority is doing is what I learn from you people."[3]

By this time, the fiscal-cliff wrangle had been a media staple for weeks, replacing the presidential election as the standard bill of fare. On December 2, Treasury Secretary Timothy Geithner had appeared on four of the five main Sunday morning shows (all but NBC's) to lay out Obama's plan for averting the fiscal cliff. He set out new tax rates for the top income bracket, plus higher taxes on investment income and a variety of other priorities. Once these demands were met, Geithner said, the President would be willing to negotiate. Geithner's appearance on these shows, far from a distraction from his duties, constituted the main presentation of the administration position on the overriding public issue of the day. A host of Republican leaders and would-be leaders scrambled to counter the administration message on the same talk shows and in news conferences of their own hastily called that same Sunday afternoon.[4]

It was not hard to see why sophisticated and unsophisticated audiences alike got the impression that their nation's fiscal future was being deliberated, debated, and determined in a handful of TV studios. And they could form that impression even before seeing countless reactions and rereactions in social media (Facebook, Twitter, Skype, and many others) or reading about it all again on news websites that evening and in the newspapers the following morning.[5]

So it was with the issue of Susan Rice, the US Ambassador to the United Nations, who had been a contender to succeed retiring Secretary of State Hillary Clinton. That mere suggestion, widespread in the media, prompted strong objections from Senate Republicans, several of whom went out of their way to publicize their misgivings. Although there were other issues, the focal point of the controversy was a series of TV appearances Rice had made ("on all five shows") on the Sunday after terrorists attacked the US consular mission in Benghazi, Libya, on September 11, 2012. That attack had killed four Americans, including US Ambassador to Libya Christopher Stevens.

Appearing on those programs, Rice had linked the Benghazi attack to an outburst of angry demonstrations around the Islamic world that same day protesting an American-made video that demeaned the Prophet Muhammad. It later became known that there had been no such protest in Benghazi that day. The fatal attack had instead been a planned terrorist thrust. Rice subsequently acknowledged this and said she had initially given the TV audience the only version she had from the CIA—their proffered "talking points" as of that stage of the investigation.[6]

Republicans saw something more afoot than an incomplete CIA report. They saw Rice striving to defuse a potential political improvised explosive device (IED) less than two months before Election Day, and regarded her possible promotion to secretary of state as a reward. The Benghazi-Rice imbroglio simmered through the final weeks of the campaign and became the headline from the reelected Obama's first postelection news conference. He publicly challenged Rice's critics to come after him, not her. But it was Rice who, still not officially nominated, went quite publicly to the Hill to engage the senators who had been so public in their opposition. Three of these senators, after meeting with Rice behind closed doors, went immediately to TV camera positions to proclaim themselves unmoved. Publicly humiliated, Rice soon asked that her name be withdrawn from consideration.

However serious the president had ever been about making Rice his secretary of state, her candidacy became a media fascination, which in turn created an opportunity for contentious interests to contend in the public eye through the media. This continued for days even after she had withdrawn. The media could not let go of a story that combined a strong personality, hot issues (with tape of fires and fighting), racial and gender sensitivities, and a whiff of political payoff to boot. This kind of a story is manna to the media, especially after a long election season has left the cupboard bare, with holidays rolling in. Anything that sustains the human machinery of news programming is also sustenance for the countless individuals and groups organized to practice politics and influence policy in the media. Rice provided a new and vivid occasion for just such combat and a new topic with which to attract and hold an audience. This is what the media demand, and there exists in Washington a limitless supply of officeholders and stakeholders determined to meet that demand.[7]

THOUGH WORLDS APART, TOGETHER IN THE MEDIA REALM

The worlds of the White House and that of Capitol Hill have always been separated by more than just sixteen physical blocks of Pennsylvania Avenue. The gulf yawns widest when one party has the presidency but does not control both chambers of Congress. In such moments, absent more civil means of communicating, the two sides often conduct their combat through the media. In their account of the budget wars of the late 1990s, George Hager and Eric Pianin describe House Republican Whip Tom DeLay screaming at President Bill Clinton, or rather at an image of him on a TV screen.

> Tom DeLay screamed at Bill Clinton, fighting the urge to throw something. It was 1:30 a.m. on a winter night in January 1996 in the living room of his high rise apartment building in Alexandria, Virginia. DeLay, the third most powerful man in the House of Representatives . . . sat raging at his television set . . . the lying, disingenuous, smarmy son of a bitch. DeLay howled at the TV.[8]

But even when one party or the other has controlled "both ends of the Avenue," the competition and animosity have often been intense—with the media in the middle. When Clinton appointed his wife Hillary to lead the drive for a new health-care system in 1993, they found themselves in a nasty media feud with a man they had thought would be an ally: Senator Daniel Patrick Moynihan of New York. As chairman of the Senate Finance Committee, Moynihan wanted to reform welfare first and build momentum for health-care legislation later. Someone in the White House anonymously told a reporter the administration "would roll right over" the chairman. In response, Moynihan made a series of damaging remarks on TV about the Clintons' plans and publicly doubted their numbers, helping send the entire undertaking to oblivion.[9]

It is surely not new for the media to be involved in the struggle between the branches. Viewers of the 2012 Steven Spielberg film *Lincoln* see the sixteenth president in 1865 battling for the Thirteenth Amendment to enfranchise former slaves. Lincoln manipulates the herd instinct and headline hunger of reporters in the House gallery just in time to turn a crucial vote. Four score and several years later, when radio and fledgling TV were the latest "new media," President Harry Truman used them to publicize his 1948 whistle-stop campaign and hammer home his attack on the "Do Nothing 80th"—a Republican Congress that blocked his bills and passed its own over his veto.[10]

The rivals for power in Washington have long regarded the media as a conduit for information, a tool of persuasion, and a cudgel with which to pummel the opposition. But in our time the media are all these things and more. In our new century, for reasons as much technological as political, policy actors are forced to participate in the media realm in ways that are more important than ever—with implications for process, substance, and outcomes. The media now define the speed of information sharing as instantaneous, the distribution of it as ubiquitous, and access to it as universal.

The latest wave of change in the media world has accompanied and in some measure worsened a deterioration of relations between the branches. Once, the no-man's-land between them could be crossed, formally and informally, by principals as well as their designees. These contacts led to information sharing and at times to negotiating, which with luck could culminate in legislating. But such efforts have attenuated in recent years, weakened by disuse, greater partisanship, and changing customs in the capital—including changes driven by the media.

Yet even as the media contribute to the division, they are also increasingly the realm in which the two worlds of the presidency and Congress can interact and communicate—willingly or otherwise.

The media of this new century still include the major franchises of print and broadcasting, now referred to, often dismissively, as "legacy media." At their zenith, not many years ago, these media were accessible to the broad public, persistent about the news, and likely to be present in important places at important times. They were also organized around commercial enterprises—newspapers and broadcasters—with the resources to send professional representatives to "cover the news" in Washington. All this, in some measure, still exists.

But added to it is another dimension of telecommunications that has enveloped the legacy media, along with both branches and the rest of political Washington and all the audiences to whom they would appeal. The media dimension is now omnipresent and constant. It is not driven by established and familiar hierarchies but by its participants, whoever they may be. And these self-selected individuals can have remarkable access to the technology and share in shaping the content and direction of political communication.

The new dimension features highly active participants who are more likely to call themselves bloggers than news professionals. Many do not think of themselves as journalists at all but as activists, advocates, social commentators, or entertainers—or some combination of all the above. Some work largely for themselves or for tiny entities with very low capital costs compared to a daily newspaper, a weekly newsmagazine, or a national TV network. Others work for political organizations that expect them to be polemic by definition. They fit every description and yet defy definition.

In his book *Blogwars*, David D. Perlmutter says blogging is a political act that makes you a political consultant—or even a politician. It is a form of human interaction through the media that differs from journalism but differs, too, from ordinary politics. Bloggers may never see their work distributed in print, and may not care. It is enough that they are blogging, being noticed is extra. Having an impact is better yet. The important thing, to use the argot of the era, is to be "out there."

This is not the standard observed by the best journalism, and much of the blogosphere's raw material is of uncertain provenance. Yet how different is it in spirit from the prerevolutionary zeal of Ben Franklin and Peter Zenger and others who set their own type and turned their own press by hand?[11]

WHO DO THE MEDIA THINK THEY ARE?

The term "media" is thrown about as casually as any serious term in the language, and it may have as many multiple meanings. We should be clear that we are concerned here primarily, but not exclusively, with the news media—people and organizations that report and comment on events and issues and personalities for the consumption of an audience—and particularly those news media that focus on politics and government. These are the media that carry on a tradition stretching back to the early days of the Republic and the earliest national political conversation. From town criers and quill-pen authors of "letters of correspondence" to hand-cranked presses and early magazines, rudimentary media helped spread the revolutionary fervor of 1776 and create the fledgling nation's sense of itself. In the nineteenth century, the development of the postal service, the telegraph, the telephone, and the high-speed press set the stage for the mass media of the twentieth.[12]

The legatees of this tradition are still with us, but rapidly declining. For example, the number of newspapers sold in the United States each day was equal to 35 percent of the population in 1950, but the comparable figure today is less than 15 percent. In 1980, more than fifty million Americans watched one of the three network news shows each weeknight. That number is now twenty-two million, a loss of 54.5 percent of audience.[13]

But any discussion of the media must now include nonnews media that have an increasing influence and impact on those who make news and on those who report it. One cannot speak of the interaction of Congress, the president, and their shared national public without considering the influence of entertainment programs such as Jon Stewart's "Daily Show" or Steven Colbert's "Colbert Report." Although comedy programs, to be sure, these topical half hours are also highly informative and totally political. Surveys find considerable numbers of younger voters consider them their most valuable source of news. Comedy shows have tended to be a lopsided success for liberals, even as talk radio has been primarily a home run for conservatives from Rush Limbaugh to Sean Hannity and Glenn Beck.

Beyond the intrusion of blogs and entertainment programming, the journalists of the new century find themselves confronting the competition of personal Internet-based "social media"—Twitter feeds, Facebook pages,

LinkedIn, YouTube, and so on. Not so long ago, journalists regarded these as a fad or a dating service. That was before Twitter reached two hundred million accounts (including one for every news organization and most national reporters) and Facebook achieved several times that many "friends."

Bill Lambrecht of the *St. Louis Post-Dispatch*, a thirty-year veteran of Washington news, says the social media have become an entire separate channel for many Hill offices that once practiced more conventional news operations. "I had a communications director for a senator tell me he was no longer answering phone calls from the second largest newspaper in the state because there are so many other ways to get the senator's message out."[14]

These media may convey relatively little news and information directly, and they typically offer little or no original work in the sense of reporting or actually observing news events directly. But they direct an enormous amount of traffic to Internet sites that do offer news or comment on the news. Some of the latter are "aggregators" that collect links to other sites and "curate" them, promoting some links over others and adding commentary of their own. While these direct visitors to other sites, the web is also home base for more conventional news operations with sizable reporting and editing staffs—such as *Politico*, *The Huffington Post*, and the *Daily Beast*—that in some cases also produce a print version for subscribers and street distribution.

For those who do not pay much attention to changes in the "media space" the numbers of new media entities can be startling. Adam Thierer of the Progress and Freedom Foundation compiled statistics in 2010 and reported nearly six hundred cable TV channels to go with 2,200 broadcast TV stations, thirteen thousand over-the-air radio stations, twenty-thousand magazines, and over 276,000 books published annually. At that time, Thierer said there were 255 million websites on the Internet, twenty-six million blogs, and over 266 Internet users in North America alone. YouTube was reporting twenty hours of video being uploaded every minute and a billion videos served up to users daily.[15]

THE LATEST NEW MEDIA TSUNAMI

How did the media come to matter so much more in Washington life? Why is the media space now the dimension where the games are played? First, because the media have become more enmeshed in the daily lives of nearly all Americans. It has been commonplace for a generation that Americans were spending more time with their TVs and less with their families, friends, or other interests. That is a trend that has generally continued, as one 2010 industry study by Forrester Research found TV-watching time had increased nationally by 5 percent from 2005 levels. But the real news in the same study was that time spent on the Internet had more than doubled (120 percent) in the same period. The Internet accounted for nearly all the increase in time spent with various media overall (with the portions allotted to reading magazines down 18 percent and newspapers down 26 percent). The study found the Internet use accounted for nearly all the increase in overall household media time from thirty hours to thirty-seven. That is a considerable increase in total media time in just five years. [16]

Moreover, the Forrester study was looking only at home use, and the popularity of the mobile device has greatly expanded the hours we spend looking at screens elsewhere. Another study sponsored by the Nielsen company (longtime providers of TV and radio ratings) found US adults exposed to screens—TVs, cell phones, computers, and GPS devices—for an average of 8.5 hours each day. That suggests that they were spending half their waking hours in the presence of some form of media. [17]

So if we spent meaningful amounts of our time with media in the mid-twentieth century, and media experiences became culturally dominant late in the century, living in and through various media has become an even more immediate, pervasive, and normative lifestyle since the year 2000. And this is not exclusively, or even primarily, a phenomenon of the young. Researchers conducting the Ball State study were struck by how the number of screen hours was "almost identical for every age group." [18]

Truth be told, talking about cable TV and personal computer screens begins to sound a bit old-fashioned now that new generations of media consumers experience the world through mobile devices that meet all their information and communication needs—and create new ones all the time. The Pew Research Center Project for Excellence in Journalism, in its closely followed State of the News Industry 2012 report, said the tipping point has already been reached, with 50 percent of US adults now owning either a tablet device or a smartphone that connects to the Internet. Of these owners, two-thirds say they get news from these devices. And nearly half (43 percent) say their use of the news from tablets is an add-on to their overall news consumption. [19]

Producers of data and information are responding, and scrambling to stay ahead of the tide. The *New York Times* has said it will soon be publishing more material digitally than in print. How soon? One company estimate is 2015. That's the same year when, according to Mary Meeker, Morgan Stanley's "Queen of the Net," mobile devices will surpass the personal computer as the access/download device of choice for all forms of digital material. [20]

From a political standpoint, of course, the focus is not the sheer availability of online material, nor the particular unit a given user chooses. What matters to policy makers is the increasingly powerful lure and hold that some of the emerging media have on the very people the president and Congress care most about reaching: high-end consumers of news who are highly likely to be voters.

The former news editor and online entrepreneur Alan Mutter notes in his blog "Reflections of a Newsosaur" that the Internet and newspapers were about even in audience numbers for news about the presidential election in 2008. But in 2012, he adds with what seems to be glee, "the internet absolutely buried newspapers as the preferred source of campaign news." Citing figures from the Pew Research Center, Mutter notes that newspapers and the Internet were cited by about one third of Americans as "go-to outlets for political news" in 2008. Four years later, the Internet was the choice for 47 percent and the paper for 27 percent. The lines have crossed and the data points are still diverging. On Election Night, according to Pew, 39 percent of all voters between the ages of eighteen and thirty-nine (and 28 percent between forty and sixty-four) were watching the returns on TV and online at the same time. Multiscreening is the new walking while chewing gum.[21]

THE MEDIA REALM ON THE HILL

If some Washington veterans find it difficult to believe the new media mood of the capital's officialdom, it is because in the not-so-distant past the prevailing order was quite different. Any member who pursued publicity was regarded as running for statewide office or pursuing some other grand design, risking being tagged as what totemic Speaker Sam Rayburn called a "show horse." Rayburn and his inner circle strongly preferred the "work horse" member who did his job, went to his committee meetings, and voted correctly on the floor. Even in the 1990s there were still some members who said "the less I get covered the better," according to David Price, a North Carolina Democrat and a political scientist turned legislator. In previous generations, Price added, "that was standard."[22]

In his 1989 book *Making News and Making Laws*, political scientist Timothy Cook observed that "for most of the 20th century, the way to get things done and advance a career in Washington was to play an inside game, building relationships with colleagues, deferring to senior colleagues and bargaining while slowly building up the legislative longevity necessary to achieve a position of power."[23]

But many of the new members arriving after Vietnam and Watergate were impatient with the old House ways. "Visibility leads to credibility," said George Miller, a California Democrat in the "Watergate Class" of 1974. Another Democrat in that class, Tim Wirth of Colorado, was anointed its TV symbol and featured on three broadcasts before he was sworn in. That nettled Jamie Whitten, an old-school Dixiecrat from Mississippi and chairman of the

Appropriations Committee, who took Wirth aside to tell him he himself had not been on TV even once in thirty-five years.[24]

Whitten is long gone, and the Watergate babies as well, and the Congress of today is more media-oriented than either could have imagined. Now even the most dedicated work horse must be prepared to define that work in the media. This means not only an avid interest in TV of any kind, any time, but eager outreach via a host of new technologies from e-mail to Skype. Two Congress scholars who observed the phenomenon in recent sessions call this the new norm.

> While this new understanding of the proper relationship between congression-
> al members and their constituents began to increase the frequency and expand
> the aims of members' publicity activities, it also began to change the pace and
> tone of congressional discourse. In today's variegated, competitive and more
> partisan breaking-news environment, speed and drama increase the chances
> that any one political actor's voice will be heard amidst all the others clamor-
> ing for attention.[25]

Members must be concerned about the messages they convey because the media environment is full of other messages about them already—ranging from critical to negative to scabrous. Often, they come from people already organizing for the next primary or general election. So it is not enough to support, for example, the Second Amendment right to bear arms. It is not enough to vote for it and be on record somewhere for doing so. You must aggressively promote and advertise your stance through every means avail-able—which means every kind of media you can be in as often as you can swing it.

"There is no such thing as an inside game anymore," says Anita Dunn, who worked for members of Congress and Democratic campaigns before becoming White House communications director for Obama and later a pri-vate consultant. She notes that in another era, members had more relation-ships with the other party and centrists of both parties felt free to cross the aisle on votes. "Even five or ten years ago, tough problems got dealt with because centrists came together. It used to happen, now it doesn't happen."[26]

What happens instead is that even the lowliest backbenchers feel free to pursue a media-heavy set of priorities, taking on the president and bearding the congressional leadership in floor speeches and news conferences. They know they will attract media attention and provoke comment in the blogo-sphere. They are simply copying the behavior they have seen work for oth-ers.

It could be said that the media orientation is a species of response to the other problems affecting the current Congress, a reflection of breakdown of "regular order" in proceedings in both Senate and House.[27] It must seem increasingly futile to pursue a classic "inside strategy" when the inside workings of the institution produce so little. [28]

Nonetheless, the hyperconsciousness about media and constituent standing disrupts every other aspect of the old Washington system. It enforces a focus on self and image, carrying what has always been a common characteristic among politicians beyond vanity and creating a barrier to governing. When one's media profile matters more than one's actual work, it distracts from that work and prevents the kind of personal interaction and group organization on which successful political systems thrive. It means members must be careful about crossing the aisle to work with the other party—or the other party's president.

Once upon a time, official Washington had ways of socializing new arrivals and stiff-necked independents who thought themselves immune to "Potomac fever." In more genteel times, members of Congress and an administration would meet at parties, dinners, and other social gatherings. Spouses, primarily wives, attended many of these events, because spouses came to Washington for extended periods. In the later twentieth century, when the world wars and air conditioning had stretched congressional calendars more or less across the four seasons, long-term members of Congress typically had their primary residence in Washington or its nearby suburbs, often raising their children there and socializing with other members and their families.

This dynamic has weakened with each of the turnover wave elections that make members at all stages of seniority feel insecure. As far back as the Reagan years, members were talking about how little they knew about their colleagues anymore. Political scientist Burdett Loomis noted then that "much of what the 535 members of Congress know of each other and their policy initiatives comes through the media, not person-to-person contact." [29]

Meg Greenfield, the legendary editorial page editor of the *Washington Post*, also had a blast for the new order she saw emerging at the turn of the millennium:

> Political people can now deal directly with their audiences of choice. They need not depend so much on party organizations. Individuals do their own hustling, run their own campaigns and do their own deals, as do special interest caucuses and lobbies. They feel less bound to stay in tune with their group or its leaders. They often feel more bound to stay in tune with the anti-authority ethic of what has become a kind of electronic national conversation—part gripe session and part political bathing suit contest—from which they increasingly take their cues. [30]

The current members of Congress are far less likely to move their families to Washington, or even to buy a home in the area. It has become standard since the 1990s to fly to the capital in time for Tuesday afternoon sessions and go home after Thursday evening sessions. The leadership in both chambers is generally amenable to scheduling votes to accommodate this schedule (although the House Majority Leader announced in January that the body would meet on fifteen Fridays in 2013). Regular trips back home do little to build relationships in Washington, but they do facilitate the steady contact with constituents that is continued through the work week via Skype and various social media.

Despite the media-centric nature of the moment, these members are less likely to establish relationships with national reporters in Washington. Janet Hook, who has been covering Congress for more than thirty years for *Congressional Quarterly*, the *Los Angeles Times*, and the *Wall Street Journal*, sees the shifting media climate making more traditional journalistic relationships impossible.

"In the 1980s and into the mid-1990s," says Hook,

> I felt that as a print reporter I could have a lot of conversations with members of Congress that were honest and unscripted. . . . interviews or background "dishing" that could really help me understand an issue or a political situation. Lawmakers then seemed to see reporters as conduits for understanding. Now, even with members of Congress I have known for decades, it is almost all talking points and party line stuff. The media is seen just as a conduit for their message.[31]

Indeed, members' perception of reporters now has largely been shorn of its collegial aspect, just as reporters now regard far fewer members with the respect and affection they once reserved for a select few.

Some of this messaging that Hook described is intended for general consumption by wider circles of media and other communicators, and some of it is meant for voters. But much of it is directed at the most circumscribed of audiences, the other participants in the internal Washington conversation. This is true among members and it is true between Congress and the White House. Don Foley, whose many jobs in Washington since 1976 have included being press secretary to former Democratic Leader Dick Gephardt as well as chief of staff in the Senate and the executive director of the Senate Democratic Campaign Committee, says the "triangulation" among the legislative and executive branches and the media has reached a baroque stage.

"The online news organizations have added a logarithmic acceleration of news," says Foley.

> That in turn has greatly increased the prospects for a variety of players—policymakers, lobbyists and others with an interest in Washington output and outcomes—to provide input to shape or make the town's agenda. And while the politicians still pay homage to the need to bring the interests of their constituents to the daily battles, they are quite comfortable simply communicating with one another and to the interest groups. A lot of what emanates from here as news just stays here in Washington.[32]

Members also communicate with each other in much the same way as their teenaged offspring communicate with their peers—via mobile device. Indeed, as Congress has been becoming a less cooperative and less communicative human environment, technology has continued to race ahead. The cell phone replaced the pager, the smartphone replaced the cell. Now the mobile device that combines computer and phone calls has become as ubiquitous as the index cards on which members once carried their daily schedules, or the lapel pins that identify them as members. Thus is created the vicious cycle of social media substituting for actual social life. And if members seem isolated from one another, they are all the more removed from the daily concerns, moods, and issue ferment going on within the White House and the larger executive branch.

GOING AFTER THE PRESIDENT

Another example of the recent media effect is the heightened temptation of the junior member to take on the top of the power structure. Only in the current climate would a second-term House member such as Michelle Bachmann of Minnesota be able to see herself as a rival for power—not only within the House Republican Conference or the House as a whole—but in presidential politics. After frequent appearances on C-SPAN, Fox, and other cable outlets during her first term, Bachmann felt herself quite ready to offer her own response to the State of the Union address in January 2011 (backed by a Tea Party group) and to seek the White House in 2012.[33]

The media world is also the best place in which to understand why Representative Joe Wilson of South Carolina, another Republican backbencher in the House, felt free to shout "You lie!" during a presidential address to a joint session of Congress in 2009. Wilson apologized the next day, but he also quickly issued a fundraising appeal—cashing in on being a hero and even a martyr in conservative media outlets. The House later approved a "resolution of disapproval," but even that mild discipline was opposed by nearly every Republican in the chamber.[34]

While these are egregious cases, the ego-promoting practices of the social media and local news media that preoccupy many members make it seem natural and even irresistible to see one's self—and not the Congress as a whole—as the president's power rival. It is not hard to see how quickly and thoroughly this complicates the task of governing for two branches that must cooperate in order to succeed.

And speaking of ego, the temptation for many reporters to become stars has been too much to resist, even if it meant abandoning their ethos of objectivity.

"Many in the media have shed any semblance of neutrality," says Don Foley, "and have found it more profitable to pick sides and rather than reporting on the debate, they provide a bigger megaphone and have joined the debate. So the message senders in the White House and Congress get to choose their messengers and can do so without being challenged from the neutral position of old. We have returned to the days of hand-selected couriers of our messages."[35]

That includes, of course, the frank embrace of the conservative viewpoint by Rupert Murdoch's Fox News, founded and run by Roger Ailes, a campaign consultant for Presidents Nixon, Reagan, and George H. W. Bush. In 2011, Fox's evening news shows were drawing about two million viewers while ABC, CBS, and NBC combined were drawing more than twenty million. Yet Fox's viewers were watching more loyally and for longer hours, giving Fox more profit for its comparable operations than the three legacy networks combined.

Given Fox's dominance on cable, CNN has tried a variety of approaches and abandoned each—culminating in a shakeup that removed all its commentators early in 2013. MSNBC, the hybrid of Microsoft and NBC, has adopted a candid mirror image of Fox, filling its lineup with liberals from Chris Matthews to Rachel Maddow.

THE MEDIA REALM OF THE WHITE HOUSE

The president, of course, has his own paths to a media connection. His is the one political actor's voice that will always be heard, if only because his singular position of speaking individually for one branch of government has no equivalent. In the pre-Internet era, a president could simply notify the networks he would be out to make a statement and he could count on prime-time coverage. But that habit weakened in the network headquarters as the privilege was used often by Presidents Clinton and George W. Bush. Moreover, in the age of cable TV news, C-SPAN, and the Internet, the networks have felt less and less obligation to sacrifice precious primetime minutes when audiences have so many other media available. The president, after all, has his own White House program online.

And after some uncertainty in the first term, the president and his team showed signs after his reelection that he would be using that pulpit the way Teddy had in mind. In just the first weeks of January he was well out in front in restricting guns and liberalizing immigration—dominating the media and antagonizing Republicans in Congress. Dealing with these new media realities has caused the never-too-cozy relationship between the executive and legislative branches new problems.

"The growth of the media, and its transformation from print to electronic to pervasive, has contributed to the sharp divide between the Hill and the White House," says Carl P. Leubsdorf, who has covered Washington for the *Dallas Morning News* and the Associated Press for more than forty years. Leubsdorf can hark back to the marathon wrestling matches between Congress and successive presidents over Vietnam and Watergate, which "created a unique, intensive period of antagonism." But even then, he notes, "it did not pervade every issue the way it does today."[36]

Leubsdorf and other veteran journalists have watched the figurative Pennsylvania Avenue lengthen over the decades as the relatively clubby world of print (where many reporters covered both Congress and the president) gave way to the electronic media, with their unprecedented audience and hyper-competitive internal dynamics. "The increasing domination of television has changed things. Network correspondents on Capitol Hill are eager to get on the air as much as their White House counterparts, and the way to do that is to portray the sharp opposition of members of Congress to the administration. That is even more so because of the rise of cable and, now, Internet on-line instant reporting by the likes of Politico."

Leubsdorf notes that the heightened emphasis on conflict, and especially on defiance of higher authority, has been a boon to new members.

> Where once the daily coverage was driven by party leaders or members who were issue experts, now even a freshman is as likely to be featured on the evening news . . . and the sharpest voices get the most coverage. Look at the coverage accorded Joe Walsh, a totally insignificant Illinois Republican House member, in the [112th] Congress. And within two weeks of coming to Washington, Senator Ted Cruz of Texas is becoming a regular on the Sunday shows because he's an outspoken critic of the president.[37]

President Obama had a special set of problems with the media in his first term because he had been such a media favorite in his 2008 campaign. Once he was in office, many news managers felt it was time to take off the gloves—or at least be seen as getting tougher with the president. Obama and his team quickly perceived a comparative coolness in many of the same journalists who had covered the campaign. Despite sometimes Herculean efforts to woo the media, Obama found the multiple crises of 2009 and the rapid deterioration of his honeymoon poll numbers quickly cost him the magical aura of 2008.[38]

But Obama as president pursued a long-run strategy, much as he had done as a candidate. At news conferences and other media availabilities, he took care to call on representatives of online news organizations and other new faces. "He kept the older established media happy with a lot of one-on-one interviews, especially at key points in the term," says Richard Benedetto, longtime national correspondent and columnist for *USA Today* and now teaching at American University. [39]

But Obama was not focused on keeping Congress happy, either through the media or through personal contact. He had done little schmoozing in his four years in the Senate (two spent largely running for president), and he had little inclination to romance the Hill—even when Democrats had about three-fifths of the seats in both chambers. He decided to leave the negotiating of key legislation on health care and financial regulations and climate change largely to the relevant committee chairs in the Senate, with mixed results. In the end, his health-care bill lost momentum and lost public support because it had not been promoted effectively to the public—a task that had to be achieved through the media and was not. [40]

Geoff Garin, a pollster who was not working for the White House at the time, bemoaned the problems of selling the Obama stimulus and health-care plan to a distracted country. Longing for the days when a president might grab the nation's attention with a primetime address on all three networks, Garin asked: "How do you drive a national political conversation, when there are 100 voices and sources of information instead of three?" [41]

The White House team did not have a compelling answer to that question in 2010, when Garin asked it. But by 2012 they did, for the campaign if not for their dealings with Congress. "These guys understand the media," Benedetto said. "The Obama guys know what media reaction is going to be and they're on top of it. I think they understand the media better than a lot of the media do." [42]

David Axelrod, a *Chicago Tribune* reporter and columnist before becoming Obama's top strategist, once explained the halting White House media performance on health care by saying "When you've got the greatest running back in history in your backfield, you're tempted to give him the ball on every play." [43]

That worked in the campaigns of 2008 and 2012, but not on health care. On the other hand, it is always tempting to blame a bungled issue—and health care was a political bungle even though it eventually passed—on a failed media strategy. As the veteran White House watcher Stephen Hess has noted, this assumes a president can really execute a media strategy. Hess worked for Presidents Eisenhower and Nixon before joining the Brookings Institution as a media scholar.

> [Senator] Al Simpson used to say "You can have a media impact, but can you really have a media strategy?" It implies the president can do something to change the media. The media march left and then right; and whether their shifts are rational or not, they are not driven by the president. [44]

Among other rough patches in the first term, Obama and his team were often at odds with bloggers for firedoglake.com and other liberal and civil libertarian cites. Bloggers such as Glenn Greenwald at Salon.com (later at the *Guardian*) were unrelenting in their denunciations of the president, and at times it seemed the communications team was mystified by their anger over Guantánamo, drone strikes, and stepped-up deportations of illegal immigrants.[45]

Obama seemed far more sure-footed in 2012, however, when in the midst of his reelection campaign. Campaign adviser David Plouffe returned to run the message and turnout operation, a strikingly successful encore to his 2008 performance. Also back was the candidate's steely discipline and focus on a few states, a few constituencies, a few issues, and even a few sentences that he repeated endlessly without complaint. After the election, Plouffe again left the scene, as he had after 2008. But the Obama team still maintained it could deploy the campaign organization again as a lobbying force behind gun and immigration legislation—as well as for the 2014 midterms. Similar goals were set four years earlier, and went unfulfilled.

Obama in 2011 also settled in with a new press secretary, Jay Carney, a former *Time* reporter who knew personally most of the heavyweight reporters he was dealing with in the briefing room. Carney brought an air of almost academic solemnity to his job, along with a lawyerly adherence to the case he was given and an almost Jesuitical willingness to argue fine points of language. Unlike Robert Gibbs, Obama's first press secretary, Carney rarely made news. Some of this was his style, some was his rather owlish appearance on TV. But mostly, he did not begin with a history of campaign combat and newsmaking interviews in 2008. Cable TV rarely aired his briefings and excerpted them only sparingly. And that was fine with the White House, where there was always the website for Obama fans to watch the daily briefing and other exhaustive coverage of the day at 1600.

The White House team also benefited greatly from the shift of media attention after 2010 to the boisterous new Republican majority in the House, which threatened to shut down the government and then came close to forcing a US default by refusing to raise the debt ceiling. The political newshounds were also baying in Iowa and New Hampshire and covering more than a score of televised debates between the Republican contenders for the 2012 nomination. Like Bill Clinton in 1995, Obama got a boost toward reelection when he lost full control of Congress in the midterm.

WHO'S AFRAID OF THE MEDIA REALM?

As we have noted, there are negative aspects to the surprising rise of the latest media in Washington. Should the nation be worried if our elected leaders at the highest levels of the federal establishment are more concerned than ever with their media personae? While there may be cause for concern at any time about these relationships, it is not clear that the era at hand is fundamentally more hazardous to the Republic.

There are some basic elements of all media coverage that raise questions. One is what media historian Michael Schudson has called the "politics of the narrative," or the inherent rhetorical effects of relating news events in story form. Schudson notes, for example, that in the twentieth century, the national media began making the president the lead character in every story they possibly could. That obviously creates an impression—not only over a presidency but over a lifetime—that has political implications. [46]

The fact is that the story form is so basic to journalism that most practitioners scarcely think about it. It could be called the universal bias of the media. A story is, by its nature, a re-presentation of a set of facts. It is not the same thing as the plain unvarnished facts. And sometimes our desire to sell that story to an audience gets the better of us. This does not mean that reporters—or for that matter bloggers or the authors of the day's best Tweets—are making things up. They are merely making them more clear and comprehensible, and that can be distorting.

This fact has proven very bothersome to some of the more high-minded critics of the news business, such as Paul H. Weaver, who was an editor at *Fortune* and a teacher at Harvard and a fellow at the Hoover Institution. Weaver wrote a book called *News and the Culture of Lying*.

> Contrary to the way we usually speak of it, news isn't simply a report of what happened yesterday, it's a story with characters, action, plot, point of view and dramatic closure. Moreover, it's a story about crisis and emergency response, about the waxing and waning of urgent danger to the community and about the actions of responsible officials to cope. Thus, officials in search of publicity and journalists in search of news . . . enact, select and narrate events in the image of the genre's overarching drama of urgent public danger. [47]

What Weaver calls fabrication may also be called art, although even that is a term most working journalists would find discomfiting. It is too close to artifice and implies something is not quite factual. Even Weaver is willing to concede that most news is factual: "Facts in the news generally remain true, that much being necessary to maintain the credibility of the entire exercise. However, sooner or later almost everything else becomes a fabrication."

What bothers Weaver and others about media practice is the insistence that reality be packaged for eager, easy consumption. For starters, media representations are usually quite short and relatively simple, whereas the realities being described tend to be complex and long-lasting. Reducing the complexities and contradictions of Pakistan, say, to a single book or magazine article is difficult enough. Reducing them to a thousand-word news-paper story, or a broadcast report measured in seconds, is quite impossible.

Thus the work of the media, in news as in entertainment, is to capture an essential impression in miniature. And the way this is done is through story form. The term "storify" is not new, but it has come into greater use in recent years, and it is now the trademark of a social network service on which anyone can create stories of their own using Facebook, Twitter, or Instagram. A variety of cooperating news organizations' logos appear on the website, and many more have started using the service to provide grass-roots material for stories. The Canadian Broadcasting Corp. used it to cover the London riots in 2011, and Al Jazeera has used it for a program called "The Stream."

The narrative imperative matters because in the daily struggle between the president and Congress, the day is won by the side that provides the better story—or the better elements for the story the media will make of it. This does not mean the most accurate or balanced or elegantly written story but the most cogent. This is usually the one that is easiest for the audience (on whatever platform) to comprehend and relate to in the most personal terms possible. The media look for stories wherein real people tell their own stories. "It draws the reader in," the editor will say. That is an intuitive reaction, borne out by many a reading and viewing experience; and there is certainly objective research to support it as well. [48]

THE TYRANNY OF THE VISUAL

The need for narrative is further dramatized by the value of visuals. When C-SPAN arrived in the House (1979) and Senate (1986) the demand for charts and graphics increased exponentially. Suddenly, members wanted something to point to. The chamber rules have not yet bent to allow members to show video, or use audio, but it seems logical that members giving floor presentations would eventually be able to present them in a multimedia fashion. Witnesses might be called to appear at hearings not in person but as holograms. [49]

Visuals are obviously part of the narrative imperative. Video is to news reporting what movies are to novels. It adds tremendously to the audience fascination, and it makes the underlying story far more powerful. Consider the effect a few seconds of videotape shown repeatedly on cable news had on the House of Representatives in the spring of 2005. The tape showed a Florida woman named Terri Schiavo, who had been in a persistent vegetative state for years, turning toward the sound of her mother's voice and apparently making a sound of her own. Driven by these images, the House reconvened on Palm Sunday weekend to pass an emergency order stripping the Florida courts of their jurisdiction over the woman's fate. President Bush flew back from Texas to sign the legislation. The effort was soon rebuffed in federal court, the House had to back down, and Schiavo died after being taken off life support. [50]

The narrative imperative also matters because stories take on a life of their own. Writers of fiction often report that a tale they began with one ending in mind eventually came to a different one, or that characters they had created began evolving and altering the plot. Some of that happens in the writing of news, as well, as the writer strains to make new events fit the existing storyline. For example, as it emerged that the Troubled Asset Relief Program (TARP)—better known as the bank bailout—would actually recover the funds provided to various banks and financial firms, this information presented an enormous challenge to the media.

If the government had recovered virtually all its invested funds by the end of 2012, how could that be reconciled with the deeply ingrained conviction that it had all been a boondoggle (a conviction ingrained in large part by the media)? The outlines of the reality were clear by the fall of 2010, but the issue of TARP's gradual success and recovery did not receive much play and was not much discussed in the 2010 midterm election cycle, the 2012 presidential primaries, or the 2012 federal elections. [51]

LOOKING TO AN UNCERTAIN FUTURE

David Folkenflik, media reporter for NPR News, has compared the place of the legacy media in the present landscape of Washington to the importance of historical buildings in London. "It's a city of enormous modernity, with high tech and futuristic stuff all over the place. But people do still want to go to see Westminster Abbey and Whitehall and the recreation of the Globe Theater—even the Roman ruins. There's a demand for all of it." [52]

Like the landmarks of old London—and the aging ceremonies and social events of official Washington—the legacy media will almost surely survive in some form and maintain some semblance of significance for the foreseeable future. They will retain some value as occasions for communication, comprehension, and negotiation. But in another generation it is hard to imagine we will not be electing our president and Congress largely through electronic means and following their performance in office the same way.

These new means, now in a nascent state, change constantly. And they may keep changing indefinitely. But we can already see they will be the battleground for the political forces of the next era, not only in campaign season but in governing as well. The struggle for power between the president and Congress will no longer begin and end at their traditional points of intersection but in the media space—and increasingly in media cyberspace.

Those who value the relationships that once prevailed among policy actors—and between them and the media—need to ask why we still wish to retain these arrangements. Do we simply prefer the devil(s) we know? Or is there something we can honestly and persuasively say has been lost in the move to the new landscape? Many of us in the Washington world—the political and media establishment, if you will—revere democracy but have doubts about populism, which is political energy mobilized against elites. The rise of the nonprofessional exchange of information through the Internet is a populist cause. In this case, we the media have met the elite, and they are us.

The latest generation of self-made media participation draws deeply on our national mythology about individuals who strike out on their own, strike their own bargain, and, if need be, strike back at those who would restrain them. Much of our political culture harks back to this impulse, and its creative and destructive forces are evident throughout our history.

Still, there is an egalitarian spirit in the most recent media technologies, a leveling effect that gives far more people access to far more information—and the inherent empowerment that goes with it. Few journalists or officeholders would be prepared to argue against anything so democratic and transparent as the Internet ideal. And in the end, this would be arguing against the future; and that is surely futile, especially against a future that has already arrived.

NOTES

1. Alan Ota and Meredith Shiner, "Fiscal Cliff Agreement Continues to Elude Senators," *CQ Roll Call*, December 30, 2012, www.rollcall.com/news/fiscal_cliff_agreement_continues _to_elude_senators-220418-1.html.

2. Jonathan Weisman, "Seesaw Talks Produce No Accord on Fiscal Crisis," *New York Times*, December 31, 2012.

3. C-SPAN live coverage of the Capitol, unscheduled news conference by Speaker Nancy Pelosi, December 31, 2012.

4. Dominic Rushe, "Tim Geithner's Fiscal Cliff Plan Leaves Boehner 'Flabbergasted,'" *Guardian*, December 3, 2012, www.guardian.co.uk/world/2012/dec/02/boehner-flabbergasted -geithner-fiscal-cliff.

5. The Sunday morning shows have proved remarkably durable as media icons ("Meet the Press" began in 1947, "Face the Nation" in 1954). Despite their modest audience (the top-rated show barely tops three million viewers in most weeks), their power to drive media decisions in the new week, coupled with the close scrutiny they receive from newsmakers and policy actors, make these programs disproportionately influential. An issue that arises in these venerable venues can suddenly leap to prominence in other media, which translates into de facto prominence in reality; see David Bauder, "Sunday Mornings Heat Up: CBS 'Face the Nation' Gets under Skin of NBC 'Meet the Press,'" *Huffington Post*, September 16, 2012, huffington-post.com/2012/09/16/Sunday-mornings-cbs-face-the-nation-nbc-meet-the-press_n_1887911 .html.

6. David Weigel, "Sunday Morning Quarterback," Slate.com, November 19, 2012, www.slate.com/articles/news_and_politics/politics/2012/11/john_mccain_vs_susan_rice_on _sunday_morning_tv_talk_shows_are_site_of_battle.html.

7. Peter Nicholas and Julian Barnes, "Susan Rice Ends Secretary of State Bid amid Criticism," *Wall Street Journal*, December 14, 2012.

8. George Hager and Eric Pianin, *Mirage: Why Neither Democrats Nor Republicans Can Balance the Budget, End the Deficit and Satisfy the Public* (New York: Random House, 1997).

9. David Broder and Haynes Johnson, *The System: The American Way of Politics at the Breaking Point* (New York: Little, Brown, 1996), 351.

10. James T. Patterson, *Great Expectations: The United States 1945–1974* (Oxford: Oxford University Press, 1996), 158–63.

11. David D. Perlmutter, *Blogwars* (Oxford: Oxford University Press, 2008), xx–xxiv.

12. Paul Starr, *The Creation of the Media: Political Origins of Modern Communication* (New York: Basic Books, 2004); Michael Schudson, *Discovering the News: A Social History of American Newspapers* (New York: Basic Books, 1978); Michael Schudson, *The Power of News* (Cambridge: Harvard University Press, 1995), 53–71. For book-length considerations of these historic progressions and their relation to other developments in American history, the most complete discussion is Paul Starr's magisterial *Creation of the Media* (2004). All the writings of Michael Schudson are also provocative and eye-opening, in addition to being delightful reading.

13. Newspaper data from Editor and Publisher Yearbook and U.S. Census Bureau, cited in "State of the News Media," *Pew Research Center's Project for Excellence in Journalism*, 2004. Network evening news program audience figures from Nielsen Research, cited in "State of the News Media," *Pew Research Center's Project for Excellence in Journalism*, 2012.

14. Bill Lambrecht, interview with Ron Elving, January 25, 2013.

15. Thomas Mann and Norman Ornstein, *It's Even Worse Than It Looks: How the American Constitutional System Collided with the New Politics of Extremism* (Oxford: Oxford University Press, 2012), 59.

16. Forrester Research, Cambridge, MA, 2010, mashable.com/2010/12/13/internet-tv-for rester/.

17. Brian Stelter, "Study: Americans Spend 8 Hours a Day in Front of Screens," *New York Times*, August 26, 2009, www.huffingtonpost.com/2009/03/27/study-americans-spend-8 -h_n_179921.html.

18. "The researchers found that the number of minutes with media is almost identical for every age group. [One researcher] called the amount of time 'amazingly consistent across the age groups.' Remarkably, the one outlier among age groups was the cohort from 45 to 54, who spent an extra hour in front of screens despite (or perhaps because of) being cross-pressured by work and families."

19. Rick Edmonds, Emily Guskin, Tom Rosenstiel, and Amy Mitchell, "State of the News Media 2012," *Pew Research Center, Project for Excellence in Journalism*, 2012. The report of the Pew Research Center's Project for Excellence in Journalism had other forms of bad news for the newspaper and broadcast industries. Circulation has declined for thirty-four consecutive quarters. Classified ads fell from $20 billion in 2000 to $5 billion a decade later, while daily ads fell from nearly $50 billion in the late 1990s to $20 billion in 2011. The best newspaper companies are now trading at one-half their peak stock value, while others are as low as one-tenth.

20. Mathew Ingram, "Mary Meeker: Mobile Internet Will Soon Overtake Fixed Internet," GIGAOM, April 24, 2010, gigaom/2010/04/12/mary-meeker-mobile-internet-will-soon-over take-fixed-internet/.

21. Alan Mutter, "Web Election Audience Overtakes Newspapers," *Reflections of a Newsosaur*, November 19, 2012, newsosaur.blogspot.com/2012/11/web-election-audience-over takes.html.

22. David Price, interview with Ron Elving, April 2, 1993.

23. Timothy Cook, *Making News and Making Laws* (Washington, DC: Brookings Institution, 1989), 26–29. Cook notes that after the famous Senator Estes Kefauver hearings on organized crime became a distraction in the early 1950s Rayburn banned both cameras and microphones from hearing rooms. He often referred to national correspondents as various kinds of carrion-eating birds, while reserving a certain affection for his Texas contingent of more respectful scribes. The Rayburn ban survived his death in 1961 and was not fully rescinded

until the House, noting the image of the highly televised presidency, opened its doors to C-SPAN in 1979.

24. Hedrick Smith, *The Power Game: How Washington Works* (New York: Random House, 1988), 135.

25. Gary Lee Melecha and Daniel J. Reagan, *The Public Congress: Congressional Deliberation in a New Media Age* (New York: Routledge, 2012), 145.

26. Anita Dunn, remarks to Public Affairs Institute, Laguna Beach, California, January 13, 2013.

27. Mann and Ornstein, *It's Even Worse Than It Looks.*

28. Sarah Blackwill, "112th Congress Set to Become Least Productive in Decades," *MSNBC*, December 31, 2012, tv.msnbc.com/2012/12/31/112th-congress-set-to-become-least-productive-in-decades/. The 112th Congress was by some measures the least productive in history, having passed just 219 bills that were signed into law, compared to 383 in the previous Congress and 460 in the 110th. The members left town at the end of 2012 with a disapproval of 82 percent in the NBC/*Wall Street Journal* Poll, also a record.

29. Burdett Loomis, *The New American Politician: Ambition, Entrepreneurship and the Changing Face of Political Life* (New York: Basic Books, 1988), 76–77.

30. Meg Greenfield, *Washington* (New York: Public Affairs, 2001), 58.

31. Janet Hook, interview with Ron Elving, January 21, 2013.

32. Donald Foley, interview with Ron Elving, January 18, 2013.

33. Ryan Lizza, "Leap of Faith: The Making of a Republican Front-runner," *The New Yorker*, August 15, 2011.

34. Mike Soraghan, "Wilson Not Going to Apologize Again, Despite Threat of Sanction from Dems," *The Hill*, September 13, 2009.

35. Foley interview.

36. Carl P. Leubsdorf, interview with Ron Elving, January 19, 2013.

37. Leubsdorf interview.

38. Ron Elving, "Fall of the Favorite," in James Thurber, ed., *Obama in Office* (Boulder, CO: Paradigm Press, 2011), 147–48.

39. Richard Benedetto, interview with Ron Elving, January 31, 2013.

40. George C. Edwards, III, *Overreach: Leadership in the Obama Presidency* (Princeton: Princeton University Press, 2012), 89–99, 179–84.

41. Elving, "Fall of the Favorite."

42. Benedetto interview.

43. David Axelrod, interview with Juan Williams and Ron Elving, October 22, 2010.

44. Stephen Hess, interview with Ron Elving, August 30, 2010.

45. Elving, "Fall of the Favorite."

46. Schudson, *The Power of News.*

47. Paul H. Weaver, *News and the Culture of Lying: How Journalism Really Works* (New York: Free Press, 1994), 2–3.

48. One recent study by a team at Pennsylvania State University and the University of Indiana–Fort Wayne actually quantified the degree to which audiences respond to a story with a person's name and personal details in comparison to a "policy story" approach based on objective data; see Mary Beth Oliver, James Price Dillard, Keunmin Bae, and Daniel J. Tamul, "The Effect of Narrative News Format on Empathy for Stigmatized Groups," *Journalism & Mass Communication Quarterly* 89, no. 2 (June 2012), journalistsresource.org/studies/society/news-media/effect-narrative-news-format-empathy-stigmatized-groups.

49. Attention should be paid to the fact that the first experiments with holograms in the news business were not a rousing success. CNN on Election Night 2012 had veteran anchor Wolf Blitzer live in a studio talking to a hologram of Jessica Yellin, a CNN reporter who was actually at Mitt Romney's headquarters in Boston. The question on this occasion was: why would you prefer to see her glowing in the studio rather than reporting from the actual location where the news was happening?

50. Larry Copeland and Laura Parker, "Schiavo Case Doesn't End with Her Passing," *USA Today*, March 31, 2005.

51. Jackie Calmes, "TARP to Cost Less Than Once Anticipated," *New York Times*, October 1, 2010. Senator Robert Bennett of Utah, who had been labeled "Bailout Bob" and denied renomination by Utah Republicans, expressed resignation. "My career is over," he said, "but I do hope we can get the word out that TARP, number one did save the world from a financial meltdown and number two . . . won't cost the taxpayer anything." Bennett also noted ruefully that the man who challenged him for his Senate seat had been motivated to run by an email full of false accusations about ObamaCare that "went viral."

52. David Folkenflik, interview with Ron Elving, January 31, 2013.

Chapter Nine

Presidents, Congress, and Budget Decisions

Joseph White

Budgeting might be considered the thermometer of presidential-congressional relations. Sometimes it shows a balanced, healthy, normal body politic. Sometimes it reveals a dangerous fever. And sometimes the thermometer breaks and glass and mercury are spilled all over the floor.

Budgeting is at the heart of government, because it is the most direct example of the authoritative allocation of values. The framers of the constitution expected Congress to have the largest say in budgeting decisions. Yet the constitution also, both through the president's veto over legislation and his supervision of administration, gave him a major role in the allocation of government funds.[1] Developments in the extraconstitutional political system, such as the emergence of the presidential role as a party leader and his occasional ability to appeal to public opinion, added to the president's potential budgeting power. Congress also granted presidents institutional resources—the budget bureau and its routines—that are central to the modern presidency.[2]

Budgeting also is extremely hard. Congress and the president may seem to fail because there is no result that would meet public demands that are either contradictory (avoid recession but balance the budget!); or beyond their power to meet ("manage the economy" when, to a great extent, the economy determines budget totals rather than vice versa); or require decisions for which there is not close to majority support (as will be discussed below).

Done properly, federal budgeting is an immensely technical and complicated task, involving many thousands of decisions that are supposed to be integrated into a complex web of legislation and implementation. As a result, both Congress and the presidency include specialized budgeting institutions. When the body politic is healthy, these institutions each contribute to decisions.

The congressional budget process includes specialized committees for what we now call discretionary spending (the House and Senate Appropriations committees); for revenue legislation (House Ways and Means and Senate Finance); and to provide an annual framework for decisions about spending and taxing (the House and Senate Budget Committees, through the annual Congressional Budget Resolution). A wide variety of special rules apply to consideration of revenue legislation, appropriations, and the class of laws called entitlements (or mandatory spending) that provide budget authority for more than one year (such as for farm price supports and Medicare). Congressional staff agencies oversee executive management of budget allocations (GAO, the Government Accountability Office) and advise Congress on budgetary effects of legislative alternatives (CBO, the Congressional Budget Office).

The executive (or presidential) budget process is managed by the Office of Management and Budget (OMB) within the Executive Office of the President. Budget offices within each agency and department deal with OMB. Although it has undergone reorganizations since its creation in 1921, the budget bureau[3] has always packaged agencies' budget requests into an overall bundle subject to presidential approval (the President's Budget) and then, after Congress responded with appropriations or other legislation, managed allocation of funds among agencies (budget execution). This presidential process gives the president first move in determining how specific tax and spending plans relate both to each other and to totals for taxes, spending, and the federal surplus or deficit. It also influences information provided to Congress, because agencies are expected to testify in favor of the budget bureau's proposals.

This chapter addresses how the budgeting relationship between the president and Congress has developed over time.[4] A theory based on presidential dominance was implemented, after 1921, in a manner that instead allowed positive collaboration. From the late 1960s on, this developed into a much more adversarial process, in which president and Congress competed to shape policy and avoid blame. At various times, such as 2011–2012, that has devolved into a raw struggle in which the formal budgeting process has shattered and the values it serves been nearly ignored.[5]

PURPOSES OF BUDGET PROCESSES

Specialized budget processes have a series of functions, or justifications, as part of both democratic politics and competent government. Budgeting can be a way to make government transparent and its actions predictable; a procedure to set social priorities and to pursue efficiency in the operation of public services; and can be used by government to try to manage the economy.[6]

In many people's view, however, the core purpose of any budget process should be to "balance" the budget. By this they mean have spending be no more than revenues. As Irene Rubin has written, this is just one possible balance (in the sense of a balance sheet)[7]; and there are many situations in which a "balanced budget" is neither necessary policy nor good economics. Even if one does not think deficits are evil, however, there should be some balance—a level of deficit or surplus—that seems advisable for a combination of economic purposes (such as manipulating aggregate demand) or a version of household management (such as accumulating resources in case of later hard times).

The fundamental challenge for any budget process is that preferences about details are highly unlikely to add up to preferences about total spending, total taxes, and the resulting budget balance. Hence processes are needed to *adjust preferences about totals and details to each other*, in such a way that the combination in the end is as satisfactory as possible to the decision-making person or group.

As this problem is normally posed, a set of fragmented decisions about programs and taxes, which is what would happen if agencies simply proposed their own budgets and Congress responded committee by committee, must be resisted by central "guardian" bodies in Congress or the executive branch. Yet the challenge is not simply that short-sighted claimants might ignore totals. Most participants in budget-making can identify *somebody else's spending* that they would be willing to eliminate, or *somebody else's taxes* that they would be willing to raise, so that they could justify their details within their preferred total. Then budget deficits can exceed public and elite views of what is proper *not* because individuals are hypocrites and want to have their cake and eat it too, but because each would bake the cake in a different way.[8] During the budget battles of the 1980s, for example, conservative Republicans could consistently favor a balanced budget because they were willing to slash social programs to achieve the goal, while liberal Democrats could favor balance because they were willing to cut defense spending and raise taxes on corporations and people with higher incomes.[9]

Under these circumstances, all sides can treat some level of deficit as a horror and a sin, and attack the others without any sense of shame. Other participants in budget debate, such as editorial boards and economists, will talk about the need to reduce deficits yet view the details as other people's problem. Budgeting, therefore, tends to generate a great deal of blame that politicians want to avoid. There will be blame for specific decisions to cut spending or raise taxes, but also blame for *not* cutting *programs in general* or for *not* raising *taxes in general.* Blame is so pervasive that budget politics cannot be understood separate from the allocation not only of values, but blame.

THE PRESIDENTIAL BUDGET AS A BASIS FOR COOPERATION

The core institutions of the presidential budget were created in the Budget and Accounting Act of 1921, emerging from an elite executive budget movement. The dominant trend in this movement distrusted both the legislature and the public, and believed the chief executive and administrators should be free to make decisions that served their view of the public interest. [10] Many subsequent reformist analyses have followed in this tradition. [11] This executive dominance view was (and is) "at odds both with contemporary practice and the separation of powers." The process Congress supported in 1921 therefore retained "legislative initiative in appropriations" and stressed "the executive budget as a means of gaining executive responsibility and strengthening legislative budgetary control." [12]

How could the same process both make the executive more responsible and strengthen legislative control? It could help *both* president and Congress control the executive agencies.

DEVELOPMENT OF THE CLERK/BROKER PATTERN

Agency behavior can create problems for both Congress and the president. The first is "coercive deficiencies": an agency runs out of money and its political overseers feel compelled to appropriate more, rather than stop the activity. The process created by the 1921 Act, in which the budget bureau apportions funds to agencies, greatly reduced this problem. [13]

Both could also gain if agencies were operated more efficiently. Efficiency is not the same as economy. [14] As one senior OMB career official put it in an interview, "the idea I grew up with was to be a neutral competent budget analyst. As I told my staff, that meant *if it was a Republican administration trying to minimize cost; if it was a Democratic administration, how to maximize value for the money we had.*" The executive process could provide a "scrub" of agency requests and prevent them from submitting "blue sky" requests to Congress.

Both branches might also benefit from better coordination across programs, which could reveal if agencies were working at cross-purposes or uncover the "wasteful" opposite, redundancy or overlap of functions. Congress might choose not to use such information, but providing it would improve Congress's options. [15] Efficiency *might* be served if the budget bureau improved management. In practice, Congress has been conflicted on this topic, with some legislators at any given time hoping that central management initiatives will yield economies, and others fearing interference with their own influence over the agencies. We will see that recent management initiatives, even if mandated by Congress, appear to have done more harm than good. Nevertheless, there have been periods when the management activities of the budget bureau played a positive role. The Division of Administrative Management established within the budget bureau by Director Harold Smith in 1939 contributed in ways that are still recalled as a kind of "golden age" of the budget bureau. [16]

Most significantly, the president's budget can serve Congress by dispersing blame. If the president proposes measures that Congress can accept, legislators get to share the blame. If Congress rejects a presidential proposal, so must replace it with another, legislators can gain credit from the interest they protect, somewhat offsetting blame from the interest they hurt. The president gains policy influence from the initiative and agenda-setting effects of the presidential process.

In these ways, the presidential process helped both president and Congress match details to totals, and the budget system developed into a rough equilibrium of shared expectations and mutual adjustment. [17] It fit into the presidential role that Richard Neustadt described as "clerkship." Neustadt described the budget as "among the cardinal services the president-as-clerk performs for Congressmen and bureaucrats and lobbyists." [18] A better term might be brokerage: the president sits at a key point within a complex system of bargaining. In return for facilitating transactions, he collects resources that he uses for his own purposes. Because it was created by an intensive process within the executive branch; because it represented commitment in its most concrete form, money; and because the nature of appropriations meant that Congress had to respond to those proposals; the budget became the year's premier initiator.

Budgeting in this period was hardly a nonpartisan lovefest. There were occasional fevers, sometimes severe. Nevertheless, what Allen Schick termed the "Seven Year Budget War" from 1966 to 1973 initiated a transition to a much more adversarial role for the president's budget. [19] The clerk/broker role depended on conditions that diminished in the late 1960s and nearly disappeared in the 1980s.

TOWARD ADVERSARIAL BUDGETING

The first condition for cooperation was that Congress and the president have similar goals for budget totals. Liberal Democrats and conservative Republicans had very different fiscal policy views, but the conservative coalition that dominated Congress in the 1950s largely agreed with President Eisenhower, and disagreement only became systematic when President Nixon faced a more liberal Congress.

The second condition was that the instruments available within the budget process be adequate to the task of making details fit the totals. The process that had emerged only guaranteed action on annually appropriated programs, what would later be called "discretionary" spending. The growth of entitlements such as Social Security and Medicare, followed by military spending's decline as the Vietnam War wound down, meant that by 1973 annual appropriations were less than half, and a declining share, of spending.

The third condition was that the president and congressional majority be in rough agreement on program details or priorities. Again, this disagreement appears to have widened during the Nixon presidency. The fourth condition was that the apportionment power be used in a way that was remotely acceptable to Congress. Instead, President Nixon used it to impound (refuse to spend) appropriations for purposes that he did not approve and had not been able to veto. A constitutional crisis over budget powers was avoided only because another, culminating in Nixon's resignation, took its place.

Congress responded by passing the Congressional Budget and Impoundment Control Act of 1974. The Budget Act created the Budget Resolution process, through which Congress, before passing other spending and tax legislation, would lay out targets for spending and revenue totals and priorities. This process would be reformed and strengthened in 1980 by implementing *reconciliation*, a process through which legislative committees would be given targets for spending cuts or revenue increases in the Budget Resolution. Reconciliation had strong procedural protections against filibuster in the Senate. It therefore provided a vehicle through which Congress was much more likely to respond to presidential proposals to alter entitlement programs such as Medicare and Medicaid, or to change tax law, than had been the case before 1980. This extended the potential influence of the president's budget through both agenda-setting and blame-sharing, and the Budget Act therefore helped President Reagan win spending reductions in 1981.[20]

Yet the Budget Act also reduced Congress's dependence on the president for information, through creation of the Congressional Budget Office and the Budget Committee staffs. Budget Resolutions enabled Congress to set its own standards for totals, so its details would not be judged by the president's totals. CBO provided Congress's own source of economic analysis, to counter the president's judgments. The resolution further forced Congress to explicitly state its own fiscal policy and overall priorities, making any conflict more explicit.

After 1981, systematic deficits that were unprecedented during peacetime increased the blame for budget totals. Intense disagreement between the president and much of Congress (including moderate Republicans) about other budgetary values led to battles about budget resolutions and diminishing attention to the president's framework. Either Congress took the lead, as in 1982 and 1984, or leaders maneuvered to create some form of "budget summit," as in 1987 and 1990.

In 1985 a coalition of conservative radicals (e.g., Senator Gramm) and budget hawk moderates (Senators Rudman and Hollings) took legislation to increase the debt ceiling hostage in order to force procedural changes that, they believed, would force agreement on deficit reductions. Democratic leaders decided they could not increase the debt ceiling without something like that proposal, so worked to make it as bad for the president and his allies as possible. They succeeded enough that House Majority Whip Tom Foley was able to describe the Gramm-Rudman-Hollings law (GRH) as "about the kidnapping of the only child of the President's official family that he loves [defense], holding it in a dark basement and sending the President its ear."[21]

One OMB senior career official described budgeting with GRH as a game of "deficit-reduction roulette." The only way OMB could look like it was proposing doing "enough" on the deficit was to submit proposals that were obviously unacceptable (so in no sense constituted an "agenda"). As one agency budget officer expressed it, some proposals did not pass the "laugh test . . . the committees regard it with utter disdain, with laughter. Even around this table we laugh." The president's budget was commonly viewed as fake, impossible, or both, so "dead on arrival." In response, OMB released the fiscal year 1987 plan by sending it to Congress in an ambulance, in the form of a staffer on a stretcher. He jumped up to reveal a shirt proclaiming, "The FY87 Budget Lives."

The adversarial relationship between the branches led to changes in OMB's role and capacity. The professional staff redeployed from analyzing programs to supporting the political staff in negotiations with Congress. One of Director David Stockman's top aides explained that rationales for cuts were sought as weapons; "the notion was . . . one could find reasons to fit whatever our goal might be." The cost of this approach was in organizational capacity to identify efficiencies: to understand programs well enough to tell how they could do as much with less. In the background, some of the logic of the clerk/broker era remained. If the president proposed an increase within the budgetary environment of the 1980s, it would get more attention than if it came from anyone else. OMB might still find what one senior OMB civil servant called "the least provocative minuses"—proposals Congress could accept. But this became both less common and less of a focus for the process.[22]

In the circumstances of the 1980s there was far too much blame to share.[23] Both president and Congress had incentives to enact pure gimmicks, as in the 1989 "summit agreement" between president and Congress that included about $39 billion in smoke and mirrors out of a $47 billion total.[24]

The George H. W. Bush administration amended the outgoing Reagan administration's FY90 plan by specifying increases and calling for unspecified cuts. In the words of one House Appropriations Committee aide, "We didn't really feel we ever had a President's Budget." By 1990, the president's men were blaming Congress for not changing his budget enough.[25] Such developments led budget scholars to ask whether the presidential process had outlived its usefulness.[26]

PRESIDENT AND CONGRESS IN THE 1990S

During the first two years of the George H. W. Bush administration, the president's proposals appear to have been placeholders for eventual negotiations, at best. Nevertheless, in 1990 OMB Director Richard Darman managed to negotiate both significant deficit reduction and procedural rules, the Budget Enforcement Act, that eliminated the absurdities of GRH and provided totals with which it was possible to budget somewhat more regularly for the rest of the term. In order to do this, however, President Bush had to court blame by abandoning his 1988 campaign pledge of "no new taxes." Both the president and Congressional leaders felt they had to disguise the ways there were repealing the worst aspects of Gramm-Rudman, so they would not be accused of abandoning commitment to a balanced budget.[27]

By taking on blame, President Bush enabled a package that significantly reduced future deficits. He then ran for reelection against a Democrat who accused him of not being in touch with economic problems he had tried to fix through the conventional wisdom nostrum of deficit reduction; with a base that objected to his raising taxes; and with a third-party candidate (Ross Perot) attacking both parties for not caring about the deficit for which Bush had angered his base. Bush lost. The next President Bush appears to have concluded that compromise in order to reduce deficits is not a great deal for presidents.

Compared to 1990, 1993 was much more clearly a case of presidential leadership, in that the Clinton administration laid out a direction and some details that were largely followed—unlike the bargaining process for the 1990 deal. In its first two years, the Clinton administration's budgets related details to totals in a way that considered both short- and long-term effects. However, this was made possible by a newly united government; the legislation passed by one vote in both the House and Senate; united government focused partisan blame; and in the 1994 election congressional Democrats paid the price by losing control of both houses of Congress for the first time in forty years.

The Republican takeover of Congress in 1994—and especially the capture of the House by Republicans led by Speaker Newt Gingrich, who sought to revolutionize American government—created extreme disagreement with little room for the clerk/broker role. The budgetary relationship between Clinton and the Republican Congress was among the worst in American history, with the logical result that, as two budget process experts expressed, "It often seemed that policy proposals were designed more for partisan posturing than for effectiveness and efficiency."[28]

OMB in 1995 returned to the Reagan-era role of serving the president in continual pitched battles and negotiations with Congress. In both chambers, the leadership wanted the president to make proposals that would reduce the blame they could get for cutting programs, and would take almost any savings he could find so long as they weren't in defense, but this was not a matter of seeking clerical or analytic services. The president didn't want to be so helpful; meanwhile delays in one year's appropriations made it rather difficult to produce a plan for the next year's. As one administration official put it, "Anything would be flawed, so we punted."

After Clinton's reelection and the turn of events that followed the Balanced Budget Act of 1997 (BBA-97)—including, to general surprise, a balanced budget—one might have expected that extra money in a budget surplus would lubricate compromise. It did not for two reasons. First, the preferences of the president and of the Congressional majority leadership differed too greatly. The second problem was discretionary spending caps built into the deficit reduction legislation of 1997.

Clinton sought new spending and congressional Republicans sought new tax cuts. But the administration was also concerned about the long-term financing of Social Security, and concluded that future pensions could be made more affordable by reducing the federal debt and thereby future interest expenses. Therefore the Clinton administration promoted a standard of "saving Social Security first," by which it meant balance the budget without counting the Social Security surpluses. It therefore increased budgetary pressure on the details.[29]

Multiyear caps respond to pressure to reduce deficits by ignoring or hiding specifics. The 1990 budget deal had also created five-year caps, but they were not so tight. Those caps were revised and extended in 1993 as part of a strong push within Congress for savings from discretionary spending, with much less attention to the details that would result.[30] The 1993 targets were met only with assistance from the Gingrich Congress that the Clinton administration did not seem to appreciate at the time. The BBA-97 caps required that outlays be cut by about three percent relative to their real value in FY98 for FY99, and then be flat from FY99 through FY2002—in spite of economic growth, budget surpluses, and predictable events such as the decennial census.[31]

The problem with caps is that they do not resolve the details, which still must be appropriated each year. The Clinton administration wanted to spend above the caps, and proposed to pay for the extra spending with measures such as increased tobacco taxes and user fees. Congressional Republicans saw this as welching on a deal to constrain domestic spending, and objected to the offsets. Majorities in Congress neither wanted to violate conservative principles by raising the caps, nor fulfill them by spending as little as the caps required, nor enact the offsets.

So, each year, the administration insisted on its spending; appropriations were delayed by intense conflict; congressional Republicans largely gave in; and the caps were evaded with maneuvers that mainstream observers viewed as "gimmicks," such as shifts of payment dates from one year to another, declaring census spending an "emergency," and declaring somewhat predictable spending for military deployments in Bosnia an "emergency." By the end of 2000, discretionary spending was nearly $100 billion above the cap set in the BBA.[32] But this had been achieved in an entirely uncooperative way, in which the president's budget was viewed as unrealistic in Congress. OMB officials admitted as much; in one's words, "You do what you can to legitimately and sensibly come up with a total that is consistent with the overall decision of the president about what level of spending he wants to propose for the next year, and then turn it over to the appropriations process to change. Sometimes you propose things that you know aren't going to be enacted; it's a feature of the process."

BUDGETING DURING THE
GEORGE W. BUSH ADMINISTRATION

The George W. Bush (Bush 43) administration inherited a massive budget surplus and had, for most of its time in office, a supportive Congress. One might have expected presidential leadership and a process that fit common views about what a good process would do. Instead, events demonstrated that an administration's own preferences control how the presidential process fits into federal budgeting. This administration had little interest in totals as conventionally defined (the budget balance), and not much more in many details (particularly for discretionary domestic spending).

Process breakdowns approached levels seen at previous heights of conflict. Congress failed to pass budget resolutions for fiscal years 2003, 2005, or 2007. In 2004 nine of the thirteen appropriations bills did not pass until they were packaged together in an omnibus bill after the election, on November 20. In 2006, the Republican Congress not only failed to agree with the Republican president to pass nine of the bills before the election, but then passed only a short-term continuing resolution, leaving the new Democratic Congress to deal with those bills in 2007. The Bush administration expressed its disappointment, but had done nothing to make agreement more likely.

Although the Bush 43 deficits were not large by historical standards, they appeared larger given the preceding surpluses and a fear campaign about future costs from retirement of the baby boomers.[33] Perhaps as a result, blame-avoidance may have been taken to new heights (or lows) by a series of maneuvers to obscure policy choices and their consequences. These included suppressing the administration's own cost estimates for its Medicare pre-scription-drug legislation, manipulating sunset dates of tax legislation, con-tinual failures to honestly address the Alternative Minimum Tax, and system-atic funding of an ongoing war through supplemental appropriations.

Although it did not want blame for deficits, it is not clear that the Bush 43 administration much cared about the deficit as policy. In its view lower taxes were good,[34] lower spending on domestic programs was good, defense spending was not to be constrained by budget concerns, privatizing social programs was good even if it increased spending,[35] and the overall balance mattered much less than the results on the component parts. A senior political official's description of how the budget was assembled shows the pattern. He reported that they focused on "what is appropriate, needed and fair for nonse-curity . . . We ended up with some increase, just below inflation, and building from that. So then you ask what is the increase on the security side, you build in that. Then there is DOD, and you can imagine there were discussions on that. *There was no magic on the top line, it's just the sum of the parts.*" This is remarkably different from standard ways of thinking about the budgeting task. Yet career OMB staff broadly supported this description.

Even if the administration had wanted to take leadership on the details, it had diminished capacity to do the work of the clerk/broker model. OMB analysts spent much less time monitoring the appropriations process, because of the administration's disengagement from the details. But both Clinton and Bush had reduced OMB personnel, and the remaining staff was buried under new "management" work, both from the 1993 Government Performance and Results Act (GPRA) and the Bush Administration's Program Assessment and Rating Tool (PART) process.[36] "There has been a gradual expansion of legislated tasks," one senior career official observed, "and the result is that there is a substantial amount of examiners' time that gets consumed with responding to requirements that are either mandated or legislated on the institution." Another said that "one thing I used to do was sit down with examiners and identify two or three things we would need to learn more about from March to September . . . we could no longer do that, because PART sucked up every moment between February and September." The gravest problem, a third observed, was that there was "a whole lot of paper there, but we don't have the time to see if any of it is actually representative of anything."[37]

Thus Bush 43 budgets were criticized in the same terms as the late Rea-gan budgets, at a time of lower deficits. Some claims about flawed proposals involved traditional worldview differences between OMB and appropriators, such as whether agencies could find savings to offset pay increases (OMB finds that more reasonable). Legislative budgeters also will blithely adapt "OMB tricks" they've criticized to avoid blame themselves. So they are hardly pure; but they legitimately felt they were not getting the analysis that the presidential process is supposed to provide: in one appropriations veteran's words, "a sense of how our agencies are doing."

Even at the height of conflict, appropriations staff have believed that the president's budget *could* be helpful by providing some constraints on agency requests and vetting agency details. One illustrated the need by saying the National Cancer Institute's "bypass budget," in which NCI presents its "needs" without OMB interference, "is just too expensive. No one can use it." So Congress wants information about how to prioritize inputs into individual programs. But the Bush 43 administration showed "blatant disregard" for giving Congress the detailed budget justifications appropriators want to use.[38]

All this was true before the Democrats retook Congress in 2006. At that point Congressional Democrats, who had to get to work on the bills for 2008, enacted the remaining 2007 bills in a full-year Continuing Resolution for the first time since 1986. The new Democratic majorities did pass a Budget Resolution, but did not pass appropriations for all of the government except the Pentagon until an omnibus bill on December 19. Such a sweeping bill had not been necessary since 1987.

How cabinet secretaries allocated their budgets was basically their problem, as one OMB veteran reported, "so long as it meets the totals." The administration took much the same view in its negotiations with Congress. In a July 11, 2007 press conference, outgoing Budget Director Rob Portman declared, "I think the position of the administration has been clear, which is, $933 billion is the top line, and the flexibility occurs under that top line."[39] A congressional source commented that "for the most part this administration cared about the top line and didn't care much about the detail under that top line . . . (in 2007) we got down to the President's number by cutting $10 billion out of our bills, and we did it without them in the room. There was literally no involvement, which was completely different from the Clinton years."

In 2008 Congress, faced with certain vetoes and the possibility of a different president if it waited long enough, passed only the three bills that covered security related spending (Defense, Homeland Security, and Military Construction/Veterans Affairs), and didn't even bother bringing other bills to the floor of the House and Senate. The new president and Congress were left, again, to deal with the problem after the Inauguration.

Hence the president's budget process in the second Bush presidency was a strange amalgam of relevance and irrelevance from an adversarial stance.

Both because of his veto and his party's control of Congress for most of the period, President Bush largely got his way on both totals and the details he cared about. Discretionary domestic "nonsecurity" spending was substantially constrained; military spending was not; two large tax cuts were passed along with a major expansion and "reform" of Medicare. But his success had little to do with the apparatus of presidential budgeting.

Disinterest in the usual activities of the clerk/broker role makes "adversarial" the default description of Bush 43 presidential budgeting. So does that administration's complicity in process breakdowns even during united government. An alternate interpretation, however, would be that both the Bush administration and Congressional Republican leadership were more interested in attacking the federal government than in making budgets. In this sense they were allies, not adversaries.

THE OBAMA FIRST TERM: PLAYING CHICKEN AND CHICKEN-LITTLES

The Bush 43 years should have clarified a simple point: relations between the president and Congress on budget decisions depend on how the president's process is managed. Obama's first term illustrates another simple point: it's dangerous to talk about conflict between "president" and "Congress" if it's difficult to figure out what either "side," especially the president, wants in the first place.

Congress, after all, is supposed to be divided; presidents not so much. But the Obama administration suffered from a peculiar budgetary schizophrenia, talking and acting in multiple voices. This could be viewed as an attempt to be moderate and balanced, but did not work out so well.

As Barbara Sinclair argues in this volume, Obama and the Democratic majority in the 111th Congress cooperated to pass major legislation related to taxing and spending. These included the economic stimulus package in February of 2009; cleaning up the remaining appropriations for Fiscal Year 2009 in March of 2009; and the health-care reform legislation that was passed in March of 2010 and included restructuring of the federal student-loan programs.[40] As she also shows, the 112th Congress was dominated by bitter conflict between the Obama administration and the House majority. This conflict included hostage-taking over the debt ceiling that reenacted the worst patterns of the Reagan years. To a great extent, budgeting became a game of chicken between the two parties in government.

Another part of the story, however, was how horrific economic and budget conditions, amid immense pressure from much of the press and the Washington and financial establishments to take major steps to reduce future deficits, exacerbated divisions within the administration and Congressional (especially Senate) Democrats. This pressure enabled and in some cases supported taking the debt ceiling hostage as well as other efforts to budget outside the regular process. Once again panic about the totals led to irresponsibility about the details.

The Obama administration, in dealing with these pressures, sent mixed and inconsistent messages about its goals. How one interprets the pattern will depend on one's policy view. If you believe the nation was gravely threatened by the prospect of very large deficits a decade in the future, or that the extremely large deficits (over 10 percent of GDP) caused by the recession were bad policy, then the Obama administration's vacillation was simply a lack of courage and the attempts to bypass traditional budgeting were necessary. If you believe that the deficits during Obama's first term were a proper response to macroeconomic conditions, and the idea that future deficits were the nation's greatest problem was misguided, then the focus of political analysis should be on the forces that pushed to prioritize "fixing" future deficits rather than the immediate economy. From this perspective, elite deficit hysteria helped break the budgeting thermometer—and not for the first time. [41]

I am in this second camp. Budgetary Chicken Littles claimed the sky was falling based on analyses that were simply wrong. The most egregious arguments asserted that what Paul Krugman called the "bond market vigilantes" would punish the United States for its deficits by driving up interest rates. [42] In fact, interest rates on US Treasury securities were persistently so low that federal government interest expenses as a share of GDP were lower in 2012 (1.4 percent) than in 2008 (1.8 percent)—even as the federal debt owed to the public grew from 40.5 percent of GDP to 72.5 percent. [43]

Presidents and Congress operate within a context of not only mass opinion but also elite opinion. [44] An exaggerated sense of the deficit's economic significance was promoted by Democratic and centrist economists throughout the 1980s and 1990s, and this made deficit-hawk attitudes, especially the belief that "entitlements" were a grave threat to the nation, conventional wisdom. [45] When Republicans claimed the deficit was a huge problem they met ready agreement from centrist Democrats in Congress and cheers from much of the press and Wall Street. This did not mean either that voters wanted to cut entitlements (far from it); or that investors were seriously concerned (as shown by the low interest rates); or that what Republicans meant by "the deficit" was the same as what centrists meant (like President Bush, when Republicans during the Obama administration said "deficit" they basically meant "spending"). It did mean that the Obama administration appears (I'm no mind reader and their words deserve as much trust as any politician's words) to have drawn five conclusions:

- They had to at least publicly agree that the deficit was a big problem and priority.
- For much of the administration, it actually was a big problem and priority.
- The Republicans had to get the blame for the failure of any negotiations.
- Deficit reduction should not occur quickly enough to endanger the economy and, thereby, the president's reelection.
- And it would be nice to do some things that pleased the Democratic base and gave reason to be president in the first place—like come closer to the party's dream of health insurance for all.

Resolving these conflicts was made more difficult by budget scorekeeping. Budgeting includes a literal score (the deficit, or changes in the deficit) that outsiders believe reveals how well the incumbents are doing. Scoring only by the deficit is misleading but common.[46] The baselines used by CBO in 2009 assumed various laws would expire, automatically changing policies. All of the 2001 and 2003 "Bush" tax cuts would expire at the end of 2010; the Alternative Minimum Tax would suddenly apply to an extra twenty million people at the beginning of 2010; physician fees in Medicare would be cut by about 21 percent at the same time; and other highly unpopular and so unlikely events would occur as well. This meant, however, that even compromises that changed the budget policies in effect in 2009 to reduce deficits, such as letting some but not all of the 2001 and 2003 tax cuts expire, could be condemned by both partisan opponents (e.g., for raising taxes) and moderate sometime-allies (because they increased deficits above the baselines!).

The administration attempted to resolve the conflicting pressures, first, with a detailed and ambitious budget agenda.[47] After enacting the large (if possibly not large enough) economic stimulus package described by Professor Sinclair, the President's Budget proposed new taxes and spending cuts to Medicare and Medicaid to help pay for health-insurance expansion; extending the 2001 and 2003 tax cuts for people with incomes up to $200,000 for individuals and $250,000 for joint filers, but not above that level; taxing emissions of pollution and using the proceeds partly to cut taxes for lower-income workers and partly to fund new energy programs; and phasing out the military commitments in Iraq. It compared all its policies not to CBO's "current law" baseline but to existing policies. The administration hoped that health-care reform would help control health-care costs so further improve the budget and economy; that its energy policies would jump-start new industries and so improve growth; and so that its policies would form a virtuous circle of deficits now but growth and lower deficits later.

More conservative Democrats in Congress, however, did not favor much of this. They did not pass legislation to change the baselines. They postponed acting on the tax cuts. They showed no interest in adopting the pollution taxes. This refusal to deal quickly with the tax cuts and baselines would prove especially damaging in the long run.

The failure of the President's Budget to shape the Budget Resolution was hidden by passage of the stimulus package and the dramatic battle over health-care reform. The latter battle also, however, showed the same pattern. The conservative Democrats who most emphasized deficits also blocked the provision, the public option, which was most likely to help control health-care spending. The final legislation included many measures that were widely promoted in the health-policy community but that CBO, looking at the evidence, could not project would reduce spending anytime soon.[48] Similarly, in the fall of 2010 the Obama administration could not get the Senate to vote on extending a portion of the tax cuts on its terms (and so guaranteeing the others would expire) before the 2010 election; again it was blocked by conservative Senate Democrats who thought the vote might hurt their reelections (and apparently did not think making the Republicans vote in favor of the rich and against everyone else would be any help).

In short, it would be wrong to ascribe the Obama administration's struggles with the budget simply to partisan opposition. Democrats, particularly in the Senate, were quite divided. Budgeting by 2010 had devolved into a complex mess in which the administration could enact very little but there were continual efforts to change procedure, either because some legislators sincerely (regardless of decades of evidence) thought it would help, or to fool voters into thinking they were "doing something."[49] At the beginning of 2010, moderate Democrats led by Senate Budget Committee Chair Kent Conrad held an increase in the debt ceiling hostage, demanding creation of a special deficit-reduction commission that would create a deficit-reduction package on which Congress would be forced to vote outside of the regular order. They could not pass their proposal because Republicans, fearing the commission would propose tax increases, blocked it. But President Obama was only able to get the debt ceiling increased by promising to create a commission by executive order.[50]

By this point, formal budget procedures, other than scorekeeping rules, had become irrelevant to budget making—except to the extent they provided opportunities to take hostages. The relationship between president and Congress could be better understood from the basic power relationships involved.

The proper question is: *how can presidents change what Congress would do, compared to what Congress would do if there were no president?* The major answers are:

- The president can frame an issue in a way that exerts public or interest group pressure on the opposite party. This happens rarely, since members of the other party already got elected without his support. The president also is only one voice amid a cacophony of public advocacy—think of speaking from a bully pulpit next to a busy airport runway, or three.

- The president can take a stance that identifies his party with an initiative. This creates a cost to the party label from failing, so that conflicted members of the party may see a risk in defeating the initiative even if they also see risks in supporting it. This appears to be one reason some Democrats from more conservative districts voted for health-care reform. In the words of a participant and leading health-politics scholar, "The real story of health reform's enactment is how the legislative battle got Democrats so invested that they could not afford to fail."[51]

- The president can sell out his own party, promoting a policy that is more acceptable to the opposition. Then his partisans must face the charge that they are being partisan extremists if they do not go along. President Clinton's welfare reform and NAFTA legislation are examples of this pattern; arguably so is President Reagan's tax reform. This only changes policy, however, if the opposition accepts the deal.

After health-care reform there were no examples of the second pattern. The tension was between the first and third, and both Obama's behavior and the results tended towards the third.

Thus Obama appointed six of the eighteen members of the National Commission on Fiscal Responsibility and Reform, including the cochairs, former GOP Senator Alan Simpson and former Clinton Chief of Staff Erskine Bowles. Although the committee did not report by a margin sufficient to trigger a vote in Congress, eleven of the eighteen expressed support for the cochairs' highly conservative plan. It set a limit of 21 percent of GDP on federal revenues (which had been a conservative constitutional amendment in the 1980s); included large cuts in Social Security and Medicare; relied much more on spending cuts than tax increases; and called for tax "reform" that would cut rates on higher incomes, supposedly paid by reducing tax preferences. Five of Obama's six appointees endorsed the plan, and the positions of each could have been predicted from their previous records.

The legislation that extended all of the Bush tax cuts at the end of 2010 could, as Sinclair argues in her chapter, be viewed as a "victory" in some sense. If so, it was from a position of great weakness: it made the budget situation worse (continuing the pressure) and transformed the stimulus law's main tax cut for middle- and lower-income Americans into a payroll tax "holiday" that conservatives could use to attack Social Security by saying its trust funds were fake. Social Security advocates were enraged.[52]

This was the background to the bitter partisan warfare with the House majority and Senate minority in the 112th Congress. When the House held the debt ceiling hostage, it was doing what supposed moderates had done the year before. The president was unwilling or unable to make the case that the debt ceiling itself was a mindless law, and should be repealed. The hostage-takers were supported by ostensibly centrist organizations such as the Committee for a Responsible Federal Budget (CRFB), which saw this as yet another opportunity to force action. "Failing to raise the debt ceiling," CRFB pronounced, "would likely lead to a fiscal and financial crisis, but failing to address the debt would eventually do the same."[53]

During the debate the president seemed to want to agree with House Speaker Boehner on a deal that would have been almost as bad, from Democratic perspectives, as Bowles-Simpson.[54] The settlement included a deficit-reduction package consisting entirely of spending cuts. It also included yet another "action forcing" device, a new version of the Gramm-Rudman-Hollings sequester, designed to be just as mindless as the original. That ostensibly would be avoided by yet another deficit-reduction "Supercommittee," tasked with reporting an alternative $1.2 trillion in deficit cuts (over ten years) by November 23, 2011. It failed.[55]

Nothing else much happened on the budget for the next year, until after the election. Hardly anything was passed remotely on time. In September of 2012, Congress passed and the president signed a Continuing Resolution to fund all discretionary programs through March 27, 2013. Even the defense appropriations could not be enacted separately.

As 2013 began, there was movement, of sorts. After massive publicity about the "fiscal cliff" the economy would fall off if the planned sequester were to happen and all of the various tax cuts expired, President Obama and House Republicans agreed to pass the American Taxpayer Relief Act of 2012. It made the 2001 and 2003 income tax cuts permanent up to incomes of $400,000 for individuals and $450,000 for couples; fixed the Alternative Minimum Tax for three years; extended some unemployment benefits for a year; and postponed the sequester for two months.[56] It did not, however, either repeal the sequester, or do anything about the government shutdown that loomed at the end of March if there were no agreement on appropriations; or address the fact that the debt ceiling was going to become a major problem again in mid-May. Some observers viewed the result as a new, tougher Obama using public support from the election to gain the upper hand. Others thought the result was worse than Congressional Democrats could have negotiated if the administration stayed out of the bargaining.[57]

CONCLUSION

This chapter began by arguing that budgeting is extremely important and that there were reasons why both Congress and the president could gain from cooperation.

The first remains true; the latter not so much. At least, presidents and party leaders only believe it if they are of the same party; and even then, as the Bush 43 administration shows, presidents these days may neither understand nor care about how they could make the system work better.

Budget-process collapse, however, is not simply due to partisanship or presidents' disinterest in the more clerical functions. Budgeting has involved too much blame for the political system to manage. This blame results mainly from a failure among political elites to understand that other budgeting outcomes and values are as important as the deficit. Budgetary hostage-taking has continually been as common among centrists as radicals.

Under these circumstances, it may not be surprising that a president, particularly one who instinctively seeks a "center," would try to have it both ways—to pressure for a "grand bargain" on the deficit but somehow pursue his own party's priorities. Yet, after his early victories, President Obama lost more than he won. Handcuffed by the Chicken Littles, Obama lost most of the games of chicken.

He did a bit better at the end of 2012. Readers will know how he did in the battles that occur in 2013. Political scientists should not pretend to guess—and readers should be aware that at some point a game of chicken can look, for the country, like Russian roulette.

NOTES

The research for this chapter includes interviews that the author conducted for numerous projects since 1983; interviews focused on executive budgeting were conducted mainly in 1990–1991 and in 2008. All interviews were conducted on condition that comments would not be attributed to the respondents, so quotations from those interviews are not attributed.

1. The basic statement of both the need to combine authority and the expected greater role of the Congress over spending matters is Alexander Hamilton, James Madison, and John Jay, *The Federalist Papers*, e.g., the Bantam Classic edition (New York: Random House, 2003), especially papers 47 and 48, by Madison.

2. Larry Berman, *The Office of Management and Budget and the Presidency* (Princeton, NJ: Princeton University Press, 1979); Richard E. Neustadt, *Presidential Power: The Politics of Leadership from FDR to Carter* (New York: Wiley, 1980); Aaron Wildavsky, *The Politics of the Budgetary Process* (Boston: Little, Brown, 1964); Joseph White, "Presidential Power and the Budget," in Thomas D. Lynch, ed., *Federal Budget & Financial Management Reform* (New York: Quorum Books, 1991).

3. The term "budget bureau" will be used in this chapter when I refer to the basic functions performed by both the Bureau of the Budget (pre-1971) and Office of Management and Budget (1971 and after).

4. Accounts of the 1980s and 1990s include Elizabeth Drew, *Showdown: The Struggle between the Gingrich Congress and the Clinton White House* (New York: Simon & Schuster, 1996); David Maraniss and Michael Weiskopf, *Tell Newt to Shut Up! Prize-winning Washington Post Journalists Reveal How Reality Gagged the Gingrich Revolution* (New York: Simon & Schuster, 1996); Joseph White and Aaron Wildavsky, *The Deficit and the Public Interest: The Search for Responsible Budgeting in the 1980s* (Berkeley and New York: The University of California Press and The Russell Sage Foundation, 1991). For an overview that focuses more on congressional procedures, see James A. Thurber, "The Dynamics and Dysfunction of the Congressional Budget Process: From Inception to Deadlock," chap. 13 in Lawrence C. Dodd

and Bruce I. Oppenheimer, eds., *Congress Reconsidered*, 10th ed. (Washington, DC: CQ Press, 2012).

5. This chapter updates the chapter in the previous edition of this book. A more detailed account of 2009–2010 is Joseph White, "From Ambition to Desperation on the Budget," in James A. Thurber, ed., *Obama in Office: The First Two Years* (Boulder, CO: Paradigm Publishers, 2011). More detail on the George W. Bush administration is in Joseph White, "What Not to Ask of Budget Processes: Lessons from George W. Bush's Years," *Public Administration Review* 69, no. 2 (March/April 2009): 224–32.

6. For typical lists of functions see Donald Axelrod, *Budgeting for Modern Government* (New York: St. Martin's Press, 1988); Irene Rubin, *The Politics of Public Budgeting: Getting and Spending, Borrowing and Balancing*, 3rd ed. (Chatham, NJ: Chatham House, 1997); and Allen Schick, "Twenty-five Years of Budgeting Reform," *OECD Journal on Budgeting* 4, no. 1 (2004): 81–102

7. Rubin, *The Politics of Public Budgeting*.

8. Joseph White, "Making 'Common Sense' of Federal Budgeting," *Public Administration Review* 58, no. 2 (1998): 101–8; a classic statement of the social choice paradoxes is Anthony Downs, "Why the Government Budget Is Too Small in a Democracy," *World Politics* 12, no. 4 (1962): 541–63.

9. For details see White and Wildavsky, *The Deficit and the Public Interest*.

10. Irene Rubin, "Early Budget Reformers: Democracy, Efficiency, and Budget Reforms," *American Review of Public Administration* 24, no. 3 (1994): 246.

11. Paul Posner, "The Continuity of Change: Public Budgeting and Finance Reforms over 70 Years," *Public Administration Review* 67 (November/December 2007): 1023.

12. Naomi Caiden, "Paradox, Ambiguity and Enigma: The Strange Case of the Executive Budget and the United States Constitution," *Public Administration Review* 47, no. 1 (January/February 1987): 84.

13. United States Senate Committee on Appropriations, *Committee on Appropriations U.S. Senate: 1867–2008*, 110th Congress, 2nd Session, Document No. 14 (Washington, DC: US Government Printing Office, 2008).

14. Allen Schick, "The Road to PPB," *Public Administration Review* 26, no. 4 (1966): 243–58.

15. The coordinating function expanded to legislation, and even that can have benefits to Congress by revealing problems before extensive investment in an initiative. Richard E. Neustadt, "Presidency and Legislation: The Growth of Central Clearance," *American Political Science Review* 48, no. 3 (1954): 641–71.

16. Mathew J. Dickinson and Andrew Rudalevige, "Worked Out in Fractions: Neutral Competence, FDR, and the Bureau of the Budget," *Congress & the Presidency* 34, no. 1 (2007): 1–26; Donald Stone, "Administrative Management: Reflections on Origins and Accomplishments," *Public Administration Review* 50, no. 1 (1990): 3–20.

17. Wildavsky, *The Politics of the Budget Process*; for a larger emphasis on the budget bureau's role see John P. Crecine, M. S. Kamlet, D. C. Mowery, and M. Winer, "The Role of the Office of Management and Budget in Executive Branch Budgetary Decision-Making," in J. P. Crecine, ed., *Proceedings of the First Annual Research Conference on Public Policy and Management* (Greenwich, CT: JAI Press, 1980).

18. Neustadt, *Presidential Power*, 83.

19. Allen Schick, *Congress and Money* (Washington DC: Urban Institute Press, 1980).

20. Reconciliation in the Reagan years was led as much by the chairs of the Ways and Means and Finance committees as by the administration. See White and Wildavsky, *The Deficit and the Public Interest*, and John B. Gilmour, *Reconcilable Differences? Congress, the Budget Process, and the Deficit* (Berkeley: University of California Press, 1990).

21. White and Wildavsky, *The Deficit and the Public Interest*, 431–32. The president thought he was taking domestic programs hostage.

22. For more detail see White, "Presidential Power and the Budget."

23. Joseph White and Aaron Wildavsky, "Public Authority and the Public Interest: What the 1980s Budget Battles Tell Us About the American State," *Journal of Theoretical Politics* 1, no. 1 (1989): 7–31.

24. Statement of Rep. Lee Hamilton in the *Congressional Record* for May 3, 1989, H1553-56.

25. White, "Presidential Power and the Budget."

26. Bernard T. Pitsvada, "A Call for Budget Reform," and see also Fred Thompson, "Reforming the Federal Budget Process: A Symposium Commemorating the 75th Anniversary of the Executive Budget," both in *Policy Sciences* 29 (1996); quote p. 225.

27. Postscript to White and Wildavsky, *The Deficit and the Public Interest*; Shelley Lynne Tomkin, *Inside OMB: Politics and Process in the President's Budget Office* (Armonk, NY: M.E. Sharpe, 1980).

28. Philip G. Joyce and Roy T. Meyers, "Budgeting During the Clinton Presidency," *Public Budgeting & Finance* (Spring 2001): 2. Also Drew, *Showdown*; Maraniss and Weiskopf, "Tell Newt to Shut Up."

29. Daniel J. Parks, "Between the Lockbox and a Hard Place," *CQ Weekly Online*, September 8, 2001, library.cqpress.com/cqueekly/weeklyreport107-0000003061-17. Also Joseph White, *False Alarm: Why the Greatest Threat to Social Security and Medicare Is the Campaign to "Save" Them* (Baltimore: Johns Hopkins University Press, 2003).

30. The administration was divided about the 1993 caps; Tomkin, *Inside OMB*.

31. See United States Congressional Budget Office, *The Economic and Budget Outlook: Fiscal Years 1999–2008* (Washington, DC: Congressional Budget Office: 2008), 67.

32. On process see Joyce and Meyers "Budgeting During the Clinton Presidency"; for numbers US Congressional Budget Office, *The Budget and Economic Outlook: Fiscal Years 2004–2013* (Washington, DC: Congressional Budget Office, 2003).

33. White, *False Alarm*.

34. For a good example of the fundamentalist view about the evils of taxes see White House Office of Homeland Security, *National Strategy for Homeland Security* (July 2002), 65.

35. Jonathan Oberlander, "Through the Looking Glass: The Politics of the Medicare Prescription Drug, Improvement, and Modernization Act," *Journal of Health Politics, Policy and Law* 32, no. 2 (2007): 187–220.

36. For a fuller account of this story, see Joseph White, "Playing the Wrong PART: The Program Assessment Rating Tool and the Functions of the President's Budget," *Public Administration Review* 72, no.1 (January 2012): 112–20. For a summary of other management initiatives during the 1990s, see Posner, "The Continuity of Change."

37. The account here is amplified by others' recent research. See Scott Lilly and Eleanor Hill, "Broken Budgeting: A View of Federal Budget Making from the Trenches," Center for American Progress, August 2012, www.americanprogress.org/wp-content/uploads/issues/2012/08/pdf/broken_budgeting.pdf.

38. Lilly and Hill, "Broken Budgeting," 27; see also White, "Playing the Wrong Part."

39. Brian Friel, "Spending: The Power of the Purse Strings," NationalJournal.com, July 28, 2007, www.nationaljournal.com/njmagazine/print_friendly.php?ID=nj_20070728_7.

40. As Sinclair describes, this required two pieces of legislation, the Affordable Care Act and a separate Reconciliation Act, so was only possible due to budget-process rules.

41. White and Wildavsky, *The Deficit and the Public Interest*, explains the political origins of Gramm-Rudman-Hollings.

42. As one of many instances see Paul Krugman, "Bond Vigilantes and the Power of Three," *New York Times*, December 24, 2012, krugman.blogs.nytimes.com/2012/12/24/bond-vigilantes-and-the-power-of-three/. See also Brad DeLong's blog from December 22, 2012, delong.typepad.com/sdj/2012/12/back-when-i-feared-the-bond-market-vigilantes-maundering-old-timer-reminiscence-weblogging.html.

43. Data downloaded from Congressional Budget Office website February 18, 2013, www.cbo.gov/publication/43904.

44. One version of this is the "Washington reputation" that is central to Richard Neustadt's discussion of *Presidential Power*.

45. For the attitude and its development see White, *False Alarm*. A good example of the view in the Obama years is the offhand reference to "entitlements (the deadweight sitting on the future of the economy)" in Jonathan Alter, *The Promise: President Obama, Year One* (New York: Simon & Schuster), 424.

46. This is why "public participation" processes such as the Concord Coalition's fix-the-budget-yourself games are misleading: you "win" by reducing the deficit, while in the real world the country might be worse off and you might not be re-elected. For an example see www.concordcoalition.org/act/tools/federal-budget-challenge.

47. The argument here is made with much more detail in White, "From Ambition to Desperation on the Budget."

48. Jonathan Oberlander, "Throwing Darts: Americans' Elusive Search for Health Care Cost Control," *Journal of Health Politics, Policy and Law* 36, no. 3 (2011): 477–84; Joseph White, "Muddling through the Muddled Middle," pp. 443–48 in the same issue.

49. White, "From Ambition to Desperation on the Budget," 193–96.

50. David Clarke and Greg Vadala, "Senate Passes Debt Limit Increase after Commission, Pay-As-You-Go Agreements," *CQ Weekly Online*, February 1, 2010.

51. Judith Feder, "Too Big to Fail: The Enactment of Health Care Reform," *Journal of Health Politics, Policy and Law* 36, no. 3 (2011): 413.

52. For more explanation see White, "From Ambition to Desperation," and sources cited therein.

53. Committee for a Responsible Federal Budget, "What Needs to Come Out of the Debt Ceiling Negotiations," June 21, 2011, crfb.org/document/what-needs-come-out-debt-ceiling-negotiations.

54. For an account see Matt Bai, "Who Killed the Debt Deal?" *New York Times Magazine*, April 1, 2012. For typical presidential remarks at the time, see www.whitehouse.gov/the-press-office/2011/07/11/press-conference-president.

55. Joseph J. Schatz, "After the Fall of the 'Supercommittee,'" *CQ Weekly Report*, November 28, 2011, 2490–95; James A. Thurber, "Agony, Angst, and the Failure of the Supercommittee," *Extensions* (Summer 2012).

56. Congressional Budget Office, *The Budget and Economic Outlook: Fiscal Years 2013–2023* (Washington, DC: CBO, 2013), 12–13.

57. Noam Scheiber, "The Inside Story of How Obama Could Have Gotten a Better Tax Deal Without Biden," *The New Republic*, January 9, 2013, www.newrepublic.com/blog/plank/111749/obamas-big-mistake-in-fiscal-cliff-negotiations-letting-biden-haggle-mcconnell#.

Chapter Ten

The Politics of Federal Regulation

Congress Acts, the President Hones
His Policies by Regulations[1]

Claudia Hartley Thurber

President Obama had stunning legislative success in his first two years in office, with the passage of 334 laws including the historic stimulus package, health-care reforms, and financial-reform legislation. All embody the broad outline of what they are intended to accomplish.[2] In his second term, the Democrats, though the majority party in the Senate, are too few to overcome filibusters and the Republican-controlled House of Representatives, fraught with dissention, cannot seem to overcome its ideological recalcitrance and legislate. With what portends to be a deadlocked do-nothing 113th Congress, the president will focus on federal regulations to further implement his policies. In particular, the Patient Protection and Affordable Care Act (PPACA) and Dodd-Frank Wall Street Reform and Consumer Protection Act mandate extensive rulemaking. Federal government departments, agencies, and independent regulatory agencies have been and will continue to promulgate regulations pursuant to these new enabling statutes. In addition, major legislation from as far in the past as the 1970s also requires rulemaking. For example, in just two areas of the environment, the Clean Air Act of 1970 and the Clean Water Act of 1972 have provisions that require rulemaking, and the Occupational Safety and Health Administration (OSHA) and the Mine Safety and Health Administration (MSHA) have significant rules in the pipeline to protect workers in general industry, construction, maritime, and mining. Under the Food Safety Modernization Act, the Food and Drug Administration is addressing food safety from produce to animal feed to human food, with the goal of preventing unsafe food from reaching the market.

The executive branch, the president's administrative tool, but also answerable to the Congress and the courts, is an important component in the rivals for political power in American democracy. Congress passes broad legislation; the administrative agencies, usually through notice and comment rulemaking, take the laws and define their terms, and promulgate the specific rules that explain how an affected individual, organization, or business can meet the requirements of the law, and also set the deadlines for compliance. There are many reasons why the Congress passes laws that lack specificity, but probably the main one is the authors' need to get support for passage from their colleagues who hold different views. Regulatory policy and action in the form of rules and guidance documents have far-reaching effects on individuals, corporations, and organizations, and on state, local, and tribal governments. As the Congress and the president compete for power, the federal executive branch enhances the president's power to implement his policies through rulemakings that hone the requirements in the congressional statutes. Through regulatory policy, the president can set his political goals by prioritizing what issues will be addressed in his administration, and determining how best to make the rules cost effective, faithful to their underlying legislation, and fair.

Federal rules and regulations affect everyone as they conduct their affairs, be they personal, social, or work-related. Federal rulemaking is initiated and completed by the federal agencies pursuant to their statutory authority; the Administrative Procedure Act of 1946[3]; a myriad of legislation that has been enacted over the last half century and made applicable to the federal rulemaking process; and court decisions on rules that have become further requirements, precedents, and directions affecting not only the subject rulemaking, but also subsequent rulemakings. The rules, based upon congressional statutes that are known as enabling statutes, are legislative in nature, as they affect prospective behavior.

Rulemaking occurs throughout the executive branch of government, but certain departments and agencies promulgate a greater number of significant rules. They include the Department of Treasury, Departments of Labor (OSHA and MSHA), Health and Human Services, Homeland Security, Housing and Urban Development, Transportation, Energy, Education, and Veteran's Affairs, and agencies such as the Environmental Protection Agency (EPA) and the Food and Drug Administration (FDA). Independent federal agencies that engage in rulemaking include the Commodities Futures Trade Commission, the Consumer Product Safety Commission, the Federal Elections Commission, the National Labor Relations Board, the Social Security Administration, and the Federal Communications Commission and the Securities and Exchange Commission (SEC). Independent federal agencies can be just as powerful and usually make their rules in the same way as other agencies, but they often have fewer procedural requirements. The major difference lies in the independent agency structure, which typically is headed by a commission or board, members of which are appointed by a president, but in many cases have to be nonpartisan, which means balanced by party, and because they often serve staggered terms, they can be in office over more than one presidency. Finally, a sitting president cannot easily fire board and commission members, whereas he can fire the political appointees in the executive agencies at will.

Each person is affected by rules governing the quality of the air he breathes, the food he eats and the water he drinks, the clothes he wears (and the fabric from which they are made), the car he drives, the marshland next to his house, the conditions under which he works, the access he enjoys to health care, the information to which he is entitled in his financial dealings, the security of his investments, and the scheduling and safety of the airplane on which he travels, to name just a few areas. No one can escape the reach of federal rules from the day we are born in a hospital, through our education and employment years to our sunset years in assisted living or nursing homes; but then few of us would want to return to the days when unsafe conditions abounded in nearly all areas of life.

COSTS OF FEDERAL REGULATION

The costs of federal regulations are high, but the benefits are even higher. Major rules, as defined in Executive Order (EO) 12866 as Significant Regulatory Actions, typically result in a rule that may:

> Have an annual effect on the economy of $100 million or more or adversely affect in a material way the economy, a sector of the economy, productivity, competition, jobs, the environment, public health or safety, or state, local, or tribal governments or communities;
> Create a serious inconsistency or otherwise interfere with an action taken or planned by another agency;
> Materially alter the budgetary impact of entitlements, grants, user fees, or loan programs or the rights and obligations of recipients thereof; or
> Raise novel legal or policy issues arising out of legal mandates, the president's priorities, or the principles set forth in this Executive Order. [4]

Rulemaking can move at glacial pace, with a particular rule taking more than a decade to promulgate and defend from legal challenges, meaning regulation frequently spans several presidential terms. Of the thirty-eight thousand final rules published in the Federal Register from fiscal year (FY) 2002 through FY 2011, the Office of Management and Budget (OMB) reviewed 3,262 under EO 12866 and 13563 and considered 531 major. OMB included 106 final rules in its ten-year analysis. Table 10.1 shows that costs for the

106 major rules promulgated from 2001 to 2011 by the federal rulemaking agencies were between 43.3 and 67.3 billion (2001) dollars while benefits ranged from 141.0 to 700.6 in billions of (2001) dollars.

Often, particular agencies within a department or agency are responsible for the major or significant rules. Table 10.2 shows the agencies that promulgated the most rules or the most significant of the rules.[5]

OMB compiles statistics for fiscal years and the most recent data show that the fifty-four major rules that account for the majority of the total benefits and costs were reviewed. Of these, thirty implement federal budgetary programs, usually causing income transfers, which leaves just thirteen whose effects are primarily through private sector mandates.[6] Table 10.3 shows the thirteen rules where the agencies monetized costs and benefits.[7]

Independent regulatory agencies also issued major rules during the period from October 1, 2010 to September 30, 2011.[8] Of the seventeen rules issued by five agencies, most dealt with regulating the financial sector. The Federal Reserve System promulgated two rules on Debit Card Interchange Fees and Routing, one on Electronic Fund Transfers, and one on Truth in Lending. The Nuclear Regulatory Commission issued a Revision of Fee Schedules; Fee Recovery for Fiscal Year 2011. The SEC issued ten major rules, including: Disclosure for Asset-Backed Securities Required by Section 943 of The Dodd-Frank Wall Street Reform and Consumer Protection Act; Family Of-

Table 10.1. Estimates of the Total Annual Benefits and Costs of Major Federal Rules by Agency, October 1, 2001–September 30, 2011 (Billions of 2001 Dollars)

Agency	No. of Rules	Benefits	Costs
Department of Agriculture	5	0.9–1.3	0.8–1.2
Department of Energy	10	6.5–12.0	3.3–4.7
Department of Health and Human Services	17	16.0–47.6	2.2–4.2
Department of Homeland Security	1	< 0.1	0–0.1
Department of Housing and Urban Development	1	2.3	0.9
Department of Justice	4	1.8–4.0	0.8–1.0
Department of Labor	7	6.8–19.8	2.1–5.0
Department of Transportation (DOT)	27	16.1–27.9	7.9–15.7
Environmental Protection Agency (EPA)	32	84.8–565.0	23.2–29.3
Joint DOT and EPA	2	6.1–20.7	2.0–5.2
Total	**106**	**141.0–700.6**	**43.3–67.3**

Table 10.2. Estimates of Annual Benefits and Costs of Major Federal Rules: Selected Program Offices and Agencies, October 1, 2010–September 30, 2011 (Billions of 2001 Dollars)

Agency	No. of Rules	Benefits	Costs
Department of Agriculture			
Animal and Plant Health Inspection Service	3	0.9–1.2	0.7–0.9
Department of Energy			
Energy Efficiency and Renewable Energy	10	6.5–12.0	3.3–4.7
Department of Health and Human Services			
Food and Drug Administration	9	2.1–30.9	0.9–1.3
Center for Medicare and Medicaid Services	7	13.6–16.5	1.3–2.8
Department of Labor			
Occupational Safety and Health Administration	4	0.2–1.4	0.4
Employee Benefits Security Administration	3	6.6–18.4	1.7–4.5
Department of Transportation			
National Highway Traffic Safety Administration	12	13.3–23.9	5.6–12.1
Federal Aviation Administration	6	0.3–1.2	0–0.4
Federal Motor Carriers Safety Administration	3	1.2–1.3	1.1–1.2
Environmental Protection Agency			
Office of Air	20	82.2–556.5	21.8–27.7
Office of Water	6	1.2–3.7	1.0–1.2
Office of Solid Waste and Emergency Response	4	0–0.3	-0.3
Department of Transportation/Environmental Protection Agency			
National Highway Traffic Safety Administration/Office of Air	2	6.1–20.7	2.0–5.2

OMB notes that there is more research and analysis to resolve uncertainties in the EPA Air Rules. However, it is important to note that the benefits are mostly attributable to reducing public exposure to fine particulate matter, with benefits from $19 to $167 billion/year, but with costs of $7.3 billion/year (Clean Air Fine Particle Implementation Rule, 2007). A more complete analysis can be found in the 2012 Draft Report to Congress, pp.14–16.

fices; Issuer Review of Asset in Offerings of Asset-Backed Securities; Large Trader Reporting; Regulation SHO; Reporting of Security-Based Swap Transaction Data; Risk Management Controls for Brokers or Dealers with Market Access; Rules Implementing Amendments to the Investment Advisers Act of 1940; Shareholder Approval Compensation and Golden Parachute Compensation; and Whistleblowers Incentives and Protections. The Commodity Futures Trading Commission issued two rules, one on Whistleblower Incentives and another on Safety Standards for Cribs.

These data set forth the rulemaking entities, costs, and benefits, where available, and trends for the period, but their accuracy in showing the implementation through rulemaking of a president's policies generally increases in the later years of an administration. Because a major rule can take years, even occasionally decades to promulgate, a sitting president may have to spend the early years of his administration dismantling to the extent possible his predecessor's regulatory initiatives, a task that succeeds in proportion to the stage of the rulemaking. Final rules promulgated usually require a new rulemaking to withdraw, whereas rules in earlier stages such as preproposal and proposed can be terminated by policy direction from the president or, in the case of proposed rules, by notice of withdrawal. However, termination of a predecessor's rulemaking means less time and resources spent on promulgating one's own rules. Moreover, the often glacial pace of rulemaking means that final rules implementing a president's policy may not show up in OMB's analysis during his presidency. Still other rules are "court ordered" and may not have been within the policy of the administration at the time. These often include deadlines and cannot be ignored.

LEGAL REQUIREMENTS

The legal basis for rulemaking is the Administrative Procedure Act (APA). The APA requires agencies to publish a notice of proposed rulemaking (NPRM), provide an opportunity for public participation, and publish the final rule with its explanation.[9] These basic requirements still provide a "floor" for agency actions, but agency rulemaking requirements have been greatly expanded by the requirement of the enabling statutes, court decisions, specific legislation, executive orders, and agency practice.

Table 10.3. Estimates by Agency of the Total Annual Benefits and Costs of Major Rules: October 1, 2010–September 30, 2011 (Billions of 2001 Dollars)

Agency	No. of Rules	Benefits	Costs
Department of Energy	3	2.5–5.1	1.4–2.2
Department of Health and Human Services	2	0.9–10.2	0.3–0.7
Department of Labor	2	6.6–18.4	1.8–4.6
Department of Transportation (DOT)	2	1.7–2.5	0.6–1.5
Environmental Protection Agency (EPA)	3	20.5–59.7	0.7
Joint DOT and EPA	1	2.2–2.6	0.3–0.5
Total	**13**	**34.3–98.5**	**5.0–10.2**

In cases where a person or group of persons is dissatisfied with a rule that has been promulgated, several appeals processes are available. The first is an appeal to the agency, which is usually a letter pointing out where the writer believes the agency misinterpreted the evidence or failed to follow prescribed procedures. If satisfaction is not forthcoming from an appeal to the agency, the APA provides for judicial review.[10] Courts have defined the rights of persons aggrieved by agency action that was based on the administrative record. Judges must consider relevant factors for errors of judgment and whether the rule is based on the administrative record. The standard for judicial review is "arbitrary and capricious," which will be found if the agency failed to follow requirements in statutes (APA, and the agency's enabling statute), failed to consider important aspects of the issues, made decisions counter to the evidence, or made decisions too implausible for just a difference of views or particular agency expertise. Other statutes are stricter, requiring the rule be based on "substantial evidence in the record as a whole," and through statutes and court decisions more requirements, such as that the rule be technologically and economically feasible, have been added. Court challenges to the promulgation of a rule made by persons or groups that are affected by it are usually specified, but generally must take place within fifty-nine days of promulgation and, where there are multiple parties, the actions are combined and heard in one court. For example, in a challenge to OSHA's 2006 rule on Hexavalent Chromium, Public Citizen, United Steel, Paper and Forestry, Rubber, Manufacturing, Energy, Allied Industrial Service Workers International Union, and Edison Electric Institute, joined by the Aerospace Industries Association of America, Inc., Portland Cement Association, Surface Finishing Industry Council, Color Pigments Manufacturers Association, Inc., National Association of Manufacturers and Specialty

Industry of North America, as interveners, all sued the US Department of
Labor. The Third Circuit Court of Appeals upheld all of the rule's provisions,
save the exposure determination provisions, which were remanded to OSHA
for further rulemaking.[11] Courts can uphold the agency action, uphold parts
of the rule, or vacate the entire rule. Finally, judicial appeal can occur when
an agency action is enforced against a person or entity. In this process, the
appellant usually must present the case to an administrative law judge and a
review commission prior to the federal courts.

Since 1996, there has been another way to vacate an agency rule, and that
is by a finding of disapproval by Congress under the Congressional Review
Act (CRA).[12] Nearly all major rules, well over forty-five thousand since
1996, are submitted to Congress for review, but only forty-three resolutions
of disapproval were introduced in the Senate or the House, and of these only
two passed one house of Congress and, finally only one rule, OSHA's Ergonomics Rule, has been disapproved. Of the forty-nine rules where a joint
resolution to disapprove was introduced, none has gone further. In the 111th
Congress, a rule submitted by the National Mediation Board relating to election procedures and a rule relating to status as grandfathered health plan
pursuant to the PPACA failed to get the Senate to agree to proceed. While
these results suggest the law has not been effective, it is equally possible that
the agencies have been writing their rules to avoid the application of the Act.
If this is true, and the mere existence of the act has a chilling effect on
rulemaking, rules may well be promulgated to avoid the congressional notice
and ire that Ergonomics received, making outright disapproval under the act
unnecessary.

THE REGULATORY PROCESS

The regulatory process begins with a catalyst, which could be a specific
requirement in a new law or an action pursuant to an enabling statute that is
the result of a petition, a catastrophe, or a policy decision to address an issue.
The agency will generally collect information on such issues as costs and
benefits, necessity, risks, affected persons or groups, and the quality of available data. If the rule will have a significant economic impact on a substantial
number of small entities, the Small Business Regulatory Enforcement Act
(SBREFA) of the Regulatory Flexibility Act requires specific economic analyses. Moreover, the EPA and OSHA are required to set up SBREFA panels
made up of affected small-business representatives, and write a report of the
comments and proceedings that must be signed by the Small Business Administration, OMB's Office of Information and Regulatory Affairs (OIRA),
and EPA or OSHA. Finally, the proposing agency must address the issues
raised during the SBREFA process in the preamble to the proposed rule. The

draft proposed rule, which will become the Notice of Proposed Rulemaking (NPRM), will be reviewed by the Office of Management and Budget's OIRA for compliance with Executive Order (EO) 12866,[13] which has been supplemented and reaffirmed by the more detailed instructions on general principles, public participation, integration and innovation, flexible approaches, science, and retrospective analyses of existing rules in EO 13563, issued January 18, 2011.[14] (All regulatory agencies are focusing on the retrospective analyses and setting forth existing rules to be reviewed.) In addition, OIRA will review the draft for compliance with its guidelines on data quality and peer review, other laws such as the Paperwork Reduction Act and National Environmental Protection Act, and the president's priorities. OIRA will also send the draft to other federal entities that may have an interest in its contents for their comments. Following OMB approval, the NPRM is published in the *Federal Register* and public comment periods are set and a public hearing is scheduled, if a request has been made or is anticipated. Along with research acquired by the agency, the comments and hearing testimony and exhibits become part of the administrative record upon which the rule will be based. Following the close of the comment periods, the agency, using the entire record, drafts the final rule, which then goes through all the administrative approval processes and is submitted to Congress for review under the CRA.

THE PRESIDENT'S ACCOMPLISHMENTS AND REGULATORY PLANS

The EPA has the distinction of promulgating the most rules with the highest costs so it is not surprising that the EPA generates controversy for its past and future rulemakings. During the president's first term, the EPA's finding that greenhouse gases (GHGs) pose a threat to public health and the environment allowed the agency to move forward with proposed standards on National Emissions Standards for Hazardous Air Pollutants (NESHAP) for energy producers, industrial boilers and process heaters, commercial and industrial solid-waste incinerations, and cooling water intake structures and disposal of coal combustion residuals from electric utilities. A short list of EPA's final regulations include Revisions to the Spill Prevention; the Control and Countermeasure Rule that exempts previously covered compounds and equipment; NESHAP for Portland Cement, that adds and revises limits for mercury, total hydrocarbons, particulate matter and hydrochloric acid; National Ambient Air Quality Standards for Sulfur Dioxide, now seventy-five parts per billion with the emissions primarily from power plants; NESHAPs for Reciprocating Internal Combustions Engines; an area source rule for Industrial, Commercial, and Institutional Boilers and Process Heaters, an

Amendment to the Oil Pollution Prevention Regulation to Exempt Milk and Milk Products Containers; Greenhouse Gas Emissions Standards and Fuel Efficiency Standards for Medium- and Heavy-Duty Engines and Vehicles; and Amendments to Air Regulations for the Oil and Natural Gas Industry, which will be the first federal air standards regulating gas wells that use hydraulic fracturing technology.[15]

President Obama signaled in his second Inaugural Address that he would respond to the threat of climate change, as failure would betray children and future generations and that though some can deny science, no one can "avoid the devastating impact of raging fires, and crippling drought, and more powerful storms."[16] That response will come from the EPA using existing statutes and regulations, final, proposed and to be proposed, not congressional initiatives. The EPA's regulatory plan includes work on greenhouse gas standards for mobile and stationary sources, review and implementation of air quality standards, and addressing concerns about chemicals such as PCBs, mercury, lead, and formaldehyde under the Federal Insecticide, Fungicide, and Rodenticide Act; the Federal Food, Drug, and Cosmetic Act; the Toxic Substances Control Act; and the Pollution Prevention Act. It also includes improving accountability and oversight of hazardous secondary materials recycling, addressing America's water challenges by determining what waters are covered by the Clean Water Act, protecting aquatic organisms from cooling water intake structures, reducing discharges of pollutants from steam power plants with effluent guideline, streamlining drinking water standards, upgrading reporting requirement to electronic filing, and proposing an amendment to the National Contingency Plan that would improve the response to oil spills; among many other regulatory initiatives. The leading source of toxic air omissions is coal and stemming these emissions will lead to the greatest gains in clean air. Other air-quality regulations already proposed or in draft include: mercury and toxics standards (MATS), which is expected to be finalized March 2013; carbon pollution standards for future power plants, and new energy-efficiency standards for home appliances and buildings. Pressure is mounting on the president to approve the Keystone Pipeline. In addition to new standards promulgated pursuant to the EPA's enabling statutes, enforcement of existing standards will further his goals. Environmental groups have petitioned the EPA for disclosures of the chemicals leaked or emitted from hydraulic fracturing. Hydraulic fracturing is also the subject of regulatory activity, including standards and guidelines in the Departments of Energy (DOE), and Agriculture (USDA), the Bureau of Land Management (BLM) (soon to finalize new regulations), the Centers for Disease Control and Prevention (CDC), and the SEC. In the area of water, the EPA has already proposed guidelines. These and other environmental issues will be at the forefront of President Obama's response to climate change. Financial reform regulation has been mainly pursuant to Dodd-Frank, a law so extensive it requires the promulgation of at least 398 rules. The fact that the statute places regulation writing authority in more than four major entities including the Federal Reserve, the SEC and its new Office of Credit Ratings, the Department of Treasury and the new Office of National Insurance, and the Federal Deposit Insurance Corporation with its new Consumer Financial Protection Bureau, has not resulted in a speedier, more efficient process.

The legislation covers consumer protection by creating the Consumer Financial Protection Bureau, an independent watchdog at the Federal Reserve whose job it is to ensure clear, accurate information for consumers on mortgages, credit cards, loans, and other financial products, and protect them from hidden fees, abusive terms, and deceptive practices. The Financial Stability Oversight Council watches over banks and other financial firms such as hedge funds, looking to identify systemic risks from large companies, products, and activities. No longer can these institutions look forward to bailouts, as the council can require greater reserves to preclude the "too big to fail" debacle of AIG. A continuing source of controversy and potential litigation is the Volker rule prohibiting banks from owning and investing in hedge funds for themselves. Risky derivatives (credit swaps) are to be regulated by the SEC or the Commodity Futures Trading Commission (CFTC) in a separate exchange to encourage transparency and prevent crises. The new Federal Insurance Office is charged with identifying insurance companies whose practices and failures create extreme risk and studying the insurance industry with the goal of making affordable insurance available to minorities. Finally, Dodd-Frank encourages reporting of security violation with financial rewards.

As of February 2013, only 148 (37 percent) of the required rulemakings have been finalized and 129 (32.4 percent) have yet to be proposed. Among the major accomplishments (final rules) of the SEC, alone and sometimes in conjunction with other entities, are: a rule to remove exemptions for credit rating agencies (September 30, 2010, §975(b)), rules regarding asset-backed securities' issuers' responsibilities to conduct and disclose review of the assets (January 20, 2011, §944), rules to implement a Whistleblower Incentives and Protection Program (May 25, 2011, §922), rules requiring advisers to hedge funds to report information for use in monitoring systemic financial risk (with CFTC, October 31, 2011, §§ 404 and 406), rules regarding disclosure of mine safety information (December 21, 2011, § 1503), rules and guidelines to help prevent identity theft (with CFTC, February 28, 2012, §1088), a rule to adopt the threshold used to determine who is a "qualified client" of a registered investment adviser (February 15, 2012, § 418), rules regarding mandatory clearance of securities-based swaps (June 28, 2012, §763), rules requiring disclosure by resource extraction issuers (August 22, 2012, § 1504), and revisions to rules regarding due diligence for the delivery of dividends, interest, and other valuable property to missing security holders (January 16, 2013, § 929W). [17] This short list of some of the completed rules illustrates the breadth of Dodd-Frank with regulatory action dealing with asset-backed securities, auditing, disclosure, derivatives, enforcement, international mineral extraction, oversight of the market, and the investment advisers and broker dealers. It is no wonder that a mere third of the rules have been finalized and only a further third proposed. Clearly, regulation under Dodd-Frank will continue to play a big role in President Obama's second term.

Regulation and guidelines issued pursuant to the PPACA have been extensive, but in light of the breadth of topics covered by the act and the proposals and interim final rules [18] awaiting review and finalization, the rulemaking process will continue for at least the next four years. Health and Human Services (HHS) leads in regulation development, but other departments and agencies, such as the Internal Revenue Service and Department of Veterans Affairs, are also required to promulgate relevant rules. HHS has said it will focus on: compliance with the Patient Bill of Rights; assisting states to review unreasonable rate increases and oversee medical-loss ratios; providing oversight on the state-based health exchanges; and administering the Consumer Assistance Program, preexisting conditions insurance plans, and the early-retiree insurance program. [19] Important final and interim final rules include: rules covering group health plans and health insurance reviewers on internal claims and appeals and external review processes; summary of benefits and coverage and the uniform glossary; preexisting insurance plan program; early retiree reinsurance program; establishment of exchanges and qualified health plans; standards related to essential health benefits, actuarial value, and accreditation; standards related to reinsurance, risks corridors, and risk adjustment; application, review, and reporting process for waivers for state innovation; PPACA establishment of consumer-operated and oriented plans; incentives for wellness programs in group health plans; PPACA preexisting condition exclusions, lifetime and annual limits, rescissions, and patient protections; group health plans and health insurance issuers relating to dependent coverage of children to age twenty-six; medical loss ratio requirements under the PPACA; coverage of certain preventive services under the PPACA; and insurance rate disclosure and review; among others. In addition, over sixty-five guidance documents have been issued. Nevertheless, as the act enters its third year, new issues need to be proposed, proposed rules need to be finished, and interim rules need to be finalized, along with enforcement of the rules as they become effective.

Most federal departments and agencies will be doing significant rulemaking and regulatory reviews. For example, the USDA is focusing on improving access to nutrition assistance and will propose nutrition standards for foods sold in schools, revise regulations to address emerging food-safety challenges, finalize a rule for poultry-slaughter inspections, finalize regulations to streamline natural resources conservation, institute a national animal-disease tracking system, and finalize a standard for the humane care of dogs imported for resale, among other activities.[20] Some of the major activities in the Department of Transportation (DOT), which in its regulatory plan notes that DOT's primary focus is on safety in various modes of transportation, include work on continuing implementation of safety management systems (Federal Aviation Administration); strengthening requirements for electronic on-board recorders and revising motor carrier safety fitness procedures (The Federal Motor Carrier Safety Administration); rulemaking to reduce death and injury resulting from incidents involving motor coaches (National Highway Traffic Safety Administration); and rulemaking on aviation that will further safeguard the interests of consumers flying the nation's skies (spearheaded by the Office of the Secretary of Transportation).[21]

The Department of Labor's major rulemaking agencies are OSHA and the Mine Safety and Health Association (MSHA). OSHA is beginning to address risks to workers exposed to infectious diseases, institute new procedures for whistleblower protection, and assess and regulate the risks of crystalline silica, along with exploring rulemaking to prevent backover injuries and fatalities and the hazards of reinforcing operations in construction. Consistent with President Obama's EO 13563, "Improving Regulatory Review," OSHA will be reviewing its standards for bloodborne pathogens, permissible exposure limits for chemical standards, and confined spaces in construction. Work will continue on removing or revising duplicative, unnecessary, and inconsistent safety and health standards with the Standard Improvement Project—Phase IV, and a revision to Digger Derrick's Requirements in the recently promulgated Crane and Derricks in Construction Standard pursuant to a settlement agreement.[22] MSHA will finalize a rule to address proximity detection systems for continuous mining machines in underground coal mines, and will propose a rule to require proximity detection systems for mobile machines in underground mines. Other areas of regulation include strengthening and specifying how the Patterns of Violations provision of the Mine, Safety and Health Act will be used for effective enforcement, particularly by expanding the information that must be submitted to MSHA. In the area of risk reduction, MSHA will continue its regulatory work on lowering miners' exposure to coal mine dust, including a standard for continuous personal dust monitors, and addressing issues of rock dusting, ventilation, and operators' responsibility for certain mine examinations and certified persons stemming from recommendations resulting from the investigation of the Upper Big Branch explosion, and working on exposure limits for crystalline silica, using OSHA's findings on health effects and risk assessment.[23]

The DOE's mission is to promote dependable, affordable, and environmentally sound production and distribution of energy; advance energy efficiency and conservation; provide responsible stewardship of the nation's nuclear weapons; provide responsible resolution to the environmental legacy of nuclear weapons production and strengthen US scientific discovery, economic competitiveness, and improved quality of life through innovations in science and technology. The Energy Efficiency Program for Consumer Products and Commercial Equipment set efficiency standards in 2012 for residential clothes washers, fluorescent lamp ballasts, and residential dishwashers; work will continue on other efficiency standards. Pursuant to EO 13563, some of the existing regulations to be reviewed include: standards for battery chargers and external power supplies, standards for distribution transformers, federal building standards rule update, and, to reduce the burdens on small businesses, alternate efficiency determination methods and alternate rating methods and waiver and interim waiver for consumer products and commercial and industrial equipment.

EXECUTIVE ORDERS

A final way a president implements his policies is through executive orders, which, though they apply only to the federal government, can effectively repeal the policies of his predecessor, implement his policies, and may become voluntary standards of conduct for others outside the federal government. As former administrator of OIRA, Cass Sunstein has written,

> Executive actions are nothing new, and presidents, both Republican and Democratic, have properly undertaken a large number of them. They are an established part of our constitutional system—and are typically legitimate because Congress itself has previously authorized them. [24]

In his first term, President Obama signed 144 executive orders directing his administrative agencies on topics large and small. Some of the most important are EO 13490, Ethics Commitments by Executive Branch Personnel[25]; EO 13492, Review and Disposition of Individuals Detained at the Guantánamo Bay Naval Base and Close of Detention Facilities[26]; EO 13501, Establishing the President's Economic Recovery Advisory Board[27]; EO 13513, Federal Leadership on Reducing Text Messaging While Driving[28]; EO 13603 National Defense Resources Preparedness[29]; EO 13623, Preventing and Responding to Violence against Women and Girls Globally[30]; EO 13632 Establishing the Hurricane Sandy Rebuilding Task Force[31]; and EO 13605 Supporting Safe and Responsible Development of Unconventional Domestic Natural Gas Resources. [32] Executive orders affecting federal agency rulemaking include: EO 13479, Revocation of Certain Executive Orders Concerning Regulatory Planning and Review, revoking President George W. Bush's Executive Orders 13258 and 13422, whose policies were not in line with those of President Obama;[33] EO 13563, Improving Regulation and Regulatory Review, supplementing and reaffirming EO 12866;[34] EO 13579, Regulation and Independent Regulatory Agencies in which President Obama said that Independent Regulatory Agencies should comply with EO 12866 to the extent permitted by law;[35] EO 13609, Promoting International Regulatory Cooperation;[36] and EO 13610, Identifying and Reducing Regulatory Burdens.[37] Collectively, these executive orders give the president power in his competition with Congress over policy making. These orders address issues domestic and international covering subjects such as the armed forces, commissions and task forces, national defense, energy, environment, foreign relations including trade and human trafficking, and federal regulatory policy. President Obama has vowed to address gun safety through executive actions that presumably will include executive orders. These allow President Obama to address issues quickly and exert maximum control over his administration, thus giving him much power in his rivalry with Congress.

NOTES

1. An earlier assessment of regulatory policy in the latter part of the George W. Bush presidency and the first two years of President Obama's administration appeared in Claudia Hartley Thurber, "Obama in Office," in James A. Thurber, ed., *The Politics of Regulation in the Obama Administration* (Boulder, CO: Paradigm Publishers, 2011). Some of that material is repeated here as background for President Obama's current regulatory policy.

2. American Recovery and Reinvestment Act of 2009, Pub. L. 111-5; Patient Protection and Affordable Care Act, Pub. L. 111-148; Dodd-Frank Wall Street Reform and Consumer Protection Act, Pub. L. 111-203, HR 4173.

3. Administrative Procedure Act, 5 U.S.C. 553.

4. William J. Clinton, 1993 Regulatory Planning and Review, Executive Order 12866, *Federal Register*, vol. 58, p. 51735, October 4, 1993.

5. 2012 Draft Report to Congress on Benefits and Costs of Federal Regulations and Unfunded Mandates on State, Local, and Tribal Entities, pp. 12–13, OMB.gov.

6. OMB deems these budgetary transfers as funding programs specifically required or authorized by Congress and causing transfers, usually from taxpayers to program beneficiaries. Examples given include: "a Department of Treasury rule implementing the Small Business Lending Fund Refinance Program and the Crop Assistance Program." 2012 Draft Report to Congress on Benefits and Costs of Federal Regulations and Unfunded Mandates on State, Local, and Tribal Entities, pp. 21–23.

7. 2012 Draft Report to Congress on Benefits and Costs of Federal Regulation and Unfunded Mandates on State, Local, and Tribal Entities, p. 22, omb.gov.

8. Independent Agency Rulemaking is not subject to review under EO 12866, but the Government Accountability Office (GAO) is required to report to Congress yearly on major rules, including those promulgated by independent agencies. Therefore, the cost-benefit analysis is not required, but inclusion of such data should occur as EO 13563 on agency use of "the best available techniques to quantify anticipated present and future benefits and costs" and EO 13573 where the president said independent agencies should follow the central principles of EO 13563.

9. APA 5 U.S.C §§ 551–559; rulemaking is specific to code § 553.

10. 5 U.S.C §§ 701–706.

11. *Public Citizen and United Steelworkers v. OSHA, 2009*, 557 F.3rd 165 (3rd Cir. Court of Appeals).

12. 5 U.S.C. §§ 801–808.

13. William J. Clinton, 1993, Regulatory Planning and Review, Executive Order 12866, *Federal Register*, vol. 58, p. 51735, October 4, 1993.

14. Barack Obama, Improving Regulation and Regulatory Review, Executive Order 13562, *Federal Register,* vol. 76, pp. 3821–3823, January 18, 2001.

15. Unified Agenda and Regulatory Plan, 2012 Agency Statements of Regulatory Policy, Environmental Protection Agency, www.reginfo.gov/public/.

16. President Barack Obama's Inaugural Speech, January 21, 2013, www.whitehouse.gov/.

17. For a complete listing of the actions pursuant to Dodd-Frank, see SEC, Dodd-Frank Act, www.sec.gov/.

18. An Interim Final Rule (IFR) can be published when an agency deems it has good cause to issue it without first proposing. The IFM is effective immediately, but usually contains a section that advises the public that the agency will make change to the rule pursuant to significant public comments.

19. HHS website, www.hhs.gov/.

20. Unified Agenda and Regulatory Plan, 2012 Agency Statements of Regulatory Policy, Department of Agriculture, www.reginfo.gov/public/.

21. Unified Agenda and Regulatory Plan, 2012 Agency Statements of Regulatory Policy, Department of Transportation, www.reginfo.gov/public/.

22. Unified Agenda and Regulatory Plan, 2012 Agency Statements of Regulatory Policy, Department of Labor, Occupational Safety and Health Administration, www.reginfo.gov/public/.

23. Unified Agenda and Regulatory Plan, 2012 Agency Statements of Regulatory Policy, Department of Labor, Mine Safety and Health Administration, www.reginfo.gov/public/.

24. Cass R. Sustein, "When Presidents Wait and Act on Their Own," February 27, 2013, ed. Katy Roberts, Bloomberg.com.

25. Barack Obama, 2009 Ethics Commitments by Executive Branch Personnel, *Federal Register*, vol. 74, p. 4673, January 26, 2009; see James Thurber, "The President, Congress, and Lobbyists: Has President Obama Changed the Way Washington Works?," in James Thurber, ed., *Rivals for Power* (Lanham, MD: Rowman & Littlefield, 2013).

26. Barack Obama, 2009 Review and Disposition of Individuals Detained at the Guantanamo Bay Naval Base and Close of Detention Facilities, Executive Order 13492, *Federal Register*, vol. 74, p. 4897, January 27, 2009.

27. Barack Obama, 2009 Establishing the President's Economic Recovery Advisory Board, Executive Order 13501, *Federal Register*, vol. 74, p. 6893, February 11, 2009.

28. Barack Obama, 2009 Federal Leadership on Reducing Text Messaging While Driving, Executive Order 13513, *Federal Register*, vol. 74, p. 51225, October 8, 2009.

29. Barack Obama, 2012 National Defense Resources Preparedness, *Federal Register*, Executive Order 13602, *Federal Register*, vol. 77, p. 16651, March 22, 2012.

30. Barack Obama, 2012 Preventing and Responding to Violence against Women and Girls Globally, Executive Order 13623, *Federal Register*, vol. 77, p. 49345, August 16, 2012.

31. Barack Obama, 2012 Establishing the Hurricane Sandy Rebuilding Task Force, Executive Order 13632, *Federal Register*, vol. 77, p. 74341, December 14, 2012.

32. Barack Obama, 2012 Supporting Safe and Responsible Development of Unconventional Domestic Natural Gas Resources, Executive Order 13605, *Federal Register*, vol. 77, p. 23107, April 17, 2012.

33. Barack Obama, 2009 Revocation of Certain Executive Orders Concerning Regulatory Planning and Review, Executive Order 13497, *Federal Register*, vol. 74, p. 6113, February 4, 2009.

34. Barack Obama, 2011 Improving Regulation and Regulatory Review, Executive Order 13563, *Federal Register*, vol. 76, p. 3821, January 18, 2011.

35. Barack Obama, 2011 Regulation and Independent Regulatory Agencies, Executive Order 13579, *Federal Register*, vol. 76, p. 41587, July 11, 2011.

36. Barack Obama, 2012 Promoting International Regulatory Cooperation, Executive Order 13609, *Federal Register*, vol. 77, p. 26413, May 1, 2012.

37. Barack Obama, Identifying and Reducing Regulatory Burdens, Executive Order 13610, *Federal Register*, vol. 77, p. 28469, May 10, 2012.

Chapter Eleven

The President, Congress, and Foreign Policy

Lawrence J. Korb and Alexander Rothman

Foreign policy is undoubtedly the policy area in which the president can most easily accomplish his agenda independently—that is, without congressional approval. Not coincidentally, it is also the arena in which President Obama enjoyed the most success in his first term. While the president's domestic achievements are impressive on their own, to say the least (health-care reform, the auto bailout, and the Dodd-Frank Act come to mind), congressional gridlock prevented his administration from acting on a number of other domestic priorities, including immigration reform, climate change legislation, and more aggressive efforts to stimulate the economy.

On the other hand, when unencumbered by the need for supermajority support in Congress, President Obama racked up an impressive list of foreign policy achievements. To name but the highlights, the president ended the war in Iraq, prevented a humanitarian disaster in Libya, rebuilt the United States' battered relationships with its allies, rallied an international coalition that put in place a sanctions regime to pressure Iran to end its nuclear program, reclaimed the United States' moral authority on nuclear disarmament, killed Osama bin Laden and decimated al Qaeda's leadership, and put the United States on track to transition out of Afghanistan—and end the longest war in this nation's history—by 2014. In an odd twist of fate, foreign policy—perceived as the weakness in President Obama's 2008 campaign—became the president's strongest issue area in his 2012 reelection bid.

While the president may be the most dominant actor shaping US national security and foreign policy, Congress is hardly impotent. In fact, two of President Obama's signature foreign policy achievements—the ratification of the New START (Strategic Arms Reduction Treaty) nuclear arms control agreement with Russia and the repeal of "Don't Ask, Don't Tell"—would have been impossible without congressional approval. Similarly, it is congressional roadblocks that have thus far prevented the president from fulfilling his campaign pledge to close the US detention camp in Guantánamo Bay, Cuba and stymied his efforts to ratify the Comprehensive Test Ban Treaty (CTBT).

Even given the Obama administration's strong record on foreign policy thus far, protecting US national security and interests in the coming decade will require a better working relationship between the president and Congress. In shaping foreign policy, Congress possesses three principal powers: the power of the purse (that is, to determine federal budgets), the power to ratify treaties, and the power to shape public opinion. It will be difficult for the Obama administration to effectively address the most pressing national security challenges facing the United States—including ending the US combat mission in Afghanistan, rebalancing US security spending, and combating the threat of nuclear terrorism—without a more reasonable partner in Congress.

During his first four years in office, President Obama faced unified opposition from congressional Republicans, opposition that was, often as not, based on partisan politics rather than the substance of the president's policy proposals. After the Republican Party swept the 2010 midterm elections, Senate Minority Leader Mitch McConnell (R-KY) famously remarked, "The single most important thing we want to achieve is for President Obama to be a one-term president."[1] His colleagues in the Republican-controlled House of Representatives then proceeded to vote to repeal ObamaCare thirty-three times in their two year terms while Republicans in the Senate filibustered dozens of presidential appointees.[2]

Now that President Obama has been reelected—and considering he will be term-limited in 2016—the hope is that congressional Republicans will be more willing to work with the president for the good of the country. This chapter outlines a foreign policy wish list for the president and Congress in his second term.

1. End the war in Afghanistan: end the US combat mission by 2014, leaving behind a residual force of no more than six thousand soldiers for troop training and counter terror operations.
2. Reduce the defense budget to sustainable peacetime levels: cut $1 trillion from the defense budget over the next ten years, a 30 percent decrease that would be in line with historical postwar defense drawdowns.
3. Rebalance overall US security spending: ensure the nation's nonmilitary security programs receive the funding necessary to carry out their mission.

4. Resolve the Iranian nuclear crisis without provoking an all-out war.

In achieving these goals, the president and Congress would finally move the country past the foreign policy blunders of the Bush administration, shore up the foundations of American power, and prepare the nation to meet the threats of the twenty-first century effectively and efficiently.

AFGHANISTAN

When President Obama assumed office in 2009, he inherited a deteriorating situation in Afghanistan. As the war in Iraq descended into chaos, the Bush administration pulled resources from Afghanistan, allowing the Taliban to gain momentum and reestablish control over large parts of the country. To make matters worse, the US-backed Karzai government was not only unable or unwilling to tamp down on corruption within its ranks but had come to be viewed as illegitimate by many of its people after allegations of rampant fraud in the 2009 Afghan national elections.

As a candidate, Barack Obama argued repeatedly for a realignment of priorities back to Afghanistan, defending the conflict as the "good war"—the war that was justified on national security grounds, legitimized by the support of the international community, and begun in response to the deadliest terror attack in the history of the United States. As a result, ending the war in Iraq was an early priority for the Obama administration for not only moral but also strategic reasons: to free up resources to shift back to Afghanistan. When the president took office, the United States had only thirty-two thousand Americans serving in Afghanistan, compared with 160,000 in Iraq at the peak of war.[3]

Upon taking office, President Obama laid out three goals for US involvement in Afghanistan: to reverse the Taliban's momentum, deny al Qaeda a safe haven, and strengthen the capacity of Afghanistan's government and security forces.[4] He underscored this renewed commitment by surging US troop levels in the country, sending twenty thousand troops soon after taking office and then an additional thirty thousand when the new commander requested more troops.[5]

Yet even as he added additional troops, President Obama made it clear that the United States would not be taking on an open commitment in Afghanistan. "We will continue to advise and assist Afghanistan's security forces to ensure that they can succeed over the long haul. But it will be clear to the Afghan government—and, more importantly, to the Afghan people—that they will ultimately be responsible for their own country," he stated in a speech at West Point in 2009.[6] And even as President Obama announced the troop surge, he promised to begin bringing these service members home in

2011. In September 2012, US officials announced that the last of these surge troops had been withdrawn from the country.[7]

By dramatically increasing troop levels in Afghanistan, President Obama reversed the Taliban's momentum, providing the fledgling Afghan government with a stronger bargaining position in its negotiations with the Taliban as well as the time to work on its own internal governance issues. At the same time, by setting an end date to the surge and to US military involvement in the country, the president made it clear to the Karzai government that it cannot rely on the United States forever and therefore must make serious efforts to end corruption and bridge the country's serious domestic political divides. The end date also served to reassure the American people that the United States would not be dragged into another quagmire.

A stable Afghanistan is undoubtedly in the interest of the United States, as well as the North Atlantic Treaty Organization (NATO) and the region. Volatility in Afghanistan could spill over to destabilize the region, thereby potentially providing ungoverned safe havens for terrorist groups and adding to instability in Pakistan, Afghanistan's volatile, nuclear-armed neighbor. That said, the fate of Afghanistan ultimately lies in the hands of the Afghan people: American troops cannot be a long-term crutch for the Afghan government, and there comes a point when a large prolonged US military presence becomes counterproductive.

Eighteen months after the death of Osama bin Laden, and in the era of a degraded al Qaeda, it is time for the United States to reassess its strategy in Afghanistan. We have achieved our original goals in the country: al Qaeda's senior leadership in the region has been decimated, and it is no longer a safe haven for terrorist groups with a global reach. As the United States deals with a fragile economic recovery at home and weighs potentially devastating cuts to key domestic programs, we cannot afford to maintain a large, long-term military presence in Afghanistan. It is unclear what the United States can accomplish with an extended military commitment that it has not been able to achieve in the past decade. And in many ways, the enormous US presence in Afghanistan, both militarily and financially, enables the Afghan government to avoid making the concessions and reforms necessary to address the long-term challenges facing the country, including corruption and political fragmentation, all while enhancing the Taliban narrative that the United States is an occupying power.

These facts have not been lost on the Obama administration. During President Karzai's most recent visit to Washington in January 2013, President Obama announced an accelerated transition in Afghanistan, reiterating his commitment to end the NATO-led combat mission in the country in 2014. In spring 2013, US troops will move into a "support role," providing training and oversight to Afghan troops while allowing the Afghans to take the lead in assuming responsibility for their own security.[8] US forces will also withdraw from Afghan villages.

These two shifts are smart steps toward reducing the United States' military involvement in Afghanistan. Military action alone cannot lead to the creation of a stable Afghan state, and President Obama is right to set a firm end date for the United States' military involvement, which has been so tremendously costly in both blood and treasure. In the president's second term, in order to smoothly draw down the US presence in Afghanistan, President Obama and Congress should honor their pledge to end the US combat mission in 2014, support the political transition in Afghanistan, and plan to keep a residual force of no more than six thousand troops after 2014 for troop training and counterterror operations, provided the Afghan government grants immunity to US troops.

Afghanistan's problems cannot be solved by military force, be it foreign or not. A sustainable transition will require a political settlement among Afghanistan's many political factions, including the Karzai government, the Taliban, regional partners, and domestic groups like women's organizations.[9] The Obama administration has been wise to take steps to support free and fair presidential elections in Afghanistan in 2014—these elections present an important political transition as President Karzai must step down due to term-limit restrictions.

Additionally, the Obama administration should continue to facilitate the peace process through outreach to insurgent elements and to support dialogue among regional players.[10] Achieving a broader political settlement will be a long and complicated process. There must be major governmental reforms aimed at broadening fair participation, reducing corruption, and supporting self-sufficiency. And an electoral process must be developed to facilitate compromise between Afghanistan's dramatically diverse political factions.

As the longest war in this nation's history drags on, the American people are war weary. The solutions to the conflict in Afghanistan are not military in nature. The enormous US presence in the country may bring some semblance of stability in the near-term, but in the long-term, the US presence allows the Afghan government to avoid making the concessions and reforms necessary to form a viable state and comes at a tremendous cost to the US taxpayer. Given the extremely limited al Qaeda presence in Afghanistan, the United States can no longer justify its enormous financial and military commitment overseas. And at a time when Congress is mired in debate over whether we can afford to fund a relief package for victims of Hurricane Sandy—a disaster here at home—we must reevaluate whether it makes sense to continue spending tens of billions on reconstruction efforts in Afghanistan.[11] As the United States transfers responsibility for Afghan security over to the Afghan government, a small force—consisting of no more than six thousand

American or international troops—should be sufficient to protect US interests in the country after 2014.

DEFENSE SPENDING

In the decade since 9/11, US defense spending has increased by 46 percent in
real terms, reaching levels not seen since the end of World War II. [12] At a
time when the country faces no existential threats, the United States now
spends more on defense than we did during the Cold War, when we faced a
nuclear-armed rival superpower. This level of spending is dramatically dis-
proportionate to the threats facing the country, and in this era of fiscal austerity, we cannot afford unnecessary spending, even in the name of national
security.

In its FY 2013 budget request, the Obama administration announced
plans to cut Pentagon spending by $487 billion over the next ten years, as
mandated by the Budget Control Act of 2011. These cuts, part of a greater
effort to reduce the federal deficit, are a promising first step to rein in the
Defense Department's $620 billion per year budget, which now accounts for
about half of all federal discretionary spending. [13]

These proposed cuts, however, come from *projected increases* in the
defense budget. As a result, these "cuts" essentially hold the defense budget
steady at its current level, adjusted for inflation, over the next five years,
before allowing a return to moderate growth. In short, the Obama administration's budget plan halts the runaway growth in defense spending that has
occurred since 9/11, but it does little to bring the budget down from its
current level, near historic peaks.

Given the long-term threat the federal deficit poses to American security,
influence, and interests, it is imperative that Congress and the Obama administration make real progress toward getting our nation's fiscal house in order.
Yet it is also important that in the name of budget austerity, policy makers do
not implement measures that will hamper the United States' ability to compete in the twenty-first century global economy.

Over the past two years, the Pentagon has largely escaped real cuts to its
budget while the domestic programs that fund our national investments in
infrastructure, education, and research have seen their funding slashed repeatedly. Unnecessary defense spending does not make our nation safer;
each dollar spent on defense diverts resources away from other critical investments in the American economy—the real foundation of the United
States' global power. As President Obama begins his second term, the Department of Defense (DOD) is far better positioned to endure cuts than its
domestic counterparts, and targeted defense cuts will not undermine our
national security or economic recovery.

In recent months, Capitol Hill has been in a panic about defense sequestration, the much reviled method of cutting defense spending enacted by the Budget Control Act of 2011. Sequestration would cut all Defense Department programs by 9.4 percent—with the exception of a few accounts, such as military personnel, that are explicitly exempted by the law—in order to achieve $500 billion in reductions over the next decade. This meat-axe approach is not a smart way to cut defense spending. Not all programs are equally important to US national security, and Defense Department officials should be able to choose where cuts fall.

Yet the overall target set by sequestration—$500 billion in cuts over the next decade, in addition to the $487 billion in "cuts" already announced by the administration—presents a responsible step for the president and Congress to return defense spending to a more sustainable fiscal path. Such a cut would reduce the defense budget by about 30 percent as the United States winds down its involvement in Iraq and Afghanistan, a number in line with historical postwar defense drawdowns.[14] Furthermore, these reductions would provide significant budgetary savings without negatively impacting our national security or economic recovery.

This target of $1 trillion in cuts to defense over ten years has been echoed by a number of deficit reduction task forces from both sides of the aisle, including President Obama's own National Commission on Fiscal Responsibility and Reform, known as the "Bowles-Simpson Commission"; the commission headed by Alice Rivlin, President Clinton's former director of the Office of Management and Budget and former Republican Senator Pete Domenici; the office of Senator Tom Coburn (R-OK); and the Sustainable Defense Task Force. And despite apocalyptic rhetoric by the Republican "Three Musketeers"—Senators John McCain (R-AZ), Lindsey Graham (R-SC), and Kelly Ayotte (R-RH)—this $1 trillion target is not only eminently achievable but also fairly moderate: it would return the base or nonwar budget in real terms to its 2007 level.

In order to achieve these reductions responsibly, we would recommend reductions in the following areas of the budget:

Procurement

President Obama and Congress should reduce the procurement of platforms that serve merely to increase the United States' already overwhelming naval and air superiority. Cutting the Navy's buy of the overbudget F-35 program—in favor of the cheaper yet still effective F/A-18 E/F—while reducing the procurement of the Air Force variant by half would save $16.62 billion over the next ten years. Terminating the V-22 Osprey helicopter, which has long been hampered by cost overruns and technical problems, would save at least $9.2 billion over ten years.

Moreover, the US Navy currently possesses more firepower than the next twenty largest navies combined, many of which are US allies. With such an overwhelming advantage, the Pentagon can afford to slow the procurement of DDG-51 destroyers and littoral combat ships, which cost $2 billion and $1 billion, respectively, per ship. Similarly, stretching out the Virginia Class submarine program and pushing eight subs further into the future would enable savings of $22.3 billion over ten years.

Finally, while the United States maintains eleven aircraft carriers, no other nation has even one of comparable size and power. Eliminating the purchase of one Ford-class carrier would save $13.87 billion over ten years.

Personnel

The Pentagon's personnel budget is composed of three major items: pay, retirement, and health care. These costs have nearly doubled in the past ten years and now consume one-third of the baseline defense budget. If they continue growing faster than the overall budget, these costs will begin to divert funds from other critical national-security initiatives such as training and modernization. In fact, if personnel costs are allowed to continue growing at their current rate, they will consume the entire defense budget by fiscal year 2039 unless the overall budget is increased to accommodate them.[15]

The threat that mounting personnel costs pose to military readiness has not gone unnoticed by the nation's political and military leaders. In the Pentagon's fiscal year 2013 budget request, Defense Secretary Leon Panetta and the Joint Chiefs of Staff highlighted the need for significant changes to the Defense Department's existing pay, health-care, and retirement systems.

Congress has historically been loath to approve the Defense Department's efforts to update its personnel systems, even as these expenses have, in the words of former Secretary of Defense Robert Gates, begun "eating the Defense Department alive."[16] Yet if the Pentagon is to truly address the long-term challenges facing its personnel programs, these cost-saving initiatives will require congressional approval and vigorous administration support.

Pay

The long-term growth in the Pentagon's personnel costs stems most significantly from its health-care and retirement systems. Still, the Pentagon spends $107 billion each year on salaries and allowances, about 20 percent of its base budget.[17] These costs have grown rapidly in the past twelve years, primarily due to a series of pay raises authorized by Congress over and above the Defense Department's budget requests. Congress should pass the reforms to military pay in the Obama administration's FY 2013 budget request, updates that will save $16.5 billion over the next five years without cutting any active service member's pay.[18]

Health Care

The biggest driver of the 300 percent increase in military health-care costs over the past decade is the Tricare for Life program, instituted in 2001, which supplements Medicare coverage for military retirees and their spouses. Since Tricare for Life covers many out-of-pocket expenses for retirees on Medicare—such as copays and deductibles—it eliminates disincentives for unnecessary care. Adding measures to prevent overutilization and unnecessary care—for example, modifying Tricare for Life so it will not cover the first $500 in out-of-pocket expenses and only 50 percent of an enrollee's next $5,000, as recommended by the Bowles-Simpson deficit commission—would reduce Pentagon spending by about $40 billion over the next decade.

Furthermore, Congress should also pass the administration's proposed increases in Tricare fees, which, despite skyrocketing increases in health-care costs nationwide, have been raised by just $5 per month since the program was created in the mid-1990s. As a result, much of the cost growth in the Tricare program can be attributed not to active-duty service members—who receive health care for free—but to military retirees, who paid about 27 percent of their health-care costs in 1996 but contribute just 11 percent of these costs today.[19] These artificially low health-care premiums provide an incentive for military retirees who pursue second careers not to enroll in the health-care plans of their new employers. To put those numbers into perspective, due to congressional inaction, working-age military retirees pay just $520 *per year* for health coverage for an entire family, with the Pentagon picking up the rest of the bill.

In order to save $13 billion by FY 2017, the Pentagon has proposed responsible increases in the health-care fees paid by military retirees, indexed to retired pay.[20] Even with these increases, however, military retirees will still pay just 14 percent of their health-care costs. Congress should heed the request of the Obama administration and our nation's military leaders and pass these reforms to regain control of military health-care costs.

Retirement

The Pentagon also calls for an overhaul of its retirement program in its fiscal year 2013 budget request, perhaps the most politically toxic of its proposed personnel reforms. In the document, the Obama administration and Secretary of Defense Leon Panetta call on Congress to authorize the creation of a Military Retirement Modernization Commission.[21] The commission would be designed to help Congress and the Pentagon make the politically difficult decisions necessary to reform the military's outdated retirement system, which has been long criticized for its inequality, inflexibility, and high costs and whose unfunded liability is nearly $1 trillion.

Under the Pentagon's current retirement system, military personnel who serve for at least twenty years earn the right to a generous annual pension for life. Those who leave prior to achieving twenty years of service, however, get nothing. As a result, four out of five veterans leave the force with no retirement benefits.[22] Perhaps most troublesome, enlisted troops in ground-combat units—the men and women who have borne the brunt of the fighting in Iraq and Afghanistan—are among the least likely to achieve retirement benefits.[23]

Retirement reform may be the most politically difficult to implement of the recommendations in this chapter. Yet it also presents one of the most promising areas for savings. If left unreformed, military retirement costs are projected to grow to $217 billion by 2034, an enormous sum the Pentagon simply cannot afford to pay.[24] Implementing the recommendations of the Defense Business Board or Quadrennial Review of Military Compensation—both of which have released retirement reform plans—would bring about savings of tens of billions of dollars per year.

The Pentagon's outdated retirement system fails to provide for more than 80 percent of US service members, restricts the management decisions of Defense Department officials, and comes at a tremendous cost to US taxpayers. It may take political courage, but working together to reform this program is one of the best things the president and Congress can do for the country and our enlisted troops.

Nuclear Weapons

The Pentagon and the Department of Energy will spend about $640 billion on the US nuclear complex over the next decade. This includes the cost of maintaining and modernizing our enormous arsenal of weapons, the costs of procuring the next generation of delivery systems, funding a wide range of missile defense programs, and securing and safely disposing of fissile material.[25] Our massive nuclear stockpile—1,722 deployed warheads as of September 2012—is a relic of the Cold War.[26] This arsenal is expensive to maintain, of little value in combating the threats facing the nation today, and is composed of far more warheads than are necessary for deterrence or a second-strike capability.

In December 2012, forty-five US lawmakers signed a letter to congressional leadership calling for the nuclear weapons budget to be reduced by at least $100 billion over the next decade.[27] We also endorse this target. These $100 billion in reductions can be achieved by:

- cutting our nuclear arsenal to 1,100 nuclear weapons, about five hundred warheads below the limits required by the New START treaty;
- slowing production of the SSBNX;

- slowing design and production of the next generation bomber;
- cancelling the production of a new uranium processing facility; and
- cancelling ineffective missile defense programs.

As the Obama administration seeks to find responsible reductions in defense spending, our bloated nuclear stockpile presents a tremendous opportunity for savings. And with the election over, in his second term, the president has an opportunity to make significant progress on what has become one of his signature policy priorities: working toward a world free of nuclear weapons.

According to Air War College and School of Advanced Air and Space Studies faculty members Gary Schaub and James Forsyth Jr., the United States can maintain an effective nuclear deterrent with an arsenal of 292 operational warheads and nineteen reserve warheads—311 in total. In the near term, however, given the partisan opposition to the New START, 311 nuclear weapons may not be a feasible target politically, regardless of whether it makes sense strategically or financially.[28]

Earlier this year, however, the Obama administration was reported to be weighing cuts to a more moderate level of approximately 1,100 nuclear warheads.[29] We endorse this plan and recommend that the Pentagon achieve these reductions by the year 2022. Such a cut would bring the size of the US arsenal well below the limit of 1,550 deployed warheads mandated by New START, thereby demonstrating the country's commitment to nuclear disarmament and constituting a promising first step toward a nuclear posture more in line with the threats facing the United States.

The United States cannot buy perfect security, no matter how much we spend. But our dominance in every dimension of military power is clear. The United States' current military expenditures account for 40 percent of the world's total.[30] But the true engine of the United States' global power is our economic might. If the president and Congress are serious about tackling the deficit while preserving critical programs at home, the United States must carry out a responsible defense drawdown as we transition away from the wartime budgets of the Bush administration.

REBALANCE US SECURITY SPENDING

Given the deficit woes facing the nation, the Obama administration is right to weigh responsible decreases in defense spending. But not all of these savings should be used for deficit reduction. Rather, in order to most effectively and efficiently protect US national security, the president and Congress should shift some of these freed-up funds to the United States' chronically underfunded nonmilitary security programs, run primarily through the Department of State.

With its $600 billion per year budget, the Defense Department receives a grossly disproportionate share of the nation's security funding. To compare, the FY 2013 budget request for US international affairs budget, which covers funding for the State Department and the United States Agency for International Development (USAID), came to just $51 billion. While international affairs budget has increased significantly in the decade since 9/11, it has come nowhere close to closing the gap with a military budget that has grown even more exponentially.

The militarization of American foreign policy damages US national security for two reasons. First, military action alone will not be sufficient to counter the threats of the twenty-first century. For example, the United States cannot manage failed states and nonstate actors—which are at the center of many modern conflicts—with tactics designed for the Cold War.

Second, even when successful, military action is often an ineffective means of addressing the threats facing the country. As evidenced by the wars in Iraq and Afghanistan, solving the underlying causes for conflict through diplomacy and development comes at a fraction of the cost compared to military intervention. Expanding foreign aid and diplomatic efforts will help the United States mitigate future threats to national security before they disintegrate into situations that require military action, which is too often extremely costly in both American blood and treasure.

Yet as President Obama begins his second term, it is a very real possibility that our international affairs capabilities will be reduced even further. The State Department budget is perennially on the chopping block. House Budget Chairman Paul Ryan's (R-WI) "Path to Prosperity," for example, would require an $11 billion cut in international affairs spending while raising the Pentagon budget even higher above its already historic peaks.

The Department of State and USAID are already struggling to maintain an effective global presence with a budget that is less than a tenth of what their DOD counterparts receive. Additionally, underfunding international affairs programs has a tangible impact that strikes deeply at core diplomatic missions. The recent attacks on Benghazi certainly underscore the risks Foreign Service Officers take for their country and our duty to give them the support they need, something the State Department will be unable to do if it is continually subjected to budget cuts.

The military can become leaner and stronger, but politicians need to consider the broad array of security tools at their disposal. In order to most effectively and efficiently protect US national security, the president and Congress should invest in the nonmilitary security programs that prevent global crises from escalating into military confrontations. If we allow all of our nonmilitary security programs to atrophy, military action, so costly in both American lives and dollars, will be the only tool left in our arsenal.

IRAN

For the past decade, Iran has repeatedly undermined the strategic interests of the United States, its allies, and the international community in general. Probably the world's most dangerous state, Iran is a known sponsor of terrorism and has a history of funneling money and recruits to groups like al Qaeda and Hezbollah while supporting dictators like Bashar al Assad in Syria. Additionally, Iran's decision to enrich uranium to 20 percent—far more than the 3.5 percent necessary to produce nuclear energy for civilian energy production—as well as its decision to store this fuel in an underground bunker has long suggested that its nuclear program is not designed solely for peaceful purposes, as the Iranians claim.

In the past, counterproductive military action by the United States has strengthened Iran's hand. Iran is perhaps the clearest winner from our mindless, needless invasion and occupation of Iraq—it was able to capitalize on the overwhelming anti-American sentiment generated throughout the Arab and Muslim world by our invasion of Iraq under false pretenses.

Since taking office, however, the Obama administration, after reaching out to the Iranian regime, has successfully mustered international support for increased sanctions against Iran, an agenda that has tremendously weakened the country. Numerous states and multinational entities have imposed sanctions against Iran including the United Nations, the EU, Canada, Australia, South Korea, Japan, Switzerland, India, Israel, and the United States. These sanctions have had adverse effects on the Iranian nuclear program as well as the Iranian economy. More specifically, the sanctions have resulted in many oil companies withdrawing from Iran as well as a decline in oil production and reduced access to technologies needed to improve their efficiency. Additionally, many international companies have been reluctant to do business with Iran for fear of losing access to larger Western markets and global financial institutions.

Going forward, the United States should further focus its energy on the initiatives that have so successfully defrayed Iranian power and influence over the past two years: assembling a unified international coalition that condemns Iranian bad behavior, imposes multilateral sanctions, and isolates the country internationally, and reaching out to engage the Iranian government directly or through the P5-plus-1 group in order to deny Iran's leaders their most effective method of uniting their people—the specter of an "evil America."

The Iranian government is divided, widely viewed as illegitimate by its people, and isolated internationally. Moreover, Iran's economy is in shambles and its nuclear program has stalled, partly as a result of the sanctions. While the United States should not take any options off the table in responding to the Iranian nuclear developments, our military and intelligence leaders and most of the foreign-policy establishment agree that a military strike would likely be counterproductive. Iran is plagued by internal unrest, and an American or Israeli attack would no doubt unify the country.

Instead, the United States should strengthen its own sanctions regime and press for the strongest international sanctions that can garner the support of our allies in this coalition. The sanctions on Iran draw legitimacy from the fact that they have been approved by the United Nations and even involve some of Iran's former allies, such as Russia and China. Maintaining the support of this robust coalition should be one of the primary goals of the US response.

In determining the United States' policy toward Iran, the president and Congress should keep in mind what has made its efforts to contain Iran so effective over the past two years: international consensus. It is important that the US policy and rhetoric towards Iran furthers our long-term goals: deterring Iranian aggression and protecting US national security. Doing so will require us to work multilaterally with our allies. Military action would be counterproductive.

CONCLUSION

In the second Obama administration, the president and the Congress will be forced to deal with these four challenges as well as many others, including the continuing fallout from the Arab Spring, the crisis in Syria, the rise of al Qaeda in the Islamic Maghreb (AQIM), the increasing assertiveness of China, the growing threat of cyber attacks, the leadership change in North Korea, and the policies for using drones. But if the president and Congress can work together to carry out the wish list outlined in this chapter, they will possess the tools to handle these other challenges effectively.

In analyzing the factors that have and should determine how much the United States can spend on defense, it is clear that the current level of defense spending can be reduced. We face no existential threats abroad at a time when we are long overdue for investment at home. The federal deficit is increasing, and the Obama administration, with the support of the majority of the Congress and the American people, is shifting to a less expansive military posture and ending two wars. Rather than the Reagan policy of peace through strength, the new mantra is strength through peace.

The United States is one budget deal away from ensuring its strategic preeminence for the foreseeable future. Our dominance in every dimension of military power is clear. Rather, the greatest threat to US power and influence—our inability to come to a fair and balanced budget agreement—is self-inflicted. In his first term, President Obama protected the United States' national interests and security in spite of Congress. In his second term, the world's greatest legislative body will need to do better.

NOTES

1. Michael A. Memoli, "Mitch McConnell's Remarks on 2012 Draw White House Ire," *Los Angeles Times*, October 27, 2010.

2. Gail Collins, "Looking Forward," *New York Times*, January 2, 2013.

3. Barack Obama, "Obama's Address on the New Strategy in Afghanistan and Pakistan," *New York Times*, December 2, 2009.

4. Obama, "Obama's Address on the New Strategy in Afghanistan and Pakistan."

5. Sheryl Gay Stolberg and Helene Cooper, "Obama Adds Troops but Maps Exit Plan," *New York Times*, December 1, 2009.

6. Obama, "Obama's Address on the New Strategy in Afghanistan and Pakistan."

7. Rod Nordland, "Troop 'Surge' in Afghanistan Ends with Mixed Results," *New York Times*, September 21, 2012.

8. Scott Wilson and David Nakamura, "Obama Announces Reduced U.S. Role in Afghanistan Starting This Spring," *Washington Post*, January 11, 2013.

9. Caroline Wadhams, "Managing Afghanistan's Political Transition between Now and 2014," Center for American Progress, January 7, 2013.

10. Wadhams, "Managing Afghanistan's Political Transition between Now and 2014."

11. George Washington University, "US Spends More Rebuilding Iraq, Afghanistan than Post-WWII Germany," October 16, 2012, www.facethefactsusa.org/facts/us-spends-more-rebuilding-iraq-afghanistan-than-post-wwii-germany/.

12. Office of the Undersecretary of Defense, "Fiscal Year 2013 Budget Request," US Department of Defense, February 2012, comptroller.defense.gov/defbudget/fy2013/FY2013_Budget_Request.pdf.

13. Todd Harrison, "Analysis of the FY2013 Defense Budget and Sequestration," Center for Strategic and Budgetary Assessments, August 24, 2012, www.csbaonline.org/publications/2012/08/analysis-of-the-fy2013-defense-budget-and-sequestration/.

14. Lawrence J. Korb, Laura Conley, and Alex Rothman, "A Return to Responsibility: What President Obama and Congress Can Learn About Defense Budgets from Past," Center for American Progress, July 14, 2011.

15. Office of the Undersecretary of Defense, "Overview: Fiscal Year 2013 Budget Request," US Department of Defense, February 2012, comptroller.defense.gov/defbudget/fy2013/FY2013_Budget_Request_Overview_Book.pdf.

16. Thom Shanker, "Gates Takes Aim at Pentagon Spending," *New York Times*, May 8, 2010.

17. Elisabeth Bumiller and Thom Shanker, "Defense Budget Cuts Would Limit Raises and Close Bases," *New York Times*, January 26, 2012.

18. Lawrence J. Korb, Alex Rothman, and Max Hoffman, "Reforming Military Compensation: Addressing Runaway Personnel Costs Is a National Imperative," Center for American Progress, May 7, 2012, www.americanprogress.org/issues/security/report/2012/05/07/11573/reforming-military-compensation/.

19. Office of the Undersecretary of Defense, "Overview: Fiscal Year 2013 Budget Request."

20. Office of the Undersecretary of Defense, "Overview: Fiscal Year 2013 Budget Request."

21. Office of the Undersecretary of Defense, "Fiscal Year 2013 Budget Request," US Department of Defense, February 2012, comptroller.defense.gov/defbudget/fy2013/FY2013_Budget_Request.pdf.

22. Defense Business Board, "Report to the Secretary of Defense: Modernizing the Military Retirement System," 2011, dbb.defense.gov/pdf/DBB_Military_Retirement_Final_Presentationpdf.pdf.

23. Defense Business Board, "Report to the Secretary of Defense."

24. Defense Business Board, "Report to the Secretary of Defense."

25. Ploughshares Fund, "What Nuclear Weapons Cost Us," Ploughshares Fund Working Paper, September 2012, www.ploughshares.org/sites/default/files/resources/What%20Nuclear %20Weapons%20Cost%20Us%20Final%20(100212).pdf.

26. Jorge Benitez, "US Has More Nuclear Warheads and Delivery Vehicles Deployed Than Russia," *NATOSource: Alliance News Blog*, October 3, 2012, www.acus.org/natosource/us -has-more-nuclear-warheads-and-delivery-vehicles-deployed-russia.

27. Congressman Ed Markey, "Markey, House Dems to Leadership: Unneeded Nuclear Weapons Spending Should Be Cut to Help Avoid Fiscal Cliff," December 4, 2012, http:// markey.house.gov/press-release/markey-house-dems-leadership-unneeded-nuclear-weapons -spending-should-be-cut-help.

28. Gary Schaub Jr. and James Forsyth Jr, "An Arsenal We Can All Live With," *New York Times*, May 23, 2010.

29. Fox News, "US Edging toward Decision on New Nuclear Arms Cuts," July 2, 2012, www.foxnews.com/politics/2012/07/02/us-edging-toward-decision-on-new-nuclear-arms-cuts/

30. Peter W. Singer, "Comparing Defense Budgets, Apples to Apples," *TIME*, September 25, 2012, nation.time.com/2012/09/25/comparing-defense-budgets-apples-to-apples/.

Chapter Twelve

Obama's Constitutional Conflicts with Congress

Louis Fisher

As with other presidents, Barack Obama collided often with Congress in the exercise of what he considered the scope of his independent constitutional powers. The controversies include his executive order to close the detention facilities at Guantánamo, the abortive attempt to prosecute Khalid Sheikh Mohammed in New York City, use of signing statements, initiating military force in Libya without congressional authority, making recess appointments, and the "Fast and Furious" gunrunning program that resulted in the House citing Attorney General Eric Holder in contempt followed by Obama invoking executive privilege.

CLOSING GUANTÁNAMO

On his second day in office, January 22, 2009, President Obama issued an executive order to close the detention facilities at the naval base "as soon as practicable, and no later than 1 year from the date of this order."[1] As many as eight hundred individuals had been held there after the terrorist attacks of 9/11. The Bush administration returned more than five hundred either to their home country or a third country. The Defense Department concluded that additional detainees were eligible to be transferred or released. President Bush realized that Guantánamo had become an international symbol of American lawlessness and human rights abuse.

Obama's decision to sign the executive order marked an extraordinary mistake, damaging him at the very start of his administration. He had all the elements of a greenhorn, someone coming into office untutored on the use of political power, raising serious questions about his understanding of

American government. Did he think a mere signature would close the facility? Where were the experienced adults in the administration to warn him that there had to be careful *preparation* before issuing the executive order? It was essential to check with members of Congress, both Democrat and Republican, to know how they would respond. Did they have legitimate concerns about closing the facility? What steps could the administration take to alleviate those concerns? How would the public react? Would they be fearful about the transfer of terrorist suspects from Guantánamo to prisons in America? There needed to be a concerted effort by the administration, particularly by President Obama, to explain that hundreds of terrorists had already been prosecuted in US courts and held in US prisons, without incident.

Before issuing the executive order, the administration should have first located a prison in the United States that could safely take detainees. By the second month, White House aides identified three possible sites: a state prison in Thomson, Illinois; a Navy brig in Charleston, South Carolina; and the Army's maximum-security prison in Fort Leavenworth, Kansas.[2] None of those choices panned out. During the early months, the mood on Capitol Hill grew steadily more hostile to Obama's plan. Opposition came from both Democrats and Republicans. Senate Democratic Leader Harry Reid insisted on a comprehensive, responsible proposal from Obama: "We will never allow terrorists to be released into the United States."[3] One of the casualties in the failed Guantánamo initiative was White House Counsel Greg Craig, who left the administration by the end of the year.[4]

Congress passed several legislative efforts to block closure of the detention facility. One provision, signed into law on January 7, 2011, prohibited the use of military funds to transfer or release Guantánamo detainees into the United States.[5] In signing the bill, Obama said this section "represents a dangerous and unprecedented challenge to critical executive branch authority to determine when and where to prosecute Guantanamo detainees, based on the facts and circumstances of each case and our national security interests."[6] Dangerous or unprecedented, Obama had to live with it. He paid a price because he decided to act unilaterally (like President George W. Bush) instead of working jointly with Congress. Another provision, which became law on April 15, 2011, also denied funds to transfer or release Guantánamo detainees to the United States.[7] Once again Obama used a signing statement to protest against this "dangerous and unprecedented challenge" to executive power.[8] Once again Congress, not the president, prevailed.

Another early embarrassment concerned the administration's decision to try Khalid Sheikh Mohammed, the most senior al Qaeda detainee, in New York City. As with the attempt to close Guantánamo, the administration failed to reach out to lawmakers in Congress and to political leaders in Manhattan. Mayor Michael Bloomberg estimated the trial could cost $1 billion.[9] The statutory provisions mentioned above specifically named Khalid

Sheikh Mohammed. Eventually the administration conceded it would lose this battle also. The defeat was humiliating to Obama and particularly to his attorney general, Eric Holder.

SIGNING STATEMENTS

During his campaign to be president, Obama offered views on signing statements to *BostonGlobe* reporter Charlie Savage. He said it was appropriate to use signing statements "to protect a president's constitutional prerogatives."[10] However, he added: "It is a clear abuse of power to use such statements as a license to evade laws that the President does not like or as an end-around provisions designed to foster accountability. I will not use signing statements to nullify or undermine congressional restrictions as enacted into law."[11]

After taking office, Obama made it difficult for journalists and academics to track signing statements. His administration discontinued publication of the *Weekly Compilation of Presidential Documents*, which had provided a very convenient way to keep up with signing statements. Researchers now had to rely on the White House website to find signing statements. Anyone who has tried to navigate the website will attest that it is not user-friendly.[12]

On April 15, 2011, President Obama raised objections to a bill that defunded certain "czar" positions.[13] He spoke of the president's "well-established authority to supervise and oversee the executive branch" and the president's "prerogative to obtain advice that will assist him in carrying out his constitutional responsibilities."[14] Yes, the president has authority to supervise the executive branch and obtain advice, but he has no authority to create and fund White House positions. That authority belongs to Congress, which can increase or decrease the number of White House officials and increase or decrease their salaries. His signing statement claimed that the statutory restrictions "violate the separation of powers by undermining the President's ability to exercise his constitutional responsibilities and take care that the laws be faithfully executed." That was far too abstract and airy. Congress decides how many aides a president may have and how much they will be paid. Obama referred to a "prerogative" that does not exist.

In *INS v. Chadha* (1973), the Supreme Court struck down the "legislative veto," which Congress had used for more than a century to control delegated authority.[15] Sometimes it acted either with a House or Senate resolution (one-House veto). On other occasions it used a concurrent resolution (two-House veto). It also required executive officials to seek the approval of designated committees. The court's decision supposedly invalidated every form of legislative veto. According to the court, if Congress wanted to exercise control of individuals outside the legislative branch, it had to pass legislation by both houses (bicameralism) and submit the bill to the president for his signature or veto (presentation). However, the court had no understanding of the political accommodations entered into by both branches over the years. The executive branch often invited legislative vetoes as a way of receiving more generous delegations of statutory authority. [16]

Unsurprisingly, the committee vetoes that existed before *Chadha* continued to exist after *Chadha*. When bills containing committee vetoes reached the White House, presidents would routinely announce in a signing statement that they were invalid under *Chadha* and instruct agencies not to abide by them. Just as routinely, agency officials continued to meet with designated committees to seek their approval when they wanted to move money from one purpose to another. Agency budget manuals identify the types of funding shifts that require committee approval. [17]

As with previous presidents, Obama objected to committee vetoes. In a signing statement on December 23, 2011, he said: "Numerous provisions of this bill purport to condition the authority of executive branch officials to spend or reallocate funds on the approval of congressional committees. These are constitutionally impermissible forms of congressional aggrandizement in the execution of the laws." [18] Bold, but empty, words. He explained: "Although my Administration will notify the relevant committees before taking the specified actions, and will accord the recommendations of such committee appropriate and serious consideration, our spending decisions shall not be treated as dependent on the approval of congressional committees." Wholly illusory.

What Obama and other presidents do not want to acknowledge is that agencies need discretion and flexibility once a fiscal year begins, and new problems emerge they did not anticipate. To keep faith with Congress, they notify committees of these changes and, in some cases, seek their approval. It was far-fetched and inaccurate for Obama to call this kind of executive-legislative accord "Congressional aggrandizement." Both branches recognize that agencies need greater flexibility in spending money. That process worked well before *Chadha*; it continues to function after it. If Obama and other presidents really wanted to eliminate committee vetoes, they could send a memo to executive agencies and command them to delete from their budget manuals all references to a committee veto. That would be a very foolish step. The federal government needs to perform effectively. Committee vetoes help serve that purpose. [19]

MILITARY ACTION IN LIBYA

While escalating the war in Afghanistan and attempting to withdraw US forces from Iraq, President Obama in March 2011 opened a new war in Libya without obtaining authority from Congress. Instead, he claimed legal support from two outside organizations: the United Nations (UN) Security Council and the North Atlantic Treaty Organization (NATO) allies. Harry Truman was the first President to circumvent Congress by receiving UN resolutions for the war in Korea. President Clinton on a number of occasions skirted legislative control by claiming authority either from the UN or NATO.[20]

During his presidential campaign, Obama was asked by reporter Charlie Savage under what circumstances a president possessed constitutional authority to bomb Iran without Congressional authority. The question was aimed specifically at the strategic bombing of suspected nuclear sites in Iran that did not involve an "imminent" threat. Obama replied: "The President does not have power under the Constitution to unilaterally authorize a military attack in a situation that does not involve stopping an actual or imminent threat to the nation." He added that the president, as Commander in Chief, "does have a duty to protect and defend the United States" in case of actual or imminent threats. Otherwise, he said that history has shown that military action "is most successful when it is authorized and supported by the Legislative branch. It is always preferable to have informed consent of Congress prior to any military action."[21]

Steps toward military action against Libya began with the decision of the Security Council on March 17, 2011, to pass Resolution 1973. After earlier expressing concern about the escalation of violence and heavy civilian casualties in Libya, the Security Council established a ban on "all flights in the airspace of the Libyan Arab Jamahiriya in order to help protect civilians." Of course the ban did not apply to "all" flights. It covered only those by the Libyan government. Military flights by coalition forces were necessary to enforce the ban by bombing air defense systems and other targets. On March 21, Obama notified Congress that two days earlier, at 3 p.m. EST, US forces "at my direction" commenced military operations in Libya to assist the UN action.

Expectations and plans about the military action began to shift, week by week. Obama predicted that military operations would last "days, not weeks."[22] The operations lasted seven months. Unable to predict with any accuracy a military commitment, it would have been wise for Obama to avoid the "days" imagery. But he had political reasons to be specific. He wanted to assure Congress and the American people that his initiative, no matter how questionable legally and constitutionally, would be of short duration. Basically: a constitutional violation that would not last very long. Specificity in this case proved politically costly. Either Obama was being deliberately misleading or he lacked the capacity to judge military commitments.

On March 21, Obama announced at a news conference: "It is U.S. policy that Qaddafi needs to go."[23] The initial policy of protecting innocent civilians now included a new purpose: regime change. Initially, General Carter F.

Ham, in charge of the coalition effort, stated that the United States was not working with the rebels: "Our mission is not to support any opposition forces."[24] The Allied bombing mission in Libya soon proceeded to do precisely that. On April 21, the Pentagon announced that President Obama had authorized the use of armed Predator drones against Qaddafi forces.[25] On April 25, NATO directed two bombs into a residential and military complex used by Qaddafi in central Tripoli.[26] On May 5, the Obama administration announced it had begun efforts to release some of the more than $30 billion in assets it had seized from Libya and divert some of that money to rebel forces. Secretary of State Hillary Clinton said the administration would ask Congress for legislative authority to shift some of the frozen assets to help the Libyan people, including assistance to the rebels.[27]

On March 28, President Obama announced he was prepared to "transfer responsibilities to our allies and partners." As he explained, NATO "has taken command of the enforcement of the arms embargo and the no-fly zone."[28] None of these public statements could justify Obama's actions. Like the UN Charter, NATO was created by treaty. The president and the Senate through the treaty process may not shift the Article I powers of Congress to outside international and regional bodies like the Security Council and NATO. Section 8 of the War Powers Resolution (WPR) specifically states that authority to introduce US armed forces into hostilities or into situations where involvement in hostilities is clearly indicated by the circumstances "shall not be inferred . . . from any treaty heretofore or hereafter ratified unless such treaty is implemented by legislation specifically authorizing the introduction of United States Armed Forces into hostilities or into such situations and stating that it is intended to constitute specific statutory authorization within the meaning of this joint resolution."[29] The authorizing body is always Congress, not the Security Council or NATO.

On October 30, 2006, Obama spoke about the power of the presidency. The biggest problem, he said, "is to lie about the choices that have to be made. And to obfuscate and to fudge."[30] He didn't follow that advice with military operations in Libya. The initial goal was to protect civilians. Quickly it morphed into removing Qaddafi. On April 1, 2011, the Office of Legal Counsel (OLC) concluded that the operations in Libya did not constitute "war." According to OLC, satisfying the standard of war requires "prolonged and substantial military engagements, typically involving exposure of U.S. military personnel to significant risk over a significant period."[31] The WPR does not speak of "risk." It refers to "hostilities." OLC reasoned that if US casualties can be kept low—no matter the destruction and loss of life to another nation—war would not exist within the meaning of the Constitution. A powerful nation could pulverize another country, including the use of nuclear weapons, and there would be no war if it did not suffer casualties.

As military operations in Libya continued, the Obama administration would once again interpret words beyond their ordinary and plain meaning. By early June 2011, US involvement exceeded the sixty-day clock of the WPR. Under the terms of that statute, presidents who engage in military operations for up to sixty days without congressional authorization must begin withdrawing troops and complete that step within the next thirty days. Because of that timetable, the House passed a resolution (H. Res. 292) to direct President Obama to submit a report to the House within fourteen days describing the national security interests in Libya, including the "President's justification for not seeking authorization by Congress for the use of military force in Libya." The resolution passed by a vote of 268 to 145.

On June 15, the Obama administration submitted a thirty-two-page report to the House. It concluded that "the current U.S. military operations in Libya are consistent with the War Powers Resolution and do not under that law require further congressional authorization, because U.S. military operations are distinct from the kind of 'hostilities' contemplated by the Resolution's 60 day termination provision" [32] Not only did no war exist in Libya but not even hostilities. This interpretation ignores the context under which the WPR was debated and enacted: the decision of the Nixon administration to conduct a massive bombing operation in Cambodia, which did not involve US ground troops or substantial US casualties. [33] Nothing in the WPR waives the sixty- to ninety-day limitation if US military operations are "limited" and there are few US casualties. According to the legal analysis by the Obama administration, if the United States conducted military operations by bombing at thirty thousand feet, launching Tomahawk missiles from ships, and using armed drones, there would be no "hostilities" in Libya (or anywhere else) under the terms of the WPR, provided that US casualties were minimal or nonexistent.

Having secured from OLC a memo stating that "war" did not exist, Obama now needed a legal judgment that there were no "hostilities." This time OLC refused to provide such a memo. Jeh Johnson, general counsel in the Defense Department, also refused. Eventually Obama received from White House Counsel Robert Bauer and State Department Legal Adviser Harold Koh statements that no hostilities existed in Libya. [34] If President Obama did not anticipate hostilities in sending US forces to Libya, he had no obligation to report to Congress within the forty-eight-hour deadline of the WPR. Yet he did so. Through his public action he acknowledged hostilities or imminent hostilities. [35]

Various administrations, eager to press the limits of presidential war power, appear to recognize that they may not—legally and politically—use the words "war" or "hostilities." They seems to recognize that using words in their normal sense, as understood by members of Congress, federal judges, and the general public, would acknowledge Congressional preeminence. Other than repelling sudden attacks and protecting American lives overseas, presidents may not take the country from a state of peace to a state of war without seeking and obtaining statutory authority. To sidestep that constitutional limit, Presidents go to great lengths to explain to Congress and the public that what they are doing is not what they are doing.

When President Truman went to war against North Korea in 1950 without coming to Congress, he knew the power to go to war rested with the legislative branch. He was asked by a reporter: "Are we or are we not at war?" He replied: "We are not at war."[36] Another reporter asked: "Would it be correct, against your explanation, to call this a police action under the United Nations?" He agreed: "Yes. That is exactly what it amounts to."[37] When presidents and executive officials attempt to defend military actions that cannot be justified by talking straight, they resort to what can accurately be called "double-talk." Perhaps that term may seem crude and unscholarly when analyzing the presidency, but consider how it is defined: "language used to deceive, usually through concealment or misrepresentation of truth."[38] Another dictionary explains that the term "appears to be earnest and meaningful but in fact is a mixture of sense and nonsense." It produces in the listener "a strong suspicion that he is either hard of hearing or slowly going mad." The language is typically "inflated, involved, and often deliberatively ambiguous."[39]

Drew Westen, writing for the *New York Times* on August 7, 2011, confessed: "Like most Americans, at this point, I have no idea what Barack Obama—and by extension the party he leads—believes on virtually any issue." He noted Obama's pattern of "presenting inconsistent positions with no apparent recognition of their incoherence."[40] An example is a major speech Obama delivered at the State Department on May 19, 2011. The topic: the Arab Spring. Repeatedly he defended the principle of nonviolence. "The United States opposes the use of violence and repression against the people of the region." Toward the end of the speech he strongly supported "the moral force of nonviolence."[41] Yet at that moment the United States and NATO were bombing Libya.

In that same address, Obama reminded the audience that one of his first acts as president was a speech in Cairo where he began "to broaden our engagement based upon mutual interests and mutual respect." He believed then "and I believe now—that we have a stake not just in the stability of nations, but in the self-determination of individuals." There could be "no doubt that the United States of America welcomes changes that advances self-determination and opportunity." He explained that the United States "supports a set of universal rights" and among those rights are free speech, the freedom of peaceful assembly, the freedom of religion, equality of men and women under the rule of law, "and the right to choose your own leaders."[42] At the very moment he uttered those words, Obama was in the process of driving Colonel Qaddafi out of power.

MAKING RECESS APPOINTMENTS

The framers understood that the Senate would not always be in session to give advice and consent to a presidential nomination. They therefore empowered the president "to fill up all Vacancies that may happen during the Recess of the Senate by granting Commissions which shall expire at the End of their next Session." The delegates at the Philadelphia Convention accepted this language without a dissenting vote.[43] There is little in the convention record to fix the intent and scope of this presidential power.

The word "recess" requires interpretation. It means more than final adjournment at the end of the first session of a Congress or at the end of a Congress. A temporary recess of the Senate, "protracted enough to prevent that body from performing its functions of advising and consenting to executive nominations," permits the president to make recess appointments.[44] A Senate adjournment from July 3 to August 8, 1960, constituted a "Recess of the Senate" as interpreted by the Justice Department.[45] There is general acceptance that a Senate recess of a month, or more, constitutes a recess of sufficient length to permit a recess appointment.

What of shorter periods: two weeks, a week, or less than a week? According to an Attorney General opinion in 1921, brief adjournments "for 5 or even 10 days" do not "constitute the recess intended by the Constitution."[46] A Justice Department brief in 1993 suggested that recess appointments might be valid for recesses in excess of three days, but the litigation that prompted that analysis was not decided on that ground.[47]

In November 2007, the Senate began holding pro forma sessions every three business days to prevent recess appointments by President Bush. One Senator calls the Senate into session and then adjourns, usually in less than a minute. An example is the action of Senator Patrick J. Leahy, who called the Senate to order on October 27, 2011, at ten seconds after 11:00 a.m. After assuming the chair as Acting President pro tempore, he ordered the Senate to stand adjourned until 3 p.m. on Monday, October 31, 2011. The Senate adjourned thirty-three seconds after 11:00 a.m.

Beginning on October 17, 2011, and projected to end on January 23, 2012, the Senate held a series of pro forma sessions, intended this time to prevent recess appointments by President Obama. However, on January 4, 2012, after a pro forma session, he made four recess appointments: Richard Cordray to be director of the Consumer Financial Protection Bureau (CFPB) and three members of the National Labor Relations Board (NLRB). In a memo dated two days later, OLC decided that the holding of pro forma sessions in which no business is to be conducted does not have the legal effect of interrupting what OLC called a functional recess of twenty days. Under that interpretation, President Obama possessed authority to make the recess appointments.

The constitutional issue is complicated by several factors. Under the president's constitutional obligation to take care that the laws be faithfully executed, if a position is vacant and the Senate is unavailable to confirm, a recess appointment is understandable. Yet designating a director of the CFPB did not seem an urgent matter to President Obama. The Dodd-Frank statute created the CFPB position on July 21, 2010. Obama did not submit Cordray's name until almost a year later, on July 18, 2011.[48] OLC reasoned that the Senate is not in session during pro forma periods because party leaders announce "in advance that there is to be 'no business conducted' at such sessions." It concluded that "the President may determine that pro forma sessions at which no business is to be conducted do not interrupt a Senate recess for purposes of the Recess Appointment Clause."

OLC chose to rely on what party leaders *said* rather than on what the Senate *did*. In fact, business was conducted during these pro forma sessions, including Senate action on a temporary payroll tax bill on December 23, 2011.[49] When Obama signed the bill into law, the administration understood that the Senate in pro forma session has the capacity to conduct business. If the Senate can pass legislation at such times, it could confirm nominees if it wished to do so. OLC's memo raises two other issues. Article I, Section 5, of the Constitution provides that neither house of Congress may adjourn "for more than three days" without the consent of the other house. The House of Representatives did not consent to a Senate adjournment beyond three days. Furthermore, Article I, Section 5, stipulates that each house "may determine the Rules of its Proceedings." The Senate determines its rules, not the president or OLC.[50]

OLC acknowledged that Obama's actions presented "novel" issues. It noted that "substantial arguments on each side create some litigation risk for such appointments." Shortly after he made the recess appointments, several lawsuits were filed. If the administration lost a legal challenge, decisions made by the NLRB and CFPB could be nullified. In 2010, the Supreme Court voided more than five hundred decisions by the NLRB because it attempted to operate with a two-person quorum in an agency authorized to have five members.[51]

On January 25, 2013, the DC Circuit ruled that President Obama violated the Constitution when he used recess appointment power to select the three NLRB members.[52] In deciding *Noel Canning v. NLRB*, the court ruled that the president may make recess appointments only between sessions of Congress, not during an intrasession recess. By invalidating Obama's action, the decision left the NLRB without a quorum, which could possibly nullify more than three hundred of the board's decisions.[53]

The Senate has full constitutional authority to withhold confirmation over a particular nominee because of qualifications and many other factors. The issue with Cordray was unique, however. In mounting a filibuster against his nomination, it was clear from the debate that on the cloture motion Republican senators did not block confirmation because he was unqualified.[54] Senate Minority Leader Mitch McConnell explained that the Republicans were opposed to *any* nominee for the position unless and until President Obama and Congress rewrote the underlying statute to satisfy three conditions: "replace the single Director with a board of directors," subject the bureau "to the congressional appropriations process" (the bureau depends on funds transferred to it from the Federal Reserve), and "allow other financial regulators to provide a check on CFPB rules."[55]

In no previous instance has a group of senators refused to confirm a nominee unless the authorizing statute was rewritten in accordance with their specifications. Senator Sherrod Brown asked Senate Historian Donald Ritchie if, in the past, "one political party tried to block the nomination of a Presidential appointee based on wanting to change the agency." Ritchie could locate no precedent.[56] Could this legislative tactic be used against any nominee chosen to head an executive department, agency, or bureau? Under this interpretation, a minority of senators could prevent confirmation of a secretary of defense, attorney general, EPA administrator, and other nominees unless enabling statutes were revised to satisfy their instructions. Such actions have the potential to cripple government.

"FAST AND FURIOUS"

"Fast and Furious" was a gunrunning operation carried out by the Alcohol, Tobacco, and Firearms (ATF) agency. The program went tragically awry, allowing about two thousand assault weapons to leave US gun shops and enter Mexico, leading to the deaths of hundreds of Mexicans. What makes the story of special interest is the misguided attempt by the Justice Department to limit the damage. Actions by officials in Main Justice ended up making the problem far worse, leading the House to cite Attorney General Holder for contempt. At that point President Obama invoked executive privilege to prevent House access to executive branch documents. He never actually explained the legal basis for his decision. "Fast and Furious" is a textbook example of an administration unable to handle a political scandal without exacerbating it.

Gunrunning

The issue of weapons flowing from the United States into Mexico predates President Obama. The administration of George W. Bush created a program called "Operation Wide Receiver." The purpose was to monitor "straw buyers"—customers who purchase guns for someone else. Instead of immediately seizing the weapons, ATF decided to follow the guns to major crime syndicates. The strategy: let straw buyers lead ATF to firearms traffickers and Mexican drug cartels. The program was finally closed down after ATF concluded it lost track of too many guns. One of the mysteries of the Obama administration is why it decided to renew a failed program.

In 2006, ATF agents in Phoenix, Arizona initiated Operation Wide Receiver. With the assistance of local gun dealers, the agents watched straw buyers purchase guns with the intent to transfer them to other parties. After numerous unsuccessful efforts to interdict the weapons at the Mexican border, the lead ATF agent in charge of this program acknowledged a year later: "We have reached that stage where I am no longer comfortable allowing additional firearms to 'walk.'"[57] In late 2007, the operational phase of this program was terminated. In the Obama administration, a Justice Department prosecutor reviewed the file for Operation Wide Receiver and remarked that "a lot of guns seemed to have gone to Mexico" and "a lot of those guns 'walked.'"[58]

Given the evident difficulty of tracking weapons from gun shops to the border and into Mexico, why would this type of program be revived by the Obama administration? What safeguards could be added to avoid the problems experienced by the Bush administration? When reports of gunrunning gained public attention, the Obama administration initially denied that guns had walked to Mexico. Independent investigations by members of Congress and the media forced the administration to admit that its denials were false, but the manner in which it made that admission added to the scandal, as will be explained.

Senator Grassley's Letter

On January 27, 2011, Senator Charles E. Grassley wrote to Kenneth E. Melson, ATF acting director. Grassley said that members of the Senate Judiciary Committee received "numerous allegations that the ATF sanctioned the sale of hundreds of assault weapons to suspected straw purchasers, who then allegedly transported these weapons throughout the southwestern border area and into Mexico." According to those allegations, one of those individuals purchased three assault rifles with cash in Glendale, Arizona on January 16, 2010, and two of the weapons "were allegedly used in a firefight on December 14, 2010 against Customs and Border Protection (CBP) agents, killing CBP Agent Brian Terry." As noted in his letter, the allegations were accompanied by "detailed documentation" that appeared to lend credibility to the claims "and partially corroborates them." Grassley expressed concern that ATF "may have become careless, if not negligent, in implementing the Gunrunner strategy."[59]

Under ATF policy, weapons should be interdicted before falling into the hands of criminals. Instead, despite the protests of many ATF agents, the weapons were allowed to reach Mexico and be used by drug cartels. After the death of Brian Terry, Attorney General Holder took steps to close down Fast and Furious. Two months later, on February 28, he ordered the inspector general in the Justice Department to conduct an investigation.

Drafting a Letter to Grassley

Although Grassley wrote to Melson, the Justice Department decided the response letter would go out of Main Justice. How that letter was drafted is fairly clear from 1,364 documents (mainly e-mails) the Justice Department made available to the House Committee on Oversight and Government Reform. I have read those documents and will describe some here. The easiest way to identify the documents is by the number assigned to them, such as "HOGR DOJ 003665." HOGR stands for House Committee on Oversight and Government Reform. DOJ stands for Department of Justice. I will just use the number.

Officials in the Justice Department should have taken the Grassley letter very seriously. Grassley and his staff have excellent reputations for conducting thorough and credible investigations. Frequently they receive documents and testimony from agency whistleblowers who decide to reveal actions within the executive branch that are wasteful, abusive, and often illegal. If Grassley took the time to write to Melson, he had strong grounds. The wise thing to do was to ask him what documentation he possessed about gunrunning. That was not done.

Gregory Rasnake, ATF's chief of legislative affairs, e-mailed Ronald Weich, head of DOJ's Office of Legislative Affairs, on January 27, 2011. Rasnake reported: "They claim to have 'documentation' that confirms their concerns" (003637). On that same day, Rasnake was asked by Melson: "Can you ask them for documentation?" Rasnake received this advice from James McDermond, ATF's assistant director for public and government affairs: "They will never share the documentation at this time" (003660). Rasnake responded: "No way. We can't even ask" (003662). McDermond agreed: "I concur with the fact that we can't ask" (003665). From the positions they held, Rasnake and McDermond should have been capable of knowing what members of Congress will and will not do. Grassley wanted to know about gunrunning. He said he had documentation. No conceivable harm could come from asking him to share the documents. Why not ask?

Rasnake e-mailed Melson on January 27, at 5:31 p.m.: "The bottom line is we couldn't even ask them for it. It would be viewed as impolite. You see—they have no reason to share. . . . The likelihood that they would give it to us is so remote, that I suggest it is not worth the risk of offending them" (003673). A remark by Rasnake to Melson is revealing: "My initial thoughts were to hide and punt, but after my conversation with Grassley's staffers—I don't believe that dog is gonna hunt" (003673). Clearly Rasnake found Grassley's staffers professionally competent and determined to find the truth. It appears that Rasnake and McDermond didn't ask Grassley for documents for fear he possessed credible evidence about gunrunning. If ATF officials in Phoenix (and some in Main Justice) had decided to send a strong letter of rebuttal to Grassley, telling him his allegations were false, they may have decided it was better not to ask for information he had.

Why would a request to Grassley's office for documentation be "viewed as impolite" and carry the risk of "offending them"? I cannot imagine any grounds for those concerns. Asking a member of Congress and his staff for documents is not impolite or offensive. ATF officials in Phoenix were key players in drafting the letter that informed Grassley that his allegations were false. What could be more offensive to Grassley than being told by the Justice Department that his legitimate concerns were lacking in merit? What turned out to be false were not Grassley's allegations but rather the letter Main Justice sent him.

A number of Justice Department officials were prepared to vigorously defend ATF and rebut Grassley. Dennis Burke, US attorney in Phoenix, e-mailed Main Justice on February 3, at 8:05 p.m.: "I am personally outraged by Senator Grassley'[s] falsehoods. It is one of the lowest acts I have ever seen in politics" (004647). Several officials in Main Justice also strongly defended ATF. Jason Weinstein, deputy assistant attorney general in the Criminal Division, e-mailed William Hoover, assistant director for field operations (ATF) on February 1, 2:15 p.m., stating that Lanny Breuer, assistant attorney general in the Criminal Division, "is one of ATF's biggest supporters—he has encouraged me to do whatever we can to help" (004026). Weinstein e-mailed Rasnake on February 2, 1:36 p.m.: "My boss and I are fervently supportive of ATF, and these allegations are infuriating" (004212).

For some reason, the Justice Department felt under pressure to respond by letter quickly. They received Grassley's letter of January 27 and immediately began the drafting process. The letter went out February 4. The report by the Office of Inspector General, released on September 19, 2012, notes: "We believe that in his zeal to protect ATF's interests, Weinstein 'lost perspective' and provided distorted information. In helping to draft the February 4 letter, he 'failed to act in the best interests of the Department by advocating for ATF rather than responsibly gathering information about its activities.'"[60] The OIG report concluded that the February 4 letter "was the byproduct of rushed and sloppy drafting by uninformed and misinformed officials."[61]

The larger question is why the Justice Department felt compelled to send a letter to Grassley within a matter of days. His letter of January 27 did not set a deadline for a written response. He only requested that his staff be briefed "by knowledgeable ATF supervisors no later than February 3, 2011." The Justice Department had plenty of time to prepare an informed and accurate letter. I think the reason for the "rushed" letter lay in the intent of ATF and Main Justice officials to strongly repudiate Grassley's allegations about gunrunning, especially the connection between the purchase of weapons in Glendale, Arizona and the death of Brian Terry.

The February 4 Letter

Ronald Weich, head of the Office of Legislative Affairs (OLA), signed the response letter to Senator Grassley on February 4, 2011. The value of an OLA letter is that it allows the Justice Department to speak decisively with a single voice and put an issue behind it. That is possible only when the letter is accurate and informed. The February 4 letter was false and misinformed, as the Justice Department eventually admitted, but it took ten months to retract the letter. Looking back, Main Justice would have been better off had the letter gone out under Kenneth Melson's name. It would have looked like a Phoenix cover-up instead of obstruction by Main Justice.

The February 4 letter must be read with great care. It states: "At the outset, the allegation described in your January 27 letter—that ATF 'sanctioned' or otherwise knowingly allowed the sale of assault weapons to a straw purchaser who then transported them into Mexico—is false." On the surface, it makes Grassley look like he possessed false information, but a key part of the sentence is whether straw purchasers transported weapons to Mexico. Quite likely they did not. Their function was to purchase weapons and give them to other parties, who would take the weapons to Mexico. In a letter to Senator Patrick Leahy two months later, on April 19, Weich made that distinction clear by referring to straw purchasers "who purchase the weapons not for themselves, but with the purpose of transferring them to others who then facilitate their movement across the border to the cartels."

If straw purchasers did not transport weapons to Mexico, it was technically true that ATF did not "sanction" or "knowingly allow" straw purchasers to buy weapons and bring them to Mexico. But it is also true that ATF did sanction and knowingly allowed straw purchasers to buy weapons, transfer them to third parties, and the third parties transported the weapons to Mexico. Grassley was correct about gunrunning, which was his principal concern. Of subsidiary interest was how the guns reached Mexico.

The February 4 letter also stated: "ATF makes every effort to interdict weapons that have been purchased illegally and prevent their transportation to Mexico. Indeed, an important goal of Project Gunrunner is to stop the flow of weapons from the United States to drug cartels in Mexico." Referring to "every effort" and "important goal" did not address Grassley's question: did assault weapons in US gun shops end up in Mexico? The answer is yes, as the Department would eventually have to concede.

Slow Motion toward Retraction

The February 4 letter, highly suspect when issued, declined in credibility with each passing week. On February 23, a CBS broadcast reported that ATF had facilitated the delivery of thousands of guns into criminal hands. In response, Attorney General Holder advised his chief of staff, Gary Grindler, and Deputy Attorney General James Cole: "Ok. We need answers on this. Not defensive bs—real answers."[62] Apparently a substantive, informed challenge by Senator Grassley (the ranking member of Senate Judiciary) could be pushed aside, but a television program reaching millions of viewers could not.

By March 30, Phoenix supervisors concluded that the February 4 letter contained inaccuracies, especially after reviewing material in wiretap affidavits. They took the initiative to recommend to Main Justice that it should read the affidavits, but did not connect that advice to particular deficiencies in the February 4 letter.[63] Weich wrote to Grassley on May 2 that "it remains our understanding that ATF's Operation Fast and Furious did not knowingly permit straw buyers to take guns into Mexico." "Did not knowingly" is a far cry from denying that assault weapons had walked.

The report by the inspector general criticized the May 2 letter: "Regardless of whether there was an intent to draw a distinction between straw purchasers and third parties, senior Department officials knew or should have known that while ATF may not have allowed straw purchasers to buy firearms so that they themselves could take the guns to Mexico, ATF had in many instances allowed straw purchasers to buy firearms knowing that a third party would be transporting them to Mexico."[64] The report further noted: "We believe that to Congress and the public the Department's May 2 letter reasonably could be understood as at least a partial reaffirmation of the February 4 letter at a time when Department officials knew or should have known that the February 4 letter contained inaccurate information."[65]

On May 4, at a Senate Judiciary Committee hearing about whether ATF had interdicted weapons, Attorney General Holder responded: "I frankly don't know. That what the [Inspector General's] investigation . . . will tell us."[66] After those concessions, why not withdraw the February 4 letter? On June 15, the House Oversight Committee listened to ATF agents describe how the agency failed to track the purchase of weapons at gun shops by straw buyers.[67] At that same hearing, Assistant Attorney General Weich told the committee that "allegations from the ATF agents . . . have given rise to serious questions about how ATF conducted this operation," adding: "We are not clinging to the statements" in the February 4 letter.[68] In November, both Holder and Assistant Attorney General Lanny Breuer testified before the Senate Judiciary Committee in separate hearings that the February 4 letter "inadvertently included inaccurate information."[69]

Finally: Retraction

On December 2, 2011, the Justice Department finally decided to withdraw the February 4 letter. Deputy Attorney General James M. Cole wrote to Darrell Issa, chairman of the House Oversight Committee: "As indicated in congressional testimony by senior Department officials on several occasions, . . . facts have come to light during the course of this investigation that the February 4 letter contains inaccuracies. Because of this, the Department now formally withdraws the February 4 letter."

The retraction letter is strangely constructed. Instead of saying "We want to acknowledge that a previous statement by us was in error and we apologize," the letter begins with a defensive tone. It states that Issa earlier sought "highly deliberative internal communications" relating to the drafting of the February 4 letter to Grassley. The next paragraph discusses the DOJ's "long-held view, shared by Administrations of both political parties, that congressional requests seeking information about the Executive Branch's deliberations in responding to congressional requests implicate significant confidentiality interests grounded in the separation of powers under the U.S. Constitution."

Having discoursed on constitutional principles of high moment, agreed to in the past by administrations of both parties, Cole proceeds to tell Issa that DOJ "will make a rare exception to the Department's recognized protocols" and provide documents explaining how the February 4 letter was drafted. He said he was sending Issa "1364 pages of material" to help explain how inaccurate information was included in the letter.

Paragraph 5 of Cole's letter discusses how the letter was drafted. He states: "First, to respond to the allegations contained in Ranking Member Grassley's letters, Department personnel, primarily in the Office of Legislative Affairs, the Criminal Division and the Office of the Deputy Attorney General, relied on information provided by supervisors from the components in the best position to know the relevant facts: ATF and the U.S. Attorney's Office in Arizona, both of which had responsibility for Operation Fast and Furious. Information provided by those supervisors was inaccurate."

That argument is unpersuasive. Main Justice said it relied on information from officials in Phoenix because they were "in the best position to know the relevant facts." They were also in the best position to deny fault, dissemble, and obstruct the inquiry, which they proceeded to do. The Justice Department should have been wary of claims coming from a field office in deep trouble. It was a mistake to rely solely on ATF supervisors and US attorneys. As Weich told the House Oversight Committee on June 15, 2011, information obtained from ATF agents produced an entirely different picture of gunrunning.

The retraction letter advised Issa that ATF supervisors made six claims to the Justice Department: (1) "We didn't let guns walk"; (2) "We . . . didn't know they were straw purchasers at the time"; (3) "ATF had no probable cause to arrest the purchaser or prevent action"; (4) "ATF doesn't let guns walk"; (5) "We always try to interdict weapons purchased illegally"; and (6) "We try to interdict all that we being [sic] transported to Mexico." Cole did not say so, but all six claims are false. Remarkably, nothing in the four-page letter from Cole to Issa expressly identifies the portions of the February 4 letter that were "inaccurate."

Steps toward Contempt

On March 16, 2011, Chairman Issa wrote to ATF Acting Director Melson requesting documents and information on Project Gunrunner and Operation Fast and Furious, to be provided to the committee no later than March 30, 2011. A series of committee subpoenas, including March 31 and October 11, 2011, were issued to obtain agency documents and testimony. On July 4, 2011, the House Oversight Committee interviewed Melson. When asked about the need for congressional oversight, Melson replied:

> My view is that the whole matter of the Department's response in this case was a disaster. That as a result, it came to fruition that the committee staff had to be more aggressive and assertive in attempting to get information from the Department, and as a result, there was more adverse publicity towards ATF than was warranted if we had cooperated from the very beginning. And a lot of what they did was damage control, after a while. Their position on things changed weekly and it was hard for us to catch up on it, but it was very clear that they [Main Justice] were running the show.[70]

Melson said he was aware that the Justice Department was drafting a letter to Senator Grassley, advising him that he would not receive materials because he was only a ranking member and not the chair of Senate Judiciary. Melson told a colleague: "This is really just poking him in the eye. What's the sense of doing this? Even if you say you can't give it to him, he's going to get it through the back door anyhow, so why are we aggravating the situation [?]"[71]

On January 31, 2012, Issa wrote to Holder to establish new deadlines for documents. In referring to his committee subpoena of October 11, 2011, he concluded that the Justice Department was "actively engaged in a cover-up" and set a new deadline of February 9, 2012, to produce the requested documents. Failure to provide the documents, Issa said, would lead the committee to find Holder in contempt. A letter from Speaker John Boehner to Holder on May 18, 2012, also warned of the risk of contempt.

Issa wrote to Holder on June 13, narrowing the categories of materials needed by the committee. Two days later, Issa referred to this "subset of post-February 4 documents" to be delivered before the committee's scheduled consideration of contempt at 10:00 a.m. on June 20. Receipt of those documents, Issa said, would be sufficient to postpone contempt proceedings while the committee reviewed the materials. This effort at accommodation failed. Issa met with Holder on June 19 at the US Capitol, along with Ranking Member Elijah Cummings and Senators Leahy and Grassley.

The meeting lasted about twenty minutes. Holder agreed to provide Issa with a "fair compilation" of documents on three conditions: that Issa permanently cancel the contempt vote, agree that the Justice Department was in full compliance with the committee's subpoenas, and accept the documents—in Issa's words—"sight unseen." That is, Issa would have to take Holder's word that the documents would settle the dispute. Issa considered the three conditions as "unacceptable, as would have my predecessors from both sides of the aisle."

On a 23 to 17 party-line vote on June 20, the House Oversight Committee found Holder in contempt. After Issa refused Holder's offer of June 19, Holder wrote to President Obama that same day, requesting him to assert executive privilege, which Obama did. It is discussed in the next section. On June 28, the House voted 255 to 67 to support a resolution finding Holder in contempt. The relatively few votes against the resolution reflect the decision of 109 Democrats to leave the chamber and not vote. Seventeen Democrats voted in favor of the resolution.[72]

Obama's Executive Privilege

There are many interesting issues about President Obama invoking executive privilege. You might think he signed a document and gave reasons. He did not. Instead, Deputy Attorney General Cole wrote to Chairman Issa on June 20, 2012, stating: "the President has asserted executive privilege over the relevant post-February 4, 2011 documents." Cole argued that any effort to compel production of internal executive branch documents generated in the course of the "deliberative process" would have "significant, damaging consequences." According to Cole, release of the documents would "inhibit the candor" of future executive branch deliberations and "significantly impair" the executive branch's ability to respond to congressional oversight. Any compelled disclosure, Cole said, "would be inconsistent" with the separation of powers and "potentially create an imbalance" between the executive and legislative branches.

This analysis is not credible. When Holder met with Issa on June 19 he offered to produce a "fair compilation" of post-February 4 documents. He was prepared to release documents on the internal "deliberative process" within the executive branch. In making the offer, did Holder intend to "damage" the executive branch, "inhibit" the candor of future executive branch deliberations, "significantly" impair the capacity of the executive branch to respond to congressional oversight, act inconsistently with the doctrine of separation of powers, and "create an imbalance" between the two branches? Obviously not. When the Inspector General issued his 471-page report in September 2012, providing details on Fast and Furious and releasing new evidence and documents, did he inflict all those injuries on the executive branch? No.

When Holder wrote to Obama on June 19, 2012, asking him to invoke executive privilege, his eight-page letter relied heavily on a Justice Department legal opinion issued in 1981. It argued that executive documents need to be withheld from Congress to protect the deliberative process, especially "predecisional, deliberative memorandum." Yet Congress often gains access to predecisional, deliberative memoranda in the executive branch. In 1981 and 2011–2012, the Justice Department gave such documents to Congress and was prepared to surrender others to reach an accommodation.

On another point, Holder relied on the 1981 precedent to claim that Congress is more entitled to documents if part of a "legislative task" and its access is "considerably weaker" if done for legislative oversight. There is nothing to support that distinction. The first major congressional investigation—General Arthur St. Clair's military defeat in 1792—was not conducted for the purpose of passing legislation. It was purely a matter of oversight. The House of Representatives received all the documents it requested.[73] Congress could easily neutralize Holder's theory by introducing a bill whenever it wants to conduct oversight.[74]

On the same day that the House cited Holder for contempt, it passed a resolution authorizing the House to seek a declaratory judgment from a federal district court affirming Holder's duty to comply with the subpoena on Fast and Furious. On August 13, 2012, the House filed its civil action. On October 15, the Justice Department filed a memorandum requesting the court to dismiss the House action. The DOJ brief contemplates a drastically reduced role for committee investigations, forcing Congress to generally request documents through the full legislative process.[75] On November 21, the House filed its opposition to the motion to dismiss.

CONCLUSIONS

The failure to close Guantánamo revealed a new president seemingly clueless about the limits of issuing an executive order. Someone should have insisted that the political ground be tested first. Apparently no one did. As a result, Obama began his term looking like an amateur. His record on signing statements displays little understanding of the federal government. Military action in Libya initially brought praise in some quarters, but it created an expectation for intervention abroad that could not be satisfied when violence swept Syria. The legal arguments for his recess appointments were strained. If courts rule against him the political and legal cost will be substantial. With regard to Fast and Furious, the bungling was primarily in the Justice Department. For some reason, Obama decided to join the cause. We await court action on that dispute.

NOTES

1. Executive Order, "Review and Disposition of Individuals Detained at the Guantánamo Bay Naval Base and Closure of Detention Facilities," January 22, 2009, sec. 3.
2. Richard Wolffe, *Revival: The Struggle for Survival Inside the Obama White House* (New York: Crown Publisher, 2010), 217–18.
3. Wolffe, *Revival*, 219.
4. Wolffe, *Revival*, 225–26
5. P.L. 111-383, sec. 1032; 124 Stat. 4351.
6. Statement by the President on H.R. 6523.
7. P.L. 112-10, sec. 1112; 125 Stat. 104.
8. Statement by the President on H.R. 1473.
9. Daniel Klaidman, *Kill or Capture: The War on Terror and the Soul of the Obama Presidency* (Boston: Houghton Mifflin, 2012), 182.
10. Todd Garvey, "The Obama Administration's Evolving Approach to the Signing Statement," *Presidential Studies Quarterly* 41 (2011): 395.
11. Garvey, "The Obama Administration's Evolving Approach to the Signing Statement," 395.
12. Christopher S. Kelley, "Rhetoric and Reality? Unilateralism and the Obama Administration," *Social Science Quarterly* 93 (2012): 1146.
13. Mitchel A. Sollenberger and Mark J. Rozell, *The President's Czars: Undermining Congress and the Constitution* (Lawrence: University Press of Kansas, 2012), 170–71.
14. See note 8.
15. 462 U.S. 919 (1983).
16. Louis Fisher, *Defending Congress and the Constitution* (Lawrence: University Press of Kansas, 2011), 189–97.
17. For details on agency budget manuals that require agencies to seek committee approval for certain kinds of actions, see Louis Fisher, "Committee Controls of Agency Decisions," Congressional Research Service, Report RL33151, November 16, 2005, loufisher.org/docs/lv/2626.pdf.
18. Statement by the President on H.R. 205, www.whitehouse-gov/the-press-office/2011/12/23/statement-president-hr-2055.
19. Louis Fisher, "Obama's Objections to Committee Veto Misguided," *Roll Call*, January 19, 2012, 4, www.loufisher.org/docs/lv/comveto.pdf.
20. Louis Fisher, "Sidestepping Congress: Presidents Acting under the UN and NATO," *Case Western Reserve Law Review* 47 (1997): 1237; www.loufisher.org/docs/wp/424.pdf.
21. "Barack Obama's Q&A," *Boston Globe*, December 20, 2007, boston.com/news/politics/2008/specials/CandiateQA/ObamaQA.
22. David Bromwich, "Obama: His Words & His Deeds," *New York Review of Books*, July 14, 2011, 8.
23. Elizabeth Bumiller and Kareen Fahim, "U.S.-Led Assaults Hit Tripoli Again: Objective is Near," *New York Times*, March 22, 2011.
24. Bumiller and Fahim, "U.S.-Led Assaults Hit Tripoli Again."

25. David D. Kirkpatrick and Thom Shanker, "Libyan Rebels Advance in West; U.S. Will Deploy Armed Drones," *New York Times*, April 22, 2011.

26. Simon Denyer and Leila Fadel, "NATO Bombards Gaddafi Government Complex in Tripoli," *Washington Post*, April 25, 2011.

27. Steven Lee Myers and Rachel Donadio, "U.S. Seeks to Aid Libyan Rebels with Seized Assets," *New York Times*, May 6, 2011.

28. Remarks by President Obama, March 28, 2011, www.whitehouse.gov/the-press-office/2011/03/28/remarks-president-address-nation-libya.

29. 87 Stat. 555, 558, sec. 8(a)(2).

30. Lisa Rogak, ed., *Barack Obama in His Own Words* (New York: Public Affairs, 2007), 145.

31. Office of Legal Counsel, "Authority to Use Military Force in Libya," April 1, 2011, 8, www.justice.gov/olc/2011/authority-military-use-in-libya.pdf.

32. "United States Activities in Libya," report submitted by the Obama administration to Congress, *New York Times*, June 15, 2011, www.nytimes.com/interactive/2011/06/16/us/politics/20110616_POWERS_DOC.html?ref=politics.

33. Thomas F. Eagleton, *War and Presidential Power* (New York: Liveright, 1974), 150–83.

34. Charlie Savage, "2 Top Lawyers Lose Argument on War Power," *New York Times*, June 18, 2011. The title refers to Jeh Johnson in the Pentagon and Caroline Krass in OLC "losing" the argument.

35. Louis Fisher, "Military Operations in Libya: No War? No Hostilities?," *Presidential Studies Quarterly* 42 (2012): 176.

36. *Public Papers of the Presidents*, 1950, p. 503.

37. *Public Papers of the Presidents*, 1950, p. 504.

38. *Merriam Webster's Collegiate Dictionary*, 10th ed. (Springfield, MA: Merriam-Webster, Inc., 1993), 347.

39. *Webster's Third New International Dictionary* (Springfield, MA: Merriam-Webster, 1993), 679.

40. Drew Westen, "What Happened to Obama?," *New York Times*, Sunday Review, August 7, 2011.

41. "Remarks by the President on the Middle East and North Africa," State Department, May 19, 2011, 2, 6, www/whitehouse.gov/the-press-office/2011/05/19/remarks-president-middle-east-and-north-africa.

42. "Remarks by the President on the Middle East and North Africa," 2–3.

43. Max Farrand, ed., *The Records of the Federal Convention of 1787* (New Haven, CT: Yale University Press, 1966), 2:540.

44. *Opinions of the Attorney General*, 41:466 (1960).

45. *Opinions of the Attorney General*, 41:466 (1960).

46. *Opinions of the Attorney General*, 33:25 (1921).

47. "Memorandum of Points and Authorities in Support of Defendants' Opposition to Plaintiffs' Motion for Partial Summary Judgment," 24–26, Mackie v. Clinton, Civil Action No. 93-0032-LFO (D.D.C. 1993).

48. 157 Congressional Record S4646 (daily ed. July 18, 2011).

49. 157 Congressional Record S4646, S8789 (daily ed. December 23, 2011), unanimous consent request by Senate Majority Leader Harry Reid on H.R. 3765.

50. Some Senate rules are impermissible, such as the Senate "reconsidering" a nominee who has been confirmed, taken the oath, and entered into the duties of office. United States v. Smith, 286 U.S. 6 (1932).

51. New Process Steel, L.P. v. NLRB, 560 U.S. ___ (2010).

52. Charlie Savage and Steven Greenhouse, "Court Rejects Obama Move to Fill Posts," *New York Times*, January 26, 2013, A1; Robert Barnes and Steven Mufson, "Obama Recess Picks Invalid," *Washington Post*, January 26, 2012, A1.

53. Steven Greenhouse, "More Than 300 Labor Board Decisions Could Be Nullified," *New York Times*, January 26, 2013.

54. 157 Congressional Record S8347 (daily ed. December 6, 2011) and S8428-29 (daily ed. December 8, 2011).

55. 157 Congressional Record S8422 (daily ed. December 8, 2011).

56. 157 Congressional Record S8428 (daily ed. December 8, 2011).

57. "Fatally Flawed," 2, report prepared by the Minority Staff of the House Committee on Oversight and Government Reform, placed in the *Congressional Record* on June 28, 2012, pp. H4307–4401. Also reprinted in H. Rept. No. 112-546, 112th Cong., 2d Sess. (2012), pp. 172–266.

58. "Fatally Flawed," 2.

59. This letter and many others related to Fast and Furious are available at: over sight.house.gov/documents-in-support-of-civil-action-by-oversight-committee-vs-eric-holder.

60. "A Review of ATF's Operation Fast and Furious and Related Matters," report by the Office of Inspector General, US Justice Department, September 2012, p. 406, justice.gov/oig/reports/2012/s1209.pdf.

61. "A Review of ATF's Operation Fast and Furious and Related Matters," 411.

62. "A Review of ATF's Operation Fast and Furious and Related Matters," 365.

63. "A Review of ATF's Operation Fast and Furious and Related Matters," 375–76.

64. "A Review of ATF's Operation Fast and Furious and Related Matters," 413.

65. "A Review of ATF's Operation Fast and Furious and Related Matters," 468.

66. Letter from Deputy Attorney General James M. Cole to Darrell E. Issa, Chairman of the House Committee on Oversight and Government Reform, May 15, 2012, p. 11.

67. "Operation Fast and Furious: Reckless Decisions, Tragic Outcomes," hearing by the House Committee on Oversight and Government Reform, 112th Cong., 1st Sess., June 15, 2011.

68. "Operation Fast and Furious: Reckless Decisions, Tragic Outcomes," 170, 173.

69. Letter from Deputy Attorney General James M. Cole to Darrell E. Issa, Chairman of the House Committee on Oversight and Government Reform, May 15, 2012, p. 11.

70. Transcript of interview by the House Committee on Oversight and Government Reform, July 4, 2011, p. 31.

71. Transcript of interview by the House Committee on Oversight and Government Reform, July 4, 2011, pp. 126–27.

72. Ed O'Keefe and Sari Horwitz, "Holder is Held in Contempt of Congress," *Washington Post*, June 29, 2012.

73. Louis Fisher, *The Politics of Executive Privilege* (Durham, NC: Carolina Academic Press, 2004), 10–11.

74. For further details on the arguments by Attorney General Holder, see Louis Fisher, "An Overbroad Executive Privilege Claim," *National Law Journal*, July 30, 2012, loufisher.org/docs/ep/obamaexec.pdf.

75. Louis Fisher, "DOJ's Brief on Fast and Furious: Marginalizing Committee Investigations," *National Law Journal*, October 25, 2012, loufisher.org/docs/ep/fast.pdf.

Chapter Thirteen

Congress and President Obama

A Perspective

Mark J. Oleszek and Walter J. Oleszek[1]

When President Barack Obama and GOP presidential nominee Mitt Romney accepted their party's 2012 nomination to contest for the presidency, each addressed, respectively, the Democratic or Republican National Convention. In their remarks, each candidate highlighted their policy priorities and how they wanted to lead the nation. Understandably, the two nominees used the tried-and-true generic slogans that have been staples of electoral contests for decades: "stay the course" for incumbent Obama and "it's time for a change" for challenger Romney. In their remarks to convention delegates, neither nominee said much about Congress. In fact, the president mentioned the word "Congress" twice, Romney not at all, and neither uttered the words "House," "Senate," or "legislative." To many viewers of the proceedings on television or in other media, it might have seemed that whoever won the White House could enact their agenda priorities all on their own. The reality is much different, however.

One of the nation's most important political principles—perhaps the most consequential—is the division of power. The framers embedded this principle in the Constitution in numerous ways, such as our system of separate institutions sharing and competing for power, federalism, and the array of checks and balances, especially among the three elective constitutional units (the House, the Senate, and the White House). The legislation Congress enacts, for instance, can be vetoed by the president, but vetoes can be overridden by a two-thirds vote of each chamber. In brief, our congressional–presidential system of governance often means a lengthy and complex three-way bargaining process if measures are to become public law. As Speaker Dennis Hastert (R-IL) (1999–2007), explained: "The art of what is possible is what you can get passed in the House, what you can get passed in the Senate and signed by the president. We're playing a three-sided game here."[2] (The federal judiciary may also review the actions and decisions of the Congress and the president, as in the Supreme Court's landmark decision in 2012 upholding President Obama's health-reform law, the Patient Protection and Affordable Care Act.)

When Barack Obama took the oath of office for his first term on January 20, 2009, he confronted huge inherited problems: two wars (Afghanistan and Iraq), a financial meltdown, a slowing economy and growing joblessness, a housing collapse, and rising fiscal deficits and debt, among other major concerns. If crises, communication skills, and large partisan majorities are important factors in determining a president's legislative success with Congress, then President Obama appeared poised to win enactment into law of many of his key policy priorities. As White House Chief of Staff (now Mayor of Chicago) Rahm Emanuel put it, "no crisis should go to waste." Moreover, President Obama's communications skills are exceptional, and Democrats controlled the 111th Congress (2009–2011) by wide margins: 257 to 178 in the House and, importantly, a 60 to 40 filibuster-proof supermajority in the Senate.

And the president did enjoy landmark successes during the 111th Congress, but the 112th told a different story: a time of uncompromising partisan zeal that made lawmaking especially difficult.

Recall candidate Obama's pledge in 2008 to be a postpartisan president and to change the way Washington works by engaging cooperatively and openly with both political parties. It turned out that neither promise could be kept despite efforts by the president to reach out to GOP opponents of his program. Four years later, when the president ran successfully for a second term, these dual themes (postpartisan and more political civility) were largely absent from his 2012 campaign playbook. The hard realities of governing in a no-holds-barred, polarized political environment underscore how difficult it is to get liberal and conservative lawmakers and the two parties to work together to resolve national problems. With the November 2012 elections largely preserving the partisan status quo among the elective branches, prospects for meaningful bipartisan cooperation in pushing measures through the 113th Congress (2013–2015) appear uncertain unless various circumstances (e.g., another economic downturn) or legislative imperatives ("must pass" issues, for instance) dictate otherwise. Commentators suggest that the 113th could be even more deeply divided than its predecessor for two key reasons: the further decline of centrist lawmakers and the increasing partisan divide in the country.[3]

This chapter has four broad purposes. First, it provides a review of the major policy achievements of the Democratic-led 111th Congress and the Obama administration. These achievements occurred despite the vigorous dissents and the dilatory tactics of the minority Republicans. Second, the chapter provides a short review of the truncated 112th Congress (2011–2013)—the Republican House and the Democratic Senate—and its contentious relationship with the president. Deadlock and delay on major issues characterized the lawmaking process during this time. Our focus in this section is on a principal reason for the gridlock: the decline of compromise. We examine "compromise as principle" and "compromise as politics" to lay the groundwork for the "politics of brinksmanship" that marked the 2011 legislative-executive battle to raise the government's debt ceiling. (Virulent partisanship compounds the difficulty of reaching compromises, but we left to others in this volume the reasons for the partisan polarization that suffuses today's Congress.[4])

Our third objective is to analyze brinksmanship in action by presenting a mini-case study of the summer 2011 debt-ceiling fight. This event provoked wide media coverage both nationally and internationally. The debt issue also highlights how difficult it can be to break political gridlock when a sizable number of lawmakers are able to constrain the ability of the negotiators to reach a deal. Lastly, the chapter closes with summary observations, including prospects for the 113th Congress (2013–2015).

I. THE 111TH CONGRESS (2009–2011)

As the nation's first African American president, Barack Obama immediately became a historic figure. Expectations for his "hope and change" presidency were especially high given Obama's 53 percent to 46 percent victory in 2008, winning "a higher share of the popular vote than any other Democratic nominee in history except Andrew Jackson, Franklin Roosevelt, and Lyndon Johnson."[5] Some analysts even contended that the Democrats were on the cusp of a "new, New Deal."[6] Although there were some similarities between the two "deals" (major government initiatives to revive the economy, for example), there were also stark differences between them (the public popularity of FDR's New Deal initiatives versus considerable popular dismay with many of President Obama's programs).[7] Tellingly, President Obama wanted bold policy changes, as did the Democratic House and Senate. Republicans, facing reduced numbers in Congress, were on the political ropes. Conditions were ripe for major policy initiatives, and there were many that made it into law.

Major Policy Successes

The 111th Congress enacted much of the president's ambitious agenda. Among the major legislative successes were passage of an economic stimulus measure (the American Recovery and Reinvestment Act) to prevent the country from falling into a 1930s-like Depression; financial regulatory reform (the Dodd-Frank Wall Street Reform and Consumer Protection Act, named after the House and Senate banking chairs, Senator Christopher Dodd of Connecticut and Representative Barney Frank of Massachusetts); the bailout of the automobile industry; and perhaps the president's most significant accomplishment thus far, the overhaul of the health-care system (more on this below).

Although they may have attracted less visibility, there were many other notable bills signed into law, such as measures dealing with college student financial aid, tobacco regulation, credit card protection, safeguards against hate crimes, and fair pay for women. In 2009, the president's success score—"the share of votes on which Congress acceded to his clearly stated position"—was a historically high 96.7 percent.[8] The next year, President Obama's success score dropped to 85.8 percent, still the tenth "highest on record and the fourth highest for a president in his second year."[9] The Senate also approved the president's two Supreme Court nominees (Sonia Sotomayor and Elena Kagan), and gave him the two-thirds vote required to ratify a major arms-control treaty with Russia (called "New Start"). Many of these legislative accomplishments had long been advocated for by Democratic constituencies.

The Signature Achievement: Health-Care Reform

Enactment of the Patient Protection and Affordable Care Act will likely rank as the most significant achievement of the president's first term. Among other provisions, it provides health care to nearly every American and ends the denial of health insurance to persons with preexisting conditions. Passage of this law alone would have made the 111th Congress one of the most consequential in history. Moreover, in the view of some analysts, the health-care law elevated the president to "the pantheon of transformative presidents," because "ObamaCare" now joins "Medicare and Social Security as essential struts in the nation's social safety structure."[10]

Noteworthy is that President Obama deferred to Congress in taking the lead in drafting the health-care reform bill. He chose not to follow the approach of President Clinton, who forwarded to Congress a complex and controversial health-reform measure largely drafted in secret by a small team led by First Lady Hillary Clinton. In the end, the Democratic Congress never took up the Clinton plan, thereby sinking the proposal. The 111th House and Senate, by contrast, each managed to pass a health-reform package. In fact, the prospects for a rather speedy resolution of House-Senate policy differences on health reform and the bill's signature into law appeared to be a foregone conclusion. That forecast suddenly turned bleak when Senate Democrats lost their sixty-vote supermajority.

On January 19, 2010, Republican Scott Brown won a special election in Massachusetts to replace Democratic Senator Edward M. Kennedy, who had died. Brown even campaigned on the theme that, as the forty-first GOP senator, he would vote against a health measure that would "raise taxes, destroy jobs and run our nation deeper into debt."[11] Brown's election, viewed by various lawmakers as a message to the president to pull back from comprehensive health reform, led to intensive discussions among the president, Speaker Nancy Pelosi, and Senate Majority Leader Harry Reid. President Obama received advice from various quarters to ditch comprehensive change and back a pared-down health bill. "I begged him" not to go forward with a major health overhaul bill, said Emanuel, the president's chief of staff.[12] It was Speaker Pelosi who ended such talk and said no to any "kiddie-care" bill. "We will go through the gate. If the gate is closed," she exclaimed, "we will go over the fence. If the fence is too high, we will pole vault in. If that doesn't work, we will parachute in. But we are going to get [comprehensive] health care passed."[13] The president chose the comprehensive plan the Speaker was advocating over the advice of his chief of staff. Speaker Pelosi merits significant credit for the passage of the comprehensive health-reform law by strengthening everyone's resolve when the legislative outcome appeared darkest. (Speaker Pelosi is a historic figure in her own right as the first female Speaker.)

Health-care reform was a monumental achievement, but it also represented a presidential failure. Two key reasons account for this assessment. First, President Obama failed to win any congressional GOP support for the landmark initiative, unlike President Roosevelt for Social Security and Lyndon Johnson for Medicare. Whether that was even possible remains an open question given today's hyperpartisan environment on Capitol Hill and the deep political divisions in the electorate. Still, health care was the president's first priority, he had political momentum coming off a big electoral victory, and chief executives are expected to win at least a few votes from the opposition on major legislation.

Perhaps a more concerted "wooing" effort by the president might have produced a bipartisan product. The president, however, is not someone who enjoys routinely meeting or socializing with lawmakers.[14] His temperament did not permit him to follow President Lyndon Johnson's advice in dealing with lawmakers: "You have to court members of Congress as much as your wife."[15] Political schmoozing is essential to building personal friendships, relationships, and trust with lawmakers on both sides of the aisle. Such personal ties increase the chances that presidents can govern and governing is, noted a savvy former lawmaker, "getting to know the people in the House and Senate." It means knowing what makes lawmakers tick, and "how do you get them to say yes when everybody else is telling them to say no."[16]

The president often relies on his gregarious vice president, Joe Biden, to take the lead in maintaining personal ties with lawmakers, especially with his former Senate colleagues. In the judgment of a Washington insider, President Obama largely ignored the Republicans during his first two years in office.[17] For example, the president made little or no effort to forge a bond with either House GOP leader John Boehner or Senate GOP leader Mitch McConnell. A newspaper even carried this headline: "Obama, McConnell: Perfect Strangers."[18] Added GOP Senator Lamar Alexander, Tenn., the president has "no relationship with the Republican caucus."[19] The White House, in brief, may have embraced too often the approach to congressional Republicans articulated by White House chief of staff Emanuel: "We have the votes. F___ 'em."[20]

Second, at least a plurality of the public viewed the health law as an unwanted and intrusive "government takeover" of health care, which provoked numerous efforts in Congress to repeal or weaken the law. Yet despite his oratorical skills, plainly evident as a campaigner, the president failed to use the "bully pulpit" effectively to win the support of large segments of the populace for his health plan. As a liberal House Democrat said, "One of the best communicated campaigns I've ever seen and the worst messaging presidency."[21] One result was a public backlash against Democrats in the 2010 midterm elections. "I think we paid a terrible price for health care," declared Representative Barney Frank. Moreover, "the way the issue was dealt with by the White House cost Obama a lot of credibility as a leader," said Senator Jim Webb (D-VA).[22]

Other presidential priorities failed to pass Congress, including legislation to close Guantánamo Bay, reform immigration, revamp labor laws, or cut the deficit in half by the end of his first term. Instead, a slow economy (fewer taxes collected), more government spending on safety-net programs (unemployment compensation, for instance), and other kinds of economic stimulus created deficits that exceeded $1 trillion during each year of the president's first term.

Cooperate or Confront

From the outset of the 111th Congress, Senate and House GOP leaders— although initially dispirited by Democratic control of all three elective branches—organized to try to frustrate the Democratic agenda. Senator McConnell, for example, gathered his party colleagues together after the November 2008 elections and told his members: "Republicans need to stick together as a team." As GOP Senator George Voinovich of Ohio said of McConnell's strategy, "If Obama was for it, we had to be against it." A statement on the president's health-overhaul plan by GOP Senator Jim De-Mint (SC), now the president of the conservative Heritage Foundation, reflected the Republican strategy on other Democratic priorities: "If we're able to stop Obama on [health-care reform], this will be his Waterloo. It will break him."[23] In the House, Minority Whip Eric Cantor (VA) also met with his whip team prior to the start of the new 111th Congress. His message: "We're not here to cut deals . . . We're not rolling over. We're going to fight these guys" and win public support for our views.[24]

Early in his presidency, Obama met with the bipartisan congressional leadership to get their support for rapid passage of his $800 billion economic stimulus plan. It included tax cuts, spending on infrastructure projects, and other initiatives to kick-start the sputtering economy. The president urged the GOP leaders to share their ideas on ways to stimulate the economy, and House Minority Whip Cantor did just that. His ideas included a series of revenue-raising proposals, but without changes in marginal tax rates. He also opposed spending $800 billion to jumpstart the economy. The president and his advisers rejected the GOP's ideas, which angered congressional Republicans. In the end, not a single House Republican voted for the president's stimulus package. "How is it that we could be for your bill," asked Cantor, "if we weren't a part of [putting together] any of this" measure?[25] Ignoring GOP ideas encouraged Republican lawmakers to oppose the president and fortified their belief that the administration was not serious about working in a bipartisan manner.

Throughout the 111th Congress, the GOP strategy was to use parliamentary tactics and public relations to minimize Democratic successes in reviving the economy. This strategy aimed to increase the chances that the November 2010 elections might produce GOP majorities in one or both legislative chambers. With Democrats in charge of Congress and the White House, voters would be unlikely to blame the stalling actions of Republicans for the majority's inability to pass legislation. In the view of David Axelrod, President Obama's long-time friend and top political strategist: "We didn't realize the degree to which Republicans in Washington would make a decision from the get-go that they didn't want to cooperate because they thought bipartisan solutions would redound to the President's benefit."[26]

Summary Points

It is interesting that one of the most productive Congresses in several decades was also deeply unpopular with many in the general public. Many overlapping factors contributed to this perception, such as these three. First, President Obama and congressional Democrats failed to communicate their accomplishments to the citizenry. A consummate communicator on the campaign trail, the president neglected to use the bully pulpit to explain and defend the Democrats' landmark successes. President Obama even agreed with this criticism. As he admitted, "What I have not done as well as I would have liked to is to consistently communicate to the general public why we're making some of these decisions."[27] Or, as a Democratic senator explained, "We spent too much time legislating and way too little messaging. Essentially, when we passed a bill, we moved on to the next one . . . [W]e didn't spend time letting [the public] know what we were doing."[28] By his inattentiveness to the politics of messaging, the president won scant public credit for winning passage of path-breaking legislation.[29]

Second, the absence of effective messaging by the president and congressional Democrats allowed conservative groups, Tea Partiers, conservative media outlets, and billionaires to flood the public airwaves with negative commentary about the administration's health, financial reform, and economic stimulus legislation. According to the president, the work of conservatives "reinforced the narrative that the Republicans wanted to promote anyway, which was Obama is . . . the same old tax-and-spend liberal" who excels at "spending money like nobody's business."[30] The antipathy directed at the president's program also gave rise to an assertive and conservative Tea ("taxed enough already") Party movement that castigated Obama and challenged congressional Democrats across the nation, often aggressively and vociferously in town hall events held by lawmakers.

Third, critics argued that the public was more concerned about the state of the economy and high unemployment than revamping the health-care system.[31] Health reform dominated the attention of Congress yet it appeared secondary to what many people really wanted: jobs. As a Democratic House member recounted, "Everybody [in Washington] talked about health care, and I went home [to Kansas City, Missouri] and everyone there talked about jobs."[32] Moreover, the financial cost of the Democratic agenda created unease in the country at a time of serious economic distress and surging annual deficits and debt. In a blunt political assessment shared by many, Senate GOP Leader McConnell exclaimed that the 111th Congress "will be remembered as a classic case of overreach by a governing party that not only misread its mandate but double-downed on its various costly, government-driven domestic policy proposals" that angered large numbers of Americans.[33] To be sure, Democratic views differed considerably from those of Senator McConnell. When the 111th Congress ended, a Gallup poll found that only 13 percent of Americans approved of the way it did its job.[34]

II. THE 112TH CONGRESS

Overview

The 2010 midterm elections—the third wave election in a row—led to a "shellacking" (Obama's word) for congressional Democrats: sixty-three seats lost in the House and six in the Senate. Democrats lost the House to a

Tea Party–infused Republican majority (242R, 193D)—there were eighty-seven new GOP lawmakers—while the Democratic margin in the Senate shrank from fifty-nine to fifty-three seats. Public dismay with the weak economy, the shortage of jobs, big government, and huge annual fiscal deficits were among the factors that contributed to the 2010 electoral debacle for Democrats.

Much of the work of the 111th Congress became the agenda of the 112th House, except in reverse: repeal and replace the health law, cut federal spending, eliminate governmental programs, overturn federal regulations, and so on. Senate Republicans also pushed similar initiatives through amendments to pending legislation and in other ways because they lacked formal authority to set the chamber's agenda. Agenda-setting is the prerogative of the Senate's majority leader. Yet the Senate GOP's tactical use of parliamentary devices had a strategic purpose. As Senator McConnell said in an oft-quoted comment, his political goal was to make Barack Obama a one-term president. Many Senate Republicans viewed success as causing the president to fail.

It was not long before the public became disgusted with the 112th Congress. The GOP House passed its key priorities on largely party-line votes only to see them die in the Democratic Senate. The reverse pattern was also in evidence. Gridlock on major legislation was often the order of the day in the 112th Congress. Some analysts dubbed it the worst Congress in recent memory, calling it dysfunctional and incapable of addressing many of the nation's big problems. Others had a different view. They contended that the GOP changed the conversation on Capitol Hill from spending more to deficit reduction and that it is quality, not quantity, that matters most in enacting legislation.

The return of a truncated Congress—combined with the GOP's animosity toward many of the president's policies and the sharp ideological differences between the two parties and chambers—made problem-solving difficult and often secondary to partisan bickering and brinksmanship. Moreover, there was unwillingness on the part of numerous members to compromise, something long considered fundamental to the lawmaking process. In particular, many House GOP freshmen seemed to abhor the idea of compromise. "I came here ready to go to war. The people didn't send me here to compromise," declared freshman Representative Joe Walsh (IL).[35] (Walsh, a Tea Party favorite, failed to win reelection in November 2012.)

A statement by Senator Joe Lieberman, (I-CT), highlights the theme of an unwillingness to compromise that contributed to the controversy over raising the debt ceiling. "It's accurate to say that [unbending] partisanship dominates" in the House and Senate. "The other thing going on here . . . I would say [is] ideological rigidity, which is to say an unwillingness to compromise."[36] Intense partisanship in the House and Senate compounds the difficulty of reaching policy and procedural compromises.

COMPROMISE: VARIATIONS AND VIEWS

Overview

In general, compromise means the resolution of conflicting interests and issues where each side gives up things they want, without violating lawmakers' integrity or principles. One type of compromise—often called "classic"—occurs when the competing sides agree to modify policy objectives on a given measure in a manner that is generally acceptable to the involved parties. "True compromise," in the view of Senate Majority Leader Harry Reid, "means no one gets everything they want."[37] This type of compromise implies productive collaboration among lawmakers of different parties and views.

The nature of the bargaining process to achieve a classic compromise will vary by issue area, the array of negotiators and the choices before them, the pressures of time, and so on. Typically, when economic times are good, this type of compromise occurs when House and Senate appropriators meet to reconcile their bicameral differences over spending issues. "Let's split the difference" is the common refrain in achieving a classic compromise. Members in both chambers are satisfied with the outcome as each can claim victory because the compromise is a "win win" for both houses and parties.

Another type, which might be dubbed a "reluctant" compromise, is when the contending parties reach an agreement but remain dissatisfied with the product. Members go along with the arrangement because, for instance, it involves a "must pass" measure (such as a continuing resolution to prevent a government shutdown) or it might be the least bad idea that is acceptable to the contending parties. Lawmakers may also fear constituency retribution or primary challengers if they vote against something that many voters back home view as a top priority.

Reluctant compromises are evident during eras of fiscal austerity. Today's politics of subtraction often produce unfavorable compromises for many lawmakers. Their unhappiness largely stems from political and procedural constraints that prevent them from winning additional funds for favorite agencies and pet projects. Budgeting in this environment becomes a zero-sum game: one program gains resources at the expense of another. The shortage of money might also make the settlement a "lose lose" for both sides, especially in the event of across-the-board cuts in programs regardless of their merit. The nature of compromises reluctantly made and acquiesced in was capsulized by Senator Pat Roberts (R-KS), "While this is not the best possible bill, it is the best bill possible."[38] Nonetheless, many lawmakers may vote against "the best bill possible" because they view the legislative result as a betrayal of their personal beliefs and the promises they made to their constituents.

These two basic forms of compromise are common on Capitol Hill. To be sure, vote-gathering to pass controversial legislative compromises is difficult because lawmakers are often cross-pressured by clashing concerns: conscience, party loyalty, substantive belief, and constituency opinion. But compromises on controversial issues can be achieved even if they run counter to lawmakers' self-defined principles. As the colorful Senator Everett McKinley Dirksen (IL, the GOP's minority leader from 1959 to 1969, once said: "I am a man of principle, and one of my basic principles is flexibility." He added, "I am not a moralist. I am a legislator."[39] Stated differently, a challenge for lawmakers "lies precisely in the marriage . . . of personal compromise [involving one's principles] and the common good."[40]

In a diverse country of over three hundred million people who hold conflicting views on scores of topics, representative government demands compromise or little can be done to accomplish consequential legislative goals. Recall that the federal Constitution was "established by men who disagreed sorely, but created a government founded on the philosophy that varying views could be coalesced for the common good."[41] There would not even be a Senate if the delegates to the Constitutional Convention had not reached a compromise: two senators from each state regardless of population, with representation in the House based on population. If compromises prove to be counterproductive, the American political system does provide ample opportunities (legislative, legal, regulatory, etc.) for change and self-correction.

Compromise embraces a large array of considerations, actors, and forces that are beyond the goals of this chapter.[42] Instead, we examine two multifaceted dimensions of compromise—principle and political—that shaped legislative-executive relationships during the 111th and 112th Congresses. These two dimensions provoke questions about the process of compromise, such as: How far should federal elective officials go in supporting disagreeable concessions? How much should members and chief executives compromise for the sake of enacting legislation? When and under what circumstances is a "no compromise" strategy appropriate? Is it better to accept 25 or 50 percent of something ("half a loaf") or 100 percent of nothing? As Wisconsin Senator Robert La Follette stated during the early 1900s, "half a loaf, as a rule, dulls the appetite and destroys the keenness of interest in attaining the full loaf."[43] More recently, a current House GOP member said, "When it comes to compromise, half of a bad deal is still a bad deal."[44] On the other hand, many lawmakers may accept 50 percent or more of something and come back the next year to Congress for the remainder, a strategy provoked by the often incremental nature of congressional policy making.

Embedded in the art of compromise is a willingness to listen to and vigorously debate ideas proposed by opponents with mutual respect and decorum, rather than perceive opponents as political enemies to be demonized. Respectful behavior "among our representatives is essential for them to develop the trust that in turn enables the bipartisan compromises that are needed for American politics to function."[45] Bipartisan compromises may be good or bad, but they cannot be achieved if the two parties emulate parliamentary systems: one party governs and the other opposes. Our congressional and presidential system, with its many checks and balances, blocks governance exclusively by the majority party.

To be sure, the majority party may be riven by internal conflicts and disagreements that inhibit its ability to govern effectively. A good example is the tension among House Republicans over raising taxes. Today, there are "establishment" Republicans who are willing to accept new tax increases as part of a broader "grand bargain" deficit-reduction package with President Obama. A conservative Tea Party faction opposes tax increases period. One result of the GOP split is to weaken Speaker Boehner's negotiating leverage with the president. Time and again compromises worked out between the two have been rejected by conservative Republicans. A bipartisan House coalition might be mobilized behind the Boehner-Obama accords, but the Speaker understands that if he loses the support of about half of the GOP rank-and-file, his influence as party leader is weakened, his hold on the Speakership might be jeopardized, and he must accommodate Democratic demands to win their support.

Compromise as Principle

Like many lawmakers, the country itself is divided about compromise. A Pew Research Center poll found that about half the nation (49 percent) said "that they most admire politicians who stick to their positions without compromising." These days, considerably more Republicans (62 percent) admire politicians who do not compromise compared to 39 percent of Democrats who favor political leaders who do not compromise.[46] Many congressional Republicans, often adamant in opposing compromises with President Obama, certainly have the support of most of their constituents. Today, many legislators believe that compromise implies capitulation, political weakness, a sellout, a cave-in, or a betrayal of principle. Statements about compromise by two prominent Republicans highlight an outlook no doubt shared to some extent by Democratic lawmakers.

When Tom DeLay (R-TX) gave his 2006 farewell address to the House after serving as a powerful majority whip and majority leader, whose nickname was "the Hammer" for his often "must win" approach to lawmaking, he stated that "politics demands compromise." He also asserted that compromise is a means to an end and to be used "in the service of higher principles." He argued: "It is not the principled partisan, however obnoxious he may seem to his opponents who degrade our public debate but the preening self-styled statesman who elevates compromise to a first principle."[47] To many Democratic members, the "first principle" meant that compromise required them to change or surrender their positions and accept DeLay's.

In 2011, freshman Senator Rand Paul (R-KY) delivered his maiden address to the Senate. His views expanded on and somewhat reflected those of Representative DeLay. Senator Paul sits at the desk of Henry Clay, the most famous legislator from Kentucky and known as the "Great Compromiser" for his role in preserving the Union by minimizing for a time sectional strife over slavery between the North and South. While slaveholder Clay engaged in forging compromises, his abolitionist cousin (Cassius Clay) fought to end slavery and the slave trade. Senator Rand concluded his remarks by underscoring how each lawmaker must decide when, or if, to compromise. "I will remember [Henry Clay's] lifelong desire to forge agreement. But I will also keep close to my heart the principled stand of his cousin Cassius Clay, who refused to forsake the life of any human simply to find agreement."[48]

If compromise is to serve higher principles, as DeLay states, then the clash of views between the two Clays demonstrates that people's views of higher principles can differ profoundly: preservation of the Union (Henry Clay's position) took precedence over an end to slavery and the slave trade (the view of Cassius Clay). As Senator Paul asked in his maiden speech, "Will compromise allow us to avoid the looming debt crisis?" The answer to that question is whether the national debt rises to the level of a high or first principle, or whether it is an issue of policy that requires political resolution by members of Congress. "There is room for elected leaders who won't back down on their principles" or promises to constituents, wrote former House member Lee Hamilton (D-IN). "But if they dominate the political sphere, representative government becomes impossible, as making progress on the many ills that beset us takes a back seat to declarations of principle."[49]

There is no denying that some issues are harder to reach compromises on than others—such as moral, ethical, or religiously infused issues (same-sex marriage is an example). Today's contentious environment also makes compromise elusive. "Certainly it's not as easy as telling true believers what they want to hear," exclaimed Representative Hamilton, "and it requires special courage in a charged political environment in which prominent media figures attack anyone who deviates from their view of what is right, in which every issue is seen as a tactical battlefield for the next campaign, and in which the political parties each depend on voters who scorn the very notion of compromises."[50]

Compromise as Politics

Scores of compromises are replete with political implications. We mention five that shape contemporary policy making. First, in today's polarized legislative environment, it is not unusual for accords to be reached through intra- rather than interparty negotiations. Ours is not a parliamentary system, as mentioned earlier, but in recent years the House and Senate function at times in a parliamentary or quasiparliamentary manner. The two parties exhibit striking party unity and cohesion, especially on their preferred or "message" priorities. The majority party may strive to govern but solid or near-solid minority opposition can prevent that from happening. "We don't have a Congress anymore, we have a parliament," declared Representative Jim Cooper (D-TN).[51] He added that "we have the extreme polarization of a parliament, with party-line voting, without the empowered Prime Minister."[52]

One factor that makes deal-making difficult is the decline of centrist lawmakers like Cooper in both parties. As the number of electorally safe seats in Congress has increased significantly in recent years, fewer members of either party are willing to compromise with colleagues across the aisle. As House Minority Whip Steny Hoyer (D-MD) said of the 112th Congress, "There are fewer moderate Republicans who really want to sit down . . . and discuss compromise."[53] Similarly, the so-called centrist and compromise-minded Blue Dog Democrats in the House—lawmakers who are generally fiscal conservatives and social moderates—have dwindled in numbers from fifty-four in 2008 to just fifteen in 2013.[54] Although moderates are an "endangered species" according to Representative Cooper, "we are also a necessary ingredient for any problem solving."[55]

Second, unwillingness on the part of lawmakers to bridge their differences can be part of a "no compromise" strategy. Members may be concerned that a compromise product might not be worth passing, doing more harm than good. Gridlock might also be the preferred strategy until one side of the aisle capitulates to all or nearly all of the other's preferences. Simply put, an impasse is better than a compromise, because, politically, one party may not want to hand a policy success to the other party or to the president. Congressional parties may also avoid compromises because they want to use the issues against the opposition in the next election. It can be better electorally to highlight differences between the parties ("contrast politics") than try to find common ground. Political circumstances may also promote a "no compromise" approach if one or both parties think they will achieve a better deal by waiting.

Third, electoral fear can impede compromise. With primary elections eclipsing general elections as the most competitive contest in many states or districts across the country, cross-party collaboration can be frowned upon by party stalwarts back home or even congressional leaders. Not toeing the party or ideological line can trigger a primary challenge if a lawmaker is perceived as not being conservative or liberal enough. Moreover, outside groups affiliated with each party monitor closely the voting records of Democratic and Republican lawmakers for ideological purity.

Fourth, political cross-pressures and perceptions of the national mood of the country can impact the process of compromise. On the legislation to raise the debt ceiling in 2011, for instance, Speaker Boehner believed he had the upper hand. The general view was that President Obama simply could not accept a default that would damage the economy and his presidency. Thus, Speaker Boehner established an informal rule: he insisted that every dollar used to raise the debt ceiling had to be matched by equivalent spending cuts with no tax hikes to offset the spending reductions. Would President Obama agree to the Speaker's demand? If not, Speaker Boehner could lose the support of a majority of Republicans, including the sizable and often unbending Tea Party membership. The Speaker would then confront a difficult choice "between compromising to get Democratic votes and upsetting his base or keeping to a hard line that satisfies conservative firebrands but risks a potentially catastrophic default on the nation's debt obligations."[56] (In the end, the president agreed to the Speaker's demand.)

Fifth, campaigning by legislating is a new normal on Capitol Hill, which compounds the difficulty of bridging differences between the parties. For example, a member's intransigence is often rewarded with campaign donations. Each party, as noted earlier, may be reluctant to make concessions that anger their base supporters. Moreover, it is very common for votes in the House and Senate to be scheduled to force vulnerable lawmakers to cast ballots on "hot button" issues that provide challengers with material for campaign attack ads. Campaigning is about drawing contrasts, often harsh, with your opponent. Governing is about coming together to address the nation's problems. Today, the "permanent campaign" can be an impediment to the process of "coming together" to resolve policy or procedural conflicts.

III. DEBT-CEILING BRINKSMANSHIP

Background

The Constitution (Article I, section 8) grants Congress the power "To borrow Money on the Credit of the United States." Article IV addresses the "full faith and credit" of the nation's financial commitments. By law, the Treasury Department is assigned responsibility to conduct the sale of debt instruments (interest-bearing bonds, for instance) when the government needs to borrow money to pay its bills. With recent annual deficits exceeding $1 trillion, Congress regularly enacts legislation to increase the statutory debt ceiling.

From 1975 to 2011, debt-ceiling bills became law over sixty times, with seven debt increases in 1990 alone.[57] These statutes limit the amount of outstanding debt (the accumulation of annual deficits) on the theory that they might constrain the government from spending more than it receives in revenue.

In 2011, the nation witnessed a near default on raising the statutory debt ceiling. The real possibility of a credible, never-before default—the United States reneging on paying its debts to creditors—provoked large national attention, roiled domestic and global financial markets, and called into question the "full faith and credit" of the United States. A significant number of conservative House Republicans appeared willing to accept the consequences (domestic and global financial turmoil) of a default. "My guys don't even believe default is a problem," said House Majority Leader Cantor.[58] Many had even pledged to their constituents that they would vote against increasing the debt ceiling. President Obama noted, "You have very prominent members of the House Republicans who are not only prepared to see default, but in some cases are welcoming the prospects of default."[59] Moreover, GOP presidential candidates, such as Michele Bachmann (MN), were urging Congress not to raise the debt ceiling.

Raising the debt ceiling is generally a customary action, but it often provokes considerable controversy. Why? Because lawmakers who vote to raise the legal ceiling ($14.3 trillion in 2011) open themselves to charges of being "big spenders." Moreover, minority party members often vote against raising the debt ceiling to force the majority party to pass the politically charged bill. (During the 2011 fight, Republicans reminded the president that five years earlier as a US Senator, he voted against raising the debt ceiling. The Senate at the time was in GOP hands. The White House responded by saying that Senator Obama's vote was a mistake.)

Given electoral concerns, the Democratic House in 1979 adopted a rule that avoided a direct vote on raising the debt ceiling. The rule provided that when the House adopted the annual concurrent budget resolution, as provided by the 1974 Budget Act, it was automatically "deemed" to have enacted a bill to increase the debt ceiling. (The budget resolution identifies for a five year period the outstanding public debt and estimates the amount required for the government to meet its borrowing obligations.) For decades the House embraced the rule with only a brief two-year interlude. The Senate, then and now, has no such "deeming" procedure and votes directly on a measure to increase the borrowing authority of the federal government. When Republicans won control of the 112th House, they dropped the deeming provision from the House rulebook. As vigorous advocates of limited government, Republicans wanted to cut federal expenditures and taxes dramatically, and consideration of a stand-alone debt-ceiling bill gave them the leverage to advance their objectives.

With the seeds for a legislative showdown planted, the GOP made it clear that the president must accept deep spending cuts in federal programs and agencies or House Republicans would not vote to raise the debt ceiling. Moreover, the GOP wanted an overhaul of entitlement programs (Social Security, Medicare, and Medicaid), and opposed any tax hikes to offset the spending cuts. GOP leaders were open to "revenue" increases that might be derived from tax reforms (eliminating tax expenditures, for example) but opposed any hike in tax rates. Opposition to tax rate increases has become a key part of the GOP's collective brand and, as a matter of principle and political interest, most Republicans are unyielding on that matter. To date, thirty-nine GOP senators and 219 House Republicans have signed a "Taxpayer Protection Pledge" sponsored by antitax lobbyist Grover Norquist.[60] (Dozens of House Democrats and eleven Democratic senators have so far signed "The Social Security Protectors' Pledge," promising never to cut Social Security benefits for the elderly.[61])

President Obama was adamant that legislation to raise the debt ceiling in 2011 must provide enough money to get past the November 2012 elections. Politically, the president did not want multiple votes on raising the debt ceiling in the lead up to the November elections, embroiling him in controversy as a "tax and spend and borrow" chief executive. Congressional Democrats also shared Obama's view against multiple debt-reduction votes.

Like the president, House and Senate Democrats wanted to protect entitlement programs (Social Security and Medicare, for instance) from severe reductions. The president was open to some entitlement changes and tried twice unsuccessfully to forge a fiscal "grand bargain" with Speaker Boehner that would produce budgetary savings of $4 trillion or more with entitlement reform and additional taxes part of the grand bargain. Liberal Democrats were upset with the president for suggesting spending reductions in entitlement programs, particularly Medicare and Social Security.

President Obama understood that a default would weaken his presidency, foment domestic and global economic disarray, and call into question the nation's creditworthiness. It would also damage his legacy as chief executive. Knowing this, the opposition pushed hard and successfully to win large spending cuts that might not have occurred if the bargaining context favored the administration rather than congressional Republicans, who enjoyed a political resurgence following their big November 2010 midterm election victory.

Throughout the summer of 2011, Democrats and Republicans struggled to avoid a default. The negotiating process among the president and top congressional leaders from each chamber was mired in controversy and divisiveness, in large measure because both sides stood firm on their core principles: no new taxes for the GOP and no entitlement reform for Democrats. When Treasury Secretary Timothy Geithner provided Congress with a firm deadline (August 2, 2011) for avoiding a default by passing an increase in the debt ceiling, the stage was set for deadline brinksmanship: a game of chicken among the elective branches and the two parties. The evolution of the 2011 debt-ceiling battle is summarized in table 13.1. The eventual enactment of the debt ceiling increase can be attributed to at least four main factors.

The President Favors a "Clean" Vote

President Obama and House Democrats urged Speaker Boehner to schedule floor action on a "clean" debt bill—a $2.4 trillion increase in borrowing authority—with no other provisions embedded in the measure. House Republicans refused and insisted that there must be a dollar in spending cuts for every dollar authorized for borrowing. To demonstrate that Republicans were in the driver's seat, Speaker Boehner did comply with the repeated requests of President Obama to schedule a vote on a "clean" $2.4 trillion debt measure. The vote occurred on May 31, 2011, in unusual circumstances. First, it was brought up under a procedure (suspension of the rules) that guaranteed its defeat; suspension procedure allows only forty minutes of debate, no free-standing amendments, and, significantly, a two-thirds vote for passage. Second, GOP leaders urged their party colleagues to defeat the bill they introduced. Every Republican voted for rejection, with some relishing a default to dramatize the need for spending discipline. Third, Democrats who supported the clean bill approach "assailed Republicans for bringing it up," calling their action a political stunt and warning that the measure's "certain defeat might unnerve the financial markets."[62] (A few days after Congress passed the debt-ceiling legislation in early August 2011, Senator McConnell made this prediction: "The days of getting clean debt ceilings bills are over. . . . We will go after additional spending reductions when that request is made."[63])

The House rejected the bill by a 318 to 97 vote. That vote, according to Ways and Means Chairman David Camp, Mich., makes "clear that Republicans will not accept an increase in the nation's debt limit without substantial spending cuts and real budgetary reform."[64] It was evident that a new reality permeated Capitol Hill. House Republicans "had the leverage. Democrats were going to have to agree to large cuts in federal spending if the Republicans were going to support a debt increase. There was no way around that central truth."[65] That truth, however, also requires some modification. If the Speaker expected to avoid a default despite the preferences of many in his party, he would need to support a fiscal compromise that would attract Democratic votes.

Table 13.1.   Debt Timeline, Selected Key Dates, 2011

April 13	President outlines plan to reduce deficit by $4 trillion over 12 years ($2 trillion in spending cuts; $1 trillion in revenue; $1 trillion in interest savings).
May 2	Treasury Secretary Geithner informs lawmakers that the $14.3 trillion debt ceiling must be raised by August 2.
May 5	VP Joe Biden, as directed by the president, holds first meeting with six lawmakers from the House and Senate to develop a debt-reduction plan.
May 9	Speaker Boehner states that spending cuts must be greater than the increase required to boost the debt ceiling.
May 31	House rejects a "clean" debt bill, as requested by the president and House Democrats.
June 1 and 2	President meets first with House Republicans to discuss debt ceiling; the next day he meets with House Democrats.
June 7	Senator McConnell requires $2.4 trillion in spending cuts in exchange for the debt increase.
June 13	House Majority Leader Cantor, a member of the Biden Group, supports trillions in spending cuts, including Medicare.
June 14	Biden wants his group to reach a debt-reduction deal by July 1.
June 22	Speaker Boehner and the president meet privately to craft a deficit reduction plan called the "grand bargain."
June 23	House Majority Leader Cantor leaves the Biden Group, citing opposition to any tax hikes. He learns of secret Boehner-Obama discussions from Biden. President Obama meets with House Democratic leaders.
June 27	President Obama meets separately with Senators Reid and McConnell. A dozen Senate GOP conservatives declare they will vote against any debt plan until Congress passes a constitutional balanced-budget amendment.
June 29	Obama criticizes GOP rigidity on taxes; he's open to Medicare reforms.
July 7	President meets with bipartisan House and Senate leaders to discuss a deal.
July 9	The Speaker abandons "grand bargain" talks with the president. Each blames the other for the lack of agreement on the grand bargain: $4 trillion in spending cuts, $1 trillion in revenue, and major entitlement reforms.
July 12	Obama continues meetings with congressional leaders. Senator McConnell outlines a complex plan to reach a debt-reduction agreement (see discussion below).
July 15	Senate bipartisan leaders work to develop a deficit reduction plan, using the McConnell proposal as a starting point. Speaker Boehner reopens talks with President Obama on a "grand bargain."

July 19	House passes a bill to block the debt ceiling until both chambers enact a balanced-budget constitutional amendment, a symb olic vote.
July 22	Speaker Boehner ends "grand bargain" discussions with the president. He focuses on negotiating a deficit accord with Reid, McConnell, and Pelosi.
July 25	Speaker Boehner and Senator Reid issue competing but overlapping deficit-reduction plans. Each plan made large and immediate spending cuts, created a Supercommittee to propose other fiscal reductions, among other things.
July 29	Speaker Boehner wins adoption of his deficit reduction plan (218 to 210), after earlier delays; it ties a debt ceiling increase to enactment of a constitutional balanced-budget amendment. His plan is rejected by the Senate.
July 31	A compromise accord is agreed to by the president and congressional leaders that contains features of the Boehner, Reid, and McConnell proposals. These include a cap on discretionary spending, creation of a special joint committee to cut spending by $1.2 to $1.5 trillion over a decade, and an automatic sequester mechanism to make at least $1.2 trillion in cuts if the joint panel fails.
August 1	The House enacts the deficit reduction and deficit ceiling package by a 269 to 161 vote.
August 2	The Senate passes the debt package (74 to 26). The president signs the measure into law (P.L. 112-25).

Numerous Private Discussions

Extensive negotiations took place among the president, House leaders, and Senate leaders prior to the August 2 deadline. For example, the president directed Vice President Joe Biden to lead a bipartisan and bicameral group of lawmakers to devise a twelve-year deficit-reduction plan composed of spending cuts, entitlement reforms, and revenue increases. "We want $4 trillion in deficit reduction over 12 years. Everyone else is very close to that. Our proposal is three-to-one, cuts to revenue."[66] Republicans were fine with the spending cuts but not the revenue hikes. They also wanted Democrats to agree to a long-term deficit-reduction plan that emphasized cuts in spending but relatively little by way of tax increases. The talks ended after about five weeks. Upset at the lack of progress on raising the federal debt limit, the president held a news conference on June 29, urging lawmakers to stay in town rather then head home for the July 4 break. He pointed out that his two daughters usually finish their homework a day ahead of time. Key lawmakers were available during the break to carry on negotiations, as were their staff aides.

A second and parallel set of private meetings was underway between Speaker Boehner and President Obama. Majority Leader Cantor, who was a member of the Biden group, only learned of the Obama-Boehner sessions from Vice President Biden, which further exacerbated the tensions between the two House GOP leaders. The Obama-Boehner discussions aimed to avoid a default by producing a "grand bargain": a long-term deficit-reduction plan. The president favored a "balanced" approach, which meant tax hikes on the wealthy, spending cuts, and entitlement reforms (Medicare, for example). The Speaker appeared to support much of this framework, with more emphasis on spending cuts and tax reform. The talks abruptly ended, with each side blaming the other, when conservatives in the Speaker's party objected to the grand bargain and the president asked for more revenue for debt reduction. Trust between the two leaders deteriorated for a time.

In mid-July, the Speaker telephoned President Obama and said he wanted to resume talks on a grand bargain. He proposed $800 billion in revenue to be derived from an overhaul of the tax code, as well as entitlement reform. His plan also provided for a two-step increase in the debt ceiling. The president strongly opposed having repetitive votes on raising the debt ceiling and disagreed with the deep cuts made to various entitlement reforms. This second attempt to reach a grand bargain agreement also ended quickly.

The President's Electoral Goal

Avoiding a default was a vital goal of the president's but so was another: ensuring that enactment of a debt ceiling hike extended beyond the November 2012 elections. There was to be one vote only on raising the debt ceiling and not a series of votes raising the ceiling by relatively small increments. During a White House meeting with his top aides, the president declared, "I've decided that I am not going to take a short-term debt extension [advocated by GOP leaders] under any circumstances. I want you to understand, I am not going to do it."[67] Later, in an interview, President Obama said: "The reason that's so important is because, given how spooked the markets already are about this whole process—which is unprecedented in modern American history—for us to repeat this in increments every quarter would be disastrous for our economy."[68] After Democrats and Republicans reviewed numerous plans and proposals over several weeks, the president's electoral principle was embedded in the final compromise. The complex agreement required several votes to raise the debt ceiling to occur (see below), but the agreement did not undermine the president's electoral goal.

Various Plans Shape the New Debt and Deficit Reduction Law

During the eight-week struggle to increase the debt ceiling, the president, the leaders of the two chambers, and their top aides traded proposals on deficit reduction back and forth in a series of offer-counteroffer negotiations. For example, the president presented options to House and Senate party leaders for a small, medium, and large deficit reduction package. The small plan would produce $2 trillion in budgetary savings, just enough to push another debt increase beyond the November elections. The medium option was estimated to produce $3 trillion in fiscal savings, and the large plan would achieve $4 trillion in savings. [69]

President Obama strongly supported the large option, and urged lawmakers to back that plan. (Politically, a bold plan advantaged the president's 2012 reelection chances by demonstrating his commitment to serious debt reduction.) In a press conference, he challenged Republicans to get something big done by supporting the $4 trillion deficit reduction package. House Majority Leader Cantor proposed a $2.5 trillion deficit reduction framework. As the president exclaimed, "I've been hearing from my Republican friends for quite some time that it is a moral imperative for us to tackle our debts and our deficits in a serious way . . . So what I've said to them is, 'Let's go.'" [70] "Let's go" also meant that the party leaders of each chamber periodically had to discuss the various plans with their party colleagues and then persuade enough of the rank-and-file to vote for the ultimate compromise. Moreover, given the August 2 deadline, there would be little time for rank-and-file lawmakers to review a product that hardly any had a hand in shaping.

From the Speaker's perspective, who was upset with the lack of progress in reaching a final compromise, it was time for the top party leaders of each chamber (McConnell, Pelosi, Reid, and Boehner) to craft the debt-ceiling legislation. Speaker Boehner and Senator Reid each prepared debt-raising plans with similar provisions and that also included ideas advanced by Senator McConnell. For example, both the Boehner and Reid plans cut spending by $2 trillion and formed a new congressional committee to recommend legislation to further reduce the deficit. The plans differed in how they increased the debt limit: Boehner's proposal required a two-step process, contrary to the president's wishes, while Reid's would grant sufficient borrowing authority to avoid a second debt limit increase before the November 2012 elections.

In late July, the Speaker twice had to postpone a vote on his plan because of strong conservative opposition. The House on July 29 narrowly passed the Boehner plan, but it was not enacted by the Senate. The House also rejected Senator Reid's plan. The outlook appeared bleak. With only a few days before the August 2 deadline, negotiations intensified among the principal actors. In marathon sessions, Speaker Boehner, Senators Reid and McConnell, House Democratic leader Nancy Pelosi, and top White House advisers hammered out what became the Budget Control Act (BCA). [71] Congress enacted the complex debt-ceiling and debt-reduction bill (S. 365) only hours before the August 2 deadline was breached, which would have ended the Treasury Department's borrowing authority. President Obama signed the

BCA into law (P.L. 112-25), a statute with two fundamental goals: increase the debt ceiling and reduce federal spending.

In short, after a bitter battle between the two parties and among the elective branches over raising the debt ceiling and cutting spending, the BCA put in place a procedural process to achieve a policy result. Using process to make policy is commonplace on Capitol Hill, because it allows party leaders to shield their members from taking tough, up-or-down votes on specific policy proposals. Among the key features of the BCA are these three.

Debt-Limit Increase

The BCA increased the debt ceiling (or borrowing limit) by $2.1 trillion in exchange for equivalency in spending reductions. A little over $900 billion over a decade would largely come from annual spending caps (specified in the BCA) on discretionary spending. Congressional votes to reach that number were to occur in three stages. The other $1.2 trillion required Congress to act on at least a $1.2 to $1.5 trillion legislative package of budgetary savings over ten years crafted by a special joint panel. If Congress failed to produce that legislation, then a process called "sequestration" would automatically be triggered cutting domestic and defense programs by that amount. Sequestration and the special joint committee are discussed below.

The idea for multiple votes on raising the debt limit in exchange for equivalent spending cuts came from Senator McConnell.[72] Its purposes were several: to protect GOP senators from voting directly on the politically charged debt-ceiling hike, to put the onus of raising the debt on President Obama, and to keep the debt issue in the public eye. As journalist and author Bob Woodward explained, Senator McConnell's "complicated idea was that Obama should first raise the debt limit on his own authority, and then Congress would pass legislation disapproving of the increase. The president would then veto the legislation, but Democrats would have enough votes to sustain the veto so the debt ceiling would be increased."[73]

Under the BCA, before the administration could receive the initial $900 billion increase in the debt ceiling, the president had to certify for each of the three installments that the government was within $100 billion of exceeding its borrowing authority. The first stage occurred when the default avoidance legislation became law; the administration automatically received $400 billion in additional borrowing authority. The president issued the required certification on the same day he signed the BCA into law. The second stage provided another $500 billion increase in the debt ceiling, contingent on both legislative chambers acting on a joint resolution of disapproval within fifteen calendar days. This approach allowed lawmakers to vote for the joint resolution of disapproval and thus avoid campaign ads lambasting them for being big spenders. On September 11, 2011, the GOP House adopted (232 to 186) the disapproval resolution, only to see the Senate reject (45 yeas to 52 nays) a comparable disapproval resolution. Even if the Senate had passed the disapproval resolution, President Obama would have vetoed the legislation with little likelihood that the House and Senate each could muster the required two-thirds override vote. The third installment of $1.2 trillion occurred in January 2012 when Congress failed to enact a joint disapproval resolution.

Achieving $1.2 trillion, or more, in deficit reduction was assigned to a special joint committee with a mandate to report its product by November 23, 2011, the day before Thanksgiving. The BCA required the House and Senate to vote on the joint panel's recommendation by December 23, 2011. Moreover, the BCA included expedited procedures—no Senate filibusters, for example—to facilitate timely chamber consideration of the joint panel's recommendation.

The Joint Select Deficit Reduction Committee

This bipartisan, twelve-member joint committee, dubbed the "supercommittee" by the media, was composed of three Democrats and three Republicans from each chamber. The top party leaders of each house named their respective members. The cochairs were Representative Jeb Hensarling (R-TX) and Senator Patty Murray (D-WA). To make a long story short, the joint committee held public and private meetings during their roughly four-month reporting window. Significantly, they had sweeping authority over revenue, entitlement, and spending. However, on November 21, 2011, the joint panel announced that they had failed in their mission and went out of business. Asked why the joint committee could not produce a debt-reduction package, Representative Hensarling wrote: "We could not bridge the gap between two dramatically competing visions of the role government should play in a free society, the proper purpose and design of the social safety net and the fundamentals of job creation and economic growth."[74] The joint committee's failure to agree upon a package of $1.2 trillion in debt reduction triggered the enforcement procedure mentioned earlier called "sequestration": automatic and indiscriminate across-the-board spending cuts (or "sequesters") that would fall equally on security and nonsecurity programs, departments, and agencies. (A few budgetary areas are exempt from sequestration, such as Social Security.)

Sequestration

The reality of automatic and draconian cuts in security and nonsecurity programs was never expected to happen. Just the threat of it was supposed to force compromise between Republicans (who would oppose slashing funds for defense) and Democrats (who would resist cuts in various domestic programs). As Senator Carl Levin (D-MI) put it: "The purpose of sequester is to force us to avoid a sequester."[75] The joint select panel was expected to propose the painful budgetary reductions that Congress would accept. Defense Secretary Leon Panetta called sequestration the "doomsday mechanism"—the political equivalent of the "doomsday machine" in Stanley Kubrick's classic film *Dr. Strangelove*—because of its huge budgetary impact on the Pentagon.[76] Senator Charles Schumer (D-NY) stated that the sequester is "a sword of equal sharpness and strength hanging over each party's head."[77]

The failure of the joint select panel triggered the doomsday mechanism in mid-January 2012. However, under the BCA, the sequestration would not take effect until after January 1, 2013 (after the November 2012 elections). Meanwhile, lawmakers in both chambers and parties urged the delay or repeal of sequestration. Other members had a different view. "A commitment was made, an agreement was reached [in the BCA], and I think it is wrong," said House Democratic leader Pelosi, "to say we're just not going to honor the commitment."[78]

Adding to the end-of-year controversy was the December 31, 2012, expiration of the Bush tax cuts first enacted in 2001. Thus, after January 1, 2013, two things are poised to happen automatically over a period of time unless they are blocked by law: sequestration (indiscriminate spending cuts across nearly all departments and agencies) and a significant tax increase on most Americans. This combination of automatic actions is dubbed the "fiscal cliff." Some lawmakers and analysts favor going over the cliff, because it would dramatically reduce the fiscal deficit by raising revenue and cutting spending. Many lawmakers and economists warn against going over the cliff on the grounds that it would damage the economy, perhaps triggering a recession.

What is clear is that Standard & Poor's—a major credit rating agency—for the first time ever downgraded the creditworthiness of the United States from AAA to AA+ after the acrimonious 2011 deficit hike controversy. The 2011 downgrade means that the rating agency believes there is at least a slight possibility that at some point the United States might be unable to meet its financial obligations to its lenders. As Standard & Poor's wrote about the legislative-executive squabbling that suffused the debt-ceiling fight: "The political brinkmanship of recent months highlights what we see as America's governance and policy making becoming less stable, less effective and less predictable."[79]

IV. SUMMARY OBSERVATIONS

The November 2012 elections produced what might be called "back to the future again," because it produced another two-year period of divided government. Barack Obama won a second term with a significant Electoral College victory and a popular vote margin of 51 percent, one of only five other presidents (Jackson, Grant, McKinley, FDR, and Eisenhower) to twice win the popular vote by that margin[80]; Republicans held the House despite losing eight seats, while Democrats unexpectedly picked up seats in the Senate. Moreover, the same House and Senate party leaders remained in place, and three postponed issues—sequestration, the expiration of the Bush tax cuts, and another debt-ceiling increase—dominated the attention of the postelection "lame duck" session as well as the 113th Congress (2013–2015).

Although the 2012 elections preserved the legislative status quo, there were important differences in the political context between the pre- and postelection periods. During the summer 2011 negotiations, House Republicans were in the driver's seat in terms of bargaining leverage. They had just won a decisive midterm election victory and the president and congressional Democrats were on the defensive. Many conservative Republicans supported a default on paying the debts of the nation—a believable threat to the president and congressional leaders. As a result, GOP leaders set the terms for negotiating the deficit ceiling increase. As a seasoned analyst said of the Speaker's strategy, "Boehner rather brilliantly used the 'I have to deal with this crazy uncle [Tea Party Republicans] in the attic' gambit to extract a lot of concessions in 2011."[81]

After the November 2012 elections, Republicans were devastated by their losses. Many were convinced they would win the White House, retain the House, and take control of the Senate. They also were deeply troubled by the demographic reality that the party did not reflect the diversity of America. Republicans had become a white male–dominated political party at a time when, in a matter of a few decades, the country was projected to become a "majority minority" nation. It bears repeating that "after a decisive reelection victory and Democratic gains in Congress, [President] Obama has the stronger hand," at least for a time, in dealing with Speaker Boehner and the GOP House in finding a way to avert sequestration and tax increases, except for wealthy individuals whose incomes exceed $250,000 per year.[82]

To capitalize on dismay in GOP ranks and Democratic reelection momentum, the president took a forceful approach to Republicans. He sent GOP leaders his initial plan for a settlement—$1.6 trillion in new revenue (double what he offered Speaker Boehner in 2011), $50 billion in new spending to boost the economy, and enactment of legislation granting the president unilateral authority to raise the debt ceiling, subject to Congress's ability to pass a joint resolution of disapproval—ensuring that "negotiations began on terms dictated by the newly elected president."[83] (Both chambers agreed that during the lame-duck session Speaker Boehner would take the lead with President Obama in negotiating a deficit-reduction framework that would block sequestration, prevent tax increases on most Americans, and pass the House and Senate.)

President Obama later backed away from his proposal to raise the debt ceiling on his own, leaving unfulfilled a key objective of finding a way "to neutralize GOP threats to use votes on increasing the country's borrowing limit to force additional spending cuts."[84] Speaker Boehner and Senator McConnell strongly opposed the idea of giving the president authority to raise the debt ceiling. Both recognized the bargaining leverage it gave them to force spending cuts on the president in exchange for increasing the government's borrowing authority.

In sum, the president's opening bid called for $1.95 trillion in savings.[85] The president also wanted the top tax rate to increase by about four points to 39.6 percent (the rate in effect during the Clinton presidency) for the wealthiest Americans. Unlike summer 2011, the president offered no early concessions to the Speaker. Instead, President Obama returned to the campaign trail to generate public pressure on congressional Republicans. The president's "going above the heads of Congress," noted Senator Kent Conrad (D-ND). "He's going out to the American people to rally them to support a position to get a result here."[86] Obama visited various states to highlight his plan, using the bully pulpit to rally popular support for his agenda. His effort at "going public" aimed to put pressure on members of Congress to back his plans by appealing directly to their constituents. The president also employed social media (Facebook and Twitter), and met with governors, corporate and union leaders, and others. He also threatened to veto any budget package "that somehow prevents the top rate from going up for [the wealthiest] at the top 2%."[87] "If there's one thing that I've learned," remarked the president, "when the American people speak loudly enough, lo and behold, Congress listens."[88] In short, the president's strategy was to engage in legislating by campaigning and avoid "getting sucked into long public negotiations" with Speaker Boehner over the debt ceiling and the fiscal cliff.[89]

The president's aggressive approach surprised Republicans, but it was not long before Speaker Boehner offered a GOP plan: $800 billion in additional revenue through tax reform, $1.1 trillion in entitlement savings, and $300 billion in discretionary reductions.[90] Speaker Boehner also emphasized, as he did in 2011, that any hike in the debt ceiling had to be offset by at least an equivalent amount of spending reductions. Subsequently, with negotiations with the White House appearing futile, Boehner proposed his own "Plan B," which consisted of two separate measures. The first was a bill (the Spending Reduction Act) that would cancel for a year the looming sequester in defense and domestic programs. This measure also contained provisions designed to attract conservative support for Plan B, such as spending reductions in social safety net programs. The House narrowly passed this bill on a strictly party-line vote (215 to 209).

The second component of Plan B was a bill that would extend the Bush-era tax cuts for everyone with income under $1 million. Despite predictions from the top GOP leaders that they had the votes to pass Plan B, antitax Republicans refused to support the measure. They objected to tax increases on anyone. In a significant setback for the Speaker, the tax bill was never brought to the floor for lack of votes. (During his Speakership, Boehner has confronted more times than he would like a shortage of followers, essential to leadership.) Uncertainty about what would happen next reigned on Capitol Hill as lawmakers left town for the Christmas break.

The House and Senate reconvened on December 30, a Sunday. Speaker Boehner made it clear that it was the Senate's turn to come up with a plan to avert the fiscal cliff. Recall that the Speaker could not win the votes for his Plan B, raising taxes on millionaires while keeping tax cuts for lower incomes. Boehner said the House would vote at 6:30 p.m. "on whatever the Senate can pass, but the Senate must act" first.[91] In this way, the House could approve the Senate's product (sending it to the White House) or amend it and return it to the Senate for further review.

In the end, Congress missed by a few hours the December 31 midnight deadline that would prevent the country from going over the fiscal cliff. The economic consequences were *de minimus* because both chambers and the president moved quickly to stop the automatic tax hikes and spending cuts. During the predawn hours of January 1, 2013, the Senate enacted by an 89 to 8 vote a bipartisan compromise negotiated by Senate GOP Leader McConnell and Vice President Biden. Among the several provisions of the compromise, two specifically dealt with the fiscal cliff. First, the McConnell-Biden agreement prevented tax increases for most Americans, except for individuals earning more than $400,000 and couples earning over $450,000. Tax rates on high earners also jumped from 35 percent to 39.6 percent in keeping with a central theme of the president's reelection campaign. Second, the spending sequesters were delayed by two months. The House agreed to the compromise on New Year's Day by a 257 to 167 vote, with most Republicans opposed, including Majority Leader Cantor.

House GOP leaders won the majority support of their party colleagues even though many opposed tax increases on anyone. Republican leaders argued that members were voting to cut taxes for most Americans, not raise them. Without their support for the McConnell-Biden agreement, argued GOP leaders, higher taxes would be imposed on their fellow citizens given the expiration of the Bush-era tax cuts. Moreover, halting sequestration for a few months prevented spending cuts to the Pentagon from taking effect, a priority for many Republicans.

The summer 2011 debt-ceiling battle and the fiscal cliff controversy highlight two important aspects of congressional-presidential relations that will shape the work of the 113th Congress. First, the interparty fiscal clashes are fundamentally about the size and scope of the federal government, a persistent theme throughout American history and much in evidence during the November 2012 presidential election. From early differences between Thomas Jefferson (limited government) and Alexander Hamilton (energetic government) to the Barack Obama–Mitt Romney presidential contest, the government's role has been the source of constant debate between the two parties and among the American people.

For many Republicans, their highest priority seems less about reducing the deficit and more about shrinking the government through lower taxes (a so-called starve the beast approach). On its face, more revenue would help to reduce the deficit, but those monies would also continue to fund the federal government. Accordingly, the GOP advocates deeper spending cuts, including in entitlement programs. Speaker Boehner and other Republicans concede that more revenue is needed to meet federal obligations, but they favor tax reform and closing tax loopholes as ways to raise revenue rather than through hikes in income tax rates. For many Democrats, protecting entitlement programs from unreasonable reforms and spending cuts are top priorities. Democrats support deficit reduction but in a manner that also permits more government investment in areas such as research and development, education, and transportation. Representative Barney Frank (D-MA) posed a crucial question that has been answered differently in different eras by voters and elected officials. Today, his question is especially apt: "What is the appropriate level of public activity in our society?"[92]

Second, the practice of legislative brinksmanship may be another new normal on Capitol Hill. Ideological rigidity and partisan acrimony inhibit the politics of persuasion in harmonizing divergent party views. Scores of members in each party are in an uncompromising mood with respect to their party-preferred priorities. For example, soon after the November 2012 elections, a House GOP member said: "Compromise has a very small constituency—very small."[93] The constituency is often small in Congress in part because neither party trusts the other to deliver on their promises "without some mechanism to force action," such as self-imposed legal deadlines that "encourage a culture of brinksmanship."[94]

The result is deadline lawmaking where each side waits until the final hours before accepting a compromise in the belief that it heightens their bargaining leverage. Unwillingness to compromise gives "leverage to those legislators who are least concerned about going over the brink."[95] In the view of a congressional historian, brinksmanship is "governing by threat, high stakes, and cliffhangers. You wait until the last minute; both sides are willing to threaten shutdown. The worst scenario is that the players get used to governing this way. The more you do something like this, the more comfortable you get to do it again."[96] Added a knowledgeable analyst of political activities: "Arriving at a compromise 'too early' gives ideologues within each party an opportunity to complain that their side 'caved' prematurely and could have gotten more if their political leaders had simply acted tougher, demanded more and waited."[97]

Brinksmanship has other consequences: it consumes the time and attention of lawmakers, time that might be better spent dealing with other important issues; it saps the morale of federal workers; and it undermines citizens' trust and confidence in Congress's capacity to govern effectively. Deadline lawmaking and self-imposed crises are common to lawmaking, however. Their objective is to force action because inaction might produce dire consequences that lawmakers want to avoid. "It's under the crucible of a time constraint that this place acts," observed Representative Scott Rigell (R-VA).[98]

The 113th Congress confronts in early 2013 another series of deadline dramas involving the debt ceiling (February or March), sequestration (March 1), and the expiration (March 27) of a government-funding law which, unless renewed by Congress, will trigger a government shutdown. The government reached its $16.4 trillion borrowing limit on December 31, 2012, but Treasury Secretary Geithner "signaled that he can juggle the books for about two months before the nation runs out of cash to pay its bills."[99] Congressional Republicans are looking forward to holding the debt measure hostage until the president and congressional Democrats agree to more and deeper spending cuts, as well as entitlement reforms. "The only way we ever cut spending around here," explained Senate GOP Leader McConnell, "is by using the debate over the debt limit to do it."[100] Added GOP Senator Lindsey Graham (SC), "Round Two's coming, and we're going to have one hell of a contest about the direction and the vision of this country."[101]

To be sure, a repeat of the summer 2011 deficit hike battle would have economic and political risks. Economically, a default or credit downgrade would likely produce adverse consequences, such as a recession or stock market crash. Politically, the general public, as well as numerous business leaders, do not want a replay of another bitter battle over raising the debt ceiling. These circumstances might provide sufficient incentives for both sides to reach a bipartisan plan that reconciles the GOP's commitment to spending cuts and limits on taxes with the Democrats' emphasis on the protection of entitlements and programs that aid the poor.

In short, political brinksmanship over issues of spending cuts, taxes, deficit ceilings, and entitlement reforms appears likely to dominate congressional debate for years to come. This prediction is easy to make because ours is an aging society with escalating expenditures for the nation's two main health programs: Medicare and Medicaid. How to control entitlement spending while raising revenue to meet essential governmental functions, including debt payments, are significant domestic challenges that face President Obama and the 113th Congress.

NOTES

1. The views and interpretations discussed herein are those of the authors and are in no way attributable to the Congressional Research Service or to Albright College.

2. Mark Wegner, "Hastert: GOP to Take Political Offensive," *CongressDailyAM*, March 15, 2004, 5. National Journal, Inc., is the publisher of this legislative bulletin.

3. See Gerald F. Seib, "Election Sharpens Partisan Divide," *Wall Street Journal*, December 11, 2012, and John Aloysius Farrell, "Polarity Thwarts Compromise on Cliff," *National Journal Daily*, November 30, 2012.

4. Among the explanations for virulent partisanship on Capitol Hill are these: (1) the demographic and geographic sorting that over time has produced a more liberal Democratic party and a far more conservative Republican party; (2) the intense policy differences between the two parties because of the huge ideological gap between them; (3) the array of liberal and conservative media networks that amplify and reinforce disagreements between Democrats and Republicans; (4) the large number of special interests affiliated with each party that monitor member behavior and votes for ideological purity; and (5) the fear among many lawmakers that cooperation across-the-aisle, such as cosponsoring a measure with an opposition party member, could mean a primary challenge in the next election from someone more conservative or more liberal than they are.

5. Michael Barone, "If Obama Wins, Will He Be Another Woodrow Wilson?" *Washington Examiner*, October 21, 2012.

6. Michael Grunwald, *The New New Deal* (New York: Simon & Schuster, 2012).

7. Theda Skocpol and Lawrence R. Jacobs, "Accomplishments and Embattled: Understanding Obama's Presidency," *Political Science Quarterly* (November 2012): 1–24.

8. Shawn Zeller, "Historic Success, At No Small Cost," *CQ Weekly*, January 11, 2010, 112.

9. Joseph Schatz, "Legislative Success, Political Peril," *CQ Weekly*, January 3, 2011, 19.

10. Ezra Klein, "A High-Stakes Election: Health Care at Risk," *Washington Post*, October 27, 2012.

11. Adam Nagourney, Jeff Zeleny, Kate Zernike, and Michael Cooper, "How the G.O.P. Captured a Seat Lost for Decades," *New York Times*, January 21, 2010.

12. Michael Gerson, "In Victory, Obama Failed," *Washington Post*, October 30, 2012.

13. Sheryl Gay Stolberg, Jeff Zeleny, and Carl Hulse, "The Long Road Back," *New York Times*, March 21, 2010.

14. Laura Meckler, "Vow to Tame Partisan Rancor Eludes Obama Four Years In," *Wall Street Journal*, August 23, 2012.

15. John Dickerson, "How to Measure for a President," *Slate*, September 26, 2012, 5.

16. George Condon, "Does Obama Have Friends on the Hill?" *National Journal Daily*, July 8, 2011, 5.

17. Bob Woodward, *The Price of Politics* (New York: Simon & Schuster, 2012), 58.

18. Emily Pierce, "Obama, McConnell: Perfect Strangers," *Roll Call*, May 6, 2010, online edition. As for Boehner's relationship with the president, aides reported that the "two have spent virtually no time together," and they could not recall a single one-on-one meeting or substantive phone call. See Peter Baker, "Washington Worries About Its New Power Couple," *New York Times*, November 10, 2010.

19. David Lauter, "Obama Faces Deep Divisions," *Los Angeles Times*, September 1, 2012, online edition.

20. Woodward, *The Price of Politics*, 16.

21. Jennifer Bendery, "Democrats Want White House Help on Messaging," *Roll Call*, September 30, 2010, online edition.

22. The Frank and Webb quotes are from Gerson, "In Victory, Obama Failed."

23. Ben Smith, "Health Reform Foes Plan Obama's 'Waterloo,'" *Politico*, July 17, 2009, 1.

24. Michael Grunwald, "The Party of No," *TIME*, September 13, 2012, 44. All the quotes in this paragraph are from this source.

25. Woodward, *The Price of Politics*, 16–17.

26. Michael Scherer, "Obama Plays Hard Ball," *TIME*, September 10, 2012, 30.

27. John Harwood, "After 15 Months in Office, Policy vs. Politics for Obama," *New York Times*, April 26, 2010.

28. John Stanton, "Kaufman: Democrats Muffled Their Message," *Roll Call*, September 30, 2010, online edition.

29. Paul Starr, "Obama and the Art of Not Getting Credit," *The American Prospect* (September/October 2012): 5.

30. Quoted in Gary Lee Malecha and Daniel J. Reagan, *The Public Congress* (New York: Routledge, 2012), 117.

31. According to one account, Rahm Emanuel, the White House chief of staff, begged the president "not to tackle health-care reform first; Obama overrode his advice and that of his senior staff members. He felt morally impelled to pursue the late senator Ted Kennedy's cause . . . and concluded that Year One was the time to fight the hardest battle of all. He was 'all alone' in that decision." Matthew Dalleck, "A Gifted Orator Who Can't Make His Point," *Washington Post*, May 16, 2010.

32. Susan Davis, "Go Big and Go Home," *National Journal*, December 18, 2010, 39.

33. Sen. Mitch McConnell, "Democrats Are Leaving a Legacy of Overreach," *Politico*, September 14, 2010, 45. Also see John Stanton, "McConnell's Fighting Words," *Roll Call*, December 10, 2009, 1.

34. Davis, "Go Big and Go Home," 38.

35. Alex Altman, "A Tale of Two Members," *TIME*, March 14, 2011, 38.

36. Josh Smith, "Lieberman: 'I Did What I Believed Was Right,'" *National Journal Daily*, October 9, 2012, 1.

37. *Congressional Record*, December 3, 2012, S7311.

38. Quoted in *CQ Midday Update*, December 14, 2004, 1.

39. Neil McNeil, *Dirksen: Portrait of a Public Man* (New York: World Publishing Co., 1970). The latter quotation is found on p. 1 and the former on p. 152.

40. David Brooks, "Why We Love Politics," *New York Times*, November 23, 2012.

41. Stephen W. Stathis, "To Avoid Fiscal Cliff, Obama and GOP Should Compromise Like Founding Fathers," *Christian Science Monitor*, November 28, 2012, online edition.

42. On compromise, see, for example, Amy Gutmann and Dennis Thompson, *The Spirit of Compromise: Why Governing Demands It and Campaigning Undermines It* (Princeton, NJ: Princeton University Press, 2012), and T. V. Smith, "Compromise: Its Context and Limits," *Ethics, An International Journal of Social, Political, and Legal Philosophy* (October 1942): 1–13.

43. Matthew Rothschild, "Feet of Clay," *The Progressive*, February 2001, 43.

44. Meredith Shiner, "The Speaker of the Unruly," *CQ Weekly*, September 10, 2012, 1834.

45. David Skaggs, "Cooperation in Congress," *Christian Science Monitor*, April 4, 2011, 35.

46. "Little Compromise on Compromising," *Pew Research Center Publications*, September 20, 2010, 1. To be sure, the public's view of compromise changes, including on specific issues. As one account noted, "There is also a clear desire among the public to see opposing parties work together to find a [deficit reduction] solution. Almost two-thirds of the respondents (63 percent) said negotiators should be willing to accept things they don't like as part of a compromise, while only 26 percent said negotiators should 'stand by their principles.'" See Fawn Johnson, "Public Would Accept Tax Hikes in Debt Deal," *National Journal Daily*, October 17, 2012, 6.

47. *Congressional Record*, June 8, 2006, H3549.

48. *Congressional Record*, February 2, 2011, S433.

49. Lee H. Hamilton, "We Need To Embrace Compromise, Not Insult It," *Center on Congress at Indiana University*, May 16, 2011, 1.

50. Hamilton, "We Need to Embrace Compromise, Not Insult It," 2.

51. Jennifer Steinhauer, "Weighing the Effect of an Exit of Centrists," *New York Times*, October 19, 2012.

52. Ezra Klein, "The Unpersuaded," *The New Yorker*, March 19, 2012, 38.

53. David Cook, "The Monitor Breakfast," *Christian Science Monitor*, August 6, 2012, 15.

54. Edward Luce, "America's Thelma and Louise Moment," *Financial Times*, December 3, 2012.

55. Steinhauer, "Weighing the Effect of an Exit of Centrists."

56. Steven T. Dennis and John Stanton, "Deal or No Deal: It's Up to Boehner," *Roll Call*, June 27, 2011, 1.

57. See *Fiscal Year 2012 Historical Tables* (Washington, DC: US Government Printing Office, 2010), 143–44.

58. Woodward, *The Price of Politics*, 122.

59. Woodward, *The Price of Politics*, 189.

60. Grover Norquist, "The Case for the Tax Pledge: Political Accountability," *USA Today*, December 13, 2012. Also see Binyamin Appelbaum, "How Party of Budget Restraint Shifted to 'No New Taxes,' Ever," *New York Times*, December 23, 2012.

61. Robert L. Reynolds, "A Pledge to End All Pledges," *Wall Street Journal*, December 24, 2012. The number of House and Senate Republicans who have signed the antitax pledge is taken from this article.

62. Jackie Calmes, "Pressing Obama, House Bars Rise in Debt Ceiling," *New York Times*, June 1, 2011.

63. Fred Barbash and Richard E. Cohen "Summer of Strife," *CQ Weekly*, August 8, 2011, 1736.

64. Humberto Sanchez and Billy House, "Debt Vote Marked By Political Theater," *National Journal Daily*, June 1, 2011, 7. Also see Russell Berman, "Debt Vote Set to Trap Democrats," *The Hill*, May 25, 2011 1.

65. Woodward, *The Price of Politics*, 111.

66. Woodward, *The Price of Politics*, 112.

67. Woodward, *The Price of Politics*, 218.

68. Woodward, *The Price of Politics*, 219–20.

69. Meredith Shiner and Steven Dennis, "Obama Insists Debt Deal Extend Past 2012 Elections," *Roll Call*, July 7, 2011, online edition.

70. Rebecca Kaplan, "Obama: No Short-Term Deficit Deals," *National Journal Daily*, July 11, 2011, online edition.

71. Alexander Bolton, "Baucus Demands Seat at Table for Tax, Budget Talks," *The Hill*, November 20, 2012, 4.

72. Carl Hulse, "In Debt Crisis, a Legislative Trick Up the Sleeve," *New York Times*, July 19, 2011.

73. Woodward, *The Price of Politics*, 210.

74. Doyle McManus, "The Super Committee That Wasn't," *Los Angeles Times*, November 27, 2011, online edition. Also see, for example, Joseph J. Schatz, "On to the Next Struggle," *CQ Weekly,* November 28, 2011, 2490–507; Richard E. Cohen, "Unusual Panel Would Lead Life of Conflict," *CQ Today*, July 26, 2011, 1, 8; and Don Wolfensberger, "Panel's Failure Reflects Ambivalent Public Mood," *Roll Call,* December 13, 2011, 23.

75. Sara Sorcher, "Levin: Sequester Cuts Can Be Split to Exclude Defense," *NationalJournal.com*, January 26, 2012, 11.

76. Fred Barbash and Richard E. Cohen, "Summer of Strife," *CQ Weekly*, August 8, 2011, 1736–39 .

77. Ben Weyl, "Sequester Becomes Silver Lining," *Roll Call*, November 22, 2011, 1.

78. John Aloysius Farrell, "Divided We Stand," *National Journal*, February 24, 2012, 13.

79. Quoted in John Podhoretz, "The American Moment," *Commentary*, September 2012, 15.

80. David Lauter, "Three Lessons from the Near-Final Popular Vote," *Los Angeles Times*, December 15, 2012, online edition.

81. E. J. Dionne, Jr., "Why Sanity Looks Strange," *Washington Post*, December 3, 2012.

82. Jackie Calmes and Jonathan Weisman, "Soured History Hampers Talks between Obama and Boehner," *New York Times*, December 16, 2012.

83. Lori Montgomery and Paul Kane, "Obama Offers Plan for 'Cliff,'" *Washington Post*, November 30, 2012.

84. Peter Wallsten and Zachary A. Goldfarb, "Best Scenario for Obama Allows Only Modest Agenda," *Washington Post*, December 9, 2012. During the 2011 debt-ceiling debate, a legal argument occurred: could the president ignore Congress and raise the debt ceiling on his own, citing the Fourteenth Amendment of the Constitution. As the Fourteenth Amendment states in part: "The validity of public debt of the United States, authorized by law . . . shall not be questioned." President Obama rejected the Fourteenth Amendment argument. President Bill Clinton, however, said that he would raise the debt ceiling "without hesitation and force the courts to stop me." He added: "The Constitution is clear, and I think this idea that the Congress gets to vote twice on whether to pay for [expenditures] it has appropriated is crazy." Jonathan Epstein, "Debt Ceiling," *Politico*, July 20, 2011, 3. Also see Robin Harding, "Obama Faces Legal Dilemma If Time Runs Out," *Financial Times*, July 29, 2011.

85. Jake Sherman and Carrie Budoff Brown, "Little Movement in GOP Cliff Offer," *Politico*, December 4, 2012, 27.

86. Caren Bohan and Katy O'Donnell, "Short-Timer," *National Journal*, December 15, 2012, 4.

87. Janet Hook, "Some See Hope as Talks Resume over 'Fiscal Cliff,'" *Wall Street Journal*, December 7, 2012.

88. Christi Parsons and Lisa Mascaro, "Obama Takes 'Fiscal Cliff' Battle to Social Media," *Los Angeles Times*, November 28, 2012, online edition.

89. Paul Kane, "Nation Likely to See Effect of 'Cliff,'" *The Washington Post*, December 16, 2012.

90. Sherman and Brown, "Little Movement in GOP Cliff Offer," 27.

91. Jennifer Steinhauer, "Summoned Back to Work, Senators Chafe at Inaction," *New York Times*, December 28, 2012.

92. *Congressional Record*, July 16, 2002, H4749.

93. Doyle McManus, "The Death of the Moderate Republican," *Los Angeles Times*, November 18, 2012, online edition.

94. Steven Dennis, "A Preview of Cliffs to Come," *CQ Weekly*, December 3, 2012, 2414, 2418.

95. Donald Marron, "Does Congress Thrive on Brinksmanship? Watch This Fall," *Christian Science Monitor*, September 19, 2011, 23.

96. Chaddock, "The Politics of Playing Chicken," 16.

97. Stuart Rothenberg, "For the Fiscal Cliff Talks, It's Back to the Future Again," *Roll Call*, December 4, 2012, 10.

98. Lori Montgomery and Paul Kane, "As 'Cliff' Nears, McConnell and Biden in Talks," *Washington Post*, December 31, 2012.

99. Lori Montgomery and Paul Kane, "Senate Continues Marathon Push to Avoid Cliff," *Washington Post*, December 30, 2012.

100. Rosalind Helderman, "Talks Entangle 'Fiscal Cliff' and Debt Limit," *Washington Post*, December 7, 2012.

101. Stephen Dinan, "Congress to Punt Political Football Again Rather Than Tackle Problem," *Washington Times*, January 1, 2013.

Chapter Fourteen

Rivals Only Sometimes

Presidentialism, Unilateralism, and Congressional Acquiescence in Obama's "Ongoing Struggle" against Terrorism[1]

John E. Owens

Much has been written in recent years about heightened partisan polarization in American politics and its intensification during the presidential administrations of conservative George W. Bush and centrist Barack Obama.[2] Yet, over this period and in the context of the so-called war on terror declared by Bush in the aftermath of the terrorist attacks on New York and Washington in 2001, a simultaneous and related incremental shift occurred in the balance of power between the president, the executive, and the Congress: the presidency became more "politicized"[3] and institutional power shifted further to the White House and the executive and away from the Congress. The iconic event that was 9/11 signalled not only new directions in US foreign and domestic policy but also a new presidential era in US government and politics and a new phase in the aggrandizement of presidential power, at some cost to the system's checks and balances, to the rule of law, and to civil liberties. Twelve years on from 9/11 and notwithstanding the extra-legal killing of the alleged perpetrator of the 9/11 atrocities in May 2011, the threat from terrorism, primarily but not exclusively from jihadists, continues, as has presidential aggrandizement.

UNILATERAL POLICY MAKING

Presidents from John Adams through Lincoln to Franklin Roosevelt to Barack Obama have stretched executive power to make policy unilaterally by signing administrative, executive orders, or executive agreements; by issuing written or verbal proclamations or presidential or national security directives; by writing memoranda; by designating officials, or, more recently, by issuing "findings," some of which may be secret. They deploy these unilateral instruments for strategic purposes,[4] including when they face crises demanding swift and decisive action,[5] and on occasions when they would probably not receive congressional approval for their actions.

Franklin Roosevelt claimed and obtained executive powers on this basis; on other occasions, he simply claimed delegated powers drawing on vague references to statutes, and dared the Congress to challenge him,[6] which it frequently did not. Recent presidents have perpetrated similar power grabs—especially on national and domestic security matters,[7] but in other policy areas as well[8] —when they lacked explicit congressional approval in the first instance or were subsequently not subjected to congressional censure or prohibition.[9] In taking unilateral action, presidents effectively challenge the Congress and the courts to overturn their actions, *if they want and if they can.* And, at least in the case of the Congress, legislators usually do not—for the simple reason that they find they cannot muster majorities to overturn the president's action, even less so two-thirds majorities in both chambers if the president uses his veto.

9/11, and the fear of renewed terrorist atrocities in the United States that resulted, engendered a political and governmental context in Washington that the Bush administration effectively exploited to use the president's unilateral powers not only to advance its security agenda but more often than not to deter—and often intimidate—the Congress into *not* challenging it or overturning its actions, or doing its bidding by passing new legislation. For their part, members of Congress typically found it difficult or impossible to muster collective political will to coordinate and formulate timely and forceful rebuffs to aggressive executive claims justifying unilateral action. Many were only too ready to give away or delegate their powers to the executive. As the chapter will show, the accretion of executive power in relation to the so-called war on terror under the Bush administration has been maintained under the Obama administration and, in certain cases, accelerated, despite some softening of tone and policy changes.

9/11 AND BUSH'S PRESIDENTIALIST "WAR ON TERROR"

In many respects, President Bush and his advisers did what any successful American president would have done in response to the national calamity that was 9/11: following some initial delay, they interpreted the public and congressional mood well, and, in a series of effectively choreographed public conversations with ordinary Americans and the Congress, provided the symbolic leadership that is so important in the American system. 9/11 and the ensuing, apparently limitless, "war on terror" represented what Burnham calls a "new constitutional moment"[10] and a new stage in the aggrandizement of presidential power.[11]

Although Bush's approach to the presidency and presidential relations with the Congress was not invented in the crisis precipitated by 9/11, it was certainly crystallized by and made much more visible by that event and the subsequent, presidentially declared, "war on terror." The foundations of Bush's presidentialist philosophy lay in the perceptions of leading figures in the administration that the presidency had been emasculated by congressional actions after the debacles of Vietnam, Watergate, and the Iran-Contra scandal.[12] Its theoretical origins lay in a legal doctrine developed by conservative constitutionalists in the 1980s and 1990s that extolled the virtues and necessity of a "unitary executive."[13] Its leading exponents in the Bush administration were "old hands" from previous Republican administrations and included, most notably, Vice President Cheney, Cheney's chief of staff, David Addington, and Secretary of Defense Donald Rumsfeld. The Bush administration's presidentialism, then, was a part of a bold and strategic political project that is consistent with Moe's "politicized presidency" concept. Its conception of the presidency was "ultra-separationist."[14] It was a philosophy designed to extend executive and presidential power—or, in Jones's more benign phrase, "to capitalize on [Bush's] position" as chief executive[15] and govern "executively"[16] with or without the Congress.

Unitary power is exactly as it sounds: all embracing, indivisible, inherent, plenary, exclusive, and absolute. All executive powers are invested personally in the president and subject to his direct command. The doctrine effectively permits the president to define policy in any area more or less unilaterally with or without congressional consent by claiming and actually exercising unlimited and exclusive power based on inherent and implied discretionary, independent, and formal powers derived from a very expansive interpretation of Article II of the Constitution and from congressional statutes. As a theory of governance, almost by definition, it relegates the role of the Congress, the courts, and other important actors because it seeks to insulate the president from the constitutional checks and balances in ways unknown to and antithetical to the framers of the Constitution. It is a theory, then, which is fundamentally incompatible with notions of a Madisonian or separated system in which the different institutions share power.

The Bush administration's presidentialism not only relegated the roles of other governmental actors, it was an approach to presidential power and governing that did not attach great importance to achieving or maintaining political legitimacy, reputation, prestige, or public approval—all important sources of presidential power identified as being important by Neustadt[17] and others.[18] Position was almost everything for Bush and his colleagues.[19] Political influence would follow primarily, if not exclusively, from the president's formal position as chief executive. It was a doctrine that melded well with Bush's personal leadership style.[20]

Conceptually, at least, Bush's presidentialism need not have led inexorably either to his administration's domination of the Congress in respect to his so-called war on terror—or to the Congress's followership; the rivalry and give and take intended by the Constitution's framers might have remained in operation. And, indeed, in the aftermath of 9/11, despite Bush's appeals and his administration winning strong congressional support for a series of significant new legislative proposals in pursuit of its "war on terror," Bush did not win approval for *all* he wanted from the Congress[21]; and, occasionally, his administration had to succumb to some congressional preferences—consistent with ongoing executive-legislative "conversations" that resulted in some compromises and concessions in final legislation.[22] Congressional-presidential conversations can be one-sided, however. Congressionally imposed restrictions on presidential and executive action provide only part of the story. A more important question is the preponderant balance of relations both in respect to legislation and the extent to which the Congress effectively checked the Bush administration's aggressive presidentialist claims.

As far as legislation was concerned, the Bush administration demanded revised legal definitions of terrorism; new search, arrest, and surveillance powers; and huge increases in federal spending on the military, law enforcement, surveillance, database management, border control, capital control, and intelligence capacities—and Democratic and Republican majorities in the Congress largely agreed to these demands. Equally important, however, were the administration's unilateral actions, based both on dubious claims of "inherent" and "plenary" powers, and the expanded foundational authority provided by the Congress in the apparently limitless 2001 "use of force" resolution (PL 107-40), the PATRIOT Act, the 2002 Homeland Security Act and the Iraq "use of force" resolution, the 2005 USA PATRIOT and Terrorism Prevention Reauthorization, the 2005 Detainee Treatment Act, the 2006 Military Commissions Act, and the 2008 amendments to the 1978 Foreign Intelligence Surveillance Act.[23] On these bases, Bush administration officials effectively authorized and organized state kidnapping of alleged terrorists both in the United States and abroad ("extraordinary rendition"); interned suspects in military facilities in the United States and abroad without legal redress; sanctioned abuse and torture of detainees by US personnel, private contractors, and foreign governments; and authorized warrantless electronic surveillance. Although Congress undertook a considerable amount of oversight of the so-called war on terror, the effects on policy were marginal.[24] Most of the time, the Congress bent its knee to the administration,[25] under Democratic as well as Republican majorities. The typical pattern of policy making was one of strong executive action, with or without congressional knowledge or consent, and invariably accompanied by aggressive administration assertions of "inherent" executive power and/or foundational congressional

authorization. Sometimes, strong executive action was followed by partial congressional or judicial challenge (primarily but not exclusively from Democrats), and a certain amount of congressional-presidential negotiation with particularly skillful tactical plays by the administration (Howell and Kriner's "skillfully and accurately gauging congressional opposition").[26] But, regardless of whether or not the Congress collectively challenged the administration, ultimately, the legislature deferred to the president. Exceptions were rare; stunning congressional silences, inaction, and acquiescence were common.

OBAMA'S PRESIDENTIALISM AND THE "ONGOING STRUGGLE"

Bush's presidentialism, the accretion of presidential power under his administration, and the Congress's concomitant quiescence not only prompted important questions about unchecked executive power, but also—given its elite rather than popular origins[27]—whether, at least in respect to counterterrorism policy, the stretching of presidential power and the consequent shift in the balance of presidential-congressional relations would outlive Bush's presidency. Indeed, such a development was wholly predictable given the virtual blank check handed the president in the 2001 "use of force" resolution.

During his 2008 presidential election campaign, Senator Barack Obama strongly criticized the expansive nature of the 2001 and 2003 congressional "use of force" resolutions and the Bush administration's assertion of "plenary power" in the "war on terror." Specifically, he rejected "the view that the President may do whatever he deems necessary to protect national security," disavowed "the use of signing statements to make extreme and implausible claims of presidential authority," and promised to "follow existing law." "When it comes to US citizens and residents," he insisted, "I will only authorize surveillance for national security purposes consistent with Foreign Intelligence Surveillance Act (FISA) and other federal statutes."[28]

Once in office, President Obama rejected the "war on terror" nomenclature in favor of the "enduring struggle against terrorism and extremism" or the "ongoing struggle,"[29] and appointed as head of the Office of Legal Counsel (OLC) and Solicitor General prominent constitutional lawyers fiercely critical of the Bush administration's expansive view of executive power.[30] In his first two days in office, the new president also signed executive orders revoking the Bush administration's severe limits on public access to presidential records, closing Guantánamo promptly "consistent with the national security and foreign policy interests of the United States and the interests of justice" and ending the military tribunals, creating a special task force to review detainee policy, and prohibiting the CIA from maintaining its own prisons overseas; and at a stroke the new president revoked Bush's Executive Order (EO) 13440 (2007) and every executive directive, order, and regulation relating to the detention or interrogation of individuals issued by any executive branch lawyer after 9/11. The new administration also announced that primary authority over detention policies would move from the Pentagon to the Justice Department.

Inherent in the new president's statements and early actions was his signaling of a much less aggressive and more respectful approach to Congress, which was also reflected in statements by executive nominees during their Senate confirmation hearings. Obama's nominees for attorney general and CIA director, Eric Holder and Leon Panetta, for example, repeatedly stressed their wishes to work with Congress to write new detention and other antiterror legislation and keep legislators better informed of their activities. Echoing Obama's election pledge, Holder categorically rejected the view that the president possessed "inherent" power to override congressional statutes: "No one is above the law," he insisted. "The president has the constitutional obligation to make sure that the laws are faithfully executed."[31]

Ominously, however, these friendly statements had been preceded, following Obama's election victory, by former Vice President Cheney averring that the new president would "appreciate" the expansions of executive power achieved during the Bush administration and "not likely . . . cede that authority back to the Congress. I think they'll find that due to the challenges they face, they'll need all the authority they can muster."[32] Indeed, notwithstanding early eschewal of his predecessor's "inherent" powers doctrine and him proposing "conversations" with the Congress on new counterterror legislation, many of President Obama's subsequent actions have failed to confound Cheney's prediction and come to resemble the presidentialism evinced by his predecessor, albeit without some of the more confrontational public rhetoric.

Detainee Policy

While seeking to draw a line under the previous administration's policies, Obama's executive orders to close Guantánamo and the CIA's so-called black sites (where torture was endemic), suspend military commissions, and renounce the Bush administration's "enemy combatant" label for designating terrorist suspects were carefully written to include several subtle loopholes that left the new president with plenty of room for maneuver to continue many of the Bush administration's tough policies, beyond the public gaze.

Notwithstanding Obama demanding in May 2009 that the Congress write a new law of "preventive detention" coupled with a commitment to working with the Congress to "develop an appropriate legal regime so that our efforts are consistent with our values and our Constitution," the administration sent no new detainee legislation to the Congress. Instead, the administration opted to retain the Bush administration's policies of "prolonged" detention without trial, albeit within the US mainland rather than at Guantánamo, as well as by military commissions.[33] When liberals in the Congress controlled by his own party objected to the administration continuing previous policies and proposed new legislation on which House and Senate hearings were held in June and July 2009, Obama did not support it—preferring instead to retain discretion without a new congressional statute. Moreover, when the Congress fiercely resisted administration proposals in the FY 2010 Defense Appropriations bill to provide $100 million to facilitate the closure of Guantánamo and the transfer of fifty or so of more than two hundred terrorist suspects to the United States for trial in federal courts— and went so far as to prohibit any funds from being used for the transfer to, release, or incarceration of Guantánamo detainees in the United States—the White House loath to expend any more political capital than necessary in sorting out what it saw as a problem inherited from his predecessor signaled its preference for concentrating on other legislative issues and did not put up a fight.[34] Constrained by the Congress, the upshot was that the Obama administration retained the Bush administration's policy of indefinite detention without trial,[35] denied torture victims access to the US courts, and without congressional statute limited any executive accountability for the detention or brutalization of detainees held at Guantánamo or in secret prisons elsewhere.

In December 2011, congressional lawmakers went even further in seeking to limit the president's discretion in detaining alleged terrorists—evidently, against the wishes of the FBI, the Pentagon, and the Office of National Intelligence.[36] In the FY 2012 National Defense Authorization Act (NDAA), lawmakers continued to prohibit funds for the transfer of Guantánamo detainees to the United States or elsewhere but sought to expand further the detention authority implicitly granted the presidents in the 2001 use of force resolution. Effectively, by this legislation, the Congress gave the Obama administration—and its successors—the broad authority to detain individuals captured anywhere in the world indefinitely, in military rather than civilian custody without charge or trial, and regardless of whether they were actually involved in armed combat. The bill that passed the Republican-controlled House 322 votes to 96 would deny these prisoners access to the federal courts—*contra* the Court's 2008 *Boumediene* decision[37]—and provide the president with new authorization to use military force against terrorist organizations; while the Democratic-controlled Senate version (opposed by the administration but approved 93-7) would have made it almost impossible for any suspect to be tried in a federal court and would have consolidated exclusive military control over detainees. Senator Lindsey Graham (R-SC) reflected the strength of congressional sentiment:

> We need to let this President know, and every other President . . . that if you capture someone in the homeland, on our soil—American citizen or not—who is a member of al-Qaida, you do not have to give them a lawyer or read them the rights automatically. You can treat them as a military threat under military custody, just like if you captured them overseas.[38]

An amendment offered by Mark Udall (D-NM) to strike the provision denying access to the federal courts and allow the administration to devise a new plan failed 38-60, as sixteen Democrats joined forty-four Republicans in opposition. Another amendment offered by Dianne Feinstein (D-CA), which would limit mandatory military custody to those captured outside the United States, failed 45-55, with only three Republicans voting in favor. The bill that emerged from the conference committee dropped the House provisions banned using civilian courts to prosecute terrorist suspects and a new authorization to use military force against terrorist organizations, but included a Senate provision further enhancing the 2001 "use of force" resolution by authorizing the detainment without trial of suspected members of terrorist organizations or their allies or those who "substantially supported" them. Obama threatened to veto the bill on the grounds that it would infringe on executive branch powers, limiting presidential discretion in dealing with accused terrorists, but ultimately signed it with "serious reservations" stating that he would "not authorize the indefinite military detention without trial of American citizens."

Amid fears voiced by conservatives as well as liberals that US citizens could be sent to Guantánamo by any future president,[39] and provisions of the bill being challenged in the courts, various bills were introduced into Congress designed to prohibit the administration from detaining any US citizens or permanent residents against their will without due process. However, in its FY 2013 NDAA approved in December 2012, the Congress again insisted on the same controversial provisions, which were overwhelmingly approved in both chambers notwithstanding inclusion of an apparently meaningless amendment that reasserted US citizens' rights to *habeas corpus* while denying these rights to terrorist suspects.[40] A Senate-approved amendment offered by liberal Feinstein and conservative Mike Lee (R-UT), which would prohibit detention without charge or trial of US citizens accused of terrorism and apprehended in the United States without Congress's express authorization, was opposed in the House and dropped in the conference committee.

Lawmakers, then, were certainly active in seeking to restrict the rights of terrorist suspects—and restrict the administration's discretion to a much greater extent than it wished—and as a result the president was denied his wish to close Guantánamo and no detainee identified for release by the administration's review task force has been certified for transfer overseas or to the United States in over two years.[41] Yet, at the same time, congressional assertiveness was *ad hoc*, and potentially threatening to the civil liberties of US citizens. Despite the numbers of detainees increasing since Obama took office, neither the administration nor lawmakers have made concerted efforts to write a new general legislative framework governing who may be detained, a coherent set of evidentiary and procedural rules to determine who is an enemy, or guidance in respect to the government's obligation to disclose evidence to detainees' lawyers or on the rights of detainees. The consequence was that the president has continued to determine detainee policy more or less unilaterally—which, of course, was his intention in resisting congressional restrictions. However, leaving discretion to the president has also meant that detainee policy is *ad hoc* because, in the absence of congressional statute, the US District Court in Washington, D.C., to whom Congress delegated responsibility, must hand down judgments and create a *de facto* legal framework case-by-case[42] according to "different rules and procedures . . . different rules of evidence . . . [and] substantive law."[43]

Not that the administration has welcomed court interventions any more than those by the Congress. Thus, when suspected terrorists held in detention sought *habeas corpus* relief pursuant to the *Boumediene* decision, Obama's Justice Department filed legal memoranda in the US District Court in Washington, D.C. holding to the Bush administration's position that the president had the unilateral authority (based on the 2001 congressional "use of force" resolution and law-of-war principles, which Obama had condemned as a senator and presidential candidate) to detain terrorist suspects indefinitely without criminal charges or *habeas corpus* rights, even when originally detained outside a traditional "battlefield"[44] and moved around the world by the administration, beyond the reach of the US Constitution, effectively subjected to indefinite detention without trial. The Obama administration used the same law-of-war principles as its predecessor in a further two hundred cases.[45]

Furthermore, following the passage of the FY 2010 DDAA enacting restrictions on the transfer of detainees from Guantánamo, instead of going to the Congress with a new set of proposals for the detention of terrorist suspects (including those already at Guantánamo), Obama again opted for unilateral action to maintain more or less the same position as its predecessor: by the stroke of his pen, he rescinded his 2009 order suspending the Bush administration's military trials, issued a new executive order (13567) that deployed the same laws-of-war justification as his predecessor. Effectively, the president formalized indefinite detention and trial by military commission outside the US judicial system, and without external independent review.[46] Although evidence obtained via "cruel" or "inhuman" means would not be admissible and detainees would be given access to defense lawyers, be able to file *habeas corpus* petitions in the federal courts, and forsee the prospect of being released, the 2012 DDA effectively made release or transfer of many detainees impossible. Given the failure of the administration and the Congress to pass statutory legislation governing detainees, although Obama's unilateral action had the inadvertent consequence of detoxifying once-controversial indefinite detention policies introduced by the Bush administration policies, it left him with more discretion than he would have obtained from a Congress likely determined to approve even more draconian detention measures to deal with high-profile terrorist suspects.

Drone Targeting and State Assassinations of Terrorist Suspects Outside the United States

In a second and increasingly central area of US counterterrorism policy, the Obama administration has been even more unilateralist in its approach to terrorist suspects located outside the United States, and congressional-presidential relations have been even more one-sided.

In his 2008 presidential election campaign, Senator Obama coupled withdrawing the US troops from Iraq with more concentrated efforts on destroying al Qaeda and other terrorist networks outside the United States, notably those in Pakistan.[47] Indeed, while often criticizing President Bush for being too aggressive in many of his counterterrorism policies and actions, Obama was critical of his predecessor for not being aggressive enough in "go [ing] after al Qaeda's leadership." "I would be clear," he told the *Washington Post*, "that if Pakistan cannot or will not take out al Qaeda leadership when we have actionable intelligence about their whereabouts, we will act to protect the American people. There can be no safe haven for al Qaeda terrorists who killed thousands of Americans and threaten our homeland today."[48]

Just three days after assuming office, Obama followed through by authorizing an armed drone strike in the tribal areas of Pakistan, in the process reportedly killing numerous innocent people as well as "a high-value target."[49] Although barely acknowledged, since 2008 the Obama administration has made much greater use of armed Predator drones, controlled remotely from a base in Saudi Arabia or elsewhere, to find and kill terrorist suspects, including US citizens, and Taliban leaders.[50] The culmination of this policy was, of course, the targeted killing of Osama bin Laden by US Special Forces in Pakistan in May 2011. The US military have not conducted these operations, however, as part of some general orders from the president in pursuance of a declared war. Rather, the president himself has been intimately involved in targeting and attack decisions—evoking older images of President Lyndon Johnson personally determining bombing targets in Vietnam in the 1960s. According to interviews with Obama's current and former advisers, the president has "placed himself at the helm of a top secret 'nominations' process to designate terrorists for kill or capture, of which the capture part has become largely theoretical . . . approving every new name on an expanding 'kill list,' poring over terrorist suspects' biographies . . . personally overseeing the shadow war with Al Qaeda . . . even when it comes to killing an American cleric in Yemen."[51] It was not surprising then that when bin Laden was killed, the president claimed some personal political credit.

Like its predecessor, the Obama administration justified these targeted killings by invoking the same legal rationale and the same foundational legislation as the Bush administration to stretch presidential power *viz.* "as an act of national self-defense" consistent with the Congress's 2001 use of force resolution, which authorized the president "to use all necessary and appropriate force,"[52] even though the United States is not formally at war. Taking unilateral presidential action to help find and kill terrorist suspects, of course, had the double political advantage for the Obama administration of eliminating (or at least minimizing) US casualties—unless, of course, the suspects were US citizens[53] —and, equally important, of avoiding the complications of detention and trial of suspects at Guantánamo and elsewhere that the current and previous administrations encountered[54]: simply, if the United States did not capture terrorist suspects (and almost invariably it did not), the number of suspects held at Guantánamo and elsewhere did not increase and the use of military commissions or civilian courts became moot.[55]

Still, the Congress has not given formal specific authority for these high-technology assassinations, which the administration calls "acts of war." Nor has the Obama administration gone out of its way to converse with the Congress on these targeted killings—which might readily be characterized as extrajudicial executions. Seventy years ago, following the bombing of Pearl Harbor, Franklin Roosevelt asked the Congress for a declaration of war against Imperial Japan, and followed several days later with separate requests for declarations against Nazi Germany and Fascist Italy. Rather, like its predecessor, the Obama administration relied for its legal and constitutional authority on the Congress's 2001 resolution, which provided for no geographic or time limits for presidential action against those who "planned, authorized, committed or aided" the 9/11 attacks, as well as on legal precedents. Like the Bush administration, which conducted military and intelligence operations in almost any state around the world without any time limit, the Obama administration has exploited the expansive nature of this resolution to launch antiterrorist operations, including drone attacks and targeted assassinations in Libya, Pakistan, Somalia, Yemen, and most recently in or from Burkina Faso, Djibouti, Ethiopia, Mali, and Niger,[56] often without that country's authorization.

For its part, the Congress collectively has made next to no effort to conduct oversight, let alone expand or restrict the 2001 use of force resolution, notwithstanding the important question as to whether "killings carried out in 2012 [or later] can be justified as in response to [events] in 2001"[57] and the simple fact that the process of targeting and killing alleged terrorists provides for no due process or for the person being charged formally with a crime or convicted at trial. Certainly, the Congress has not launched anything like the Church Committee's or subsequent efforts to regulate CIA activities, which led to a ban on state assassinations,[58] let alone write statutory guidelines for these operations[59] —or, for that matter, legislate immunity from prosecution by some jurisdiction or international tribunal for civilian or military personnel who carry them out. The Oversight and Government Reform Committee's National Security and Foreign Affairs Subcommittee convened hearings in 2010, as it was particularly concerned that targeted killings by drones might be illegal under international law. However, the committee was very careful to limits the testimony it received. Most importantly, the United Nations's special rapporteur on extrajudicial killings, summary or arbitrary executions, Christof Heyns, was not called, and no legislation was forthcoming.

Republican Senator Roy Blunt (R-MO) tentatively raised issues of oversight and accountability in regard to drones and targeted killings during Senate Intelligence committee hearings on the nomination of David Petraeus as CIA Director in June 2011, only to be put off by Committee Chair Feinstein. With the administration's targeted killing of three US citizens suspected of membership of al Qaeda in Yemen in late September 2011, however, the Congress became a little more testy. Republican and Democratic members of Congress sent letters asking the administration to explain the legal justification for the deaths.[60] No answers were forthcoming. Demands by various senators, including Feinstein, Ron Wyden (D-OR), Patrick Leahy (D-VT), Charles Grassley (R-IA), and John Cornyn (R-TX)—that the administration release an OLC memo outlining what, if any, authority the president was acting under—also went unanswered. Apparently, Obama's OLC had prepared a lengthy secret legal memorandum justifying the president's action, which asserted that due process required by the Fifth Amendment applied and that this *requirement could be satisfied by internal deliberations within the executive branch.*[61] A Department of Justice White Paper (not the OLC's memo) sent to lawmakers seven months after the assassination of a suspected US terrorist in Yemen, and subsequently leaked to "NBC News" in advance of Senate Select Intelligence Committee hearings on the nomination of John Brennan as CIA director, provided further details of the administration's justifications. Citing the United States' right to self-defense as well as the laws of war as justification, the paper troublingly asserted that it would be lawful to target and kill a US citizen (without charge or trial) if *"an* [undefined-JEO] *informed, high-level official"* *of the government decided* that the target was a ranking al-Qaeda figure who posed "an imminent threat of violent attack against the United States" and if his or her capture was not feasible.[62] During the Brennan hearings, Feinstein complained that the CIA had told her that she could not disclose publicly the number of civilians inadvertently killed each year by drone attacks, which she suggested "has typically been in the single digits," even though other sources suggest the number was much higher. Other senators suggested that an independent court should review drone-targeting decisions in the same way that the FISA court reviews secret intelligence eavesdropping warrants. Nonetheless, by February 2013, neither the Senate Intelligence nor the Armed Services committee had convened a hearing on drones and targeted killing, despite an estimated 3,500 people dying in 420 drone strikes.[63]

The Obama administration justifications betrayed the same expansive unilateralist approach and presidentialist tone as its predecessor. Leaving aside that the administration was operating in countries with which the United States is not formally at war and that the law it apparently drew on to justify its actions was secret (a practice frequently used by the Bush administration and condemned in Senate testimony by Obama's first choice as head of the OLC), the assertions and justifications embodied in this secret legal memo from Obama's OLC were substantively indistinguishable from the Bush's secret legal memos published by the Obama administration on assuming office in 2009 and justifying abusive interrogation techniques. Most important for the purposes of congressional (and possibly judicial) oversight, the memo did not indicate specific thresholds of evidence seen as sufficient to trigger an assassination, which would necessarily be far from any battlefield. Not limited to attacks in progress, moreover, its definition of "imminent threat" was very elastic. Notwithstanding the memo's assertion that the president's power "is subject to appropriate limitations and safeguards," its terms aped the separationist tone of the Bush legal memos in specifically excluding the courts from reviewing or restraining such executive/presidential decisions, and, indeed, the paper argued that courts and the Congress did not have the right to rule on or intervene when decisions were made "in the heat of battle." While refusing to release the OLC's memo, the best oversight mechanism that Attorney General Eric Holder allowed was that "the Executive Branch regularly informs the appropriate members of Congress about [their] counterterrorism activities . . . where lethal force is used."[64]

As, however, congressional and public pressure mounted, the issues surrounding the legality of the targeted killing program and the extent of congressional oversight acquired a distinct partisan hue. Although Democratic Judiciary Committee Chair Leahy again asked Holder for sight of the OLC's memo in March 2012, he did not press the issue.[65] Four months later, as the Judiciary committee considered the must-pass 2012 intelligence authorization bill, an amendment offered by Republican Senators Cornyn and Grassley mandating the administration to share its OLC memo with the Congress was voted down by Democrats. In the colloquy that followed Cornyn and Grassley offering their amendment, it became unclear as to which members of the so-called Gang of Eight, who are supposed to receive intelligence briefings from the administration, were actually told of the drone strikes, and at what stage in the decision process. Committee Democratic Senator Dianne Feinstein (D-CA), who also chaired the Senate Select Committee on Intelligence, was dismissive: Feinstein asserted that she and the committee's Republican ranking member "provide[d] all the oversight on this front that is needed" (rather than the entire "Gang of Eight"), and briefings on targeted killings are provided "sometimes before, sometimes during, sometimes just after."[66] According to the *Los Angeles Times*, these briefings—instigated by Feinstein—were apparently informal and after-the-event, and amounted to "a group of staff members from the House and Senate intelligence committees [and sometimes Congress members] driv[ing] across the Potomac River to CIA headquarters in Virginia, assembl[ing] in a secure room and begin[ning] the grim task of watching videos of the latest drone strikes. . . . [Apparently, i]f the congressional committees objected to something, the lawmakers could call CIA leaders to testify in closed investigative hearings. If unsatisfied, they could pass legislation limiting the CIA's actions." At least one House Democrat member of the House Intelligence Committee was satisfied: "If the American people were sitting in the room [during these presentations]," he averred, "they would feel comfortable that it was being done in a responsible way."[67] Besides, many Congress members, including most Republicans, agreed with the administration that it already has "both the authority and the obligation to defend the country."[68]

Certainly, this kind of informal monitoring is part of the congressional oversight process. Leaving aside important policy questions over the long-term effectiveness of the program in reducing terrorism, and whether or not so-called collateral damage (i.e., killing innocent, even anti-al Qaeda, civilians, including family members) is justified and may actually have negative consequences[69] —all matters that might well be the subject of congressional investigation—the major weakness of these and other oversight efforts is lawmakers' failure to write any statutory guidance, which might limit—or at least regulate—a president's authority to conduct these actions in countries with which the United States is not formally at war. Absent that statutory framework, the president authorizes the use of force *ad hoc* and unilaterally, in the process risking violating the rule of law in the United States and international legal norms. As former Bush's CIA director, Michael Hayden, has observed: "Secrecy has its costs . . . This program rests on the personal legitimacy of the president, and that's not sustainable. I have lived the life of someone taking action on the basis of secret OLC memos, and it ain't a good life. Democracies do not make war on the basis of legal memos locked in a DOJ safe."[70]

Amongst the questions left open by unchecked presidential authority is how terrorist suspects are included on the administration's "kill list," including when it is targeting its own citizens to be killed. Despite Obama originally campaigning against the Bush administration's increased use of the state's secrets doctrine, in respect to targeted assassinations (and other aspects of US counterterrorism policy), his administration continued to draw on this doctrine as justification *not* to provide the Congress with information, including how a "kill list" is compiled. The blank check provided by the Congress in September 2001, and used both by the Bush and Obama administrations to justify their actions, is hardly consistent with the US Constitution, which supposed that the Congress will monitor, challenge, and ultimate prevent the overreach of unilateral presidential power. Leaving aside the risks of violating international legal norms and that US action might encourage other states, like North Korea and Iran, to do the same, allowing the president to order targeted killing without congressional limits provides any president with the opportunity to manipulate force in the name of national security, as some previous presidents have done.[71] Conversely, if guidelines are debated and understood, decisions to execute are likely to acquire much greater public legitimacy and support. The Congress has a constitutional obligation to determine when force is appropriate—under what circumstances the president can authorize the killing of an individual once he or she joins a particular organized group—and a constitutional right to be briefed by the president on how his or her proposed targeted killings comply with congressional guidelines. "Oddly," a former general counsel to the Senate Select Committee on Intelligence and former deputy legal adviser to the CIA's Counterterrorism Center has observed, "under current law, Congress and the courts are involved when presidents eavesdrop on Americans, detain them or harshly interrogate them—but not when they kill them."[72] As on detainee policy, so with targeted assassinations, lawmakers have not risen to the task of conducting meaningful oversight or accepting responsibility for determining policy.[73] Indeed, besides likely violating "the sovereignty of more countries, more times, than any other administration,"[74] at least some aspects of the targeted killing program might well be unconstitutional.[75] Still, when several senators suggested to CIA nominee Brennan in January 2013 that the Congress might create a special court similar to the FISA Court to review killing targets, the idea was scotched as divisions quickly emerged as to how this might be achieved while others dismissed the notion as an intrusion on the president's authority as commander in chief.[76]

Rendition and Torture

In his 2008 presidential election campaign, Obama insisted that "America doesn't torture and I'm going to make sure that we don't torture. Those are part and parcel of an effort to regain America's moral stature in the world."[77] These commitments were intended to contrast with the policies, actions, and constitutional justifications claimed for those policies and actions by the Bush administration.[78] On the basis of legal advice from Bush's Attorney General Alberto Gonzales that "a new kind of war . . . renders obsolete Geneva's strict limitations on questioning of enemy prisoners and renders quaint some of its provisions,"[79] President Bush had written a classified memorandum to administration officials insisting that, although the United States would continue to treat detainees humanely and support the Geneva Conventions, none of the Geneva Conventions would apply to al Qaeda.[80] Claiming "inherent" and "plenary" powers, Bush authorized and organized state kidnapping of alleged terrorists both in the United States and abroad ("extraordinary rendition"), and sanctioned abuse and torture of detainees by US personnel, private contractors, and foreign government. On the basis of these huge claims for the president's incidental power, reinforced by secret legal memoranda beyond congressional or public discussion or debate, the Bush administration unilaterally reformulated US torture policy without seeking or being subject to new congressional legislation, and in the process ignored existing US statutory and international treaty obligations.[81] Indeed, as in other areas, the implicit and often explicit assumption in Bush's separationist approach to governing—and especially in respect to his so-called war on terror—was a rejection of congressional challenges and interventions, which were not only unwelcome but more often than not actively and successfully deterred. For their part, members of Congress typically found it difficult or impossible to muster collective political will to coordinate and formulate timely and forceful rebuffs to aggressive executive claims justifying unilateral action. Many were only too ready to give away or delegate their powers to the executive.

Certainly, the Congress undertook oversight during the Bush administration—and a considerable amount of it, including a six-thousand-page report on abuse of terrorist suspects after 9/11[82] —but lawmakers were generally quiescent. Following press reports of prisoner abuse, torture, rape, and murder at Abu Ghraib and elsewhere, and the findings of the Taguba military inquiry, lawmakers passed the McCain amendment, which became the 2005 Detainee Treatment Act, but this legislation essentially confirmed existing legislation and, more importantly, included the Graham-Kyl amendment, by which for the first time the Congress legitimated the use of torture by allowing the courts to consider evidence obtained through torture.[83] Even then, Bush refused to accept congressional intervention.[84] Even after the Supreme Court criticized the administration in its 2006 *Hamdan vs. Rumsfeld* decision for allowing suspects brought before military tribunals to be convicted on evidence that might have been extracted by torture, the Senate rejected on a party-line vote an amendment proposed by Senator Edward Kennedy (D-MA) to the Military Commissions Act that sought to prohibit specific interrogation techniques, including waterboarding, and then in 2007, an amendment to the conference report on the FY 2008 intelligence authorization bill banning the CIA and all other US intelligence agencies from using harsh interrogation techniques died when the House sustained President Bush's veto.[85]

Once elected, Obama coupled aggressive counterterrorism policies in respect to drone strikes, military commissions, indefinite detention, and the PATRIOT Act with new limitations on prisoner abuse. In the absence of significant congressional action, one of the new president's first acts was to issue EO 13491, which restricted those interrogating suspects "in armed conflicts" to a list of "nonabusive" tactics approved in the Army Field Manual and excluded waterboarding used by the Bush administration. Still, although Obama's executive order apparently ruled out torture and abuse, its careful wording left the new president with plenty of discretion and did not restrict the continuation of "extraordinary rendition."[86] Like Bush's actions, Obama's more expansive definition of torture and policy revisions was implemented by unilateral presidential action, without congressional statute. Obama or a successor could very well issue another executive order rescinding the old one. Indeed, fears about the integrity of the new policies were raised almost immediately when the new president proceeded to nominate as CIA director, John Brennan, who been the CIA director's chief of staff. Ultimately, Brennan was forced to withdraw,[87] but Obama's second choice, Leon Panetta, also failed to assuage many congressional concerns: while promising to keep the Congress better apprised of the CIA's activities, Panetta told the Senate Intelligence Committee in January 2009 that, in certain circumstances, he would seek presidential approval for the CIA to use methods that went beyond the president's new order; he left open whether such methods would amount to torture, as defined by congressional legislation.[88]

As with the Bush administration, congressional oversight of Obama's actions in respect to torture and extraordinary rendition has been problematic. Like its predecessor, the Obama administration has frequently invoked the "state's secrets" doctrine to suppress evidence and shut down cases when plaintiffs have reached the federal courts to allege extraordinary rendition and torture, as in early February 2009 in a case before the Ninth Circuit Appeals Court involving a Guantánamo detainee.[89] Similarly, it has kept classified the results and recommendations of its Special Task Force on Interrogations and Transfer Policies. Nonetheless, in early 2009, while announcing that it would continue to send individuals to other countries, ostensibly contrary to the Bush administration's stance, the Obama administration would seek "assurances from the receiving country" that a suspect would not be tortured.[90] The Obama administration has also "placed a much greater emphasis on asking foreign intelligence and security services to take the lead in arresting terrorism suspects around the world,"[91] often in countries known to abuse suspects, including Afghanistan.[92] With the administration unwilling to incarcerate more suspects in military custody at Guantánamo or elsewhere, and the Congress unwilling to allow trials of terrorist suspects in civil courts in the United States, the administration has combined targeted killing with an active renditions policy, which in late 2012 resulted in three Europeans with Somali backgrounds being secretly arrested and detained in Djibouti, having committed no crime in that country, and clandestinely rendered by the FBI into a New York court, where they were indicted under US law.[93]

CONGRESSIONAL-PRESIDENTIAL RIVALRY?

Since 9/11, congressional-presidential relations in respect to US counterterrorism policy provide few examples of vigorous institutional rivalry, let alone congressional dominance.[94] Certainly, the Obama administration's public interpretation of the separated system is some distance from the Bush administration's aggressive unitary executive doctrine, but the accretion of presidential power in this expanding area of policy has continued unabated, and often by stealth—notwithstanding some softening of tone, rhetoric, and policy packaging, and some congressional challenges, which have constrained the president's discretion. Indeed, in regard to targeted assassinations, drone attacks, and the military campaigns in Afghanistan and Pakistan, the Obama administration enhanced executive power even further than Bush. But, it is important to note that even the most significant congressional check on the administration's counterterrorism policies—over Guantánamo—had the intended effect of *maintaining* rather than weakening executive discretion and the unintended effect of propelling the administration into new areas where it could exercise maximum discretion without congressional scrutiny *viz.* targeted assassinations. Other significant attempts by lawmakers to monitor and curtail executive power failed, notably over targeting killing, state secrets, torture, and a detention-policy framework.

Why the balance of power is so tilted toward the president is explained first by strong and continued government and public perceptions of terrorist attacks, notwithstanding the actual risk to life remaining far less than the perception.[95] Reinforcing Obama's unilateralism was the knowledge gained early in his presidency—and especially after the Fort Hood shootings in November 2009 and the Christmas Day attempts to blow up an airliner in Detroit—that a single successful terrorist attack would not only validate Republican criticisms of his administration as being "soft" on terrorism, but also jeopardize the priority given by the president to his domestic-policy agenda.

Second, notwithstanding the United States' separated system, as commentators from Machiavelli forward have observed, the executive is far better placed than a legislature to take the policy initiative, and act swiftly and decisively at a time of national danger.[96] And, in the contemporary period, US presidents have been good at assuming the mantle of a plebiscitary leader[97] in times of national danger, in so doing clothing themselves in symbolic authority and applying appropriate security rhetoric and public appeals.

Obama's counterterrorism rhetoric has been more nuanced and his policy actions more softly packaged than Bush's. His counterterrorism policies have also focused primarily outside the United States, but their effect on the balance of presidential-congressional power has been the same. Strong presidential and executive action has been reinforced by broad public and legislative support, even when actions touch on civil liberties. Poll results show strong public support for and acceptance of counterterrorism measures,[98] including use of intelligence obtained through torture.[99] When, moreover, a terrorist attack has occurred or been foiled—as in 2009 in Detroit—public pressure mounts and presidents are bound to act, often at the expense of civil liberties, particularly among those most concerned about being a terrorist victim.[100] Ultimately, as with the Bush administration, public safety and strong executive power trumped the Madisonian expectation that "ambition [would] counteract ambition," and lead to vigorous congressional oversight and regulation of the Obama administration's discretion. From the perspective of early 2013, the practice of the Obama administration's counterterrorism policies and the inability—or unwillingness—of the Congress to challenge the president collectively on these issues, provides further evidence of the consolidation of the new constitutional equilibrium wrought by Bush and 9/11.[101] Presidential power is not only the power to persuade, it is also about what a president can get away with—and whether the Congress and the courts will stop him or her. As this discussion has shown, the Obama administration, like its predecessor, went to great lengths both to protect presidential and executive privileges and to resist accountability by the Congress and the courts. Twelve years after 9/11, we can already see the continuation of a presidential shift of power to the executive instigated by George W. Bush.

NOTES

1. I am grateful for the interview time and assistance with this project provided by various House and Senate committee staffers and the congenial intellectual home provided by Jim Thurber at the Center for Congressional and Presidential Studies, American University, Washington, D.C.

2. Gary C. Jacobson, *A Divider, Not a Uniter: George W. Bush and the American Public* (New York: Longman, 2006); Gary C. Jacobson, "Public Opinion and the Presidency: The Obama and Anti-Obama Coalitions," in Bert A. Rockman, Andrew Rudalevige and Colin Campbell, eds., *The Obama Presidency: Appraisals and Prospects* (Washington, DC: CQ Press, 2010), 94–122; Gary C. Jacobson, "Legislative Success and Political Failure: The Public's Reaction to Barack Obama's Early Presidency," *Presidential Studies Quarterly* 41, no. 2 (2011): 220–43; Barbara Sinclair, *Party Wars: Polarization and the Politics of National Policymaking* (Norman: University of Oklahoma Press, 2006).

3. Terry M. Moe, "The Politicized Presidency," in John E. Chubb and Paul E. Peterson, eds., *The New Direction in American Politics* (Washington, DC: Brookings Institution, 1985), 235–71.

4. Kenneth R. Mayer, "Executive Orders and Presidential Power," *Journal of Politics* 62, no. 2 (1999): 445–66; Kenneth R. Mayer, *With the Stroke of a Pen: Executive Orders and Presidential Power* (Princeton, NJ: Princeton University Press, 2001).

5. Edward Corwin, *The President: Office and Powers* (New York: New York University Press, 1948), 304–5.

6. Edward Corwin, *Total War and the Constitution* (New York: Ayer Co., 1947); John P. Roche, "Executive Power and the Domestic Presidency: The Quest for Prerogative," *Western Political Quarterly* 5, no. 4, (December 1952): 592–618.

7. Louis Fisher, *Presidential War Power*, 2nd rev. ed. (Lawrence: University Press of Kansas, 2004).

8. Richard P. Nathan, *The Administrative Presidency* (New York: Wiley, 1983); Phillip J. Cooper, "George W. Bush, Edgar Allan Poe, and the Use and Abuse of Presidential Signing Statements," *Presidential Studies Quarterly* 35, no. 3 (September 2005): 515–32.

9. Louis Fisher, *The Politics of Executive Privilege* (Durham, NC: Carolina Academic Press, 2004), 134–61; Fisher, *Presidential War Power*; Francine Kiefer, "Clinton Perfects the Art of Go-Alone Governing: Feeling Stymied by GOP on Hill, President Pushes Agenda through Executive Orders, Vetoes, and Publicity," *Christian Science Monitor*, July 24, 1998, 3; Andrew Rudalevige, *The New Imperial Presidency: Renewing Presidential Power After Watergate* (Ann Arbor: The University of Michigan Press, 2005); Charles Tiefer, *The Semi-Sovereign Presidency: The Bush Administration's Strategy for Governing without Congress* (Boulder, CO, and Oxford: Westview Press, 1994), 1–5.

10. Walter Dean Burnham, "Constitutional Moments and Punctuated Equilibria: A Political Scientist Confronts Bruce Ackerman's *We the People*," *The Yale Law Journal* 108 (1999): 2239.

11. John E. Owens, "Presidential Aggrandizement and Congressional Acquiescence in the 'War on Terror': A New Constitutional Equilibrium?," in John E. Owens and John W. Dumbrell, eds., *America's "War On Terrorism": New Dimensions in United States Government and National Security* (Lanham, MD and Oxford: Lexington Books, 2008), 25–76.

12. Jack L. Goldsmith, *The Terror Presidency: Law and Judgment Inside the Bush Administration* (New York: Norton, 2007), 85–88; Barton Gellman, *Angler: The Cheney Vice Presidency* (New York: Penguin, 2008), 100–2; Alexis Simendinger, "Andy Card on Power and Privilege," *National Journal*, April 17, 2004, 1173.

13. Steven G. Calabresi and Kevin H. Rhodes, "The Structural Constitution: Unitary Executive, Plural Judiciary," *Harvard Law Review* 105 (1992): 1153–216; Steven G. Calabresi, "Some Normative Arguments for the Unitary Executive," *Arkansas Law Review*, 48, no. 23 (1995): 90–104; Steven G. Calabresi and Saikrishna B. Prakash, "The President's Power to Execute the Laws," *Yale Law Journal* 104 (1994): 541–665; Christopher S. Yoo and Steven G. Calabresi, "The Unitary Executive during the Second Half-Century," *The Harvard Journal of Law & Public Policy* 26, no. 3 (June 2003): 668–802; Christopher Yoo, Steven G. Calabresi,

and Anthony J. Colangelo, "The Unitary Executive in the Modern Era, 1945–2004," *Iowa Law Review* 90, no. 2 (2005): 601–732.

14. Charles O. Jones, "The US Congress and Chief Executive George W. Bush," in George C. Edwards and Desmond S. King, *The Polarised Presidency of George W. Bush* (Oxford and New York: Oxford University Press, 2007), 401.

15. Charles O. Jones, "Capitalizing on Position in a Perfect Tie," in Fred I. Greenstein, ed., *The George W. Bush Presidency: An Early Assessment* (Baltimore, MD: The Johns Hopkins University Press, 2003), 173–96.

16. Jones, "The US Congress and Chief Executive George W. Bush," 399.

17. Richard E. Neustadt, *Presidential Power and the Modern Presidents: The Politics of Leadership from Roosevelt to Reagan* (New York: Free Press, 1990), 150.

18. Theodore J. Lowi, *The Personal President: Power Invested, Promise Unfulfilled* (Ithaca, NY: Cornell University Press, 1986); Samuel Kernell, *Going Public: New Strategies of Presidential Leadership* (Washington, DC: CQ Press, 2007), 18–27.

19. Jones, "The US Congress and Chief Executive George W. Bush," 400–1.

20. Bob Woodward, *Bush at War* (New York and London: Simon & Schuster, 2002), 256.

21. John E. Owens, "Rivals Only Sometimes: Presidentialism, Unilateralism, and Congressional Acquiescence in the US 'War on Terror,'" in James A. Thurber, ed., *Rivals for Power: Presidential-Congressional Relations* (Lanham, MD: Rowman & Littlefield, 2009), 309–24.

22. Charles O. Jones, *The Presidency in a Separated System*, 2nd ed. (Washington, DC: The Brookings Institution); Barbara Sinclair, "The President and the Congressional Party Leadership in a Polarized Era," in James A. Thurber, ed., *Rivals for Power: Presidential-Congressional Relations* (Lanham, MD: Rowman & Littlefield, 2009).

23. Louis Fisher, "Invoking Inherent Powers: A Primer," *Presidential Studies Quarterly* 41, no. 1 (2007): 1–22; Nancy Kassop, "A Political Question by Any Other Name: Government Litigation Strategy in the Enemy Combatant Cases of Hamdi and Padilla," in Nada Mourtada-Sabbah and Bruce E. Cain, eds., *The Political Question Doctrine and the Supreme Court of the United States* (Lanham, MD: Lexington Books, 2007); Owens, "Rivals Only Sometimes."

24. Owens, "Rivals Only Sometimes."

25. William G. Howell and Douglas L. Kriner, "Bending So as Not to Break: What the Bush Presidency Reveals about the Politics of Unilateral Action," in George C. Edwards and Desmond S. King, eds., *The Polarized Presidency of George W. Bush* (New York: Oxford University Press, 2007), 96–141.

26. Howell and Kriner, "Bending So as Not to Break."

27. Bruce Ackerman, "Revolution on a Human Scale," *The Yale Law Journal* 108 (1999): 2312.

28. Charlie Savage, "Barack Obama's Q&A," *Boston Globe*, December 20, 2007, www.boston.com/news/politics/2008/specials/CandidateQA/ObamaQA/. Subsequently, however, Senator Obama voted for the FISA Bill in June 2008, which allowed retroactive amnesty for telecomm companies for participating in Bush administration's illegal spying program on American citizens.

29. Barack Obama, interview with Al Arabiya News Channel, January 27, 2009, www.alarabiya.net/articles/2009/01/27/65087.html#004.

30. Eric Lichtblau, "Obama Pick to Analyze Broad Powers of President," *New York Times*, January 8, 2009.

31. US Congress, Senate Committee on the Judiciary Hearings, Executive Nomination of Eric H. Holder Jr. to be Attorney General of the United States, 111th Congress, First Session, January 15, 2009.

32. Quoted in Alexander Bolton, "Cheney Says Obama Should Be Grateful to Bush," *The Hill*, December 15, 2008.

33. Peter Baker and David Herszenhorn, "Obama Planning to Keep Tribunals for Detainees," *New York Times*, May 14, 2009; William Glaberson, "U.S. Won't Label Terror Suspects as 'Combatants,'" *New York Times*, March 13, 2009; Barack Obama, "Remarks by the President on National Security," National Archives, Washington, DC, Office of the Press Secretary, The White House, May 21, 2009.

34. Although Secretary of State Hillary Clinton and Attorney General Eric Holder had offered to fight for the legislation (see Jo Becker and Scott Shane, "Secret 'Kill List' Proves a Test of Obama's Principles and Will," *New York Times*, May 29, 2012), such was public, media, and congressional hostility to terrorist suspects being tried in US civil courts that many civil liberties groups feared that, had the Congress asserted itself collectively and repealed or at least amended its 2001 use of force resolution so as to confine the president's discretion, legislators might very well have enacted an indefinite detention law that would not be limited by wartime conditions and, therefore, have serious implications for civil liberties in peacetime (see Peter Finn, "Administration Won't Seek New Detention System," *Washington Post*, September 24, 2009).

35. Several news stories documented the Obama administration's secret detention of terrorist suspects outside the US criminal justice system, including on a warship (e.g., Ken Dilanian, "Terrorism Suspect Secretly Held for Two Months," *Los Angeles Times*, July 6, 2011), and in Afghanistan, Iraq, and Somalia (Rod Nordland, "Detainees Are Handed Over to Afghans, but Not Out of Americans' Reach," *New York Times*, May 30, 2012; Ned Parker, "Secret Prison Revealed in Baghdad," *Los Angeles Times*, April 19, 2010). Apparently, by the end of 2011, some three thousand detainees were held at Parwan in Afghanistan, formerly Bagram (Rendition Research Team, "Secret Detention: Indefinite (Non-secret) Military Detention," University of Kent, Canterbury, UK, 2012, www.therenditionproject.org.uk/the-issues/indefinite-non-se cret-detention.html.

36. Frank Oliveri and Emily Cadei, "Defense Authorization: Conflict and Compromise," *CQ Weekly*, December 5, 2011: 2548–49.

37. By a five-to-four vote, the US Supreme Court held in *Boumediene v. Bush*, 553 U.S. 723 (2008) that the Congress had unconstitutionally stripped the federal courts of jurisdiction over cases filed on behalf of the Guantánamo detainees without providing for any acceptable substitute procedure. The court insisted that detainees were permitted to file *habeas corpus* suits to challenge their continued detention.

38. Lindsey Graham, "Remarks on National Defense Authorization Act for Fiscal Year 2012," *Congressional Record*, 112th Congress, First Session, November 17, 2011, S7669.

39. For example, see Brad Knickerbocker, "Guantánamo for US citizens? Senate Bill Raises Questions," *Christian Science Monitor*, December 3, 2011.

40. Josh Gerstein, "Conference Committee Drops Ban on Indefinite Detention of Americans," *Politico*, December 18, 2012, www.politico.com/blogs/under-the-radar/2012/12/ conference-committee-drops-ban-on-indefinite-detention-152352.html.

41. An immediate consequence of the legislation was that twenty terrorist suspects, whom the courts had ordered be released from Guantánamo after eight years' detention, were subsequently obliged to remain at the facility. By February 2013, 166 men remained in indefinite detention at Guantánamo, seventy-six fewer than when Obama took office.

42. Chisun Lee, "Their Own Private Guantánamo," *New York Times*, July 23, 2009.

43. Judge Thomas F. Hogan quoted in Lyle Denniston, "Commentary: Did Boumediene Leave Too Much Undone? A Key Judge's Lament over Detention," December 22, 2009, scotusblog.com, www.scotusblog.com/2009/12/commentary-did-boumediene-leave-too-much -undone/.

44. Center for Constitutional Rights, *Obama Administration Offers Essentially Same Definition of Enemy Combatant Without Using the Term* (New York: Center for Constitutional Rights, 2009).

45. William Glaberson, "President's Detention Plan Tests American Legal Tradition," *New York Times*, May 22, 2009.

46. Although US intelligence assessments concluded that about fifty Guantánamo detainees remained a serious threat and could not be safely repatriated or resettled in a third country, the administration's Periodic Review Board composed of lawyers and officials from the Departments of Homeland Security, State, and Justice had determined that they could not be prosecuted in military commissions or in federal court because of evidentiary problems, such as evidence provided by torture victims would be inadmissible (see Peter Finn and Anne E. Kornblut, "Obama Creates Indefinite Detention System for Prisoners at Guantánamo Bay," *Washington Post*, March 8, 2011). In May 2012, Khalid Shaikh Mohammed, the self-styled

mastermind of 9/11, and four other detainees accused of conspiring in the same attacks were arraigned on war crimes charges before a military tribunal at Guantánamo Bay. In practice, however, the Obama administration's efforts to "try" suspects by military commission have proved as problematic as those of the Bush administration, as military lawyers appointed to these commissions have resisted politically appointed civilian lawyers' attempts to impose more flexible (and expedient) interpretations of military law, particularly in relation to the applicability of the Geneva Conventions on Human Rights (see Charlie Savage, "Who Decides the Laws of War?" *New York Times*, January 26, 2013). An executive agency, known in military legal terms as an "Original Classifying Authority" (OCA) was also allowed to censor closed-circuit broadcasts of hearings by the military tribunal Guantánamo, where journalists monitor proceedings, and questions were raised as to whether defense counsels' consultations with suspects have been confidential (see Carlo Muñoz, "Unseen Censor Can Black Out Broadcast of Guantánamo Tribunal Hearings," *The Hill*, January 20, 2013).

47. Jeff Zeleny, "Obama Calls for Military Shift in U.S. Focus on Terrorism," *New York Times*, August 2, 2007.

48. R. Jeffrey Smith, Candace Rondeaux, and Joby Warrick, "2 U.S. Airstrikes Offer a Concrete Sign of Obama's Pakistan Policy," *Washington Post*, January 24, 2009; Karen DeYoung, "Obama Tends Toward Mainstream on Foreign Policy," *Washington Post*, March 3, 2008: A7.

49. Smith, Rondeaux, and Warrick, "2 U.S. Airstrikes Offer a Concrete Sign of Obama's Pakistan Policy."

50. President Bush executed about fifty drone attacks on suspected terrorists (see Geoff Dyer, "Brennan Faces Drone Attack from Senators," *Financial Times*, 6 February 6, 2013) whereas, according to a report from the Council of Foreign Relations (see Micah Zenko, *Reforming US Drone Strike Policies: Council Special Report No. 65* [New York: Center for Preventive Action, Council of Foreign Relations, January 2013]), the Obama administration have conducted over four hundred drone attacks against al-Qaeda targets in Pakistan, Somalia, and Yemen, as a result of which some 3,500 people have been killed. As of April 2012, the Pentagon had 7,500 aerial drones, compared with fifty in September 2011 (Zenko, *Reforming US Drone Strike Policies*, 3). In its 2012 budget request, the Pentagon asked for almost $5 billion, just for drones (see Tom Tschida, "Predator Drones and Unmanned Aerial Vehicles [UAVs]," *New York Times*, March 20, 2012).

51. Jo Becker and Scott Shane, "Secret 'Kill List' Proves a Test of Obama's Principles and Will," *New York Times*, May 29, 2012.

52. Harold Koh, remarks at the Annual Meeting of the American Society of International Law, Washington, DC, March 25, 2010; John O. Brennan, "Strengthening Our Security by Adhering to Our Values and Laws," remarks to the Harvard Law School-Brookings Institution Conference, Cambridge, MA, September 16, 2011; John O. Brennan, "The Ethics and Efficacy of the President's Counterterrorism Strategy," Woodrow Wilson International Center for Scholars, Washington, DC, April 30, 2012; Eric Holder, "Targeted Killing," Northwestern University School of Law, Chicago, March 5, 2012; Jeh C. Johnson, "National Security Law, Lawyers and Lawyering in the Obama Administration," Yale Law School, New Haven, CT, February 22, 2012; John Rollins, "Osama bin Laden's Death: Implications and Considerations," *CRS Report for Congress Report R41809*, Washington, DC: Congressional Research Service, 2011; Pete Williams, "Bin Laden Killing Was Legally Justified, Holder Says: 'It Was a Kill or Capture Mission . . . He Made No Attempts to Surrender,'" *NBC News,* May 4, 2011, www.msnbc.msn.com.

53. In several cases, suspects have been US citizens; see Daniel Klaidman, *Kill or Capture: The War on Terror and the Soul of the Obama Presidency* (New York: Houghton Mifflin Harcourt, 2012).

54. Apparently, Obama intended to try Osama bin Laden in a federal court. "We worked through the legal and political issues that would have been involved, and Congress and the desire to send him to Guantánamo, and to not try him, and Article III . . . But, frankly, my belief was if we had captured him, that I would be in a pretty strong position, politically, here, to argue that displaying due process and rule of law would be our best weapon against al-Qaeda, in preventing him from appearing as a martyr"; Mark Bowden, "The Hunt For 'Geronimo,'"

Vanity Fair, November 2012, www.vanityfair.com/politics/2012/11/inside-osama-bin-laden -assassination-plot. But, of course, bin Laden was not captured, so we will never know whether this aspiration would have been realized.

55. By February 2013, the Obama administration had incarcerated one terrorist suspect.

56. Eric Schmitt, "U.S. Weighs Base for Spy Drones in North Africa," *New York Times*, January 28, 2013.

57. Christof Heyns quoted in Owen Bowcott, "Drone Strikes Threaten 50 Years of International Law, Says UN Rapporteur," *Guardian*, June 21, 2012; see also Robert Chesney, "Beyond the Battlefield, Beyond Al Qaeda: The Destabilizing Legal Architecture of Counterterrorism," *Michigan Law Review*, forthcoming.

58. In the public and congressional outrage that followed revelations in the 1970s that the CIA had attempted to assassinate various foreign political leaders, the Ford administration issued EO 11905 banning US government employees from engaging in or conspiring to engage in political assassination. The order was subsequently reissued by Ford's successors and finally reissued by Reagan in the form still in force today (EO 12333). However, the application of this order to contemporary US counterterrorism efforts is open to many different interpretations and remains untested in the courts. For all practical purposes, the order neither inhibited Reagan's attempt to assassinate Muammar Qaddafi nor Bush's or Obama's authorization of the killing of Osama bin Laden.

59. Congressional proposals to create a comprehensive charter for the CIA charter made in the 1970s, including a prohibition of acts like assassinations of foreign leaders, died of its own weight amid cries of congressional micromanagement and dangerously limiting presidential and executive discretion; George Lardner, "Senate Panel Drops Efforts to Obtain Intelligence Charter," *Washington Post*, May 2, 1980.

60. Jeremy Herb, "Lawmakers want legal justification for drone strikes," *The Hill*, June 13, 2012: A1.

61. Becker and Shane, "Secret 'Kill List' Proves a Test of Obama's Principles and Will"; Charlie Savage, "Secret U.S. Memo Made Legal Case to Kill a Citizen," *New York Times*, October 8, 2011.

62. US Department of Justice, "Lawfulness of Lethal Operation against a US Citizen Who Is a Senior Operational Leader of Al-Qa'ida or an Associate Force," White Paper, 2013, obtained by NBC News, openchannel.nbcnews.com/_news/2013/02/04/16843014-exclusive-justice-de partment-memo-reveals-legal-case-for-drone-strikes-on-americans?lite. At the time of writing, facing the prospect of a possible filibuster of Brennan's nomination as director of the CIA following hearings before the Senate Select Committee on Intelligence the following day, the White House announced that the president would direct the Justice Department to disclose to the committee unspecified classified documents discussing the legal justification for the assassination of a US terrorist suspect in Yemen in 2011.

63. Zenko, *Reforming US Drone Strike Policies.*

64. Holder, "Targeted Killing."

65. Charlie Savage, "A Not-Quite Confirmation of a Memo Approving Killing," *New York Times*, March 8, 2012.

66. Adam Serwer, "Congress Wants to See Obama's 'License to Kill,'" *Mother Jones*, July 31, 2012, www.motherjones.com/politics/2012/07/congress-disclose-obama-targeted-killing -memos; Marcy Wheeler, "Targeted Killings: When John Cornyn Makes Better Sense Than Democrats . . . ," *emptywheeel blog*, July 19, 2012, www.emptywheel.net/2012/07/19/targeted -killings-when-john-cornyn-makes-better-sense-than-democrats/?utm_source=rss&utm_med ium=rss&utm_campaign=targeted-killings-when-john-cornyn-makes-better-sense-than-demo-crats.

67. Ken Dilanian, "Congress Zooms in on Drone Killings: A Staff Team Reviews Classified Videos in an Effort to Hold the CIA More Accountable," *Los Angeles Times*, June 25, 2012. A *Washington Post/ABC News* poll published in February 2013 showed that 83 percent of respondents approved of the Obama administration's use of unmanned drones against suspected terrorists overseas (76 percent of Republicans, 58 percent of Democrats), with 59 percent strongly approving the practice.

68. Congressman Mike Rogers quoted in Carlo Muñoz and Amie Parnes, "White House, Congress Square Off over Justice Dept. Rules for Drone Strikes," *The Hill*, February 5, 2013.

69. Center for Civilians in Conflict/Human Rights Clinic, *The Civilian Impact of Drones: Unexamined Costs, Unanswered Questions* (New York: Columbia Law School, 2012); Robert F. Worth, Mark Mazzetti, and Scott Shane, "Drone Strikes' Dangers to Get Rare Moment in Public Eye," *New York Times*, February 5, 2013; Zenko, *Reforming US Drone Strike Policies*, 9–17.

70. Becker and Shane, "Secret 'Kill List' Proves a Test of Obama's Principles and Will."

71. Obama's escalation of targeted killings of alleged al-Qaeda leaders by drones, of course, helped neutralize political attacks from Republican presidential challenger Mitt Romney, who spared no opportunity during the 2012 presidential election campaign to accuse the president of being weak on matters of national security.

72. Vicki Divol, "Who Says You Can Kill Americans, Mr. President?," *New York Times*, January 16, 2013.

73. Not, however, on the matter of funding the Pentagon to buy more drones. In August 2012, the Senate Appropriations Committee voted funding for US Air Force to buy Global Hawk Block thirty drones, costing $218 million each, it had not requested in its budget. The entire Global Hawk drone program costs $12.4 billion. The Air Force wanted to continue buying other Global Hawk drones that are cheaper and more effective, but the Senate committee required it to buy both types; see Pat Towell and Daniel H. Else, "Defense: FY2013 Authorization and Appropriations," *CRS Report for Congress R42607*, Washington, DC: Congressional Research Service, September 5, 2012, 13.

74. David Rothkopf quoted in Geoff Dyer, "Drones: Undeclared and Undiscussed," FT.com, October 21, 2012, www.ft.com/cms/s/0/7a4114be-19ce-11e2-a379-00144feabdc0.html#axzz2JYddAsMK.

75. In June 2012, the American Civil Liberties Union and the Center for Constitutional Rights filed a lawsuit challenging the administration's targeted killing of the three US citizens in drone strikes far from any armed conflict zone on the grounds that it violated the Constitution's fundamental guarantee against the deprivation of life without due process of law under the Fifth Amendment. This case followed a suit filed by the American Civil Liberties Union (ACLU) and Center for Constitutional Rights (CCR) in 2010 challenging one of the deceased's inclusion on government kill lists, before his death.

76. Carlo Muñoz, "No Court for Drone Oversight, Says GOP," *The Hill*, February 13, 2013.

77. Barack Obama, "Obama On Economic Crisis, Transition." *60 Minutes*, CBS News Interview with Steve Kroft. February 11, 2009, http://www.cbsnews.com/stories/2008/11/16/60minutes/main4607893.shtml.

78. Owens, "Rivals Only Sometimes."

79. Alberto Gonzales, "Memorandum for the President," *Decision Re Application of the Geneva Convention on Prisoners of War to the Conflict with Al Qaeda and the Taliban*, January 25, 2002, wid.ap.org/documents/doj/gonzales.pdf.

80. Indeed, according to Gonzales, under the "inherent" powers provided the president by the US Constitution, he had the authority to suspend the application of the Conventions (2002). While Gonzales's memo argued that the president need not adhere to traditional principles of international law, a later opinion—the notorious (and subsequently rescinded) "torture memo" written by Jay Bybee, assistant attorney general in the OLC—went even further: the president could *choose* not to follow international law (2002).

81. As Goldsmith (*The Terror Presidency*, 149) noted subsequently, such an extreme conclusion went far beyond the memo's legal opinion on interrogation practices or the United States' torture statute (notably, the 1998 Torture Victims Relief Act) because it implied that many other laws—including, for example, the 1996 War Crimes Act and the Uniform Code of Military Justice—were also unconstitutional; it also ignored the Congress's competing wartime constitutional authorities and the Supreme Court's numerous decisions to the contrary.

82. Scott Shane, "Senate Panel Approves Findings Critical of Detainee Interrogations," *New York Times*, December 13, 2012.

83. Emily Bazelon, "The Get-Out-of-Torture-Free Card: Why Is Congress Banning Torture but Allowing the Use of Torture Testimony?" *Slate*, December 15, 2005, www.slate.com/id/

2132572/; John W. Dean, "Senators Kyl and Graham's *Hamdan v. Rumsfeld* Scam: The Deceptive Amicus Brief They Filed in the Guantánamo Detainee Case," *FindLaw*, July 5, 2005, writ.news.findlaw.com/dean/20060705.html.

84. In his 2005 signing statement, Bush reserved the right to "construe the 2005 Detainee Treatment Act in a manner consistent with the constitutional authority of the president as Commander in Chief" and "the shared objective of the Congress and the President . . . of protecting the American people from further terrorist attacks." Seeking to nullify the act's effect, Bush's new acting head of the OLC also wrote a secret legal opinion averring that even the harshest tactics used by the CIA were not "cruel, inhuman or degrading" (David Johnston and Scott Shane, "Debate Erupts on Techniques Used by C.I.A.," *New York Times*, October 5, 2007)—the phrase used in McCain's amendment.

85. Scott Shane, "Lawmakers Back Limits on Interrogation Tactics," *New York Times*, December 7, 2007; Steven Lee Myers, "Bush's Veto of Bill on C.I.A. Tactics Affirms His Legacy," *New York Times*, March 9, 2008.

86. Apparently, White House Counsel Gregory Craig assured the CIA's General Counsel that "the new president had no intention of ending rendition—only its abuse"; Becker and Shane, "Secret 'Kill List' Proves a Test of Obama's Principles and Will."

87. Joby Warrick, "Brennan Withdraws from Consideration for Administration Post," *Washington Post*, November 25, 2008. Brennan was formerly chief of staff to the previous CIA director and during the Bush administration had endorsed abusive interrogation techniques, including waterboarding, and extraordinary rendition to transfer terrorist suspects to the CIA's "black sites" outside the United States.

88. Mark Mazzetti, "Panetta Open to Tougher Methods in Some C.I.A. Interrogation," *New York Times*, February 5, 2009. As the earlier discussion noted, efforts by several senators to pass a State Secrets Protection Act, requiring a court to rule whether the administration may claim states secrets privilege to suppress evidence, came to naught.

89. John Schwartz, "Obama Backs Off a Reversal on Secrets," *New York Times*, February 10, 2009.

90. David Johnston, "U.S. Says Rendition to Continue, but With More Oversight," *New York Times*, August 24, 2009. In the event, this announcement turned out to be less than met the eye. In his answers to questions from members of the Senate Select Committee on Intelligence, prior to his nomination hearings as CIA director, Leon Panetta quoted the weak standard used by the Bush (and Clinton) administration, which prohibited rendition only when it is "more likely than not that the suspect will be subjected to torture" (US Congress, Senate, Senate Select Committee on Intelligence, *Additional Prehearing Questions for The Honorable Leon E. Panetta upon His Selection to Be the Director of the Central Intelligence Agency*, January 22, 2009,   https://docs.google.com/viewer?a=v&q=cache:0CwPR7CtRx8J:www.fas.org/irp/con gress/2009_hr/panetta-questions.pdf+&hl=en&gl=uk&pid=bl&srcid=ADGEESj3RFzKJsveD QdDAlX5Xo8a4aePE6Ayp-hf3En56ujyPmYj5WVdx6FlAR76sJF3oAXGamOQS1RuGAQ-1 yM8iKFRwdeOIjHcnSQ3dkyVe0qDPXxV25GF1OEomC7Do6-VCpagWPA9&sig=AHIEtbQ o9AMaMr01Tjdcfs2tBocDZYa86w.

91. Tom Malinowski quoted in Louis Jacobson, "Extraordinary Rendition Officially Ruled Out, but Secrecy Makes Its Elimination Hard to Prove," Politifact.com, December 4, 2012, www.politifact.com/truth-o-meter/promises/obameter/promise/176/end-the-use-of-extreme-ren dition/.

92. See, for example, Rod Nordland and Thom Shanker, "U.S. Military Stops Sending Detainees to Some Afghan Prisons on Rights Fears," *New York Times*, January 16, 2013; UN Assistance Mission in Afghanistan, *Treatment of Conflict-Related Detainees in Afghan Custody* (Kabul, Afghanistan: UN Office of the High Commissioner for Human Rights, 2011).

93. Craig Whitlock, "Renditions Continue under Obama, Despite Due-Process Concerns," *Washington Post*, January 1, 2013.

94. Three other areas of counterterrorism policy that space precludes from discussing fully, the administration and congressional majorities exhibited similar patterns to those during the Bush administration. One concerned the renewal of the 2001 PATRIOT Act. The minority Republican ranking member of the Intelligence Committee did not even want a debate on renewal, simply approval. When a handful of senators led by Rand Paul (R-KY) proposed

modest amendments to eliminate some of the documented abuses of the Act, Senate Majority Leader Harry Reid (D-NV) accused him of grandstanding and "threatening to take away the best tools we have for stopping [terrorists] plotting against our country undetected" (2011: S3319). The amendments were soundly defeated and the bill passed unamended. A second concerned the 2008 FISA amendments in 2012. During consideration of the 2008 legislation, lawmakers had insisted on legalizing warrantless electronic surveillance of individuals by the Bush administration, including persons in the United States. The Obama administration supported a simple renewal bill passed by the Republican-controlled House. In the Senate, however, several Democratic and Republican senators sought to require modest levels of transparency and oversight over much more invasive and extensive eavesdropping than publicly recognized or reported to the Senate Intelligence Committee. The amendments were rejected with almost solid Republican support and almost solid Democratic opposition. Finally, in the absence of congressional legislation, the Obama administration has also enunciated cyber security policy unilaterally (David E. Sanger and Thom Shanker, "Broad Powers Seen for Obama in Cyberstrikes," *New York Times*, February 3, 2013).

95. John Mueller, "Simplicity and Spook: Terrorism and the Dynamics of Threat Exaggeration," *International Studies Perspectives*, 6 (2005): 208–34; John Mueller, "Is there Still a Terrorist Threat? The Myth of the Omnipresent Enemy," *Foreign Affairs*, September/October 2006.

96. John E. Owens and Riccardo Pelizzo, "The 'War on Terror' and the Growth of Executive Power?," in John E. Owens and Riccardo Pelizzo, eds., *The 'War on Terror' and the Growth of Executive Power?* (New York: Routledge, 2010), 1–32.

97. Lowi, *The Personal President*, xi–xii, 180; Craig A. Rimmerman, *Presidency by Plebiscite: Reagan-Bush Era in Institutional Perspective* (Boulder, CO: Westview Press, 1993); Andrew Rudalevige, *The New Imperial Presidency: Renewing Presidential Power After Watergate* (Ann Arbor: The University of Michigan Press, 2005).

98. Pew Research Center, "Continued Positive Marks for Government Anti-Terror Efforts. But Many Say U.S. Has Been Lucky in Avoiding Attack," October 22, 2010 (Washington, DC: Pew Research Center for the People and the Press), people-press.org, accessed March 22, 2013 http://www.people-press.org/2010/10/22/continued-positive-marks-for-government-anti-terror-efforts/.

99. Jennifer Agiesta, "Torture: The Memos and Partisan Reaction," *Washington Post*, April 26, 2009, voices.washingtonpost.com/behind-the-numbers/2009/04/torture_the_partisan_playing_f.html.

100. Jennifer L. Merolla and Elizabeth J. Zechmeister, *Democracy at Risk: How Terrorist Threats Affect the Public* (Chicago: University of Chicago Press, 2009); Darren W. Davis, *Negative Liberty: Public Opinion and the Terrorist Attacks on America* (New York: Russell Sage Foundation, 2007).

101. Owens, "Presidential Aggrandizement and Congressional Acquiescence in the 'War on Terror.'"

Chapter Fifteen

Assessing Presidential-Congressional Relations

A Need for Reform?

James A. Thurber

As analyzed by the authors in this book, President Obama's relationship with Congress illustrates both the capacity for presidential and legislative productivity when faced with crisis and under unified party control. There is also a strong tendency toward gridlock when Congress is divided as it has been for all but two years in the Obama presidency. Whether party government is unified or divided has a major impact on Congress. The 111th Congress, which spanned the first two years of the Obama presidency with a Democratic majority in both chambers, was exceedingly productive. Unified party government and strong party unity on the Hill allowed the Democrats to pass significant legislation to address instability in the financial sector, supply stimulus to an economy in recession, and reform the nation's health-insurance system. The 2010 midterm elections changed the dynamic in Congress as Republicans gained a majority in the House and narrowed the Democrats' advantage in the Senate. The 112th Congress saw historically limited legislative productivity in the run up to the 2012 elections. In the fall of 2012, President Obama won a second term in office, the Democrats expanded their majority in the Senate to fifty-five to forty-five (with two independents voting with the Democrats), and Republicans maintained their hold on the House (234 to 201). These results raised significant questions about the ability of a divided Congress to go beyond deadlock and address major issues facing the nation in the 113th Congress and beyond.

After the 2008 elections, Democrats controlled both chambers of Congress and the presidency. Between July 7, 2009 and February 4, 2010, the

Democrats held a filibuster-proof super majority of sixty votes in the Senate.[1] They used this advantage to enact major legislation including the American Recovery and Reinvestment Act (economic stimulus), the Patient Protection and Affordable Care Act (health-insurance reform), and the Dodd-Frank Wall Street Reform and Consumer Protection Act (financial reform). This period of legislative productivity in part inspired a conservative backlash in the 2010 midterm elections. The Republican Party gained control of the House and narrowed the Democratic majority in the Senate.

The success of Republican candidates in 2010, which many associated with the Tea Party movement, came to dominate coverage of the midterm elections and had a significant effect on the workings of the 112th Congress. A response to what was seen as an unwarranted expansion of the power of the federal government, the Tea Party movement involved a loosely organized collection of conservative groups focused on influencing policy and electing conservative candidates. Tea Party groups effectively exercised this power in, and after, the 2010 elections.[2]

During the 112th Congress, divided government led to gridlock in Congress and conflict with President Obama. Tensions between President Obama and congressional Republicans came to a head in May of 2011 when they objected to raising the debt ceiling without instituting a plan to reduce the deficit. This impasse between the president and Congress resulted in a downgrade of the nation's credit rating and the creation of a bipartisan congressional committee (the "Supercommittee") to recommend a deficit reduction plan. The Supercommittee failed to reach an agreement, triggering significant cuts to military, education, transportation, and health-care spending (referred to as sequestration), set to take effect in January 2013. Sequestration is a budget procedure created in the Gramm-Rudman-Hollings Deficit Reduction Act of 1985 in which appropriations in excess of the spending caps adopted in the annual Budget Resolution are "sequestered" by the Treasury Department and not allocated to agencies.

The combination of a large deficit and debt, automatic sequestration of defense and domestic discretionary spending, and the expiration of previously instituted "Bush" tax cuts, also in 2013, came to be known as the fiscal cliff. How to address these looming deadlines became a primary theme of the 2012 campaign. In November of 2012, Republicans retained control of the House, Democrats retained control of the Senate, and President Obama was reelected to a second term. These 2012 election results set the stage for continued conflict and divided government as Congress was faced with how to address the fiscal cliff and other pressing policy issues in the 2012 lame duck session and beyond.

EVALUATING THE FUNCTIONS OF CONGRESS

Public dissatisfaction with Congress reached a historic low in February and August of 2012, just before the presidential election, with 10 percent of the public expressing approval of the way Congress was doing its job, as shown in figure 15.1. At the same time, presidential job performance was over 50 percent.

Congress serves multiple functions, including lawmaking, representation, deliberation, and oversight. With regard to each of these functions, the current deadlocked and politicized environment in Congress limits the effectiveness of the institution.

The President and Congressional Rules and Procedures

Congressional procedural changes have undermined the normal legislative process in the past four decades. For the most part, these changes have not been structural, but merely the use of long standing legislative tools. However, they have helped to undermine trust in the institution. Current concerns focus on today's majority congressional leadership, but the same tactics were practiced in the past by the minority party leadership. Thus, this process cannot be blamed solely on one political party. Both parties use House and Senate rules to deny the opposition and the president a full debate or effective votes and to make significant alterations to legislation passed by the committees of jurisdiction.

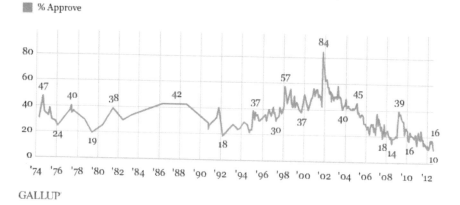

Do you approve or disapprove of the way Congress is handling its job?

■ % Approve

GALLUP

Figure 15.1.   Congressional Job Approval. Source: Gallup 2012.

An additional problem for the president is the increasing use of filibusters, amendments, and holds to clog the legislative work in the Senate. Figure 15.2 shows the rise of cloture motions to stop filibusters in the Senate since 1967. The term "filibuster" is applied to many different actions in the Senate including: objections to unanimous consent requests, efforts to delay proceedings, and the anonymous "hold" that originally was meant as an informational tool for majority leaders trying to arrange floor schedules. "Holds" are an informal senatorial custom unrecognized in Senate rules and precedents. They allow senators to give notice to their respective party leader that certain measures or matters should not be brought up on the floor. The party leaders will usually honor holds placed by a member. Holds provide significant leverage to members who wish to delay action on nominations of legislation. The mere threat of a filibuster prompts the majority leader to halt action on a bill, or to quickly move to cut off debate, meaning that the minority can block legislation without actually holding the floor and talking for hours on end. Filibusters are currently rarely invoked but often threatened to gain political bargaining power and negotiating leverage. After Democrats retained control of the Senate in the 2012 elections, Majority Leader Harry Reid indicated a desire, with the support of President Obama and some other Senate Democrats, to reform the cloture process in order to reduce the amount of obstruction in the Senate. In December of 2012, Reid announced, "We're going to change the rules. We cannot continue in this way." In response, Minority Leader Mitch McConnell expressed opposition to proposed reform. A bipartisan group of senators led by Republican John McCain of Arizona and Democrat Carl Levin of Michigan put forth a proposal to provide the Senate majority leader the ability to limit debate on some motions and to speed consideration of lower-level nominees to the executive and judicial branches. A separate proposal by Democratic Senators Jeff Merkley of Oregon and Tom Udall of New Mexico garnered the support of almost fifty Democratic senators. The Merkley-Udall proposal would ban filibusters on motions to proceed and would require senators to speak continuously on the floor to keep a filibuster going. Without action in the 2012 lame duck session, filibuster reform was left to the 113th Congress.

The President, Congress, and the Power of the Purse

The Constitution gives the Congress the power of the purse by providing that "No money shall be drawn from the Treasury, but in Consequence of Appropriations made by Law" (Article I, Section 9). The entire government will shut down if appropriations are not enacted annually. In recent years, there has been heavy reliance on omnibus appropriations bills, "minibus" appropriations, and additional riders and earmarks added to must-pass appropriation bills. There is also a growing tendency toward government by continu-

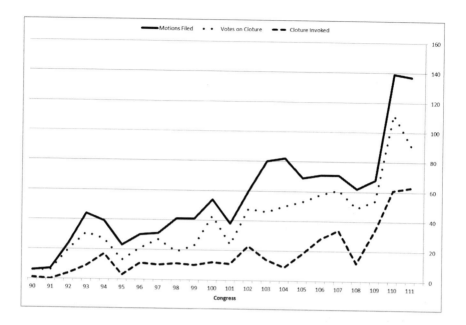

Figure 15.2. Cloture Motions Filed in US Senate, 1967–2010. Source: Wolfensberger (2012); excerpted from "Action on Cloture, Present–1917," US Senate website.

ing resolution. Continuing resolutions are a temporary stopgap funding measure whenever Congress cannot complete action on one or more of the twelve regular appropriations bills by the beginning of the fiscal year (October 1). In the past, continuing resolutions were only used for short periods (one or two months). However, the concurrent budget resolutions have been passed on time only twice since 1976. The federal government has been forced to run on continuing resolutions and supplemental appropriations. Partisan deadlock over a continuing resolution in the spring of 2012 came within a few hours of shutting down the federal government as happened in late 1995–early 1996. The 2011 experience with multiple continuing resolutions and the debt-limit negotiations revealed a deadlocked Congress. In addition, the failure of the Supercommittee to reach any agreement on deficit reduction and the self-imposed "fiscal cliff" of 2012 reinforced the perception of dysfunction. A last minute deal on the final day of the 112th Congress to avert automatic tax increases and spending cuts did not involve an agreement to address long-term deficit reduction.

Presidential Power and Congressional Committees

Committees are necessary for Congress to have a rational division of labor and to work both effectively and efficiently. However, the proliferation of committees and other bodies has contributed to policy fragmentation and jurisdictional overlap. This was evident in the battles over health-care reform and climate change legislation. Examples of policy fragmentation are extensive: the number of committees and subcommittees with jurisdiction over homeland security is 108; for energy-environment, fifty-six; and for jobs/ economic security, potentially all 218 committees and subcommittees. There is also a problem of policy balance with committees being captured by specific interests that represent only one view of issues, such as the agriculture and armed services committees, whose members typically reside in farm states and close to military bases or defense companies. When there is little policy equilibrium within committees in the deliberation of various competing policy positions, there is a perception of unfairness and unequal access for policy preferences.

Although there have been periodic attempts to reduce the number of committees, rationalize jurisdictions, and decrease the number of committee assignments, potential reforms of the committee system in the House and Senate have all failed since the overhaul of the Senate committee system in 1976. There have been thirteen committee-reform efforts since the Joint Committee on the Organization of Congress in 1946 that established the present system of committees. The consequences of an antiquated congressional committee system are unequal workloads of committees and members, unnecessary duplication, delay, and gridlock.

The "Money Chase," the President, Congress

The drive for reelection by presidents and members of Congress is a logical part of a representative democracy, though it continues to get more expensive. The growth of the "permanent campaign," with its negative campaign tactics, threatens to weaken the institution of Congress. Deregulation of campaign finance has reduced transparency about who is giving and for what. In the wake of *Citizens United v. Federal Election Commission* (2010) an avalanche of nontransparent campaign money from corporations and unions raised questions about the fairness of the campaign process and its implications for governing.

Campaign spending has grown rapidly from $3.08 billion in 2000 to $5.29 billion in 2008 for presidential election years and from $1.62 billion in 1998 to $3.65 billion in 2010 in nonpresidential election years. According to the Center for Responsive Politics, an estimated $6 billion was spent in 2012. Campaign costs have become so monumental that members must spend most of their time raising money, leaving less time for legislating and working with their fellow legislators. There is intense pressure to constantly raise money and campaign. Moreover, members often win by criticizing Congress, undermining trust in the institution. Many members stay with their families in the home district and commute to "work." With fewer Members in Washington, the infamous "Tuesday-through-Thursday Club" is all too real. The House in 2011 spent fewer than one hundred days in session, the smallest number in sixty years, and pretty close to the 108 days clocked by the 1948 "Do-Nothing Congress."

Lobbying, the President, and Congress

Lobbyists and money from special interests in campaigns are certainly part of the dynamic Congress; however, even after President Obama's lobbying and ethics reforms in 2007 and 2009, deadlock, extreme partisanship, and the hostility the public sees in Congress continued. Nevertheless, lobbying can be an essential part of congressional policy making, as when lobbyists provide expertise that would not be available to the members. But the influence of lobbyists in Congress gives rise to concerns about conflicts of interest and whether the advent of massive lobbying campaigns wrinkles rather than levels the playing field. The numbers of registered lobbyists increased—from 16,342 in 2000 to 34,785 in 2005—but dropped to around thirteen thousand in 2010 and then to 8,500 in 2011 after the 2007 lobbying reforms were fully implemented. The drop in the number of lobbyists does not mean there is less lobbying in Washington. The decline in registered lobbyists is due at least in part to failure to register by sliding in under the requirements, in the letter but not the spirit of the reforms. In 1998, registered lobbyists reported spending $1.427 billion; in 2004, lobbyists spent at least $2.128 billion on reported activities; and in 2010 and 2011 that grew to $3.4 billion, but there is likely much more spent in "grassroots lobbying" and other unregulated efforts. Spending by registered lobbyists has grown 62 percent in the last five years. This averages out to over $9.7 million in lobbying expenditures each day Congress was in session in 2008 or over $6.5 million per year for every member of Congress. This does not include money spent for strategy, public relations, grassroots, coalition building, issue advertising on television ads and in the print media, and advocacy on the Internet. The 1995 Legislative Disclosure Act (LDA) and the 2007 Honest Leadership and Open Government Act (HLOGA) do not cover most advocacy in Washington. The definition of a lobbyist fails to capture most of the advocacy activity in Washington. HLOGA is far from being fully enforced.

President, Congress, and Deliberation

There is a difference between deliberation and dysfunction. The right to talk a bill to death, the filibuster, has been allowed by the Senate's rules since 1806, but at first it was used sparingly. Its use is on the rise, as shown in figure 15.3. Senators often feel very little compunction about stopping the work of the Senate. The collapse of comity is also a serious problem undermining deliberation. The influx of more partisan former House members into the Senate has undermined its capacity for bipartisan deliberation. There appears to be a lack of true deliberation and comity and civility in both the House and Senate. There are fewer committee meetings and hearings, conference committees meet less often, laws are frequently written or substantially revised behind closed doors by the party leadership, and there has been a general demise of the regular order. Figure 15.3 illustrates an increase in the use of closed and structured rules and a concomitant decline in the use of open rules for initial consideration for the amendment of legislation.

Congressional Oversight and the President

Rigorous oversight of the president and federal agency actions is essential to ensure Congress is aware of the president's policy initiatives and that the laws Congress has passed are properly implemented. Congress is often too timid when there is unified party government and too aggressive with divided party government. Congress practices "fire alarm" oversight, waiting until the alarms go off before it begins to review in detail agency activities, rather than "police patrol" regular, planned, and active oversight. There has been a long-term decline in the ability or even willingness of Congress to make thorough use of its oversight powers to keep the executive branch in check. Robust oversight could have potentially prevented or lessened the banking and housing crises and the Gulf oil spill and improve agency response. Members of Congress are typically not involved in laws after they are passed. In some cases, there are too many friendly alliances between committees that authorize programs, the interest groups that benefit from the programs, and the agencies that administer them. In other instances, the committee chooses to distance itself from the implementation, knowing the results will not please every constituent. All laws have intended and unintended consequences and they need to be monitored carefully by Congress. Former US Representative Lee Hamilton argues, "If we want to make sure that federal agencies are doing their jobs appropriately, with the best interests of the American people constantly in mind, then Congress must do a better job of oversight, looking into every nook and cranny of their activities."[3]

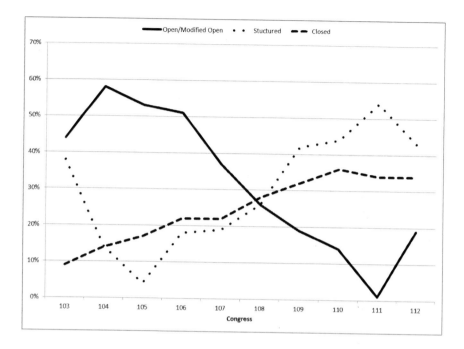

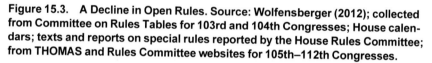

Figure 15.3.   A Decline in Open Rules. Source: Wolfensberger (2012); collected from Committee on Rules Tables for 103rd and 104th Congresses; House calendars; texts and reports on special rules reported by the House Rules Committee; from THOMAS and Rules Committee websites for 105th–112th Congresses.

THE MISSING MODERATES AND THE LIMITS OF THE LEGISLATIVE PRESIDENCY

A fundamental reason for gridlock and dysfunctionality in Congress and with the president is the disappearance of the moderates, or what some call the vital center in Congress, as discussed in many of the preceding chapters. There has been a steady decline in the number of moderates in Congress since 1960.

Four decades ago, there was a vigorous middle in Congress. Both parties spanned the ideological divide that exists today. For much of the twentieth century, each party had a large liberal and conservative wing. On divisive issues such as civil rights, liberal Democrats and Northern moderate Republicans would join forces against the conservatives of the Confederate South. Getting the votes needed to stop a filibuster required a coalition of senators from both parties. Paul G. Kirk, Jr., a former aide to Senator Ted Kennedy who was appointed to fill his seat temporarily in 2009, explains, "More commonly than not, the conservatives in the two parties would be together, the progressives in the two parties would be together, and then you'd kind of have a moderate center and find the 60. The breath of political thought overlapped."[4] Polarization has reduced these forces of moderation in both chambers.

Related to the lack of the middle in each party, it is the movement of both parties to more extreme partisanship that has also helped to create congressional dysfunction. Over 80 percent of the roll call votes have pitted a majority of Democrats against a majority of Republicans, a measure of partisanship. This is the highest percentage of party unity votes since *Congressional Quarterly* began measuring voting patterns of members of Congress in 1953. In addition, movement of former House members into the Senate has contributed to an increased partisan polarization in the upper chamber.[5]

In addition to the challenges of legislating under divided party government in an area of intense polarization, ideological divisions within the Republican Party complicated the efforts of House Speaker John Boehner and Senate Minority Leader Mitch McConnell to organize their members. In the 2011 negotiations between Speaker Boehner and President Obama to reduce the deficit and raise the debt ceiling, initial reports suggested that conservative members of the House Republican caucus rejected a tentative deal. A similar split in the Republican caucus occurred in the 2012 lame-duck session when the Speaker proposed a measure (referred to as "Plan B") to avert the fiscal cliff. Although the influence of the Tea Party seemed to be on the wane after the 2012 election, ideological conservatives, particularly in the House, continued to exert significant influence.[6]

Not only does the decline in centrist members increase polarization, but also high levels of polarization may in turn drive centrists out of Congress. The decision to forgo reelection by two moderate Senators, Democrat Kent Conrad and Republican Olympia Snowe, were attributed in part to the polarized atmosphere in the Senate. In a speech to her Senate colleagues in December 2012, Snowe decried "excessive political polarization" and argued that "It hasn't always been this way. And it absolutely does not have to be this way."

Redistricting

Among the potential causes of polarization is the redistricting of House districts. Partisan gerrymandering occurs in most states. Scholars disagree about the role redistricting has played in the increase in polarization. Some argue that redistricting is one driver of polarization in the House.[7] Others dispute the link between gerrymandering and polarization.[8] Despite this disagreement, practitioners perceive that redistricting has negatively impacted Congress and its members.

The House has been redistricted to safe seats; only eighty-five seats were competitive in 2010, and eighty-five in 2012. The creation of these safe House districts has led to the election of increasingly "ideologically pure" representatives with a relatively harmonized constituency, little institutional loyalty, and an unprecedented degree of partisan homogeneity within the two parties. This has increased the importance of the party primary, with 18.8 percent turnout on average since 1986 and activist organizers focused on getting out the ideological party vote. Moderate voters are easily shut out of the process; appeals to the "base" drown out serious debate on broad issues of national concern. This has increased the importance of ideology in legislating and lobbying activities—creating deadlock; a divided, partisan House; and a subsequent lack of comity and civility in the way decisions are made, or not, in Congress. In effect, the representatives choose their voters, hardly a democratic ideal.

PRESIDENTIAL-CONGRESSIONAL RELATIONS AND THE NEED FOR REFORM

Most of the problems in the way Congress works internally and with President Obama are linked to increasing polarization and a lack of true bipartisanship. The chambers are more partisan and deadlocked than any time since the 1860s (just prior to the Civil War). There is little consensus about major policy problems and solutions. It is harder than ever for a majority to get its way. However, important reforms could improve lawmaking and lead to more consistent and careful oversight, encourage deliberation, and fulfill Congress's Constitutional mandate to represent the people. Here are some suggestions.

Improve lawmaking through legislative procedural reforms. Return to the regular order, limit restrictive rules, and improve protection of the minority in the House. The Senate needs immediate filibuster reform. Make it easier to invoke cloture, to stop the filibuster, say with a vote of sixty on a first vote to fifty-one on the fourth vote. Moreover, Senate filibuster rules must be changed to force the members to actually perform, rather than simply threaten, a filibuster. A face-saving route to reduce frivolous filibusters and the resulting deadlock in the Senate must be found. Secretive and lengthy holds on bills and nominations must also be limited.

Of particularly critical importance is requiring members of both chambers to spend more time on their jobs in Washington. The Tuesday-to-Thursday Club needs to be stopped with an enforceable required schedule of work in Washington. Members should be in Washington doing the work of committees, oversight, lawmaking, and educating themselves. It is time for the party leadership in both chambers to set rules of attendance that have consequences. There needs to be a new schedule for Congress in session, which includes not only the show time on the floor, but the work time in committees and their offices. Congress also needs to return to real postenactment conference committees that are transparent to the public and fair to both parties.

Reforms should be made to the congressional budget process. Enforce the calendar and stop the growth of continuing resolutions and omnibus spending bills. Establish a biennial appropriations process with one year for appropriations and the next year for oversight of government programs. A two-year process is reasonable, as now the budget is often passed right on the heels of the next year's budget talks. Establish a true Pay-As-You-Go (PAYGO) rule covering expenditures, taxes, and authorizations. Abolish earmarks in both the House and Senate by requiring open access to and discussion of all narrowly cast appropriations. Stop all new "backdoor spending" by authorization committees and require all permanently authorized legislation to be reviewed on a regular basis. Wolfensberger[9] suggests restoring the use of conference committees to resolve differences between House and Senate versions of legislation.

A key part of representation in America is pluralism, the expression of interests, and lobbying through organized groups. The 2007 lobbying and ethics reforms were a weak down payment on improving the regulation of lobbying. There needs to be a better definition of lobbying and better enforcement of the congressional rules and laws. Codes of ethics in both House and Senate are rarely enforced, but coupled with greater enforcement, the Senate should create an office of public integrity and the House should step up its investigations and public reporting of ethical violations. There should be an absolute ban on lobbyists raising money for those they lobby. Leadership political action committees have no role in good government and should be abolished. Fundraising quotas set for committee chairs and ranking members are an invitation to practice undue influence; the quotas benefit no one.

CONCLUSIONS

In the absence of a vigorous bipartisan center, the inability of President Obama with the Congress to address effectively such crucial issues as job-creation programs, tax reform, the rising accumulation of public debt, a looming Medicare and Medicaid shortfall, immigration reform, gun control, a failing education system, and serious energy and environmental problems is a legitimate cause of public dissatisfaction. Our separated system of government that is polarized and ideologically deadlocked seems incapable of effectively confronting these critical public policy challenges and may lack the reserves of comity and trust to face any unknown and sudden—and perhaps even more dangerous—crises. At this point in history the public blames Congress,. Whether it is the fault of the president or Congress or their built-in rivalry, major problems facing America continue to plague our political system.

NOTES

1. 1.On July 7, 2009, Al Franken (D) won the contested Minnesota seat, giving the Democrats sixty votes. On February 4, 2010, Scott Brown (R) replaced Paul Kirk (D) in the Massachusetts delegation. However, Ted Kennedy's (D) illness kept him away from the Senate from March to August 2009. Until Kirk replaced Kennedy on September 24, 2009, the Democrats lacked the necessary sixty votes.

2. Michael Bailey, Jonathan Mummolo, and Hans Noel, "Tea Party Influence: A Story of Activists and Elites," *American Politics Research* 40, no. 5 (2012): 769–804; published online June 25, 2012.

3. Lee Hamilton, "There Is No Substitute for Robust Oversight," Center on Congress at Indiana University, June 9, 2010, http://congress.indiana.edu/.

4. James Thurber, "Corruption and Scandal in Washington: Have Lobbying and Ethics Reform Made a Difference? Exploring the Relationship among Candidates, Campaign Consultants, Lobbyists, and Elected and Appointed Public Officials," paper for Conference on Political Corruption in America at Loyola Marymount University, Institute for Leadership Studies, February 23, 2009, p. 13.

5. Sean Theriault and David Rohde, "The Gingrich Senators and Party Polarization in the U.S. Senate," *The Journal of Politics* 73, no. 4 (2011): 1011–24.

6. Vanessa Williamson, Theda Skocpol, and John Coggin, "The Tea Party and the Remaking of Republican Conservatism," *Perspectives on Politics* 91, no. 1 (2011): 25–43.

7. Jamie Carson, Michael H. Crespin, Charles J. Finocchiaro, and David W. Rohde, "Redistricting and Party Polarization in the U.S. House of Representatives," *American Politics Research* 35, no. 6 (2007): 878–904; Corbett Grainger, "Redistricting and Polarization: Who Draws the Lines in California?" *Journal of Law and Economics* 53, no. 3 (2010): 545–67.

8. Nolan McCarty, Keith Poole, and Howard Rosenthal, "Does Gerrymandering Cause Polarization?" *American Journal of Political Science* 53, no. 3 (2009): 666–80.

9. Donald Wolfensberger, "Getting Back to Legislating: Reflections of a Congressional Working Group," Bipartisan Policy Center, November 27, 2012, bipartisanpolicy.org/library/report/getting-back-legislating-reflections-congressional-working-group.

Index

About the Contributors

Gary Andres is the majority staff director for the House Committee on Energy and Commerce. Prior to joining the Committee, Andres was the vice chairman—Policy and Research for Dutko-Grayling, an public affairs and lobbying firm. In that capacity he oversaw the company's strategic communications, research and polling operations. From 2002–2010, he wrote weekly columns on politics and public policy for the *Washington Times* and the *Weekly Standard*. In 2009 and 2010, his columns were also carried nationally by the Hearst Newspapers. Andres also served in the legislative affairs office on the White House staff for President George H. W. Bush (1989-1993) and President George W. Bush (2001). Previously he also worked as a congressional aide and a corporate government affair representative. He holds a PhD in public policy from the University of Illinois–Chicago.

Roger H. Davidson is professor emeritus of government and politics at the University of Maryland and has served as professor, visiting professor, department chair, and associate dean at the University of California, Santa Barbara. He is a senior fellow of the National Academy of Public Administration. During the 1970s he served on the staffs of reform committees in both the House (Bolling-Martin Committee) and Senate (Stevenson-Brock Committee). In the 1980s he was senior specialist in American government and public administration at the Congressional Research Service of the Library of Congress. For the 2001–2002 academic year he held the John Marshall Chair in political science at the University of Debrecen, Hungary. Davidson is author or coauthor of numerous books and articles concerning legislative and presidential politics, as well as electoral politics. He is coeditor with Donald C. Bacon and Morton Keller of *The Encyclopedia of Con-*

gress (four volumes, 1995). He is senior author of *Congress and Its Members* (14th edition, 2013), the leading textbook in the field.

Ron Elving is the senior Washington editor for NPR News. He was previously political editor for *USA Today* and for *Congressional Quarterly*. He was a congressional fellow with the American Political Science Association and worked as a staff member in the House and Senate. He received his bachelor's degree from Stanford University and master's degrees from the University of Chicago and the University of California, Berkeley. He has been an adjunct faculty member at American University, George Mason University, and Georgetown University. His articles have appeared in *Media Studies Journal* and the *Columbia Journalism Review*, and he is the author of *Conflict and Compromise: How Congress Makes the Law* (Simon & Schuster, 1995).

Louis Fisher is scholar in residence at the Constitution Project. For four decades he served in the Library of Congress as senior specialist in separation of powers at Congressional Research Service (1970 to 1996) and as specialist in constitutional law at the Law Library (1996 to August 2010). He has testified more than fifty times before congressional committees on a range of constitutional issues, including war powers, executive privilege, item veto, pocket veto, legislative veto, presidential reorganization authority, NSA warrantless surveillance, CIA whistleblowing, state secrets privilege, recess appointments, covert spending, budget reform, and Congress and the Constitution. Author of twenty books and more than 475 articles, he is a visiting professor at the William and Mary Law School. His books have received a number of awards, such as the Richard E. Neustadt Award, the Dartmouth Medal, the Aaron B. Wildavsky Award, and the Louis Brownlow Book Award (twice). In 2012, he received the Hubert H. Humphrey Award from the American Political Science Association in recognition of his work as a political scientist in public service. A number of his articles, books, and congressional testimony are available on his personal webpage, http://loufisher.org. His forthcoming book, *The Law of the Executive Branch: Presidential Power*, will be published by Oxford University Press in 2013.

Patrick J. Griffin is associate director for public policy programs at the Center for Congressional and Presidential Studies Research Fellow and academic director of the Public Affairs and Advocacy Institute for CCPS. Griffin served in the White House as assistant to the president and director of legislative affairs, 1994–1996. In addition to his service in the Clinton Administration, his private sector experience includes senior VP for the worldwide public affairs firm of Burson Marstellar and founding partner of the

Washington, DC, government relations firm Griffin, Johnson, Madigan, Peck. He is currently the cofounder of the management consulting firm Griffin Williams.CPM. In the US Senate he held the elected position of secretary to the Democrats Caucus as well as senior advisor to two Senate democratic leaders. Prior to that he held professional staff positions on the Senate Democratic Policy Committee and the Senate Budget Committee. He also served as a domestic policy advisor at the United States Department of Health, Education, and Welfare and as an assistant professor of education at the University of Milwaukee, Wisconsin.

Lawrence J. Korb is a senior fellow at the Center for American Progress. Prior to joining the Center for American Progress he was a senior fellow and director of national security studies at the Council on Foreign Relations. Dr. Korb served as assistant secretary of defense (manpower, reserve affairs, installations, and logistics) from 1981 through 1985. In that position, he administered about 70 percent of the defense budget. Dr. Korb served on active duty for four years as Naval Flight Officer, and retired from the Naval Reserve with the rank of captain. He received his PhD in political science from the State University of New York at Albany and has held full-time teaching positions at the University of Dayton, the Coast Guard Academy, and the Naval War College.

Mark J. Oleszek is assistant professor of political science at Albright College where he teaches courses in American politics and the policy making process. He earned his PhD in political science from the University of California, Berkeley, in May 2010 and spent the following year serving as an APSA Congressional Fellow in the personal office of Senator Al Franken. His doctoral dissertation examines the importance of member-to-member collaboration to the Senate's lawmaking process, an interest born from previous experiences working with the Senate Democratic Policy Committee under the direction of Democratic Leader Tom Daschle.

Walter J. Oleszek is senior specialist in the legislative process at the Congressional Research Service. He has served as either a full-time professional staff aide or consultant to nearly every major congressional reorganization effort beginning with the Legislative Reorganization Act of 1970. In 1993 he served as policy director of the Joint Committee on the Organization of Congress. A long-time adjunct faculty member at The American University, Oleszek is the author or coauthor of a number of books and articles on the US Congress.

John E. Owens is professor of United States government and politics in the Centre for the Study of Democracy at the University of Westminster, faculty fellow in the Center for Congressional and Presidential Studies at the American University in Washington, DC, and associate fellow at the Institute for the Study of the Americas in the University of London's School of Advanced Study. He is the author of numerous articles in leading journals and book chapters on the United States Congress, congressional-presidential relations, and comparative legislative politics. His most recent book coedited with Riccardo Pelizzo is *The "War on Terror" and the Growth of Executive Power? A Comparative Analysis* published by Routledge in 2012. His previous publications include *Congress and the Presidency: Institutional Politics in a Separated System* (Manchester University Press), coauthored with Michael Foley; *Leadership in Context* (Rowman & Littlefield), coedited with Erwin C. Hargrove; *The Republican Takeover of Congress* (Palgrave), coedited with Dean McSweeney, and *America's "War on Terrorism": New Dimensions in United States Government and National Security* (Lexington), coedited with John W. Dumbrell. He is a member of the editorial boards of *Congress & the Presidency*, the *Journal of Legislative Studies*, and *Politics & Policy*, and a former board member of *Presidential Studies Quarterly*.

James P. Pfiffner is university professor and director of the doctoral program in the School of Public Policy at George Mason University. He has taught at the University of California, Riverside, and Cal State Fullerton and worked in the office of the director of the US Office of Personnel Management. In 2007 he was S. T. Lee Professorial Fellow at the Institute for Advanced Study at the University of London. He is the author or editor of a dozen books on the presidency and American national government, including *Power Play: The Bush Administration and the Constitution* (Brookings, 2008), and *Torture as Public Policy* (Paradigm Publishers, 2010). While serving with the 25th Infantry Division (1/8 Artillery) in 1970 he received the Army Commendation Medal for Valor in Vietnam and Cambodia. He is listed in *Who's Who in America* and *Who's Who in the World*.

Alexander Rothman is a research associate with the National Security and International Policy team at American Progress, where his work focuses primarily on US military policy. At American Progress, he has helped author studies on topics such as defense budget reform, the TRICARE military health care system, and the repeal of "Don't Ask, Don't Tell." Alex holds a bachelor's degree in international relations from Brown University. His work has been featured in *Foreign Policy, CNN Money , Politico,* and *The Bulletin of Atomic Scientists.*

Barbara Sinclair is professor emerita (formerly the Marvin Hoffenberg Professor) of political science at UCLA. She specializes in American politics and primarily does research on the US Congress. Her publications include articles in the *American Political Science Review*, the *American Journal of Political Science* , the *Journal of Politics*, and *Legislative Studies Quarterly* and the following books: *Congressional Realignment* (1982), *Majority Leadership in the U.S. House* (1983), *The Transformation of the U.S. Senate* (1989), *Legislators, Leaders and Lawmaking: The U.S. House of Representatives in the Postreform Era* (1995), *Party Wars: Polarization and the Politics of National Policy Making* (2006), and *Unorthodox Lawmaking: New Legislative Processes in the U. S. Congress* (1997, 2000, 2007, 2012). She was an American Political Science Association Congressional Fellow in the office of the House majority leader in 1978–1979 and a participant observer in the office of the Speaker in 1987–1988. She has testified before Congress on the legislative process, most recently before the Senate Committee on Rules and Administration on the filibuster in July 2010.

Claudia Hartley Thurber, a veteran of over twenty-two years of federal government service, was the US Occupational Safety and Health Administration's Counsel for Health Standards until her retirement in February 2006. She is an expert on the regulatory process, having worked on some of OSHA's most far-reaching standards that protect workers from hazards. Ms. Thurber lectures on current issues in regulation, particularly occupational safety and health, mine safety, and environmental issues. Her recent research is on "The Politics of Regulation in the Obama Administration," published in *Obama in Office* (2011).

James A. Thurber is University Distinguished Professor of Government and founder (1979) and director of the Center for Congressional and Presidential Studies (american.edu/spa/ccps) at American University. His latest publications are Campaigns and Elections, American Style (2013, 4th Ed.) with Candice Nelson. He is author and editor of numerous books and more than eighty articles on American politics including "Obama in Office" (2011) (available from http://www.paradigmpublishers.com)., "Congress and the Internet" (2002) with Colton Campbell, "The Battle for Congress: Consultants, Candidates, and Voters" (2001), "Crowded Airwaves: Campaign Advertising in Elections" (2001) with Candice J. Nelson and David A. Dulio and "Campaign Warriors: Political Consultants in Elections" (2000). He is editor of the academic journal *Congress and the Presidency*. Dr. Thurber earned a PhD in political science from Indiana University and was an American Political Science Association Congressional Fellow and is a Fellow of the National Academy of Public Administration. He served as legislative assistant to Senator Hubert H. Humphrey, Senator William Brock, Senator Adlai Stevenson III, and Representative David Obey. He received the 2010 APSA Walter Beach Pi Sigma Alpha award for his work combining applied and academic research.

Stephen J. Wayne is professor of government at Georgetown University. He is author of *The Legislative Presidency*, *The Road to the White House*, and coauthor of *Presidential Leadership*. His latest book is titled *Personality and Politics: Obama For and Against Himself.*

Joseph White is Luxenberg Family Professor of Public Policy and chair of the Department of Political Science at Case Western Reserve University. He earned his PhD in political science from the University of California, Berkeley, and before joining CWRU spent the largest part of his career with the Governmental Studies Program of the Brookings Institution. His research has focused on federal budget policy and politics; health policy and politics both in the United States and other advanced industrial democracies; and the politics of entitlement, or social insurance, programs. His budgeting publications range from *The Deficit and the Public Interest: The Search for Responsible Budgeting in the 1980s* with Aaron Wildavsky (1989), to "Playing the Wrong Part: The Program Assessment Rating Tool and the Functions of the President's Budget" in the *Public Administration Review*, January 2012.